BRITISH INTELLIGENCE
IN THE SECOND
WORLD WAR

VOLUME FOUR

SECURITY AND
COUNTER-INTELLIGENCE

BRITISH INTELLIGENCE IN THE SECOND WORLD WAR

VOLUME FOUR

SECURITY AND COUNTER-INTELLIGENCE

by

F. H. HINSLEY
Fellow of St John's College and Emeritus Professor of the History
of International Relations in the University of Cambridge

and
C. A. G. SIMKINS
Sometime Scholar of New College,
Oxford and of Lincoln's Inn, Barrister-at-Law

CAMBRIDGE UNIVERSITY PRESS
NEW YORK

Published in the USA by the
Syndicate of Cambridge University Press
32 East 57th Street, New York, NY 10022, USA

Printed in the United Kingdom for
Her Majesty's Stationery Office
Dd 291446 C75 12/89

ISBN 0 521 39409 0

CONTENTS

v

vi

PART V:

APPENDICES

Numbered notes to the text are to be found at the end of each chapter.

PREFACE

THIS BOOK forms part of the series entitled *British Intelligence in the Second World War*, of which the first three volumes, dealing with the influence of intelligence on strategy and operations, have already been published. In the course of producing it we have enjoyed the privileges that were extended to the authors of the earlier volumes, and have been governed by the same conditions. These privileges and conditions were set out in the prefaces to Volumes I, II and III and are here recapitulated.

We have been granted unrestricted access to the intelligence records for the inter-war years and the Second World War, as well as to other relevant archives, as a special measure. If any archives have escaped our attention we are satisfied that oversight on our part is the sole explanation. No constraints have been placed on us while carrying out our research. On the contrary, in obtaining access to the archives and consulting members of the war-time intelligence community we have received full cooperation from the Historical Section of the Cabinet Office and appropriate government departments.

In preparing the results of our research for publication, however, we have observed the ruling that was laid down by the Secretary of State for Foreign Affairs on 12 January 1978 in a written reply to a parliamentary question. The reply advised war-time intelligence staff on the extent to which they were absolved from their undertakings of reticence in the light of recent changes of policy with regard to the release of war-time records. He drew a distinction between the records of the Service intelligence directorates, which will be placed with other departmental archives in the Public Record Office, and 'other information, including details of the methods by which this material was obtained'. He explained that this other information 'remains subject to the undertakings and to the Official Secrets Acts and may not be disclosed'. And he concluded with a reference to this History: 'if it is published, the principles governing the extent of permitted disclosure embodied in the guidance above will apply in relation to the Official History'. The 'other information' here mentioned is information in some of the records of the intelligence-gathering bodies.

As already stated, this ruling has not prevented us from consulting these records. Nor has it prevented us from incorporating in the text the results of our work on them; we have been required to restrict our use of them only to the extent that secrecy about intelligence techniques and with respect to individuals remains essential. It has, however, dictated the system we have adopted when giving references to our sources. To the files of the assessors, recipients, and users of intelligence – government departments, inter-departmental bodies, operational commands and other executive authorities – we have supplied precise references. This applies not only to documents already opened in the Public Record Office, and those to be opened after a stated period of extended closure, but also to individual files and papers which, though they may not be available for public research for a considerable time to come, nevertheless fall into categories of war-time records whose eventual opening in the Record Office may be expected. But it would have served no useful purpose to give precise references to the domestic files of the intelligence-gathering bodies, which are unlikely to be opened in the Public Record Office.

In the present volume, dealing with Security and Counter-Intelligence, the evidence derived from these latter, restricted, files constitutes a much higher proportion of the total source material than was the case with the volumes which dealt with the influence of intelligence on strategy and operations. To a considerable extent the account we give is accordingly one for which Public Record Office references for the sources cannot be provided. But we have attempted to give such references whenever, the security and counter-intelligence authorities having brought their concerns and the results of their work to the attention of government departments and other users of intelligence, the papers remain in the archives of the recipients.

The extent to which this has been possible is not sufficient to justify the provision of a bibliography or guide to sources. It should be noted, however, that the recipients were with few exceptions identical with the recipients of the product of other intelligence-collecting bodies, and that the bibliography in Volume III, Part 2, of this series contains a comprehensive guide to the location of such of their archives as have been or will be released to the public records.

We wish to acknowledge the help given by Miss Patricia McCallum in her capacity as research assistant. We should add that the contribution made by Miss Eve Streatfeild in respect of research and administrative management to this volume, as to the earlier volumes in the series, has been invaluable.

ABBREVIATIONS

AO	Auslands Organisation
ARCOS	All Russian Co-operative Society
BSC	British Security Co-ordination
BU, BUF	British Union (of Fascists)
'C'	or CSS: Head of the Secret Service
CAS	Chief of the Air Staff
CCS	Combined Chiefs of Staff (Anglo-American)
CICI	Combined Intelligence Centre Iraq
CID	Committee of Imperial Defence
CIGS	Chief of the Imperial General Staff
COS	Chiefs of Staff (British)
COSSAC	Chief of Staff to the Supreme Allied Commander (Designate)
CPGB	Communist Party of Great Britain
CSDIC	Combined Services Detailed Interrogation Centre
CSO	Consular Security Officer
DF	Direction Finding
DMI	Director of Military Intelligence
DNI	Director of Naval Intelligence
DPP	Director of Public Prosecutions
DR	Defence Regulation
DSO	Defence Security Officer
FAK	Frontaufklärungs Kommandos
FAT	Frontaufklärungs Truppen
FBI	Federal Bureau of Investigation
FUSAG	Notional 1st US Army Group
GC and CS	Government Code and Cypher School
GPO	General Post Office
HDE	Home Defence Executive (not to be confused with the HD(S)E)
HD(S)E	Home Defence (Security) Executive (first name of the Security Executive)
HPC	Home Policy Committee
IRA	Irish Republican Army
ISO	Industrial Security Officer
ISOS	Intelligence Service, Oliver Strachey (the general term used throughout this volume to refer to decrypts and translations of German intelligence messages)
ISSB	Inter-Services Security Board

JIC	Joint Intelligence Committee
JIF	Japanese Inspired Fifth Columnist
KO	Kriegsorganisation (of the Abwehr)
LCS	London Controlling Section
LOC	Liaison Officers Conference
LRC	London Reception Centre
MEDC	Middle East Defence Committee
MEIC	Middle East Intelligence Centre
MI	Military Intelligence
NID	Naval Intelligence Division
NSDAP	National Sozialistische Deutsche Arbeiter Partei
OB	Ossewa Brandwag
OKH	Oberkommando des Heeres (High Command of the German Army)
OKW	Oberkommando der Wehrmacht (High Command of the German Armed Forces)
OSS	Office of Strategic Services (US)
PPU	Peace Pledge Union
PWE	Political Warfare Executive
RCMP	Royal Canadian Mounted Police
RSHA	Reichssicherheitshauptamt
RSHA (Mil Amt)	Reichssicherheitshauptamt Militärisches Amt
RSLO	Regional Security Liaison Officer
RSS	Radio Security Service
SCIU	Special Counter-Intelligence Unit
SCO	Security Control Officer
SD	Sicherheitsdienst
SE	Security Executive
SHAEF	Supreme Headquarters Allied Expeditionary Force
SIC	Security Intelligence Centre
SIGINT	Signals Intelligence – the general term for the processes of interception, analysis and decryption and the intelligence they produced
SIME	Security Intelligence Middle East
SIS	Special or Secret Intelligence Service
SOE	Special Operations Executive
SSM	Service de Securité Militaire
TIS	Theatre Intelligence Section
W/T	Wireless Telegraphy

PART I

CHAPTER 1

Before the War

SECURITY as it was defined by the British war-time Security Executive in 1942 – 'the defence of national interests against hostile elements other than the armed forces of the enemy: in practice against espionage, sabotage and attempts to procure defeat by subversive political activity'[1] – has been almost everywhere a major and a continuing preoccupation of governments and their citizens since the Second World War. It was otherwise before 1914. The need to protect the state against these threats has a long history – a history as long as that of government itself. But before the twentieth century it was generally the case that it was met informally, not to say casually, at the margin of the main machinery of state, by authorities whose activities were shielded from popular curiosity.

In the United Kingdom, as elsewhere, the transition from the informal to the more organised pursuit of security began in the period of mounting international tension that culminated in the outbreak of the First World War. To be precise, it began in April 1907, when a conference of officials set up by the Admiralty and the War Office in 1906 to consider 'the Powers Possessed by the Executive in Time of Emergency' recommended an immediate strengthening of the laws against espionage and a War Office investigation into 'police surveillance and control of aliens'.[2] After the completion of the conference's report, which coincided with the publication in the Press of rumours associating the existence of spies with German plans for an invasion, the European section of the War Office's Directorate of Operations (MO 2) embarked on the systematic investigation of reports on German espionage. Its findings convinced it of the need for a specially organised counter-espionage bureau and in January 1909, in a paper entitled 'Espionage in Time of Peace', the General Staff drew the attention of Lord Haldane, the Secretary of State for War, to the problem. In March 1909, to the accompaniment of mounting public concern about alarmist spy stories and lurid invasion novels, and at the request of the General Staff, the Prime Minister set up a sub-committee of the Committee of Imperial Defence (CID), with Haldane as chairman. Its terms of reference were to consider the nature and extent of foreign espionage; whether the Admiralty and the War Office should be brought into official relations with the Police, postal and customs authorities with a view to the proper

3

supervision of aliens suspected of being spies; and whether any alteration should be made in the system in force in the Admiralty and the War Office for obtaining information from abroad.

The sub-committee reported in July 1909. It found that the evidence left no doubt that 'an extensive system of German espionage exists in this country'. But it also found that 'we have no organisation for . . . accurately identifying its extent and objectives'; and it recommended that this defect should be met by the creation of a Secret Service Bureau. The purposes of the Bureau should be:

'(a) To serve as a screen between the Admiralty and the War Office and foreign spies who may have information that they wish to sell to the Government.

(b) To keep in touch through the Home Office . . . with the Chief Officers of Police and if necessary to send agents to various parts of Great Britain with a view to ascertaining the nature and scope of the espionage that is being carried on by foreign agents.

(c) To serve as an intermediary between the Admiralty and the War Office on the one hand and the agents that we employ in foreign countries on the other'.

The Bureau should be separate from any of the departments but should be in close touch with the Admiralty, the War Office and the Home Office, and also with the Police and the postal and customs authorities.[3]

The Secret Service Bureau began work on 1 October 1909 under the nominal supervision of MO 5, the special section of the Military Operations Directorate that was responsible for questions relating to enemy aliens. Within a month its leading officers had agreed on a division of labour by which one of them took responsibility for all activities in the United Kingdom while the other dealt with foreign agents and the collection of intelligence abroad. During 1910 this division of labour was formalised in the division of the Bureau itself into the Home Section and the Foreign Section.

At the outbreak of war in 1914 the Home Section, hitherto known as MO(t), was mobilised under the War Office Directorate of Military Operations as MO 5(g). In January 1916 it became part of the new Directorate of Military Intelligence as MI 5 and its relationship to the Foreign Section, which was placed under the Director of Military Intelligence (DMI) as MI 1(c), was further defined. MI 1(c) was made responsible for counter-espionage outside the British Empire as well as for the collection of intelligence abroad. MI 5 remained responsible on behalf of all departments of state for counter-espionage in Britain and for developing counter-espionage links with governments within the Empire.[4]

Until 1916 the department which then became MI 5 was almost wholly occupied with counter-espionage strictly defined and (from the outbreak of the First World War) with the threat of sabotage from foreign agents. From 1916 these threats were overshadowed in the minds of those responsible for security by the danger of political subversion. On the one hand, the threat from enemy agents had been all but eliminated. Twelve spies had been arrested before 1914, and the existence of a German network of 'stay-behind' spies had been detected. The arrest of the 21 members of this network who remained in the country at the outbreak of war had crippled the German Secret Service; 35 spies were arrested during the war, but by 1916 it had become virtually impossible for Germany to maintain agents in Britain.[5] On the other hand, symptoms of general war-weariness, the greater activity of pacifist groups and the rumbling of industrial unrest were by then emerging as grounds for anxiety.

It was the government's disquiet at the prospects of civil dissidence, a disquiet that had increased since the Bolshevik revolution in Russia in 1917, which prompted a further enquiry into the Secret Service at the end of the war. The War Cabinet appointed a Secret Service Committee in January 1919 after receiving from Mr Walter Long, the First Lord of the Admiralty, a memorandum stating that while he was no alarmist, he firmly believed that 'the elements of unrest and what we call Bolshevism are more general, more deep-seated than many of us believe . . . We must be vigilant and above all we must have an efficient . . . Secret Service on the civil side . . . under a Minister who can bring the facts to the notice of the Cabinet'. The Committee, consisting of the Foreign Secretary, the First Lord, the Home Secretary, the Secretary of State for War and the Chief Secretary for Ireland, agreed without delay. Leaving the 'military side' of the Secret Service aside for later investigation, it recommended that a new Secret Service directorate for civil intelligence should be created at once, the need for it to be reviewed when social conditions had returned to a more normal course; that it should be directed by Sir Basil Thomson, the Assistant Commissioner of Police in charge of the Special Branch of the Metropolitan Police; and that he should be responsible to the Home Secretary. The War Cabinet accepted the recommendations in March 1919.[6]

The establishment of the new Directorate of Intelligence did little more than regularise the existing situation. The Special Branch, which had long been the authority responsible for monitoring the conspiracies of the Fenians and other subversive groups, had under Thomson's direction already extended its operations in the later months of the war to cover the activities and the propaganda of pacifist and labour organisations. But the Directorate had only a brief existence. There was continual friction between Thomson and the Commissioner of the Metropolitan Police, who had disciplinary but not operational control of the Special Branch. By cultivating close relations with the Press, Thomson attracted a good deal of publicity, and his over-zealous enlistment of agents and informants incurred the hostile criticism that he was operating a secret political police. By posting liaison officers abroad, moreover, and developing collaboration with the Police in foreign countries, he threatened the established division of labour between home security and the responsibilities of the old Foreign Section, which was then coming to be known as the Special or Secret Intelligence Service (SIS). For these reasons the opportunity was taken to abolish the Directorate in 1921 when, as a result of financial stringency, the Cabinet ordered an enquiry into the whole field of expenditure on the Secret Service.[7]

The 1921 enquiry, carried out by a committee of officials under Sir Warren Fisher, the head of the Treasury, was instructed to make recommendations 'for reducing expenditure and avoiding over-lapping'. Its report, issued in July 1921, commented unfavourably on Thomson's reports on revolutionary movements overseas: they had frequently contained 'misleading if not absolutely erroneous information regarding matters by no means invariably within the purview of his work'. It noted, further, that for his information on this subject he was largely dependent on the SIS. And it recommended that the work of his Directorate should be reviewed with 'the object of ascertaining whether its incorporation in the general organisation of the Metropolitan Police would not result in an increase of efficiency and a substantial saving in the Secret Service budget'.[8] The Commissioner of Police followed up the report in memoranda to the Home Secretary. He insisted that the independence of the Directorate was a menace to the discipline of his force and that the intelligence it supplied to the force was unsatisfactory. He also argued that the Directorate had a reputation for espionage against labour organisations which was resented; public opinion accepted a Secret Service for the Army, Navy and Air Force and even for the Diplomatic Service as a necessary evil, but was suspicious of anything approaching the continental system of domestic espionage. Thomson fought back, but in October the Prime Minister ruled that he should retire, that the separate post of Director of Intelligence should cease to exist and that the Special Branch should be fully subordinated to the Commissioner of Police. The Commissioner successfully resisted a suggestion that Major-General Sir Vernon Kell (the head of MI 5 from its origin in the Secret Service Bureau) should become

Director of Intelligence with modified responsibilities, and combine the duties of this post with those of Director of MI 5.

To begin with the Fisher Committee was also sceptical about the need to retain MI 5. It eventually concluded that since the agents of several countries were showing signs of activity, and in view of the new threat of Bolshevism in the Army and Navy, MI 5 should continue to be responsible on a reduced scale for detecting espionage and protecting the armed forces against subversion. But from 1923 the existence of MI 5 was again challenged by the new head of the SIS,* who believed that the intelligence and security machinery should be amalgamated under his control. As a result of his representations Fisher was asked to revive the committee of officials in February 1925. The committee started 'with a mild disposition in favour of amalgamation', but it finally concluded in December 1925 that in view of 'the heterogeneous interests, liaisons, traditions and responsibilities of the different Services, and the marked reluctance of the majority of those concerned to advocate any drastic change, a coalition would, if it were not an actual failure, be no great improvement'. It recommended, however, that it should itself remain in existence as a standing committee (the Secret Service Committee) to act as a court of appeal which might help to bring about compromise and greater co-operation between the three Secret Service organisations.[9]

As was perhaps unavoidable when the SIS was responsible for the collection of intelligence from foreign countries, including intelligence about suspect persons and subversive political movements, when MI 5 was charged with the detection of espionage and of subversion directed against the armed forces, and when the Special Branch at Scotland Yard dealt with subversion as it affected the civilian population, confusion and friction continued. They came to a head in 1931 when Scotland Yard and MI 5 had both taken the strongest objection to SIS operations against Communist targets in the United Kingdom. The Secret Service Committee was reconvened and accepted a proposal by Sir John Anderson, then Permanent Under-Secretary at the Home Office, that responsibility for evaluating all intelligence, other than that dealing with Irish and anarchist matters, should be transferred from the Special Branch to MI 5. The change, and the move of Scotland Yard's civilian intelligence staff to MI 5, took effect on 15 October 1931, the Special Branch informing Chief Constables that it had been made 'in order to centralise the information regarding revolutionary and subversive activities, but would not affect the duties of the police as regards any executive action'.

---

* By now known as 'C' and so referred to throughout this volume.

Ministerial, indeed Prime Ministerial, approval must presumably have been obtained for this important re-adjustment of responsibilities, but no record of it has been found and the whole transaction seems to have been characterised by informality. Papers of February 1933 in an MI 5 file state that neither MI 5 nor the War Office had any accurate records of the process by which MI 5 had ceased to be a small section of the War Office entirely under General Staff control and had taken over certain civil duties from the Metropolitan Police on behalf of the Home Office. Sir Vernon Kell had agreed to take over these duties subject to the approval of the CIGS and the heads of the defence services which had been obtained by personal interview. It had been agreed that the designation MI 5 should be retained for such official convenience as it could afford, without prejudice to the appropriate internal organisation of the Security Service.

The primary motive for this re-organisation seems to have been the removal of friction. But the authorities may also have been concerned to guard against the suspicion, which had been expressed so powerfully in 1921, that they were permitting the development of a 'continental system of domestic espionage'. The important organisational consequences were left undefined, but it was clearly understood that when dealing with subversive movements among civilians the head of MI 5 would be accountable to the Home Secretary, who was constitutionally responsible for the internal safety of the country and for upholding the liberty of the subject and the rights of minorities under the law. However, the head of MI 5 was not the servant of the Home Secretary, but the servant of a number of ministers. The result of the new arrangements was that MI 5, as the Security Service, became an inter-departmental and imperial intelligence service, without executive powers, working for and with the Home Office, the Service departments, the Foreign, Dominion and Colonial Offices, the Committee of Imperial Defence, the Attorney General and the Director of Public Prosecutions and Chief Officers of Police at home and overseas. This was an anomalous position, which might become difficult if there were serious differences of opinion between departments. Lord Hankey, Secretary of the War Cabinet and Cabinet 1916–1938, would write in May 1940* that MI 5 was 'something of a lost child' and he had been aware for a long time that its head wanted it to be attached to the Committee of Imperial Defence so that it would be within the sphere of the Prime Minister.[10]

This re-organisation did not, however, affect the responsibility

---

* See below, pp 39–40.

of the SIS for counter-intelligence abroad. Outside the three-mile limits of the Empire the SIS remained responsible for the acquisition of counter-intelligence as well as of intelligence, and it alone was empowered to assess and circulate it to other authorities and to advise them on the action they should take. The SIS, on whom MI 5 in any case depended heavily for its intelligence in discharging its security responsibilities within the Empire, was thus a counter-intelligence organisation of equal status to MI 5; the division of labour between the two was geographical and not functional.

□

The division of responsibility for counter-intelligence was to produce renewed conflict between MI 5 and the SIS after the outbreak of war. In the few years before 1939, however, friction within the Secret Service community subsided, as is indicated by the fact that though the Secret Service Committee remained in being, it did not meet again after 1931. On the other hand, the inactivity of the Secret Service Committee may have increased the danger that MI 5 and the SIS, as servants of a number of different departments, would suffer from the inertia and neglect that arise when accountability is dispersed. Each underwent some expansion from 1935 in preparation for the outbreak of war, but from lack of imagination or lack of funds, and probably for both reasons, neither took adequate steps to earmark and train a war reserve and neither gave serious thought to the need for re-organisation to meet the demands which the outbreak of war would make upon it.

By 1925 MI 5's staff, which had been more than 800 at the end of the First World War, had fallen to 30. The transfer of the civilian intelligence staff from Scotland Yard in 1931 brought a small increment and from 1934 the size of the Service increased slowly. Its share of the Secret Vote, most of which was for salaries, rose from £25,000 in 1935–1936 to £50,000 for 1938. In September 1938 MI 5 had 30 officers, about 120 secretarial and registry staff and a surveillance section of six men. In the same month, in a covering note with a report summarising information from German sources on the development of German policy from 1936 onwards which reached the Foreign Secretary and the Prime Minister, MI 5 asked whether, 'apart from the paramount necessity for rapid re-armament', further measures should not be taken to develop the intelligence system and to provide a comprehensive review of the steps necessary to ensure security. Whether or not as a result of this, MI 5's share of the Secret Vote rose to £93,000 for 1939–1940. By the outbreak of war it had 83 officers and 253 other ranks (almost all of them women). These were deployed in four Branches:

A Branch, responsible for personnel, finance and administration, including the registry.

B Branch, responsible for investigating all threats to security.

C Branch, responsible for vetting.

D Branch, which advised on the security of the munitions industry and
public utilities and in war-time would carry out MI 5's responsibilities
for travel control.

The head of the Service, Major-General Sir Vernon Kell, was in
his 67th year. He had the confidence of his staff and, it appears, of
the small number of senior officials with whom he habitually dealt.
His deputy, Lt Colonel Sir Eric Holt-Wilson, had joined the
Bureau in 1912 after seventeen years in the Army. He was 64 on
the eve of war. The all important B Branch was directed by Mr O
A Harker who had joined the Indian Police in 1905 and had been
Deputy Commissioner of Police in Bombay in the First World
War. He had been with MI 5 since 1920. His Deputy, and in 1940
his successor as Director of B Branch, was Mr Guy Liddell who
had joined Sir Basil Thomson's Directorate of Intelligence after
service in the First World War and had remained at Scotland Yard
until the transfer of the civilian intelligence staff to MI 5 in 1931.

Between the wars recruitment to MI 5 was by personal introduction, which was thought to offer the best guarantee of the loyalty
and integrity required in a Secret Service. Because the salaries
which could be offered were acceptable only to men with a pension
or some private means, recruits were mainly drawn from middle-
aged retired officers from one or other of the public services and
this had tended to produce a certain rigidity and lack of imagination. However, the new intake of the immediate pre-war years
included a few younger men of more varied background. Two of
them, Mr D G White and Mr R H Hollis, would hold senior posts
during the Second World War and later in turn became head of
the Service.

In the SIS the section responsible for counter-intelligence
(Section V) consisted of only two officers until December 1938; it
was then increased to three. Until 1937 the Section had devoted
almost all its time to the study of international Communism. The
SIS's overseas stations gave low priority to counter-espionage work
until after the outbreak of war, except in Holland and Belgium
from the autumn of 1938.

□

Like the potentiality for conflict between them, the unpreparedness of MI 5 and the SIS was to have damaging consequences only after the war had broken out. Until the autumn of 1939 the evidence they obtained on espionage and (with the important exception of the Soviet-controlled Comintern) on the interest of foreign states in subversion against the United Kingdom was slight. MI 5 and the SIS were inclined to attribute the paucity of their evidence to the inadequacy of their sources of information because they did not know that it was due to the fact that the effort devoted to these activities by the Axis governments had been negligible in the case of Italy,* while restrictions by the German government on intelligence operations against the United Kingdom had lasted until late in 1937 in the hope that the United Kingdom could be persuaded not to intervene to thwart German ambitions in central and eastern Europe.[11] But the fact that they did not know this was no reflection on their peace-time efficiency. On the contrary, their anxiety, though unfounded, testified to their lack of complacency.

Although Germany had been forbidden by the Treaty of Versailles to have an intelligence service, as distinct from a counter-espionage organisation, she had resumed espionage activities in the United Kingdom from the mid-1930s. Until the re-occupation of the Rhineland in 1936 the SIS and MI 5 were not greatly disturbed, but this event gave a new impetus to Anglo-French liaison. In October 1937 the SIS drew the attention of all its overseas stations to the fact that there were serious gaps in its knowledge of the German espionage service, and of those of Italy and Japan. This followed upon discussions between the SIS and MI 5 and the French counter-espionage authorities in which the French reported that Germany had recently set up a base in Holland for operations against France and the United Kingdom, and this was later confirmed by a reliable MI 5 source who reported in 1938 that the espionage attack on the United Kingdom was to be stepped up. In the autumn of 1938 an SIS counter-espionage station was established in Holland to work in collaboration with the French, Dutch and Belgian authorities. It was reinforced in April 1939 and an officer was also posted to Brussels for counter-espionage operations.

These were modest steps, and little was learned as a result of taking them. They produced no contacts with sources who were in a position to provide comprehensive information about the plans and capabilities of the German or any other intelligence service. Before 1939 the SIS and MI 5 remained unaware even of the name of the German espionage organisation, the Amstgruppe

---

* Apart from the brief flirtation with Sir Oswald Mosley's British Union of Fascists, see below, p 16.

Auslandsnachrichten und Abwehr,* and of the fact that it was
headed by Admiral Canaris and subordinated to the Oberkom-
mando der Wehrmacht (OKW). But by the outbreak of war they
had detected the involvement of an office in Hamburg in some 30
cases of espionage or attempted espionage, four of the agents
involved being convicted under the Official Secrets Acts and a fifth
deported for failing to register as an alien. From what they learned
from these cases they might have concluded that the Abwehr's
efforts were also modest. The agents were of poor quality, their
techniques elementary and their reports to Germany contained
little of value. But MI 5 was not convinced that its findings were a
reliable guide to what the Germans were already achieving or
might be preparing to undertake. In three of the more serious
cases it investigated the agent was found to be operating as a
post-box for spies in France and the United States; this pointed to
the possibility that the more important agents in the United
Kingdom were making their reports through third countries.
Especially after 1937, an uncomfortably high proportion of the
cases detected came to light fortuitously – about a dozen because
the agents brought themselves to the notice of the British authorities – and this raised questions about the efficiency of the
surveillance system.

Among the methods of surveillance was the power to intercept
postal communications in the public interest. The legitimacy of
such interception under the warrant of a principal Secretary of
State was recognised by Acts of Parliament passed in 1710, 1837
and 1908, and the power was deemed to extend to telegrams and
telephone communications.[12] Used selectively in the inter-war
years it constituted a useful weapon against both espionage and
subversion. But its existence was well known, and under-cover
organisations have the best of reasons for taking care to evade it by
resort to other means of communication. These included diplomatic bags, private couriers, cover addresses and, increasingly between the wars if also only slowly, illicit wireless; and all or most of
them made use of secret writing or codes and cyphers. Whatever
the vigilance of the security authorities, they could never be sure
that no users of such channels were escaping detection.

The uncertainty was particularly acute in relation to the relatively new threat from illicit wireless communications. The need for a
specialist organisation for the interception of illicit transmissions
from the United Kingdom was recognised in 1928 by the Standing
Inter-Departmental Sub-Committee of the CID on Censorship. It

---

* See Appendix 1(i). Referred to as the Abwehr throughout this volume. The Nazi Party
had its own security organisation, the Sicherheitsdienst (SD), which became the Abwehr's
rival and in 1944 its supplanter (see Appendix 1 (ii) and (iii)).

recommended that the War Office should use voluntary and unpaid 'enthusiastic amateurs of unimpeachable discretion'[13] to develop such an organisation alongside the interception networks of the Services and the Foreign Office which watched transmissions within and between foreign countries for the Government Code and Cypher School (GC and CS). But attempts to carry out this recommendation came to nothing. In 1933 it was decided that, while the War Office remained responsible for general direction and the provision of funds, the General Post Office should act as its agent for the manning, maintenance and technical operation of the service[14] – later to be known as the Radio Security Service (RSS) – but progress in establishing the system continued to be slow. Not until December 1937 was it agreed that the GPO should build three fixed intercept and DF stations. The first of these was not operational until December 1938, and only then was approval finally given for the establishment at the earliest possible date of a network of fixed and mobile stations supplemented by an auxiliary observer corps of amateur operators.

No illicit transmissions from the United Kingdom had by then been intercepted, and no transmissions that were clearly intended for illicit stations in the United Kingdom. So far as is known, no such transmission had as yet been made. But as a result of the delay in providing for their interception, MI 5 could by no means be confident on this score. In the summer of 1938 it sought advice from the former Director of the Wireless and Telegraph Service in India. His report, submitted in October, reached the disturbing conclusion that interception arrangements were so inadequate that had recent developments led to the outbreak of hostilities a skilled agent could have established a reliable wireless service and maintained it for a considerable period with almost complete immunity; he added that such a service might well be already in existence.

When similar, if less pronounced, uncertainty attached to the surveillance of the other channels of illicit communication it is not difficult to see why MI 5 could not ignore the possibility that the Germans had established a stay-behind network that would begin to operate in the event of hostilities, or were at least taking steps to establish one. Nor could the Italian Intelligence Service escape suspicion, though even less was known about it than about the German, and MI 5 found no trace of its involvement in espionage.

MI 5's uneasiness was all the greater because it did not derive solely from prudence in assessing the limited positive evidence it had on espionage. In a memorandum of November 1938 it noted that 'the German Intelligence Service has us at a great disadvantage' in that it was in a position to obtain information not only from a professional spy organisation, but also from the organ of the Nazi Party in the United Kingdom and from some of the considerable number of people of German origin who served in the British armed forces and industry. In April 1940, it would again contrast its problems during the First World War, when it had had to deal only with a professional espionage network, with those it had confronted before 1939, when (as it believed) the German intelligence effort had been carried out on a 'total basis'. The problems it referred to, which it associated equally if less urgently with Italy, were those arising from the totalitarian ideologies of these states. In the 1930s Germany and Italy operated party organisations for their nationals in the United Kingdom and carried out propaganda among persons of German and Italian birth who had acquired British citizenship. They also exerted a powerful ideological attraction upon some British nationals, as did the Soviet-dominated Comintern.

The most prominent foreign party organisation was the Gau Ausland of the National Sozialistische Deutsche Arbeiter Partei (NSDAP) which had been established for the purpose of 'welding together . . . all Germans abroad . . . into one great bloc'. There was a branch in London from 1931 known as the Auslands Organisation (AO). By 1935 it had 288 members and some 1,500 contacts and these numbers had grown to 300 and 2,000 by 1937. The Fascio, organised by the Direttore Generale degli Italiani all'Estero, did similar work for the Italian colony in the United Kingdom, with branches in most of the large towns. From 1935 MI 5 warned the departments that such organisations, controlled by foreign governments, were a ready-made instrument for espionage and sabotage. In July 1936 the Home and Foreign Secretaries, prompted by MI 5, asked the Cabinet to consider whether 'informal and friendly suggestions should be made to the German and Italian Governments' that they should close down these party organisations, whose presence was 'considered unusual and undesirable'. The Cabinet thought that this would be inopportune because of attempts then under way to promote contacts between the British, French, Belgian, German and Italian governments, but invited the Home and Foreign Secretaries to bring the question up again. When they did so a year later the Cabinet agreed that the matter could not be allowed to drift indefinitely, but decided that in view of the difficulties over questions relating to the Spanish Civil War no drastic action should be taken at the moment. A parallel attempt by MI 5 to get the Chiefs of Staff to put their weight behind the drive for action was unsuccessful.[15] MI 5 accepted that, as Sir Robert Vansittart, then Permanent Under-Secretary in the Foreign Office, put it towards the end of 1937, the outlawing of the AO, which 'might have been done in comparative quiet a year ago, would now almost certainly create a first-class storm'. But in June 1938, as the international situation continued to deteriorate, MI 5 took the precaution of advising Chief Constables to be ready, on the receipt of instructions, to search AO premises, arrest all officials and known members, and take steps to prevent sabotage, and in January 1939 it asked them to prepare for similar emergency action against the Italian Fascio. In February 1939 it persuaded the Home and Foreign Secretaries to take the whole matter back to the Cabinet. In March the Cabinet authorised the deportation of a limited number of AO officials; and nine of them were expelled in April.[16]

The AO and the Fascio incorporated only a small minority of the 70,000 German and Austrian nationals in the UK and of the 19,000 Italians. Of the former particularly, the vast majority were political refugees whose sympathies could safely be assumed to lie with Britain. But as the screening of foreigners on their arrival was cursory or non-existent, and as it had also to be assumed that some of them would be open to blackmail or to appeals to latent patriotism, their large numbers obviously offered favourable opportunities for the infiltration or later recruitment of agents.

Another potential threat was the emergence of Fascist organisations for British nationals. It was first taken seriously after the foundation of Mosley's British Union of Fascists (BUF) in 1932. At a meeting at the Home Office in November 1933 attended by the Permanent Under-Secretary, the head of MI 5, the Commissioner of the Metropolitan Police and a representative from Special Branch it was agreed that with effect from April 1934 Special Branch and MI 5 should assume the same functions in respect of Fascism that they already carried out in respect of Communism: in view of the responsibility of the Police for the maintenance of public order, Special Branch should collect information on Fascism, but MI 5 would collate Special Branch's information with material obtained from other sources and be responsible for evaluating it.[17]

From the time this arrangement came into force until the outbreak of war the BUF, or the British Union (BU) as it was known from the autumn of 1937, was a source of anxiety to the authorities because its increasing anti-semitism and its campaign of confrontation with the Jewish community and the Labour movement, especially in the East End, constituted a threat to the ability of the Police to maintain law and order. It was not seen as constituting a threat to national security, as opposed to law and order. For one thing, its increasing extremism was accompanied by a decline in membership. After rising dramatically to some 50,000 by June 1934, membership was down to 8,000 by the summer of 1938, and it recovered only to about 11,000 by the summer of 1939. More to the point, MI 5 uncovered no evidence that the movement had contacts with the Axis powers of a kind that justified alarm.[18]

There was reliable information, confirmed by Italian archives after the war, to the effect that it had been subsidised by the Italian government in the early years.[19] But even after 1936, when it became more strongly orientated towards Germany, adding 'National Socialists' to its title, adopting new uniforms similar to those of the SS and condoning all Hitler's actions at its meetings and in its paper, *Action*, no evidence was found to suggest that it was being subsidised by Germany or that Germany was interested in exploiting it for the purposes of intelligence and subversion. Nor has any such evidence come to light since the end of the war.[20] In July 1939 MI 5 still took the view that the BU, like several smaller groups which subscribed to the ideology of National Socialism, and particularly to its violent anti-semitism,* presented no threat to security so long as times remained normal, but it warned that in the event of war the movement might become a serious danger. Its close association with the Nazis made it probable that individual Fascists could be used by the Germans for espionage and sabotage; there was a risk that attempts would be made to provoke disaffection in the Services through anti-Jewish propaganda and to foment anti-Jewish riots in some areas; and the activities of the movement encouraged the Nazis in their belief that the British government would not have a united nation behind it.

The IRA was another source which might be exploited by foreign intelligence services as well as being a threat to security in its own right. From the spring of 1938, when it was taken over by an extremist group advocating the use of force to bring about the fusion of Northern Ireland with Eire, the IRA was known to be preparing for an 'English campaign' of sabotage and for guerrilla operations in Ulster in the event of, or even before, the outbreak of a European war. In January 1939 it warned that the campaign would begin if the British government failed to give a satisfactory response within four days to the demand for the withdrawal of British troops from Northern Ireland; bombs duly exploded in London and the provinces on 16 January, and the attacks continued spasmodically for several months.[21] Despite the IRA's narrow appeal, the fact that Eire formed a common travel area

---

* These included The Link, founded within the Anglo-German Friendship movement by Admiral Sir Barry Domvile, a former Director of Naval Intelligence, in 1937; the Nordic League; Arnold Leese's Imperial Fascist League, established in 1937 (see Appendix 5, item 10); the National Socialist League, a breakaway group from the BU formed by William Joyce and John Beckett in 1938; and the Right Club established by Captain Maule Ramsay MP in 1939.

with the United Kingdom, with frontiers that were uncontrolled and virtually uncontrollable, and the fact that she would almost certainly remain neutral in a war, made the IRA an obvious instrument for sabotage and espionage operations in the United Kingdom by an enemy power.

Evidence obtained from some of the spies detected in 1937 and 1938 showed that Germany was alive to the possibilities of Eire as a base for operations, and several reports alleging German contacts with the IRA were received in the early months of 1939. Apart from Dr Carl Petersen, the Dublin representative of the German News Agency and a favourite suspect who was rumoured to have guaranteed that the government of Ireland would be handed over to the IRA if the IRA helped Germany to win the war, these reports implicated three Germans who were all to serve the Abwehr during the war – Franz Fromme, who was known to have made a recent visit to Eire, Helmuth Clissmann, an exchange lecturer at Trinity College, Dublin since 1933 and Dr Jupp Hoven, a student of folklore who had arrived in Eire in 1938 and paid several visits to Ulster. In July 1939 the SIS heard that an IRA representative had been promised arms and funds at a meeting 'in Berlin with Admiral Canaris of the German War Office'; the report was accurate as to the central fact that the Abwehr had established contact with the IRA, though mistaken as to the place of the meeting, the presence of Canaris and the promise of immediate help, and it was understandably accepted by MI 5 as confirming its belief that Germany had made definite plans for using the IRA against the United Kingdom.

In April 1938 an agreement was signed between the British and Eire governments which provided for the withdrawal of British garrisons from the Treaty Ports. The Eire government had not disguised its intention to remain neutral if Britain were involved in war, but had also given assurances that it would not allow Eire to be used as a base for hostile operations. On 31 August 1939, at a meeting with an officer of MI 5, the Eire Minister for External Affairs expressed his government's concern about German intelligence activities in Eire and it was agreed that there should be an exchange of information on this subject. In October liaison was established with the Eire authorities which was to prove of considerable importance. It was always strictly confined to counter-espionage.

From the foundation in 1919 of the Russian-dominated Third International (the Comintern) as 'general staff' of an international revolutionary movement avowedly dedicated to 'the forcible destruction of the bourgeois state machine', the threat of subversion from Bolshevism was the chief preoccupation of the British security authorities, and not without good reason.

Great Britain and the British Empire (and India in particular) were the prime target of the campaign of subversion which the Comintern carried out until the Fascist threat compelled it to adopt a radical change of policy in the middle of the 1930s. The knowledge that this was so, which was based on the decrypts of Russian telegrams till 1927,* had almost prevented the conclusion of the Anglo-Soviet Trade Agreement of 1920, provoked a British threat to cancel that agreement in 1923, exerted a major influence on British politics in 1924 (the Zinoviev letter) and, coupled with evidence of Soviet espionage, led to the breaking of diplomatic relations in 1927.[22] The Communist Party of Great Britain (CPGB), founded in 1920 as a fully committed member of the Comintern, was all the more suspect because, unlike the Fascist movements, it had influence in the Trades Unions and attached importance to revolutionary work in the armed forces. The General Strike of 1926 had shown that Britain was not ripe for revolution. The ineffectiveness of the CPGB as an agent of subversion had been demonstrated in 1931; it exerted no influence during the grave economic crisis which brought the National government to power, and even the Invergordon mutiny in the Navy took it completely by surprise. But from 1935, when the Comintern temporarily subordinated the ultimate goal of world revolution to the immediate objective of fighting Fascism and defending the Soviet Union as the bastion of revolution, MI 5 believed that the threat from the CPGB was becoming greater than before because it was acquiring a cloak of respectability from its Popular Front policies and its prominence in the anti-Fascist crusade. In 1935 MI 5 argued that the new tactics 'show a distinct tendency by the Comintern to face realities and to adopt methods which, had they been exploited consistently since its inception, would certainly have produced far greater results'.

There was no lack of evidence to support this anxiety. In the summer of 1937, following early setbacks in the Popular Front campaign, the CPGB was severely criticised by the Comintern and instructed to be more whole-hearted in subordinating its revolutionary aims to the search for collaboration with the Labour movement. It was to declare its acceptance of the constitution of the Labour Party, support Labour candidates, try to enter into electoral agreements with the Labour Party – in an attempt to isolate its right-wing leaders – and transform the *Daily Worker* from a Communist paper into one that appealed to the entire working class. The membership of the CPGB, which had fallen from 10,000 to under 5,000 by 1931, grew to 16,000 by September 1938

---

* See Hinsley et al, *British Intelligence in the Second World War*, Vol 1 (1979), p 52.

and 17,500 in March 1939. The expansion of its influence beyond the membership was illustrated not only by the rise in the sales of the *Daily Worker* – to about 100,000 on weekdays and 150,000 on Saturdays – but also by the striking success of the Left Book Club; established in 1936, its membership was 30,000 by the end of the year and rapidly rising, and its 'circles' were frequently led by Communists. MI 5 noted in December 1937 that the Communist Party's policies were identifying it with the 'progressive elements' in the Labour Party and, in September 1938, that its moderation had strengthened its position in the Trades Unions.

While the Communists were unrivalled in the consistency with which they opposed the Fascist states, they displayed no less consistency in their hostility to the Chamberlain government. At the time of the Munich crisis MI 5 received a report to the effect that the CPGB had been told by the Comintern that Chamberlain must be turned out of office at all costs in the event of war, an alliance between his government and the Soviet Union being logically untenable. The policy which the CPGB would adopt if the Chamberlain government led Great Britain into war with the Fascist powers remained in doubt. The correct party line was that Hitler would not fight an alliance of Great Britain, France and the USSR but that, whatever he said, Chamberlain would not fight Hitler. Accordingly, the sheet anchors of Party policy in the run-up to the war were the need for an alliance with Russia and the replacement of Mr Chamberlain by a Popular Front government. MI 5's assessment of April 1939 was that, leaving aside its long-term dedication to the destruction of all capitalist regimes, 'the outbreak of war would not of itself rally the Communist Party against a totalitarian enemy. The support of the Party could never be given to a government which contained Mr Chamberlain . . . and this ruling appears to hold good even if the USSR should be fighting on the side of this country. Not only would the Communist Party withhold support . . . but it would take active steps to embarrass the Government by hindering the prosecution of the war in the hope that it might force its resignation'. In July 1939 the CPGB was still denouncing Chamberlain's government as Hitler's Fifth Column.

There was never any doubt that the Soviet intelligence authorities would exploit Communist loyalties for espionage purposes, but few cases of Soviet espionage came to light in the 1920s and 1930s. A network, probably run by the OGPU, which was under MI 5 surveillance for several years in the late 1920s, employed both Communist sympathisers and mercenary agents (two who belonged to Special Branch at Scotland Yard were identified and removed in 1929). In 1927 Wilfred Macartney, a convert to Communism and an alcoholic, was caught trying to obtain information about arms shipments to countries bordering the Soviet Union from a Lloyds underwriter and was found to have a Soviet control and contacts with Arcos (the All Russian Co-operative Society) and the Russian Trade Delegation.[23] In 1938 Percy Glading, a prominent member of the Communist Party since the early 1920s who had resigned from the party in 1936, was found to be controlling under Soviet orders a group of agents employed at the Woolwich Arsenal. But the identity of John King as a spy in the communications department of the Foreign Office was not uncovered until September 1939, on the evidence of the Soviet defector, Walter Krivitsky,* and the success of the Russian intelligence services in the 1930s in recruiting agents with no overt Communist asociations, but with Communist sympathies and educational and social backgrounds which would be likely to ensure that they would in due course reach positions of responsibility, remained hidden until after the war.

A survey of threats to security in 1939 would be incomplete without some reference to the pacifist movement. This was organised on an unprecedented scale from 1934 through the Peace Pledge Union (PPU), founded by Canon Dick Sheppard. The so-called Peace Ballot, completed in June 1935, was in fact a ringing assertion of support for collective security by all means short of war, and in the same year the pacifist left wing was routed at the TUC and Labour Party conferences and Mr George Lansbury, a pacifist, resigned the leadership of the Labour Party. In 1936 the Spanish Civil War shook the convictions of many who had come to pacifism through their belief in socialism. Despite these developments the Peace Pledge Union continued to prosper; its membership exceeded 130,000 at the outbreak of war and the circulation of its *Peace News* was about 40,000 copies. But it increasingly encountered accusations of being pro-Nazi and pro-appeasement as a result of its support for concessions to the German government and its campaign for friendship between the British and German peoples; and it did not stop short at pronouncements that were damagingly similar to Nazi propaganda. In a handbook of May 1939 it advised its members to co-operate

---

* Born Samuel Ginsburg in 1899, Krivitsky joined Soviet Military Intelligence in 1919 and served in several western countries and also at headquarters in Moscow. He was transferred to the OGPU (later the KGB) in 1935 and was sent to Holland. He defected in 1937 when ordered to return to Russia after the defection and subsequent assassination of his childhood friend and fellow OGPU agent, Ignaz Reiss. In 1941 Krivitsky was found dead in Washington, ostensibly by suicide but probably by assassination.

A strong case has been made for thinking that information which reached the German embassy in London in the summer of 1939 about the progress of the Anglo-French-Soviet negotiations was obtained from King by his Soviet controller and used selectively to move the German government towards a pact with Russia.[24]

with The Link and *The Anglo-German Review*, and urged them to make German pen friends and visit Germany, and it held joint meetings with The Link addressed by speakers from Germany. This development was inspired not by sympathy with Nazism but by the militant opposition to war in any form which underlay the efforts of the PPU to deter young men from registering for military service when national conscription was introduced in May 1939. In these circumstances the possible effects of pacifist activities on the national war effort could not be entirely discounted.[25]

□

In their preparations for the introduction of emergency security measures to reinforce the peace-time structure in the event of war the authorities adjusted the precedents set during the First World War to take account of the precautions called for by subsequent developments.

The peace-time structure rested mainly on the Official Secrets Act of 1911, as amended by the Act of 1920, on the Aliens Restrictions Acts 1914 and 1919 and on certain statutes passed to supplement the Common Law in cases of sedition and conspiracy. The Official Secrets Acts were widely drawn with a view to easing the task of the prosecution in cases involving the unauthorised acquisition, use or retention of official information. In the 1911 Act Section 1 penalised spying by providing for punishment where the information is calculated to be, or might be or is intended to be directly or indirectly useful to an enemy, and there is a wrongful intention amounting to a purpose prejudicial to the safety or the interests of the state; and Section 2 of the 1920 Act stipulated that communication or attempted communication with a foreign agent is evidence of obtaining or attempting to obtain such information. Section 2 of the 1911 Act penalised the unauthorised disclosure or voluntary unauthorised receipt of official information or negligent conduct which imperilled it. Section 3 of the 1911 Act gave special protection to the armed forces against espionage and sabotage by making any military establishment, arsenal, ordnance factory, or other factory making 'munitions of war' a 'prohibited place' and by specifying that any person approaching, inspecting, passing over or entering a 'prohibited place' for any purpose prejudicial to the safety or interests of the state is guilty of an offence under Section 1. Section 7 of the Act of 1920 made any attempt to commit an offence, and any act preparatory to the commission of an offence, under either of the two Acts punishable as if they were the offence itself.

Against subversion the Common Law relating to sedition and conspiracy provides powerful legal defences, but it is a somewhat unreliable weapon, suitable for use only in the most serious cases. In the 1930s it was supplemented by legislation. In 1934, following the conviction in 1933 of four Communists under the Incitement to Mutiny Act of 1797, the Incitement to Disaffection Act provided a summary method of dealing with attempts to seduce members of the armed forces from their allegiance. In 1936, in response to the activities of the British Union of Fascists, the Public Order Act prohibited the wearing of uniform in connection with political objectives and the maintenance by private persons of associations of a military character. In July 1939 the Prevention of Violence (Temporary Provisions) Act conferred additional powers to deal with the IRA, including the power to deport Eire citizens from the United Kingdom.

The plans for strengthening these existing legal defences against espionage, subversion and sabotage called for the passage of an Emergency Powers (Defence) Act, which would empower His Majesty in Council to make Defence Regulations; the use of the Royal Prerogative to authorise the censorship of all postal and telegraphic communications and the internment of enemy aliens; and the assumption by Order in Council under the Aliens Restriction Acts of additional powers for the control of all aliens, neutral as well as enemy.

A comprehensive code of Defence Regulations,[26] contravention of which would under the Emergency Powers (Defence) Act be punishable either summarily or on indictment, had been drawn up by the War Emergency Legislation Sub-Committee of the CID. Some of the regulations created new offences and provided special penalties for them. Most notably:

DR 2A provided that any person committing any act likely to assist an enemy, or prejudice the public safety or the defence of the realm or the efficient prosecution of the war with intent to assist the enemy, would, without prejudice to the law relating to treason, be guilty of an offence and liable to penal servitude for life;
DR 2B provided that acts of sabotage would be punishable by penal servitude for up to 14 years;
DR 7 made it an offence punishable by up to five years penal servitude for a British subject to enter enemy territory without official permission.

In war-time control of travel is a primary security measure. The movements of British subjects in and out of the United Kingdom would be controlled under DR 18, and those of aliens under an Order in Council to be made on or immediately prior to the outbreak of war, supplementing the peace-time provisions of the Aliens Order of 1920. By these means, no one would be allowed to land or embark except at an approved port. Aliens of whatever nationality would require visas and (as in peace-time) leave to land.

Aliens and British subjects would require leave to embark, which would be conditional on the production of a permit granted by a Permit Office set up alongside the Passport Office. Applications for permits would be checked by MI 5 and the Special Branch. MI 5, operating as the Central Security Office, would station a Security Control Officer (SCO) at each approved port to work in co-operation with a detachment of Field Security Police and the Immigration Officers. The powers to be assumed would cover control of passenger traffic within the British Islands (i.e. between Great Britain, Eire, Northern Ireland, the Channel Islands and the Isle of Man) which in peace-time formed a common travel area with complete freedom of movement.

The new Aliens Order would include additional powers for the stricter control of all aliens, especially enemy aliens. All aliens over 16 would have to register immediately with the Police. The Home Secretary would have power to restrict the employment of aliens in occupations offering opportunities for espionage, sabotage or propaganda, and to prohibit, and impose restrictions on, any alien entering or remaining in an area which he designated a Protected Area. Enemy aliens would have to obtain written permission from the Police to change residence, report to the Police daily during absences of more than 24 hours from the registered place of residence, and obtain permission to travel more than five miles from the registered place of residence (except in London) or to possess such articles as cameras, explosives and large scale maps. However, it was foreseen that some measure of general internment of enemy aliens would become inevitable; this could be effected under the Royal Prerogative.*

Only enemy aliens could be interned under the Royal Prerogative. An inter-departmental committee reported in 1937 that there was serious danger that attempts to impede the war effort might be made, not from sympathy with the enemy, but by persons with 'internationalist' affiliations, or acting out of disinterested opposition to war, and the Home Secretary told the CID that most of the people working for the Comintern in this country were British nationals.[27] It had therefore been decided that the Emergency Powers (Defence) Act would state specifically that Defence Regulations could make provision for the detention of suspects whose detention appeared to the Secretary of State to be expedient in the interests of public safety or the defence of the realm. Accordingly, the Defence Regulations conferred very wide powers on the control of suspects. DR 18A would empower the Home Secretary to restrict the movements of any individual when he was satisfied

---

* See Chapter 2 for the discussions of policy regarding the internment of enemy aliens.

that this was necessary in the interests of public safety or the defence of the realm. Under DR 18B the Home Secretary would be able to make an order restricting or prohibiting an individual's possession or use of specified articles, restricting him in respect of his business, employment, association and communications with other persons and in respect of his dissemination of news and opinions, or directing that he be detained. For the purposes of this regulation the Home Secretary would be required to appoint an Advisory Committee to which the individual might make objections. It was intended that only modest use of DR 18B would be made at the outbreak of war and, contrary to their expectations, no plans were made to use it against the leaders of the BU, the CPGB or the PPU. But as we shall see,* it attracted strong criticism and survived only for a few weeks in its original form.

For the war-time control of censorship of postal and telegraphic communications, the legal basis was the Prerogative power.† Postal and telegraphic censorship was to be effected by the introduction of comprehensive regulations drawn up by the CID's Standing Inter-departmental Committee on Censorship and, subject to consultation with other governments throughout the Empire, approved by the CID in July 1938.[29] Under these regulations all communications originating from or addressed to a destination abroad would be subject to examination, including those in transit, but internal communications would be free from censorship with the exception of messages sent by radio telegraphy, which might be intercepted by stations abroad, and the communications of individuals in respect of which the Home Secretary had issued a warrant for interception.‡

As in the First World War, the postal and telegraphic censorship

---

* See below, p 35.

† Censorship of the media was to be effected under the Defence Regulations. DR 3 provided that no person should obtain, record, communicate, publish or have in his possession any document containing information which 'would or might be directly or indirectly useful to any enemy'. DR 39B empowered the Home Secretary to prevent or restrict the publication in the United Kingdom of matters as to which he was satisfied that publication would or might be prejudicial to the defence of the realm or the official prosecution of the war. The intention was to keep these drastic powers in reserve and to operate Press censorship on a modified voluntary basis. The D-Notice system which had developed during the First World War, and which had been operated entirely voluntarily through the Admiralty, War Office, Air Ministry and Press Committee since 1919, would be suspended in favour of a system by which a Ministry of Information would advise editors what should not be published, what should be submitted for approval and what could be published without official scrutiny, and by which the Ministry could issue private and confidential communications to editors without the concurrence of the Press representatives on the Committee.[28]

‡ While communications to and from Northern Ireland and Eire in transit through Great Britain were to be censored from the outset, terminal communications between Great Britain and Northern Ireland and Eire were originally treated as internal, and thus generally free from censorship.

was to be under the control of the War Office, at any rate to begin with. The organisation was to be established before the outbreak of hostilities and the Government War Book authorised the War Office to assemble the necessary staff, which included chemists, physicists and cryptanalysts for the examination of letters in code or suspected of containing secret writing, in advance of the decision to introduce the precautionary stage. While the primary object of the censorship regulations was to stop communications injurious to security, a secondary object was the collection of information for counter-intelligence purposes. This was provided for in an appendix to the regulations, which required the censorship organisation to pass to MI 5 intercepted material containing information concerning past, present or projected activity that might be prejudical to public safety or the operations of His Majesty's Forces.[30]

Provisions against the evasion of the postal and telegraphic censorship were to be included in the Defence Regulations. DR 9 dealt comprehensively with pigeons. DR 10 forbade the possession and use without permission of means of secretly conveying information, such as invisible ink, codes and cyphers. DR 11 empowered the Home Secretary to forbid the conveyance of documents and photographs into or out of the United Kingdom except by post, and conferred the appropriate power to interrogate and search travellers. DR 8 empowered the Postmaster General to make an order forbidding the possession without permission of any article designed or adaptable for the transmission of wireless communications.

Other Defence Regulations would reinforce the provisions of the Official Secrets Acts for the protection of prohibited places. Under DR 12 any place from which the Home Secretary judged it expedient to exclude unauthorised persons could be declared a Protected Place, which would also automatically become a Prohibited Place attracting the special protection of the Official Secrets Acts. Most of the potential Protected Places in a long list drawn up by the Vulnerable Points Sub-Committee of the Home Defence Committee of the CID were comparatively small areas which did not include private dwellings. In the event that it became necessary to regulate entry into areas with a resident civilian population, DR 13 would empower the Home Secretary to declare a Protected Area which no enemy alien, and no person not resident there on a specified day, might enter without permission. Protected Areas would be areas which contained numerous Protected Places or were otherwise of special strategic importance. It was intended that the Orkneys and Shetlands and a large part of the coast of Scotland would be declared a Protected Area on the outbreak of war. A less cumbersome and less public means of controlling an area, where the need for precautions had arisen urgently or was expected to be only temporary, was provided under DR 14. This conferred powers to make by-laws in respect of any place where the presence of HM Forces or munitions called for special precautions.

CHAPTER 1: REFERENCES

1. CAB 93/3, HD(5)E of 26 October 1942.
2. ADM 116/3408, Report of Conference of Representatives, April 1907.
3. CAB 16/8, Foreign Espionage in the United Kingdom report and proceedings. See also N Hiley, 'The Failure of British Counter-Espionage against Germany 1907–14 in *Historical Journal* Vol 28 No 4 (1985).
4. F H Hinsley et al, *British Intelligence in the Second World War*, Vol I (1979), p 16.
5. Hiley, loc cit.
6. Papers of the Secret Service Committee 1919. (Retained in Private Office of the Secretary of the Cabinet).
7. Unregistered Papers in Cabinet Office Archive.
8. ibid.
9. ibid.
10. ibid.
11. P Leverkühn, *German Military Intelligence* (1954) pp 91–93.
12. Cmnd 283 Report of Committee of Privy Counsellors appointed to enquire into the interception of communications, October 1957, para 113.
13. CAB 2/5, CID 235th Meeting of 22 May 1928.
14. CAB 2/5, CID 258th Meeting of 6 April 1933.
15. CAB 23/85, Cabinet Conclusions 55(36) of 29 July;
    CAB 23/89, Cabinet Conclusions 30(37) of 24 July;
    CAB 24/263, CP 206(36) of 24 July; CAB 24/270, CP 182(37) of 14 July;
    CAB 53/31, COS 584(JIC) of 5 May 1937.
16. CAB 23/98, Cabinet Conclusions 13(39) of 20 March.
17. R C Thurlow, 'British Fascism and State Surveillance, 1934–1945' in *Intelligence and National Security*, Vol 3, No 1, p 79.
18. CAB 66/5, WP (43) 148 of 14 April; R C Thurlow, *Fascism in Britain: A History 1918–85* (1987); G Webber, 'Patterns of Membership and Support for the British Union of Fascists' in *Journal of Contemporary History*, No 19 (1984), pp 575–606.
19. C Andrew, *Secret Service; The Making of the British Intelligence Community* (1985), p 373; CAB 66/35, WP(43) 148 of 14 April.
20. Thurlow, 'British Fascism and State Surveillance', loc cit, pp 84–88.
21. CAB 24/283, CP 47/39 of 17 February 1939; J Bower Bell, *The Secret Army* (1970); T P Coogan, *The IRA* (1970).
22. C Andrew, 'The British Secret Service and Anglo-Soviet Relations in the 1920s' in *Historical Journal* Vol 20 No 3 (1977) and 'British Intelligence and the Breach with Russia', in *Historical Journal* Vol 25 No 4 (1982).
23. C Andrew, 'British Intelligence and the Breach with Russia', loc cit.
24. D C Watt, 'John Herbert King: A Soviet Source in the Foreign Office' in *Intelligence and National Security*, Vol 3 Number 4, October 1988.
25. A J P Taylor, *English History 1914–1945* (1965) pp 367, 374, 379; S Morrison, *I Renounce War, the Story of the Peace Pledge Union* (1962); Hansard Vol 348, Col 1343; Vol 350, Col 264.
26. Statutory Rules and Orders (SR & O), 1939 Nos 927, 978.
27. CAB 2/6, CID 295th Meeting of 1 July 1937.
28. CAB 4/28, CID 1446B of 15 July 1938, paras 175, 176.
29. CAB 2/7, CID 331st Meeting of 27 July 1938.
30. DEFE 1/333, History of the Postal and Telegraph Censorship; CAB 15/13, CC(C) 4th Meeting of 13 September 1920; CAB 15/14, CC(C) 12 of July 1920; CAB 2/7, CID 331st Meeting of 27 July 1938; CAB 4/28, CID 1446B of 15 July 1938; CAB 15/37, Government War Book, Chapter X.

CHAPTER 2

The Twilight War

THE EMERGENCY Powers (Defence) Act was passed
through all its stages in both Houses of Parliament on 24
August 1939. An Order in Council promulgating some of
the Defence Regulations was made on 25 August; the remainder –
those affecting freedom of political discussion and the Press or
otherwise interfering with civil liberties – were brought into effect
by another Order made on 1 September. The planned amendments to the Aliens Order were also made on 1 September. The
Postal and Telegraph Censorship began to operate on 31 August.[1]

MI 5 had played a large part in devising this programme; for
months before the outbreak of war its Deputy Director, Sir Eric
Holt-Wilson, had been almost exclusively engaged in its preparation, working most of the time in the Home Office. It was thus
quite satisfied with the programme's general scope and detailed
provisions. In a memorandum in November 1939 it was to say that
'the theoretical design of the protective network may be described
as being as perfect as MI 5 advice could obtain', and to insist that
the powers it made available against espionage and leakage were
more than adequate provided they were 'fully and intelligently
exercised by those invested with their executive application'. But it
was from the outset severely critical of decisions taken by the
Home Office about the implementation of those measures which
related to aliens.

An order prohibiting anyone from leaving the country without
an exit visa was made under DR 18 at the beginning of September
but, to the annoyance of MI 5, the Home Office deferred its
enforcement till 12 September out of the wish to encourage all
aliens to leave with the exception of enemy aliens who were on the
list of those to be arrested. More seriously, relations between MI 5
and the Home Office were soured throughout the period of the
Twilight War by disputes arising from their different interpreta-
tions of the agreements reached before the war on the policy to be
adopted for the internment of enemy aliens.

In a draft memorandum of June 1938 the Home Office had
noted that MI 5, considering that general internment by classes or
ages, as carried out in the last war, 'is unnecessary on security
grounds and inflicts great hardship on innocent people', had
recommended that 'enemy aliens as a class shall not be interned
immediately on the outbreak of war and that internment be

restricted to those who are individually considered to be dangerous'. The memorandum had accepted that this proposal had much
to commend it, in that it would lighten the heavy burden that
would fall on the Police at the outbreak of war, but pointed out
that the Home Office had to consider other factors besides
security. The public would probably demand comprehensive
internment, and in districts subject to heavy air attack enemy
aliens might have to be interned for their own safety. In these
circumstances, and in view of the fact that the number of male
Germans and Austrians in the United Kingdom was increasing
rapidly, the Home Office had believed that while lists might be
prepared of refugees who, initially at any rate, might be excluded
from general internment, plans should be drawn up to ensure that
accommodation was adequate for general internment of male
aliens. In its comments on the memorandum in July MI 5 had
adhered to its view that there should not be any general order for
the internment of male enemy aliens at the outset, so that the
introduction of a category of excluded refugees would be superfluous, and while accepting that public opinion might make
general internment unavoidable, had repeated the recommendation that priority should be given to detaining dangerous
individuals.[2]

In January 1939 the CID had appointed a sub-committee to
review and co-ordinate the plans being made to control aliens in
time of war. In February the sub-committee had considered a
Home Office memorandum which argued that, while there would
be no general internment of enemy aliens at the outbreak of war, it
seemed 'almost certain that this course would very soon be forced
on the Government by public opinion, especially in the event of
serious air raids . . .'. As internment would then have to be carried
out by classes, the War Office had undertaken to find accommodation for up to 18,000 German and Italian males. The sub-
committee had also noted that plans had been made for stricter
control of all aliens and particularly of enemy aliens, including the
arrest on instructions from MI 5, issued on the authority of the
Home Secretary, of certain categories of enemy or potential
enemy aliens – suspected agents, those belonging to organisations
maintained by foreign powers, those with technical or other
qualifications which would make them especially useful to an
enemy – and for the suspension of those employed at munitions
factories and other installations of special importance. The sub-
committee had approved these plans, but had recorded that 'we
concur with the Home Office view that some measure of general
internment will become inevitable at a very early date' after the
outbreak of war. The CID had accepted the sub-committee's
report on 6 April 1939.[3]

On the strength of these discussions the Home Secretary informed MI 5 on 29 August that, as agreed by the CID, he had decided to defer general internment for as long as possible; enemy aliens on the arrest lists would be interned, but tribunals would be set up to review the cases of all other enemy aliens aged 16 and over and determine whether they should be interned (Category A) or be subject to the restrictions prescribed in the amended Aliens Order (Category B) or be subject only to the rules applicable to all aliens and allowed to take employment (Category C). MI 5 expressed general agreement with this policy, and orders to the Police to detain enemy aliens and British subjects on the arrest list were issued on 1 and 2 September.[4] Of the Germans named in the arrest lists, some 900 in number, many had already left the country. For the list of British subjects to be detained under DR18B, the Police had nominated 18 members of the IRA and MI 5 had submitted the names of 22 individuals, 19 of them being known or suspected spies or of hostile origin and only three, including William Joyce, being selected because they were 'unreservedly pro-Nazi'.[5] Joyce, also, had already left the country.

The new Home Secretary, Sir John Anderson, made a statement in Parliament on policy towards aliens on 4 September.[6] He explained how the Aliens Order had been strengthened to provide closer controls over both enemy and neutral aliens and emphasised that, while care must be taken to sift out any that were unfriendly, very many Germans and Austrians were refugees. Tribunals were therefore being appointed to review all Germans and Austrians; Czechs would not be treated as enemy aliens but would be examined by a special tribunal; and an advisory committee was being established to hear representations from those aliens who were interned. This announcement of the government's intention to avoid general internment was greeted with approval by Parliament and the Press.[7]*

In the next few months, as the circumstances of the Twilight War belied the universal pre-war expectation that public opinion would insist on the general internment of enemy aliens before long, the Home Office and MI 5 moved in opposite directions from their pre-war positions. The Home Office had previously insisted that preparations should be made for general internment; it now became convinced that there was no need for it, and that it would be politically unwise unless it was clearly justified. And more

---

* And also abroad. The United States government had invited the belligerent governments to avoid general internment of civilian enemy aliens. The British government replied in November that it intended to retain the policy of individual examination, and Germany gave a similar assurance. The US government expressed the hope that these decisions would establish precedents for international law.[8]

than that, it encouraged the tribunals to adopt a more lenient
attitude in their examinations. In September a memorandum of
guidance to the tribunals had stated that security requirements
were to be paramount; if there was any substantial doubt about an
enemy alien's friendliness to the country he should be placed in
Category A or B. But a circular of 21 October urged tribunals to
adopt a liberal interpretation of the status of 'refugee', and
another of 11 November invited them to review earlier decisions
in the light of the October circular. This resulted in the transfer to
Category C of 1,883 persons originally placed in Category B.*
MI 5, on the other hand, which before the outbreak of war had
attached far less importance to general internment than to the
arrest of dangerous individuals, insisted from early in September
that the deferment of general internment was not only dangerous
but was being forced on it in contravention of the policy agreed
before the war.

Its mounting resentment was sustained by the fact that from the
outbreak of war its staff was overwhelmed by a huge increase in its
work under which MI 5 was near to breaking down completely by
the spring of 1940. By no means all the escalation of the demands
on it was caused by the deferment of general internment; there
was a huge increase in the volume of vetting† and in the work
involved in travel control. But the flood of reports from the Police
and of denunciations of individuals by the public was in large
measure related to enemy aliens. Moreover, as it reported to the
Home Office on 16 September, it received 'many protests from
local Service authorities . . . that, at this vital period of the war,
action has been suspended as regards the many . . . enemy aliens
in this country'. And to add to its difficulties, the Service departments, which shared its view that to leave enemy aliens at large was
to run the unacceptable risk of increasing the danger from
espionage and sabotage, backed their representations with asser-
tions about leakages of intelligence that cast doubt on the efficiency of MI 5 and the SIS.

□

As early as 16 September 1939, on behalf of the Prime Minister,
Sir Horace Wilson, the Permanent Under-Secretary in the Treas-

---

* In all, more than 100 tribunals, chaired by County Court Judges, Recorders and other
experienced lawyers, dealt with 71,553 cases; of these, 572 were placed in Category A, 6,690
in Category B and 64,290 in Category C. The Police provided a secretary for each tribunal
and were responsible for bringing the cases and providing information about each individual.

† The weekly average of vetting submissions rose from 2,300 in January 1939 to 6,800 in
September and to over 8,000 iin June 1940 when the vetting of many industrial grades was
abandoned to ease the load. See further below, p 248n.

ury, asked Hankey, now Minister without Portfolio, to look into allegations by the Chiefs of Staff that the Germans were receiving intelligence, it was thought by wireless, about military operations, a less than successful sortie by the RAF against Wilhelmshafen being cited as an example, and on such other matters as the removal of government departments from London.[9] Hankey consulted MI 5 and the SIS on the possible sources of leakages. MI 5 pointed to Eire, and particularly to the German Minister in Dublin with his freedom to receive information from agents in the United Kingdom either during their visits to him or in their uncensored letters, telegrams and telephone calls, and recommended the introduction of comprehensive censorship and control of traffic between the UK and Eire and a stricter policy towards enemy aliens. The SIS thought there were several outlets: Eire, foreign embassies in London, post boxes in Holland, illicit wireless and a regular courier service of neutrals had all to be considered. Replying to the Prime Minister on 28 September, Hankey was sceptical both about the specific leakages mentioned by the Chiefs of Staff and about the value to the enemy of most of the outlets mentioned by MI 5 and the SIS, but he emphasised that the existence of illicit wireless and other technical means of communicating 'hot' information to the enemy ought to be thoroughly investigated.[10]

The uneasiness of the Service departments, which was being fed by widely circulated rumours that German broadcasts were revealing inside knowledge, was not allayed by Hankey's report. On 31 October the First Lord of the Admiralty, Mr Winston Churchill, persuaded the War Cabinet to appoint Hankey, the Home Secretary and the Dominions Secretary (Mr Anthony Eden) as a Leakage of Information Committee to report on the control of communications with Eire and Northern Ireland.[11] On the same day the Secretary of the Admiralty wrote to the Home Office proposing that the principal ports and bases should be declared Protected Areas under the Aliens Order. The committee's conclusions on Eire, accepted by the War Cabinet on 4 November, were that censorship of all postal and telegraphic traffic and the rigorous control of passenger traffic were not yet justified, as the most that could be said was that Eire was one of several sources of leakage.[12] As for the creation of Protected Areas, the Home Office would not accept the Admiralty's wish that all enemy aliens should be prohibited from residing near ports and bases and that all aliens, enemy or not, should be prevented from moving into them. Nor would it agree that the Police should have the arbitrary power of deciding which aliens should be excluded.

In the course of further discussions MI 5 repeated its view that while the powers available under the Royal Prerogative, the Defence Regulations and the Aliens Order were adequate for security purposes, the system was being undermined by the failure to intern enemy aliens and to take steps about Eire. It again argued that all able-bodied and able-minded enemy aliens should be interned and that Eire should either be treated as a neutral, which would permit the application of censorship, travel control and other security measures to her communications with the United Kingdom, or be persuaded to impose such measures herself.[13] The Leakage of Information Committee remained unimpressed. It reported to the War Cabinet at the end of December that 'the vast majority of the allegations as to leakages being revealed by German broadcasts had proved without foundation' and that, as investigations had not disclosed any leakage through Eire, there was still no case for extending censorship to her postal and telegraphic traffic. Despite a warning from the Home Secretary that the proposal would inflict hardship on aliens, it did, however, recommend that five ports (Firth of Forth, Harwich, Chatham, Portsmouth and Plymouth) should be declared Protected Areas under the Aliens Order.[14] The War Cabinet noted these conclusions and approved this recommendation on 4 January 1940.[15]

Virtually all voices raised in public had so far supported the Home Office's policy, urging that if anything there should be more generous treatment of aliens and more care on the part of the tribunals to avoid injustice to individuals. At the beginning of December a delegation from the Parliamentary Committee on Refugees pressed these points on the Home Secretary and asked for the provision of machinery for appeals from decisions by the tribunals. From January 1940, however, signs of public unease about the leniency of the policy began to appear. In that month the newspapers carried articles alleging that the Police were unhappy about the leniency of the tribunals, and the Home Secretary was asked in the House of Commons what representations he had received from the Police and the Service ministries regarding the number and character of enemy aliens granted exemption from internment. The Home Secretary replied that guidance had been issued to the tribunals after consultation with the Police and Service intelligence departments and he had no reason to doubt that in general the tribunals had followed it. Cases were, however, open to review and a scheme for reviewing certain cases was being considered.[16] The outcome was the establishment of a review committee in each Civil Defence Region, but MI 5 continued to voice its misgivings to the Home Office. The Services remained dissatisfied and thought that MI 5 was not putting its case forcefully enough.[17] On 21 March the Deputy Chiefs of Staff urged that the adoption of a stricter policy towards aliens should be considered in order to reduce the risk of sabotage and so permit a reduced scale of protection of Vulnerable Points.[18] The Home Office was preparing to answer with a full statement defending its policy when the Twilight War was ended by the invasion of Denmark and Norway on 9 April.

□

By this time the dispute about policy towards enemy aliens was becoming a controversy about the control of all potentially disloyal elements, British as well as alien.

The War Cabinet had considered whether to take action against the overt anti-war propaganda of the BU and the CPGB in October 1939. Advised by the Home Office that if action were taken against them under DR 39B it might also have to be taken against the PPU, and that this might well excite public sympathy for those who were prosecuted, it had concluded that the propaganda had so far made no headway, and that prosecution would do more harm than good.[19]

Although the authorities had no plans for immediate action against them, the BU, the CPGB and even the PPU had expected to be proscribed on the outbreak of war and had made arrangements to carry on their activities clandestinely. They were encouraged when the wide-ranging powers the government had taken to deal with subversion were emasculated following a House of Commons debate at the end of October.[20] DR 18B, DR 39A and DR 39B – which had contained wide powers against attempts to spread disaffection by persuasion, propaganda and the publication of matter prejudicial to the defence of the realm – were especially criticised; the Home Secretary was forced to consult critics in the political parties and re-submit the Regulations.[21] The powers conferred by DR 18B to issue a detention order, or to impose special restrictions, were confined to cases where the Secretary of State had reasonable cause to believe any person to be of hostile origin or associations, or to have been recently concerned in acts prejudicial to the public safety or the defence of the realm, or in the preparation or instigation of such acts. The suspect's right to make objections to the Advisory Committee was spelt out in greater detail, and the Secretary of State was required to make a report to Parliament at least once a month on the action taken under the Regulation, and as to the number of cases in which he had declined to follow the Committee's advice. The concept of 'causing disaffection' in DR 39A was limited to endeavours to seduce persons in His Majesty's service from their duty. The operation of DR 39B was confined to endeavours to influence public opinion by 'any false statement, false document or false report', and the power conferred by this Regulation to prevent or restrict publication of matters prejudicial to the defence of the realm or the efficient prosecution of the war was drastically curtailed.

In addition to publishing 'stop the war' pamphlets the PPU waged a vigorous campaign to encourage people to claim exemption from military service and provided advice on how to obtain it. The campaign was not conspicuously successful, but PPU membership may have been higher in the spring of 1940 than at the outbreak of war.[22] The BU was no less active in pursuit of the theme of the message which Mosley had issued on 1 September 1939: the government was intervening in an alien quarrel, a quarrel not of the British people but of Jewish finance, in which neither Britain nor her Empire was threatened. Defeatist, anti-Jewish and pro-Nazi propaganda was carried on by leaflets, wall slogans and chain letters. A Young Men's Advisory Committee was set up to advise BU supporters on how to claim exemption as conscientious objectors. On 15 October Mosley appealed for the acceptance of Hitler's offer of peace terms to an audience which sang the BU's marching song to the tune of the Horst Wessel Lied.[23] In January 1940 he published a pamphlet – 'The British Peace and how to get it' – with a print order of 2 million copies. The CPGB, which had announced qualified support for the war against Hitler on 2 September, soon changed its policy to that of 'revolutionary defeatism' in obedience to the Comintern's decision that the working classes of the bourgeois states should work for their military defeat and so produce a revolutionary situation. On 7 October the Party published a manifesto announcing that 'the continuance of the war is not in the interests of the people of Britain, France or Germany . . . The struggle of the British people against the Chamberlains and Churchills is the best help to the struggle of the Germans against Hitler'.[24]* The Comintern had enjoined caution in executing the new policy and it was thereafter pursued surreptitiously by encouraging attempts to foment discontent, pressure for higher wages and strikes which had no overtly political motive.[25] And after the outbreak of the Russo-Finnish war in December 1939 the CPGB mounted a major propaganda effort against 'the campaign of hatred and war-lust against the Soviet Union'. Although the *volte face* led to many resignations, the new policy enabled the CPGB to offer itself as a rallying point for opposition to a government that was receiving general support from the official Labour leadership. In January its membership was higher, at around 20,000, than it had been at the outbreak of war.

---

* For an account of the debate leading to the reversal of policy see Appendix 2, which is based on documents taken by the Police during a search carried out in June 1940.

From January 1940 misgivings that the lack of action against these groups might have dangerous consequences became widespread. On 23 February and 1 March the Home Secretary was questioned in the House of Commons about the PPU's programme of encouraging and assisting people to claim exemption from military service on conscientious grounds.[26] On 2 March he invited the Cabinet's Home Policy Committee (HPC) to consider whether it was desirable to make a new Defence Regulation forbidding incitement to evade military service.[27] On 28 February, meanwhile, at a meeting of the Cabinet's Civil Defence Committee, several ministers had expressed anxiety about subversive propaganda and the Home Secretary, acknowledging that he was receiving complaints from all quarters, had invited the Ministry of Information to circulate a memorandum.[28]

This memorandum,[29] which examined the anti-war activities of the BU, the CPGB and the PPU and concluded that neither 'political pacifism' nor 'conscientious pacifism' had yet reached dangerous dimensions, was considered by the HPC on 19 March, together with a paper from the Home Secretary on the PPU. The HPC concluded that the PPU's campaign was having little effect, the proportion of applications for exemption from military service showing a continuous decline, but that Communist and Fascist propaganda was much more dangerous. It deferred a decision as to whether to introduce a new Defence Regulation against pacifist propaganda.[30]

The memorandum had been prepared by the Ministry of Information's intelligence section which, the Ministry confessed, 'is still embryonic'. MI 5 learned only by accident that the Home Secretary had invited the Ministry to produce it, and was not consulted in its preparation. But it did not disagree with its conclusions. MI 5 recognised that the vast majority of the PPU members were genuine pacifists, though it kept an eye on its small Fascist connections – notably those who had set up the British Council for Christian Settlement in Europe, the president of which was the Marquis of Tavistock (shortly to become the Duke of Bedford), the Secretary John Beckett formerly of the BU and Joyce's Nationalist Socialist League, and the treasurer Captain Gordon Canning of the BU and The Link.* It believed that the BU should be regarded as the English branch of the NSDAP; it was 'not merely a party advocating an anti-war and anti-government policy, but a movement whose aim it is to assist the enemy in every way it can', with a core of fanatics who would be

---

* The British Council for Christian Settlement became prominent for a short time in March 1940; following a visit by its President to the German legation in Dublin, it published proposals which claimed to represent the terms on which Germany would make peace.

prepared to take active steps to this end if the opportunity occurred. But it had still found no evidence that these extremist elements had been penetrated by the enemy for espionage or subversive purposes.* As for the CPGB, MI 5 took the view in February 1940 that it was a nuisance, but not capable of seriously disrupting the war effort.

During the next two months, largely as a result of the de-briefing of Walter Krivitsky,† MI 5's attitude to the threat from the CPGB and refugee aliens who were Communists hardened. Krivitsky insisted that the Russians would use the CPGB as a Fifth Column on a large scale in the event of war with Great Britain. He also claimed that former friendly contacts between the Russian and the German intelligence services would have been revived following the German-Soviet pact and they would be collaborating against the United Kingdom, the Soviet diplomatic bag being put at the disposal of Germany for the despatch of espionage material. His opinions could not be lightly dismissed. MI 5 relied on them in a memorandum to the Home Office on 12 April, shortly after the German invasion of Denmark and Norway. This drew attention particularly to German, Austrian and Czech Communists who had arrived as refugees in 1938–1939, claiming that they were actively propagating Communist propaganda under the shelter of the Czech Refugee Trust Fund. It argued that many of them were revolutionaries carefully trained in illegal work who represented a serious threat as tools of the Russians and, at second hand, of the Germans; and it recommended the immediate internment of some 20 of them and closer control of their rank and file. It recommended, also, the detention of the leading British Communists in the event of war with Russia and, more immediately, the refusal of travel facilities to British Communists and the prohibition of the export of Communist propaganda.

The Home Office decided at the end of April that the internment of refugees solely on the ground that they were Communists was not yet justified; that it was questionable whether British Communists could be detained under DR 18B as revised in November 1939; and that travel applications had to be dealt with on the merits of each case. The banning of the export of propaganda was under discussion.

□

---

* Not even in the case of Duvivier and Crowle. Duvivier, an officer of the BU, and Crowle, employed at Devonport dockyard, were sentenced in January 1940 under the Defence Regulations for the improper communication of information about damage to British warships. This had been supplied by Crowle to Duvivier and passed by him to the editor of *Action*.

† See above p 20.

Meanwhile, early in March, Hankey had been asked to extend to MI 5 an enquiry which he had been carrying out into the SIS since December at the request of the Prime Minister, the Foreign Secretary and the Service Ministers.*

During March and April the enquiry took evidence from senior officials in MI 5, the Home Office, the Metropolitan Police, the Directors of Intelligence in the Service departments, the Director of Public Prosecutions and the Chairman of the Advisory Committee on internment cases (Mr Norman Birkett, KC). From the evidence submitted to Hankey, it is clear that relations had become so severely strained by the conflict of views, particularly about the treatment of enemy aliens, that MI 5 had become acutely restless about its constitutional position.[31]

MI 5 repeated its long-standing criticism of the Home Office's policy towards enemy aliens and of the methods of operation of the tribunals and the Advisory Committee; it complained that they were allowing the wish to avoid injustice to over-ride the requirements of security by accepting too easily the claims made for the reliability of aliens and insisting that the onus of proof was on the security authorities. It further argued that it was gravely handicapped by having no single higher authority on whose support it could rely if its advice was rejected by the departments which had the executive responsibility. It asked to be placed under a centrally placed minister who had no departmental responsibilities. The Home Office representatives retorted that except for the activities it carried out for the armed forces, MI 5 was attached to the Home Secretary; they were irritated that it should question policy decisions he had taken and seek to be in a position to get them reversed, and they believed it was over-suspicious. On this point they were strongly supported by Birkett, who claimed that MI 5 had committed 'gross mistakes and pathological stupidities' in its representations to the Advisory Committee on cases of internment. The Directors of Intelligence joined MI 5 in its opposition to the Home Office's policy, but were equally critical of MI 5 for not pressing hard enough for a change of policy.[32]

Hankey declined to recommend any change in MI 5's constitutional position. He argued that it was not as impotent as it had suggested; if it felt Home Office policy was wrong it was entitled to make representations to the Home Secretary and send copies to the Service departments, and they were not only entitled, but bound, to take the matter up with the Home Office and insist on a settlement through the normal constitutional channels.[33] This argument, though theoretically correct, took no account of the fact

---

* See Hinsley et al, *British Intelligence in the Second World War*, Vol 1, (1979), pp 91–92.

that such a course would incur the displeasure of the Home Office and put MI 5 in an invidious position. The real problem, however, lay not with MI 5's inability to make representations – it had made them often enough. It lay in the fact that, as it could produce no evidence of preparations for espionage and sabotage, it could support its demand for a change of policy towards aliens only by repeating its fervent belief that it was no longer dealing with a specialised espionage system, as in 1914, but with an intelligence organisation directed on totalitarian lines which would show its hand only when the enemy was ready.

In his report Hankey did not attempt to dispute this belief, the more so because he was writing after the German invasion of Denmark and Norway which had been welcomed by collaborators. He concluded with the following statement:

'We cannot be sure that, when the real emergency comes, the traitors within our gates, directed by some organisation which we may so far have been unable to detect, may not deal us a crippling blow. For this reason I trust that all concerned will give the fullest possible weight to any precautions which the Security Service may see fit to recommend. We simply cannot afford to take any risks, and any injustices to which such precautions may give rise are of minor importance compared with the safety of the State'.[34]

At the same time, on the grounds that the question could be decided only by results in 'the supreme emergency' which had not yet arisen, he formally reserved judgment on the question of MI 5's efficiency. Provisionally, however, he took the view that there was no evidence to suggest that it had fallen below the high standard it had maintained in the First World War.[35]

Hankey's report was not signed until 11 May, the day after the German invasion of the Low Countries and France had precipitated the Fifth Column panic. It was not circulated till the end of May. On 29 May the Cabinet Secretary sent it to Chamberlain, now Lord President, suggesting tht he should send it to the Prime Minister. There is no record that he did so, but a copy was sent on 3 June to Lord Swinton, Chairman of the newly established Security Executive.[36]*

□

In one respect Hankey's provisional commendation of MI 5's performance was not wide of the mark. With hindsight we can see that, though the results appeared to be small, it had not failed

---

* See below, p 53.

since the outbreak of war to detect any of the enemy activity that was in fact taking place in the United Kingdom.

MI 5's penetration of the Abwehr started as soon as war broke out, on the basis of small pre-war beginnings and without the benefit of any new intelligence from the SIS or any other sources. Of the six agents known to be working in Britain for the Hamburg station in September 1939, four were at once interned as being unimportant and unlikely to provide leads to other members of the German network. The other two were a Swedish woman, suspected by MI 5 since 1938 to be acting as a courier and local banker for the Hamburg station, and a Welsh electrical engineer who had been briefly employed by the SIS in 1936 before it was discovered that he was in contact with the Germans. The Swedish woman (Mrs My Ericksson) was left at liberty until December 1939, when she was arrested for giving false particulars in her application for an exit permit. Although her connection with the Abwehr was to be confirmed in the autumn of 1940,* she had produced no evidence leading to the detection of other agents. It was otherwise with the electrical engineer, known as *Snow* by the British authorities. Since 1936 he had kept in touch with the SIS and Special Branch, reporting on his contacts with the Germans and on the information they were asking him to supply. In September 1938 he had notified them that he had been appointed the chief German agent in England and had been promised a short wave wireless transceiver. This arrived early in 1939, via the left luggage office at Victoria station, and he handed it over for examination. On 11 August 1939 *Snow* travelled to Hamburg. A week later his wife and son denounced him to the Police as a German agent. He returned to England on 23 August, but he was missed at the port of entry and was not located until 4 September when he telephoned his Special Branch contact to arrange a meeting, saying that he wanted to offer his services to the British government. He agreed to continue under MI 5's control the radio contact which he had already established with the Germans. Whatever his motives – and even if his sympathies remained with the Germans rather than the British – he was thus the *fons et origo* of the use of enemy agents for double-cross purposes. In addition to maintaining the radio contact, moreover, he continued to meet Germans in Holland and Belgium with MI 5's knowledge, and was instrumental in enabling MI 5 to uncover other agents.

At one of these meetings, in Antwerp at the end of October, *Snow*, who had been asked to find a Welsh Nationalist to organise sabotage operations in south Wales, was accompanied by an MI 5

* See Appendix 6, p 324.

nominee, alias *GW*. This man was accepted by the Germans as a suitable recruit, informed of a plan to ship arms and explosives to Wales by U-boat, given some elementary training in sabotage and provided with a cover address so that he could report independently of *Snow*. *Snow* was told that he would receive money from a woman living in Bournemouth and was given a letter of introduction to a man in Liverpool. *Snow* received three remittances of money by post, the last of £20 in £5 notes marked 'S & Co' on the back. This clue led to Selfridges where the history of the notes (comparatively uncommon in 1938 and treated with becoming reverence) was traced through various departments: in each case a tall, elderly woman had asked for a £5 note in exchange for five £1 notes. A tentative identification of a woman living in Bournemouth, of German birth but British by marriage, was confirmed by two Selfridges cashiers. She was put under surveillance, but no other action was taken against her for the time being in order to avoid compromising *Snow* and in the hope that she would provide other leads. The man in Liverpool turned out to be a British subject born in the United Kingdom of a German father, who had been recruited as a spy in 1938 under threat of reprisals against a brother living in Germany. An expert photographer, he was to be used to produce and develop micro-photographs about the size of a postage stamp which the Germans planned to use for some of their communications with the United Kingdom.* He became a sub-agent of *Snow* operating with the alias *Charlie* under MI 5's control. At another meeting with the Germans in February 1940, *Snow* on MI 5's instructions got them to agree to the establishment of a link between business addresses in London and Antwerp for the exchange of messages and the despatch of equipment to him. This was set up in March.

The Abwehr and the IRA had made contact in the summer of 1939, when arrangements were made with the IRA emissary Seamus O'Donovan to establish wireless communication. This was set up at the end of October but it proved short-lived: the transmitter was seized when, following an IRA attack on an Eire Army magazine, the Eire government passed an Emergency Powers Act and carried out a series of police raids on IRA premises. In an attempt to re-establish it, the Abwehr despatched Ernst Weber-Drohl to Eire with a wireless set and money in February 1940. This improbable agent – he had worked the Irish fairs as a weightlifter and a wrestler in his youth, but spoke with a thick Austrian accent and was now over 60 – dropped the transmitter into the Irish Sea after transferring from a U-boat to a

---

* For the further development of this technique see below, p 103.

small vessel in a gale. He got ashore and delivered the money, but was arrested for illegal entry and subsequently interned.

Independently of their relations with *Snow* and the IRA, the Germans made contact with two other people who came to MI 5's notice in the early months of the war. A German businessman (Werner Unland), who had been living in England but was not on MI 5's list of suspects, had moved just before the outbreak of war to Eire, where he attracted attention by writing frequent letters in plain language code to a cover-address in Hamburg. The other man was born in England of a German mother and brought up in Germany, but had returned to England in 1938. In January 1940 he reported to the Police that a German school friend had written to him from Antwerp offering him an agency in commercial intelligence. On MI 5's instructions he met his friend in Antwerp in February and April and was recruited as a German spy. He was to operate under business cover as the agent of a Belgian firm, receiving instructions in micro-photographs on full stops in business letters and reporting in secret writing on developments in aviation, air defence and air raids. On his return to England he served as a double agent under the alias *Rainbow*.

These two cases, and the contacts given to *Snow*, made the importance of German connections obvious enough to justify the suspicion that others might be escaping notice when the enemy alien population was so large. Moreover, even if the Germans had made no preparations for such a development, the danger of collaboration and sabotage from some enemy aliens and extreme Fascist elements in the event of invasion could by no means be dismissed. But despite these considerations the limited number of agents detected, and the ease with which they had been detected, might have kept wariness short of serious anxiety that a large and well organised Fifth Column was waiting. This was all the more the case in view of the fact that by the spring of 1940 the watch for illicit wireless transmissions was beginning to provide suggestive evidence to the same effect. The organisation responsible for the interception of illicit wireless transmissions, the future RSS, continued to be controlled by the War Office – by MI 1(g) till November 1939 and by MI 8(c) after that date – with the GPO acting as its agent for the provision of men and material and the maintenance and operation of the intercept stations. By the outbreak of war its headquarters staff had been located close to GC and CS, which was to be responsible for cryptanalytic work on the intercepts, and it had finally established the beginnings of a network with the decision in March 1939 to establish three fixed and four mobile stations and the recruitment, from June 1939, of an auxiliary observer corps of amateur radio enthusiasts. But it had listened in vain for transmissions from the United Kingdom –

in vain because it was still the case that no transmissions were being made apart from those on *Snow's* set which was operating under MI 5's control. Since *Snow's* signals had not been heard before MI 5 took control of him, the failure to intercept others was understandably attributed to the inefficiency of the watch or to technical problems, notably the difficulty of picking up low-powered high frequency signals except at very close or very long range. By December 1939, however, it had been recognised that this difficulty did not apply to transmissions made from Germany to agents: they had to be able to receive their control stations signals, and if they could hear them, so could the RSS. On the strength of this elementary insight and with assistance from MI 5's operation of *Snow's* set, which had shown what type of message had to be looked for and had disclosed the characteristics of the operators at the Hamburg station, the RSS had by March 1940 intercepted wireless traffic between Hamburg and a ship, the *Theseus*, off the Norwegian coast, and between Hamburg and several agents in Holland, Belgium, Luxembourg and France, and GC and CS and the RSS itself had broken the simple cyphers used.* In April similar traffic was intercepted from a station somewhere in Eire. But apart from those exchanged with *Snow* no transmissions to or from the United Kingdom had yet been detected and it was beginning to be reasonable to assume that no others were being made.†

At this point a party was set up at GC and CS to be responsible for solving, decrypting and circulating the messages and Mr Oliver Strachey was put in charge of it.‡ But it was agreed that the RSS, originally charged with intercepting illicit traffic only from the United Kingdom, should continue to be responsible for intercepting it throughout Europe in view of its growing knowledge of the wireless procedure of the expanding German organisation.

---

* In fact the significance of the intelligence derived from them had been overlooked. The NID had failed to link the activities of the *Theseus* with other evidence for the German invasion of Norway. The decrypts of the second group, originally Gestapo-type messages enquiring about the whereabouts of individuals, had come to include enquiries about road blocks, defences and troop dispositions in the region through which the Germans eventually made their attack on France; but they do not appear to have been brought to the notice of the British and French military intelligence bodies. (See Hinsley et al op cit, Vol 1, pp 120, 131).

† See Appendix 3 for a later report on the assistance obtained from *Snow's* transmissions and the difficulties that uncontrolled agents faced in transmitting from the United Kingdom.

‡ In late October 1940 circulation arrangements were re-organised and decrypts were thenceforward issued as the ISOS series (Intelligence Section, Oliver Strachey). References to ISOS throughout this volume refer to decrypts and translations of German intelligence messages regardless of the originating service (eg Abwehr or SD) or cypher system involved; this was common practice in the Second World War.

CHAPTER 2: REFERENCES

1. Hansard, Vol 351, Cols 63–110; Lords Vol 114, Cols 895–903; SR & O Nos 927, 994; DEFE 1/333, History of the Postal and Telegraph Censorship Department, p x.
2. HO 144/21258/700463/4.
3. CAB 16/211, CAW 1, 12, 13 and 21 of 13 January, 14 and 17 February, 1 April 1939, and CAW 2nd Meeting of 20 February 1939; CAB 2/8, CID 352nd Meeting of 6 April 1939.
4. HO 144/21256/700452.
5. Thurlow, 'British Fascism and State Surveillance 1934–1945' in *Intelligence and National Security*, Vol 3, No 1, pp 86–87.
6. Hansard, Vol 351, Cols 366–370.
7. Louis de Jong, *The German Fifth Column in the Second World War* (1956) p 100.
8. CAB 67/6, WP(G)(40) 115 of 29 April.
9. CAB 76/14, LI(39)2 of 16 September 1939.
10. Hankey Papers on LI Committee. Retained in the Private Office of the Secretary of the Cabinet; CAB 76/14, LI (39)2 of 28 September 1939.
11. CAB 65/1, WM(39)66 of 31 October; CAB 65/2, WM (39)70 of 4 November.
12. CAB 76/14, LI(39) 1st Meeting of 1 November; CAB 65/1, WM (39)70 of 4 November.
13. CAB 76/14, LI(39)8 of 27 December.
14. CAB 76/14, LI(39)7 of 24 December.
15. CAB 65/5, WM(40)3 of 4 January.
16. Hansard, Vol 356, Cols 801–802.
17. Hankey Papers, 'MI 5'. Retained in Private Office of the Secretary of the Cabinet.
18. CAB 82/2, DCOS(40) 13th Meeting of 21 March.
19. CAB 67/1, WP(G)(39)36 of 14 October; CAB 65/1, WM(39)49 of 16 October.
20. Hansard, Vol 352, Cols 1829 et seq.
21. SR & O 1939 No 1681.
22. CAB 75/6, HPC(40)45 of 2 March; CAB 75/4, HPC(40) 11th Meeting of 19 March.
23. CAB 66/35, WP(43)148 of 14 April.
24. CAB 66/35, WP(43)109 of 13 March.
25. ibid.
26. Hansard, Vol 357, Cols 1504–6 and 2245–6.
27. CAB 75/6, HPC(40)45 of 2 March.
28. CAB 73/2, CDC(40) 7th Meeting of 28 February.
29. CAB 73/3, CDC(40)8, undated.
30. CAB 75/4, HPC(40) 11th Meeting of 19 March.
31. Hankey Papers, 'MI 5'. Retained in the Private Office of the Secretary of the Cabinet.
32. ibid.
33. ibid.
34. ibid.
35. ibid.
36. Folder retained in the Private Office of the Secretary of the Cabinet.

CHAPTER 3

The Fifth Column Panic

THE INVASION of Denmark and Norway immediately sharpened the discussion about the control of potentially disloyal elements. It was erroneously believed that the initial success of the attack on Norway was mainly due to the pro-German faction led by Quisling who had gained control of the broadcasting station and purported to assume governmental authority.[1] There was a spate of articles in the Press; the Home Secretary was invited to discuss the Fifth Column threat with the 1922 Committee and was asked in the House of Commons whether he was satisfied that members of pro-Nazi organisations would not meet the Germans here as they had done in Norway, and whether he would see that Sir Oswald Mosley was detained.[2]

On 22 April the Home Secretary drew the Home Policy Committee's attention to the strong feeling in various quarters in favour of more drastic action against Communists, Fascists and pacifists, lamenting that, because of the amendment of DR 39A after the Commons debate on 31 October 1939,* there was no power to deal with their propaganda.[3] The HPC invited him to consider urgently how the law could be strengthened, and on 30 April accepted in principle, and subject to consultation with the political parties, the Home Secretary's proposal to have three new regulations – DR 2C and DR 39A making it an offence to hinder the prosecution of the war by discouraging the will of the people to achieve victory, or to incite persons to evade military service, and DR 94A authorising the suspension of printing presses used for the production of documents published in contravention of DR 2C or DR 39A.[4] The HPC decided at the same meeting that the export of the *Daily Worker* and certain other Communist publications and of the BU's *Action* should be prohibited. The Home Secretary informed the Commons on 9 May that the new regulations had been made. He also announced the introduction of the Treachery Bill to impose the death penalty for acts of espionage or sabotage.[5]

Meanwhile a review of the military threats to the United Kingdom in the light of the new situation had been put in train by the Chiefs of Staff. On 23 April and 1 May the possibility of a

* See above, p 35.

47

German invasion was discussed by the Joint Intelligence Committee (JIC).[6] Representatives of the Home Office and MI 5 attended
the second meeting when Service misgivings about the adequacy
of Home Office arrangements for protection against Fifth Column
activities were frankly expressed. A report entitled 'Fifth Column
activities in the United Kingdom' was approved.[7] This summarised information about Fifth Column activities in Norway and
Denmark and identified potential Fifth Column elements in the
United Kingdom as enemy and non-enemy aliens, Fascists, Communists and the IRA. 'Direct evidence is difficult to obtain', said
the report, 'but we think it probable that the enemy has an
organisation drawn from the above categories which would act in
his support at the appropriate moment as in other invaded
countries'.

On 10 May, the Chiefs of Staff issued a report entitled 'Sea-
borne and Airborne Attack on the United Kingdom in the light of
the Situation created by the German Invasion of Denmark and
Norway'.[8] With the JIC report of 2 May as an appendix, the COS
report appreciated that 'enemy Fifth Column activities will be
designed to play an important part in any operation which
Germany may undertake against this country', and recommended
that 'the degree to which aliens can be controlled . . . should be
examined and any steps considered necessary to improve the
situation should be taken immediately'. Discussions took place on
the same day – it was the day the Germans invaded the Low
Countries – between MI 5, the DMI and others from the War
Office, and Home Office officials, and just before midnight the
Home Secretary authorised the internment of all male enemy
aliens in the east and south-east coastal area from Nairn to
Hampshire. Other aliens in the area were to be given the option of
moving; if they remained they were required to report daily to the
Police and observe a dusk-to-dawn curfew.*

On 11 May MI 5 recommended the detention of some 500
leading members of the British Union, but the Home Office
declined to advise the Home Secretary to take this action. On 16
May MI 5 asked permission to brief Chief Constables on a
contingency plan for the detention of 39 leading members of the
Communist Party if and when it became necessary to act against its
organisation of resistance to the war effort. The Home Office

---

* Earlier the same day the Home Office had received an anonymous letter purporting to
be from a German who had reached the United Kingdom two months ago and giving
warning of imminent airborne invasion and sabotage attacks in the south-east. It was not till a
fortnight later that the author was identified as a British subject with a criminal record who
had formerly been employed in the War Office. For this and subsequent discussions, see
Thurlow, 'British Fascism and State Surveillance 1934–1945' in *Intelligence and National
Security*, Vol 3, No 1, pp 89–92.

authorised the communication to Chief Constables of particulars of the British and foreign Communists on MI 5's list, but advised MI 5 that ministers had decided that it would be unwise to take action against Communists for the time being. On 15 May, however, the Home Office had issued instructions for the internment of all remaining male enemy aliens in Category B, wherever resident, following the first discussion of the Fifth Column threat by the new War Cabinet.

The War Cabinet meeting on 15 May invited the Home Secretary (Sir John Anderson), the Lord Privy Seal (Mr Attlee) and the Minister without Portfolio (Mr Greenwood) to consider what further measures should be taken and advise within a few days.[9] On 17 May they circulated a memorandum drawn up in the Home Office, which listed the precautions that had already been taken: those members of the NSDAP remaining in England had been interned at the outbreak of war; all male enemy aliens on the east and south-east coasts and all male enemy aliens in Category B had been interned recently; and arrangements had been made to intern 1,200 male members of the Fascio and all other Italian males with less than 20 years' residence if Italy entered the war. The memorandum went on to say that while the internment of all enemy aliens in Category C, some 64,000 persons, would be immediately popular, there would soon be a reaction against that step. It stressed that there was no evidence of any plans for Fifth Column activity in the United Kingdom, arguing that the enemy alien population consisted mostly of refugees from Nazi oppression who had been thoroughly screened by the tribunals, that there was no indication that members of the BU would be likely to assist the enemy and that there was no sign that Communists had been instructed to take action to bring about a Nazi victory.[10]

The War Cabinet discussed the memorandum on 18 May. It did not like it. It asked the Home Secretary to hold further discussions and make another report, the minutes recording that the Prime Minister 'thought the general view of the War Cabinet was that it would be desirable to stiffen up the measures already taken'.[11] In a note to the Chiefs of Staff on the same day, acknowledging a request just received from them for the internment of all male enemy aliens and measures to control the movement of all other aliens, the Prime Minister said that while nothing could be done without obtaining Cabinet approval, it was essential that aliens should be more strictly controlled and that very considerable numbers of Fascists and Communists should also be taken into preventive detention.[12] This was a view which many Chief Constables were expressing to the Home Office, and both Eastern and Western Commands had represented it to the War Office in the strongest terms.

The request from the Chiefs of Staff had been prompted by another meeting of representatives from MI 5 and the Home Office with the JIC on 15 May.[13] The meeting had clearly taken place against the wishes of the Home Office,* but it resolved to recommend to the Chiefs of Staff that they should press for the general internment of all enemy aliens. And after the meeting MI 5 kept up its pressure. On 20 May the head of MI 5 accompanied the DMI to a meeting with the Secretary of State for War (Eden) to seek his support against the Home Office's delay in acting against aliens; according to its records Eden commented that 'he did not want to have a lecture from John Anderson on the liberty of the subject'.

On 21 May, at a meeting to brief the Home Secretary for a War Cabinet meeting on the following day, MI 5's representatives not only discussed policy towards enemy aliens but also returned to the question of action against the BU. Their record of the meeting states that the Home Secretary 'said he needed to be reasonably convinced that the BU might assist the enemy and that unless he could get such evidence it would be a mistake to imprison Mosley and his supporters who would be extremely bitter after the war when democracy would be going through its severest trials . . .' The record adds that the MI 5 representatives 'longed to say that if somebody didn't get a move on there would be no democracy, no England, and no Empire, and that this was almost a matter of days . . .'

The Home Secretary must have known he was fighting a losing battle. The briefing had taken place because he had to report to the War Cabinet on 22 May that Tyler Kent, a cypher clerk in the US embassy, and Anna Volkov, the anti-semitic daughter of a White Russian admiral who was a principal aide to Captain Maule Ramsay MP, the leader of the Right Club, and apparently Ramsay himself, had been caught engaging in subversive activity.† The War Cabinet decided that the Home Secretary should consult the Law Officers as to whether Ramsay should be prosecuted or detained – he was detained under DR 18B(1) – and then debated whether in view of the contact Ramsay was thought to have with

---

* MI 5's archives show that MI 5 had decided to write a paper for the JIC about the end of the first week of May, and they record that Sir Alexander Maxwell, the Permanent Under-Secretary in the Home Office, wrote 'a very stuffy letter about our recommendation to the JIC . . . [He] thought it grossly improper for us to put forward any suggestions to the JIC on policy, and asked us to withdraw our paper . . .'.

† Kent and Volkov were convicted under the Official Secrets Acts in October 1940. Kent had abstracted a large number of secret documents from the embassy in the belief that they revealed a dishonest discrepancy between what the public was being told, particularly about Anglo-American relations, and the actual truth. Anna Volkov had passed copies to the Italian embassy and had introduced Kent to Ramsay, who was alleged to have had copies made of telegrams dated 19 January and 28 February from Mr Churchill to President Roosevelt.

Mosley, it could not afford to wait any longer before taking action against the BU. The Home Secretary told it that MI 5 had been unable to produce any evidence that either the leaders of the BU or the organisation itself had anything to do with Fifth Column activities, but was of the opinion that some 25 or 30 per cent of its members would be prepared to go to any lengths. He added that if the Cabinet thought that despite the lack of evidence they should run no risk, they must authorise the amendment of DR 18B. The War Cabinet authorised immediate action.[14] An Order in Council amending DR 18B was made the same day, and orders for the detention of Mosley and 33 other BU leaders were signed immediately.*

Later, in January 1941, the Home Secretary said that this action had been taken because there had been reason to believe that the Fascists, unlike the Communists, had had secret plans by which, in the event of a German invasion, they would either join the enemy or attempt to seize power and make terms with him.[15] At the time, while there were rumours to this effect, the transcripts of the hearing of appeals from some of the detainees to the Advisory Committee indicate that the evidence available to MI 5 and Special Branch was limited to the knowledge that secret meetings had been taking place between Mosley, Ramsay and people from other Fascist groups.[16] As the Home Secretary told the War Cabinet on 22 May, the problem was whether, despite the lack of evidence for the involvement of these people in Fifth Column activities, the authorities ought to run any risk.

At its next meeting, on 24 May, the War Cabinet was due to consider the recommendation from the Chiefs of Staff on 18 May that all male enemy aliens should be interned and special measures taken to control the movement of all other aliens. On the previous day the DMI, accompanied by an MI 5 officer, was called to a meeting with the Lord President (Chamberlain), the Home Secretary, the Foreign Secretary (Halifax), Attlee, Greenwood and Hankey to discuss the 'difference of opinion between the JIC and the Home Office on this subject'. The Home Secretary opposed general internment, believing that the administrative machine would be unable to handle it, but accepted that all female enemy aliens in Category B should be interned on the Isle of Man and

---

* A new paragraph 1A to Dr 18B empowered the Home Secretary to direct the detention of any person whom he had reasonable cause to believe to have been, or to be, a member of, or active in the furtherance of the objectives of, any organisation respecting which the Home Secretary was satisfied that it was subject to foreign influence or control, or that persons in control of it had associations with persons in the government of, or sympathies with the system of government of, any power with which His Majesty was at war, and that there was a danger of the organisation being used for purposes prejudicial to public safety.

that stricter controls should be imposed on the movement of all other aliens. The DMI insisted that internment of all enemy aliens was a military necessity, supporting his case with an outline of the information that had been obtained about Fifth Column activities in other countries.* The meeting failed to bridge the difference of opinion.

At the War Cabinet meeting itself the Home Secretary repeated his arguments against general internment and outlined his proposals regarding the internment of female enemy aliens and the introduction of stricter control on other aliens, which were adopted.[17] The meeting reached no further decision; but by 25 May MI 5 had been informed by Desmond Morton, the Prime Minister's assistant in intelligence matters, that the Prime Minister wanted 'all Fifth Columnists' interned and had so informed the Home Secretary, and on 27 May it learned from the Lord President that he was setting up a committee on which it would be represented.

This committee was the Home Defence (Security) Executive (HD(S)E). It was established by Chamberlain following a meeting of the War Cabinet of 27 May which considered a paper commissioned by the Prime Minister from the Chiefs of Staff on the problems that would arise if France fell out of the war. The paper, 'British Strategy in a Certain Eventuality', recommended 'ruthless action . . . to eliminate any chances of Fifth Column activities and internment of all enemy aliens and of members of subversive organisations, which latter should be proscribed'. The War Cabinet approved it forthwith and authorised the Lord President to take immediate steps to put the necessary emergency measures into operation. On 28 May it took note of Chamberlain's decision to set up the Home Defence (Security) Executive.[18]

HD(S)E was empowered to consider all questions relating to defence against the Fifth Column, and to initiate action through the appropriate departments.† It was to submit questions requir-

---

* The newspapers had carried reports from businessmen and reporters in Holland of Fifth Columnists, who had been 'proclaimed anti-Nazi and refugees', leaving their homes, heavily armed, to meet the German parachutists. (*Daily Express*, 13 May 1940; *Daily Telegraph*, 15 May). The British Ambassador had reported in similar terms to the Foreign Office on reaching London on 14 May. He had seen evidence that the German plans had been worked out in precise detail, which could only have come from agents; he did not have 'the least doubt that when the signal is given . . . there will be satellites of the monster [Hitler] all over this country who will at once embark on widespread sabotage'. The Military Attaché in Rome had reported a German businessman's claim that there were many German women purporting to come from Czechoslovakia waiting in London and the south-east to help German parachutists. The Madrid embassy had reported from a 'reliable' source that the basis of the fifth Column was Jewish refugees who were blackmailed with promises or threats.

† Its title was changed to the Security Executive (SE) in October 1941 to avoid confusion with the Ministry of Home Security and the Home Defence Executive.

ing decision by higher authority to the Home Secretary on the civil side and to the Secretary of State for War on the military side, and thereafter to the War Cabinet via the Lord President if necessary. It consisted of representatives from the Home Office, the Commander-in-Chief Home Forces, MI 5 and the SIS, and Lord Swinton, an ex-Cabinet Minister and a formidable political figure, was appointed its chairman with power to co-opt further members.[19]

The Executive met twice on the first day of its existence, Sir Horace Wilson and Desmond Morton also being present. On 28 May in the morning it heard from MI 5 that the Lincolnshire Police had reported that BU district officials were preparing to assist German parachutists. Meeting again that evening, it heard that the Home Office had decided that BU officials on a list supplied by MI 5 should be detained at once,* and went on to discuss at the request of the Home Office whether action should be taken against Communists.[20] In defence of its policy hitherto, the Home Office submitted a paper which argued that 'the essence of sound security policy is wise discrimination . . . a violent policy fitfully administered is not nearly as effective as a more moderate policy firmly and consistently applied'.[21] At the end of the discussion, in the course of which the chairman pointed out that the Fifth Column organisation had 'only a suspected existence', the meeting recognised 'the delicacy of the whole question' of acting against Communists. After the chairman had consulted the Minister of Labour (Bevin), the Security Executive concluded that while the *Daily Worker* should if possible be proscribed, further action against the CPGB was impracticable.[22]†

In the next few days the Executive was concerned with the extent to which the internment camps themselves presented a threat to security. As early as 24 May the Lord President and the Home Secretary had expressed misgivings about the lack of control over internees; they could move freely within the camps and could communicate with people outside and there was no intelligence coverage of their activities. On 3 June the executive sent a memorandum to the Lord President urging that, in view of the danger that the enemy might establish wireless communications with the camps and drop arms into them, enemy aliens and prisoners of war should as far as possible be transferred to islands off the coast. This suggestion proving impracticable, ministers

---

* An order for the detention of 345 of them was signed on 30 May.

† On 28 May the War Cabinet approved in principle a new Defence Regulation, DR 2D, directed against the *Daily Worker* and *Action*.[23] DR 2D, made on 29 May, empowered the Home Secretary to prohibit the publication of any newspaper which systematically fomented opposition to the successful prosecution of the war.

took up the possibility of sending internees and prisoners of war to the Dominions.[24]* In a memorandum to the Chiefs of Staff, which was discussed on 9 June, the CIGS stated that 'there is evidence . . . that plans for Fifth Column activities already exist and it is strongly suspected that internment camps will serve as rallying points for parachute landings . . . it appears that organisations in existing camps are in touch with Fifth Columnists outside who, it is suspected, comprise non-interned enemy aliens, and possibly British born traitors belonging to one or other of the subversive groups; any British born individual proved to be guilty of such treason should be shot at once'.[26]†

But the main preoccupation in Whitehall was the continuing demand for the internment of all enemy aliens. On 9 June the Chiefs of Staff invited the CIGS to take up with the Security Executive the argument that the only common sense course was to intern all enemy aliens forthwith without exception.[27] The county Chief Constables had urged this course on the Home Office on 28 May against a background of agitation and Fifth Column scares among the general public and in the Press: their memorandum stated that it was not true, as often stated, that the Police knew which aliens had to be watched; that as public opinion was so aroused, enemy aliens might well be attacked in the event of bombing or 'other serious occurrences'; and that it was 'imperative that there should be no misapprehension to the effect that Chief Constables as a whole are satisfied with the present position'.

In response to the representations from the county Chief Constables the Home Office had authorised them on 31 May to intern enemy aliens in Category C on their own responsibility if they felt there were good grounds for doubting an individual's reliability, but had emphasised that this was not to be regarded as authorisation for general internment of aliens in Category C. At a meeting of the Security Executive on 10 June it still upheld against the CIGS's representations its much criticised policy of selective internment; and notwithstanding a Home Office statement that it would be impracticable to exclude non-interned enemy aliens from specially vulnerable areas, and probably out of deference to Home Office views, the meeting decided against the internment of any further classes of enemy aliens for the present.[28]

□

---

* On 11 June the War Cabinet was informed that Canada had agreed to take 4,000 and by the end of the month shipments to Canada and Australia were in full swing.[25]

† The British Military Attaché in Ankara reported at the beginning of June that a senior Turkish officer who had returned from Germany had spoken of plans to drop arms to prisoners of war and internees.

On 11 June Italy entered the war and in the next ten days the Home Office's susceptibilities were finally swept aside. The Prime Minister immediately ordered the internment of Italians, and the Home Secretary informed the War Cabinet that those on MI 5's list would be detained first; followed by all males between ages 16 and 70 with less than 20 years' residence – upwards of 5,000 in all.[29] Action was then stepped up against the British Union.* On 14 June the Home Office advised Chief Constables that while there was to be no general detention, active or especially mischievous members of the BU should be detained. In the next three months detentions undertaken under DR 18B(1A), mainly on the recommendation of Chief Constables, brought the total number of BU detainees to some 750.† A few other Fascists were also detained, including Admiral Sir Barry Domvile and other leaders of The Link, Beckett and Gordon-Canning of the British Council for Christian Settlement and Arnold Leese of the Imperial Fascist League. On 22 June the Home Secretary decided to put an end to the BU's remaining activities, and on 10 July he applied to the BU the Defence Regulation 18AA which had recently been introduced to permit him to proscribe certain organisations.[30]

Meanwhile the Chiefs of Staff had renewed their pressure for the internment of all enemy aliens. On 19 June, two days after the French government asked for an armistice, they circulated a report on 'Urgent Measures to Meet Attack' in which they declared that 'the issue of the war will almost certainly turn upon our ability to hold out during the next three months; complained that 'certain of the measures recommended in our previous report have not yet been carried out on a sufficient scale'; and insisted that all enemy aliens should be interned, and most of them shipped overseas.[31] The Home Office concluded on the same day that all Germans and Austrians in Category C must be interned.[32] On 21 June the Home Secretary informed the War Cabinet that enemy aliens were being locked up as fast as accommodation could be provided,[33] and the Home Office issued instructions to the Police for the internment in three stages of all male Germans and Austrians. These stages were carried out on 26 June and 4 and 11 July; the peak number of internments, reached at the end of July, was about 27,000, including 4,000 Italians.[34]

Further measures were adopted in new Defence Regulations

---

* See above, pp 51, 53, for the detention of its leaders on 22 May and of its officials on 30 May.

† Detentions under DR 18B(1A) accounted for less than half of the total under DR 18B, which was 1,847 for the whole war. Of the others, which were under DR 18B(1), more than 1,000, including some 300 Anglo-Italians, were made on the grounds of hostile origin or association and more than 100 in respect of acts prejudicial to the public safety or defence of the realm.

extending the powers of Chief Constables and permitting the devolution of some of the powers of the Home Secretary to the Regional Commissioners. From early in June amendments to the Defence Regulations conferred on Chief Constables powers for the temporary arrest of suspects and wider powers of search.[35] During July the Regional Commissioners were authorised under a new Defence Regulation 18BB to detain any individuals believed to be of hostile origin or association, or to have been recently concerned in acts prejudicial to public safety, pending consideration by the Home Secretary as to whether an order should be made against them under 18B; and the Home Secretary's power under DR 18A to impose residence, movement and other restrictions on individuals was also delegated to the Regional Commissioners.*

The CPGB remained almost untouched by this formidable apparatus of control. Following the decision of 28 May to introduce the new DR 2D to permit suppression of the *Daily Worker*, the paper had moderated its tone and the Home Secretary had deferred taking action.[37]† But after the fall of France the Party had decided to accept the risk of the paper's suppression and the arrest of its leading members by calling for the formation of a new government, the arming of the workers, the conscription of wealth and the establishment of close relations with the Soviet Union. The Home Secretary drew the War Cabinet's attention to the increasing boldness of this propaganda, and particularly to a pamphlet entitled 'The People Must Act', early in July; the Cabinet after prolonged discussion decided to suppress the pamphlet but to stop short of suppressing the *Daily Worker*, to which the Home Secretary issued a warning, and to remit the problem to the Security Executive.[38] The Security Executive concluded on 10 July that the

---

* Still more drastic measures were envisaged in September. The power of Regional Commissioners to detain was extended to cover any person believed to be a member of, or active in the furtherance of the objectives of, any organisation to which DR 18AA had been applied, as it had been to the BU by the Home Secretary. On 19 September, a new paragraph 1 B was added to DR 18; in any area to which the Home Secretary applied it, the new paragraph empowered the Regional Commissioners to order the detention of any person who, because of recent conduct, or written or spoken words, was thought likely to assist the enemy.[36] This measure, designed for use in extreme emergency, was not brought into operation. But lists of British and non-enemy alien suspects were drawn up under it and detention orders for them were signed by the Regional Commissioners, but not dated. There were some 750 names on the lists early in 1941. With the release of DR 18B detainees the number grew to 1,150 in April 1944. The lists were abolished in 1944.

† The paper's temporary moderation was the second of three indications received that at this time the CPGB had a well-placed source reporting on the plans of the authorities for dealing with subversion. The first was the discovery that at the beginning of May the Central Committee had been told that there was no immediate danger of the Party being proscribed. The third was a report received by the Special Branch early in July that the Party believed that a source known only to one or two members would give it at least 48 hours' notice of any move made against it.

danger from Communist activity as such was not acute and that repressive action against the Party would have unfortunate repercussions.[39]

This conclusion accorded with the view of MI 5, which had undergone a marked change since May. It now argued that there was a clear distinction between Fascists, whose detention was justified in that they might directly aid the enemy, and Communists, whose main activity was propaganda and who had given no sign that they would assist the Germans in the event of invasion; moreover, action against Communists would cause resentment among industrial workers far beyond the membership of the CPGB. 'The Communist problem will be as urgent, or even more urgent, at the end of the War, and suppressive action now would sow the seeds of future ill-feeling'. It agreed with, and it perhaps initiated, the decision of the Home Secretary to warn the regional authorities to take no steps against members of the CPGB without consulting itself or the Home Office. In a circular drafted by MI 5 the Home Secretary advised all Regional Commissioners on 27 July to this effect and emphasised that the Police should behave towards a Communist exactly as they would to any other member of the public; if he was guilty of a breach of the Defence Regulations he should be dealt with under the law in the normal way.

While accepting that action against Communists as such would be unwise, the Security Executive was nevertheless seriously concerned about the effect of propaganda by the CPGB and from other quarters against all forms of constituted authority. The Ministry of Labour feared damage to production and the Ministry of Information damage to public morale and the authority of central and local government. The Security Executive thought it most desirable that this mischief should be stopped. On 10 July it invited the Home Office to consider the framing of a defence regulation making it an offence to attempt to subvert duly constituted authority. Maxwell consulted Sir Horace Wilson and the Senior Parliamentary Counsel, both of whom were strongly opposed to the idea. On 6 September Maxwell advised the Home Secretary that such a regulation would be highly controversial and provide so much ammunition that it would strengthen the subversive forces it was intended to check. 'There would be widespread opposition to such a Regulation as inconsistent with the historic notions of English liberty. Our tradition is that while orders issued by the duly constituted authority must be obeyed, every civilian is at liberty to show, if he can, that such orders are silly or mischievous and that the duly constituted authorities are composed of fools or rogues ... Accordingly we do not regard activities which are designed to bring the duly constituted authorities into contempt as necessarily subversive; they are only subversive if they are calculated to incite persons to disobey the law, or to change the Government by unconstitutional means. This doctrine gives, of course, great and indeed dangerous liberty to persons who desire revolution, or desire to impede the war effort . . . but the readiness to take this risk is the cardinal distinction between democracy and totalitarianism'. The Home Secretary called this minute 'a most admirable statement of principle' and the proposed new regulation was dropped with Swinton's agreement.[40]

□

In May the Home Secretary had foreseen that the general internment of aliens would be a popular measure, but that there would soon be a reaction. By the middle of July the reaction had already set in. It had surfaced in the House of Commons on 10 July,[41] when several members regretted that the liberal views of the Home Office had been over-ridden by the military, complained of mismanagement in the camps and criticised the selection of aliens for deportation in the *Arandora Star*, recently torpedoed with the loss of several hundred deportees.* During several discussions by the War Cabinet and Defence Committee, the War Cabinet decided on 18 July that internees known to be actively hostile to the Axis regimes, or whose detention was undesirable for other good reasons, should be released, and that the administration of the camps should be transferred from the War Office to the Home Office. On 22 July it set up an advisory committee to keep internment policy under review and an advisory council to watch over the welfare of aliens.[43] Categories of aliens eligible for release were listed in a White Paper published on 28 July and revised in August.[44] More than 5,500 enemy aliens had been released by the end of October. The internment of enemy aliens had meanwhile been suspended on 24 July for lack of accommodation; it was never resumed.

From the beginning of August the Home Office, which had earlier in the year been under so much pressure to stiffen its policy towards aliens, came under increasing pressure, from ministers no less than from the vocal public, to liberalise it further. On 1 August the Prime Minister said at a War Cabinet meeting that it should now be possible to take a less rigid attitude towards internment,[45]

---

* An enquiry ordered by the War Cabinet found that undoubted hardships had been suffered at one camp (Huyton). It also found that all Germans and Austrians in the *Arandora Star* were in Category A and that all but a handful of the Italians were on MI 5's dangerous list, but that the list was based on membership of the Fascio and included some purely nominal members whose sympathies were wholly with Great Britain.[42]

and at the beginning of September he and the Foreign Secretary were contemplating a statement in Parliament to the effect that friendly aliens might be released more rapidly in view of the improved war situation. On 22 August general internment was criticised in the House of Commons and condemned as indefensible by public figures in a letter to the editor of *The Times*. In the House of Commons the Home Secretary justified the introduction of general internment on the grounds of military necessity, and in view of the threat to aliens from the public while the fear of invasion was rife, and insisted on the need to retain it in all its essentials for the time being.[46] In a letter and a memorandum to the Prime Minister on 3 September he objected, successfully, to his making any announcement about its further relaxation, pointing out that about half the Category C Germans and Austrians would be released in the next few months under the provisions of the White Paper and arguing that a decision to release the remainder – some 6,000 – would cause alarm and bewilderment to the ordinary public, which did not write to the papers or its MPs, and arouse misgivings in the defence services.

At a time when the Battle of Britain had not yet reached its climax, the threat of invasion (Operation *Sea Lion*) was at its peak and public apprehensions were far from being allayed, it is safe to assume that the ministerial pressure for relaxation did not arise from the view that the war situation had improved but from two other considerations. On the one hand ministers were anxious about Parliamentary opinion and on the other was the fact that the interrogations and the other intensive investigations carried out had produced no evidence of any preparations for espionage or sabotage by Fifth Column elements, let alone of the existence of an organised Fifth Column movement. The Prime Minister implied as much when stating to the House of Commons in the middle of August, perhaps somewhat disingenuously, that 'a very great improvement has been effected in dealing with the Fifth Column danger. I always thought it was exaggerated in these islands'.[47] And as early as the middle of July MI 5 was, in private, 'very much inclined to doubt' whether an organised Fifth Column existed.

But MI 5 was still concerned to limit the risks from German espionage, and just as it had pressed for general internment on that ground before the onset of the Fifth Column panic, so it now supported the Home Office in its resistance to relaxation. In October it advised the Security Executive against a proposal from the Aliens Advisory Council that there should be an additional release category for enemy aliens who could satisfy a tribunal that they were sympathetic to the Allied cause, arguing that there was rarely sufficient evidence to support a reliable judgment on an individual's loyalty, that the more extreme opponents of the Nazis were foreign Communists who were also a grave danger to security, and that the labour involved in having to advise on some 10–15,000 cases of review would inevitably distract it from its counter-espionage duties. And we may be sure that it supported the JIC and the Chiefs of Staff when they objected in November to proposals from the Advisory Committee on internment;[48] these were to the effect that aliens between the ages of 18 and 50 should be entitled to release if they joined the Auxiliary Military Pioneer Corps and that an additional release category should be introduced for men over age or men who were rejected on medical grounds.

The Advisory Committee's proposals were nevertheless accepted. The Security Executive having firmly over-ruled the complaints of the Chiefs of Staff,[49] the War Cabinet approved the proposals on 21 November and the Home Secretary (Mr Herbert Morrison since 4 October) so informed the House of Commons of 26 November.[50] From that date the internment of enemy aliens ceased to be a controversial issue in Whitehall. Although the November relaxation did not produce a large number of applications for release,* three German males were at large by 1 January 1941 for every one still interned. In January, after analysing the attitude of the aliens in the light of information from all its sources, particularly from the internment camps, MI 5 concluded that only a small proportion of the Germans and the Austrians were pro-Nazi (though fewer still were pro-British) and that the majority of the Italians were harmless; it repeated that it had found no evidence of any plans for espionage, sabotage or other· Fifth Column activities.[51]

At the end of November 1940 the decision was also made to relax the measures taken against the members of the British Union and other Fascists under DR 18B. A White Paper had laid it down that under 18B, a preventive and not a punitive measure, the conditions of detention were to be 'as little oppressive as possible', and it is clear that the detainees had legitimate grounds for complaint about the conditions in which they were accommodated. But the civil liberties lobby and Parliament had shown much less concern for their plight than for those of the aliens; there was to be no full-dress House of Commons debate on 18B detainees until 10 December.[52] Several of them had resorted to the Courts and most of them had appealed to the Advisory Committee

---

* The number of aliens who obtained release by applying to join the Pioneer Corps finally amounted to no more than 2,583, of whom 800 had applied to join before they were interned.

on 18B detentions*. The Courts upheld the legality of the detention orders† and the Advisory Committee had dismissed by the end of July the objections of Mosley and the other senior officials, and recommended that they should remain in detention. The Advisory Committee had, however, been severely criticised by the Security Executive and MI 5 for undue leniency when it came to deal with the cases of lowlier officials and other active members. Swinton and MI 5 had argued that since the Home Secretary had ruled that active participation in the BU was sufficient ground for detention, the Advisory Committee should confine its enquiries to establishing the facts in that matter. The Committee had proceeded in the belief that it was its duty to consider not only whether a detainee had been an active member, but also whether, in the words of DR 18B(1A), it was 'necessary to exercise control over him'; and it had found in a substantial number of cases that the detainees were people of less than average intelligence and limited education, who could not be regarded as dangerous.

The Home Office brought this issue to a head in October. After examining some 30 of the cases that were in dispute between the security authorities and the 18B Advisory Committee, it advised the Security Executive that it was inclined to side with the Advisory Committee, and when the Security Executive protested that the Advisory Committee had abandoned the principle on which the detentions had been authorised in the first place, it admitted the charge but explained that 'the Home Office had adopted the principle in the first place in order to catch all the rogues and fanatics: it appeared that they had caught a great number of harmless people as well'. At a meeting on 31 October the Security Executive was advised by Swinton that the question had resolved itself into whether or not the releases recommended by the Advisory Committee would result in the revival of a hostile organisation, and that in his view the risk was not serious. The Executive finally agreed that in all cases where the grounds for detention rested wholly or principally on the fact that the detainee had been an officer or an active member of the BU the Home Secretary should accept the Advisory Committee's recommendation for release.[53]

MI 5 dissented from this conclusion. In September it had been satisfied by the reports of Chief Constables throughout the coun-

---

* For this committee see above, pp 24, 35.

† But it was not till October 1941 that it was established that, where the Secretary of State acting in good faith made an order reciting that he had reasonable cause to believe in the existence of particular matters, a court of law would not enquire whether in fact he had reasonable grounds for his belief, this question being one for the executive discretion of the Secretary of State.

try that the BU had ceased to exist, together with all other organised pro-Nazi activity, and had advised the Home Office that while there was 'a possibility that ... small groups may try to re-form, we do not think they are likely to be of any importance'. It now argued that this conclusion would not hold if the 100 or so persons whose cases were in dispute between itself and the Advisory Committee were released: their release would greatly encourage the rank and file of the BU, who would be likely to set about quiet propaganda and become a nuisance again in difficult times ahead. By the end of October the Advisory Committee had heard 317 cases and had recommended continued detention of 118 and release for 199. MI 5 had disagreed with 111 recommendations for release; in about 20 cases it had special reasons for its objections, over and above the individual's activity on behalf of the BU before the date of detention.

The Home Secretary reported MI 5's views to the War Cabinet but proposed that they should be over-ridden. He recommended to the Cabinet that, following the conclusion reached by the Security Executive, he should generally adopt the advice of the Advisory Committee, though not automatically. His reasons were that the BU was defunct; that he had to report cases of disagreement to Parliament under DR 18B(6) and that trouble could be expected from Parliament, the public and the Advisory Committee if their number was large; and that to prolong the detention of individuals who had satisfied the Advisory Committee would produce grievances. The War Cabinet approved his proposals on 21 November.[54]

The new policy increased the pace of releases, but not on any extravagant scale. Of the 747 BU detainees, 200 were still in detention in December 1941, 130 in the spring of 1943, 15 in September 1944.* Though MI 5 continued to register objections to the Advisory Committee, it ceased to complain of undue leniency on the part of the Committee; and in February 1941 it recorded that such continuing underground activity by former BU supporters as had come to light was insignificant.†

---

* The peak figure for all detainees under 18B – 1,428 in August 1940 – fell to 977 by December 1940, to just over 600 in December 1941, to 372 in December 1943 and to 65 in December 1944. Some of the more extreme were Fascists outside the BU whose increasingly outrageous expressions of Nazi sentiments kept them for years ahead of the increasingly lenient release policy.

† No prominent figure continued openly to express anti-war sentiments except the Duke of Bedford, who had not been detained. In a letter to the Home Secretary in August 1941 he drew a distinction between 'those who would assist a German invasion and those who, in the unhappy event of such an invasion proving successful, hope to be able to utilise their known past opposition to the war in order to secure better terms for their fellow countrymen', and stoutly insisted that the latter was a patriotic aim. His case was brought to the War Cabinet's attention in November 1941, and he was listed for detention in the event of invasion.[55]

CHAPTER 3: REFERENCES

1. T K Derry, *The Campaign in Norway* (1952), p 244.
2. Hansard Vol 360, Col 33.
3. CAB 75/7, HPC(40) 87 of 22 April.
4. CAB 75/7, HPC(40) 13th and 14th Meetings, 23 and 30 April.
5. Hansard Vol 360, Cols 1380–1382, 1412.
6. JIC(40) 24th and 26th Meetings, 23 April and 1 May.
7. JIC(40) 27th Meeting of 3 May; JIC(40) 47 of 2 May.
8. CAB 66/7, WP(40) 153 of 10 May.
9. CAB 65/7, WM(40) 123 of 15 May.
10. CAB 67/6, WP(G)(40) 131 of 17 May.
11. CAB 65/7, WM(40) 128 of 18 May.
12. CAB 80/11, COS(40) 359(JIC) of 16 May, 364 of 18 May.
13. JIC(40) 29th Meeting, 15 May.
14. CAB 65/7, WM(40) 133 of 22 May.
15. CAB 98/18, Committee on Communist Activities, 1st Meeting, 20 January 1941.
16. Thurlow, *Fascism in Britain; A History, 1918–1985* (1987), pp 185, 186, 202, 205.
17. CAB 65/7, WM(40) 137 of 24 May.
18. CAB 65/7, WM(40) 141, 144 of 27 and 28 May; CAB 66/7, WP(40) 168 of 25 May.
19. CAB 66/8, WP(40) 172 of 27 May.
20. CAB 93/2, HD(S)E 1st and 2nd Meetings, both of 28 May 1940.
21. CAB 93/3, HD(S)E 3, undated.
22. CAB 93/2, HD(S)E 4th Meeting, 29 May.
23. CAB 65/7, WM(40) 144 of 28 May.
24. ibid, WM(40) 137 and 161 of 24 May and 11 June; CAB 93/2, HD(S)E 5th and 6th Meetings of 3 and 5 June; CAB 93/3, HD(S)E 2 of 28 May.
25. CAB 65/7, WM(40) 161 of 11 June.
26. CAB 80/12, COS (40) 438 of 8 June.
27. CAB 79/4, COS (40) 17th Meeting, 9 June.
28. CAB 93/2, HD(S)E 7th Meeting, 10 June.
29. CAB 65/7, WM(40) 161 of 11 June.
30. CAB 75/8, HPC(40) 174 of 22 June; SR & O 1940, Nos 1078, 1273.
31. CAB 66/8, WP(40) 213 of 19 June.
32. CAB 93/5, SIC 2nd Meeting, 19 June.
33. CAB 65/7, WM(40) 174 of 21 June.
34. CAB 93/2, HD(S)E 8th Meeting, 26 June 1940.
35. SR & O 1940, Nos 843, 928.
36. SR & O 1940, No 1682.
37. CAB 93/2, HD(S)E 5th Meeting, 5 June 1940.
38. CAB 65/8, WM(40) 193, 194 of 4 and 5 July; CAB 66/14, WP(40) 482 of 23 December; CAB 67/7, WP(G)(40) 171 of 3 July; HO 45/25552/832463/172.
39. CAB 93/2, HD(S)E 9th Meeting, 10 July 1940.
40. CAB 93/3, HD(S)E 9 of 8 July 1940; CAB 93/2, HD(S)E 9th Meeting, 19 July 1940; HO 45/25552/832463/172.
41. Hansard Vol 362, Col 1207 et seq.
42. CAB 66/13, WP(40) 432, 463 of 24 October, 25 November.
43. CAB 65/8, WM(40) 207, 209 of 18 and 22 July; CAB 69/1, DO(40) 20th Meeting, 19 July.
44. Cmd 6217, 6223; Hansard Vol 363, Cols 587, 588; Vol 364, Col 179.

45. CAB 65/8, WM(40) 217 of 1 August.
46. Hansard Vol 364, Col 1525 et seq.
47. Hansard Vol 354, Col 957.
48. CAB 93/3, HD(S)E 33 of 14 November 1940.
49. CAB 93/2, HD(S)E 19th Meeting, 21 November 1940.
50. CAB 65/10, WM(40) 293 of 21 November; Hansard Vol 367, Cols 78–80.
51. CAB 93/3, HD(S)E 48 of 21 January 1941.
52. Hansard Vol 367, Col 831 et seq.
53. CAB 93/2, HD(S)E 17th Meeting, 31 October 1940.
54. CAB 65/10, WM(40) 293 of 21 November; CAB 67/8, WP(G)(40) 308 of 9 November; HO 45/25756/863032/17, 27.
55. CAB 65/20, WM(41) 115 of 17 November; CAB 66/19, WP(41) 267 of 14 November.

CHAPTER 4

The Re-Organisation of Security in the United Kingdom June 1940 to June 1941

WHATEVER MAY be thought of the arguments, for and against, which delayed the taking of increased security precautions until unexpected military disasters produced the Fifth Column panic, the crisis at least had salutary effects. The establishment of the Security Executive was followed by a wholesale tightening-up of the country's security arrangements and the re-organisation of MI 5.

On 10 June the Security Executive, which had been given a small staff of civil servants at the end of May, set up a larger staff to supervise the work of the departments responsible for investigating Fifth Column activities, to collate the information they collected and to issue instructions and advice as to the action they should take on it.[1] At the first meeting of this Security Intelligence Centre (SIC) on 15 June Swinton explained that while the Security Executive remained the forum for discussing issues of policy, the SIC was expected to carry out a positive drive to uncover the Fifth Column organisation: the Executive had 'no precise knowledge of the organisation they were fighting, although they were convinced of its existence. It was thus vitally necessary that every happening that might conceivably be a pointer to the whereabouts and nature of the organisation should be pooled at the Centre . . .'.[2]

On 11 June the Director and the Deputy Director of MI 5 were retired, and the head of one of the divisions was appointed Director under the supervision of Swinton as chairman of the Security Executive. A month later Swinton was formally entrusted with 'executive control' of MI 5, with responsibility for assisting the Director to re-organise the Service, and also with 'operational control' of the SIS in respect of its activities in Great Britain and Eire.[3]* These changes, which were reported to the War Cabinet on 19 July, appear to have been ordered by the Prime Minister. In

---

* At the same time Swinton was provided with a colleague, Mr A M Wall, General Secretary of the London Society of Compositors and a member of the TUC General Council, being appointed to assist him. They were joined in August by Mr Isaac Foot MP, following a suggestion in Parliament that the Executive should also include a member of the Liberal Party.

August, replying to questions in the Commons about the Security Executive and the SIC, he said that in the state of alarm following the invasion of the Low Countries the departments responsible for security had not been operating effectively. 'There were overlaps and under-laps and I felt that this side of the business of national defence needed pulling together'.[4]

By the middle of July, in order to ensure that all reports on Fifth Column activities were scrutinised and assessed, the SIC had instituted a system by which departmental representatives met regularly as a Liaison Officers Conference (LOC) to exchange all information received and to report on the action taken on it by their departments. Although the SIC ceased to meet after the end of September 1940 and its staff was dispersed in 1941, the LOC continued to function till the end of the war.[5]

The call for more vigorous action in investigating and reporting to the departments on possible Fifth Column activities, work which was carried out mainly by MI 5 and the Police,* was met in part by devolution. In MI 5 devolution was in any case overdue, the London office having long been overwhelmed by the pressure on it. In the middle of June it appointed Regional Security Liaison Officers (RSLOs) to the HQs of Civil Defence Regions Nos 4 (Cambridge) and 12 (Tunbridge Wells) – the two regions most threatened by invasion – and every region in the country had its RSLO by the end of September. He had access to the Regional Commissioner and to the representatives of government departments and the Service commands, but his chief task was to assist the Police in the exercise of their increased powers to arrest, search and interrogate suspects.

The appointment of RSLOs, which fully incorporated the Police forces into the security machine for the remainder of the war, did much to deflect from the headquarters of MI 5 the flood of reports and enquiries from the public – most of them absurd – about suspicious activities. But it by no means relieved it of the responsibility for analysing this material centrally. Its files of reports received in 1940–1941 about light signalling' reached a height of five feet, and five officers were employed in investigating them. It accumulated 16 files of reports of suspect markings on telegraph poles.† At the height of the panic, moreover, additional

---

* The Home Office told Chief Constables that 'the Police should use all possible endeavours to discover whether any specific activities or preparations prejudicial to the defence of the Realm are on foot in their area' and that 'steps should be taken to set aside for this work officers with the best available experience'.

† An MI 5 memorandum on this topic by a distinguished academic, based on a Post Office survey, Police reports, and reports from public utilities and from the general public, was submitted to the SIC in July 1940. It concluded that while the great majority of marks were innocent, it was not possible to say with certainty that all were harmless.[6]

responsibilities were thrust upon it. In the middle of July it was decided that those internees whose records seemed to warrant it should undergo close interrogation centrally. An interrogation centre with facilities for solitary confinement and eavesdropping and with staff from MI 5 was established at Latchmere House, Ham Common. The first batch of internees – some British Fascists, some enemy aliens and a handful of suspects evacuated with British troops from Dunkirk – arrived on 27 July. Not without complaints in the House of Commons[7] and expressions of anxiety from the Home Office, a total of 27 British subjects and 18 enemy aliens were interrogated in the next few months. Also in the middle of July under pressure from Swinton, MI 5 established a new division – W – headed by a man from the BBC, and including an SIS representative, with the task of searching for all possible enemy channels of wireless communication – a task which made it temporarily responsible for liaison with the RSS.*

These additional labours only emphasised, however, the need to remedy MI 5's organisational weaknesses. At the end of July Swinton brought in a specialist in business organisation and method as Deputy Director, Organisation. He quickly discerned that while the first necessity was to rehabilitate the registry with its central index, there would have to be a fundamental revision of duties and priorities throughout the office. The reform of the registry was a formidable task and it was delayed by the need to keep the machine working while the new procedures were brought in, by the fact that on 24–25 September the central index and some of the records were damaged in an air raid, and by the decision, which took effect at the end of September, to move the registry with the bulk of the Headquarters staff to Blenheim Palace for the rest of the war. But steady progress was made from that time in repairing the damage and introducing new methods.†

The wider drive for efficiency in MI 5 as a whole encountered a more serious obstacle: it aroused resentment in MI 5's Directorate. Although it was obvious that the new head of MI 5 was subject to

---

* The pressure for this originated at the beginning of May when suspicions were voiced that a German radio station posing as the New British Broadcasting Service was passing instructions to a Fifth Column in plain language code. On 15 June the SIC set up a sub-committee to report. It reported that in addition to cypher communications with high-grade agents the Germans were almost certainly using plain language in this way for Fifth Column purposes.[8]

† When he first took office as Director General (see below p 69) Sir David Petrie thought that MI 5 was recording too much. 'The omnibus indexing of names is not intelligence, it is mere nervousness'. But there was room for legitimate differences of opinion on this subject. In any case, the backlog of arrears in indexing was cleared by early in 1941. The damage took longer to repair. The index had been microfilmed but the work had been badly done and the prints were poor. The reconstruction was not completed till June 1941.

Swinton's authority, MI 5's chief officers had not been notified that Swinton had been formally entrusted with executive control. They believed, moreover, that some of his proposals were ill-judged. While they did not object to the appointment of a Deputy Director, Organisation, they resisted Swinton's suggestion that they should employ expert investigators from the Metropolitan Police and additional solicitors to improve their efficiency in investigation and interrogation; in their view he misunderstood MI 5's work, thinking of it as a large detective agency carrying out frequent raids with fast cars whereas it was an intelligence and research department which only occasionally needed to call on its own field staff or the Police to carry out discreet investigation. The outcome, at the beginning of August, was a stormy interview in which Swinton asserted that the entire investigation division (B Division) was inadequate and insisted on appointing as Deputy Director in charge of investigation a London solicitor who had recently joined the staff of the Security Intelligence Centre. This appointment, which seriously damaged MI 5's morale, was short-lived – the man resigned in September* – but MI 5 was equally opposed to an alternative scheme for reform. This involved relieving the sprawling and grossly over-worked B Division, which was responsible for counter-espionage investigations, Fifth Column investigations, the watch on Communist, Fascist and other subversive activities and many aspects of alien control as well as for supervising the new RSLO organisation, by creating two new divisions for the control of aliens and the watch on subversion. A meeting on 17 December under Swinton's chairmanship failed to reach agreement on how to proceed, Swinton regarding MI 5's own proposals as insufficiently radical.

At the end of November the Prime Minister heard from a close political associate that MI 5 was suffering from divided management, inadequate leadership and severe internal jealousies. He asked Morton to consult the Service Directors of Intelligence. On 3 December Morton reported that in their view the organisation was on the verge of collapse and that, although Swinton had taken personal control of it on account of his disquiet, this was not a satisfactory arrangement: MI 5 required a strong civilian, non-political, full-time head who would be responsible to a minister and not to Swinton.[9]

Action to remedy this situation was already in train. At the request of the Lord President (now Sir John Anderson) Sir David Petrie, a retired officer of the Indian Police then in Cairo, had

---

* But the attachment of Scotland Yard officers to MI 5 was implemented, and they gave valuable service once their functions had been properly defined.

been summoned home to carry out an enquiry.* Petrie began his enquiry on 31 December and finished his report on 13 February 1941. He found that the rapid expansion in the size of MI 5 had led to serious dislocation in the recruitment, training and organisation of senior staff.† Officer recruitment, which had formerly been by personal introduction, had become haphazard. While training could only be done on the job, supervision was rudimentary. The organisational breakdown, which had followed from the failure to develop an adequate chain of command, was chiefly illustrated in B Division. This now had 133 officers distributed among 29 sections, which were themselves divided into some 70–80 sub-sections. At the same time, however, Petrie was critical of the methods recently adopted for bringing about the necessary reform. He emphatically supported the proposal that the control of aliens, with all the problems associated with internment and appeals, and the monitoring of subversive activity should be transferred from B Division to two new divisions, but he believed that Swinton's appointment of the solicitor from the SIC, and by implication the appointment of Swinton himself, had been 'an unfortunate mistake'. Interference from outside over the head of the Director had produced resentment and lowered morale. 'Probably more highly-disciplined bodies than MI 5 would have reacted in much the same way . . . The Director must be master in his own house . . . Direction and co-ordination from above . . . are essential . . . but the principle governing the policy of direction must be that of support and not of detailed control . . .'. On the question of direction from above, the report accepted that since security was an inter-departmental matter, MI 5 should not be put under a single department, but recommended that it should be responsible to a centrally-placed minister without departmental duties, the obvious one being the Lord President. Petrie believed that 'MI 5 has suffered from the lack of this in the past, and that what it has gained in independence it has lost in support'.

Discussion of the report between the Prime Minister, the Lord President, the Home Secretary, Swinton and Petrie led during March to the appointment of Petrie as Director General of MI 5. At the beginning of April an exchange of notes between Petrie and Swinton established that while the Director General was responsible through the Security Executive to the Lord President for the

---

* Sir David Petrie KCMG (1879–1961). Joined Indian Police in 1900. Director, Intelligence Bureau 1924–1931. Member, and then chairman, Indian Public Service Commission 1931–1936.

† In September 1938 there had been 33 officers and 119 supporting staff. These figures had risen to 83 and 253 by September 1939 and to 234 and 676 (of whom 634 were women) by January 1941.

efficient working of MI 5, he would be free from interference in the day-to-day work of the office and matters relating to the staff. MI 5 was notified of Petrie's appointment and of his plans for re-organisation on 24 April 1941.

Under the re-organisation, which was completed by August, the former head of MI 5 became the Deputy Director General, three heads of divisions became Directors and B Division was relieved by the creation of two new divisions to cover aliens control and subversive movements under Deputy Directors. On the other hand, W Division was subordinated to B Division. But W Division had failed to develop any substantial function – it had for some time been referred to only as a branch or a section – and it was soon to lose all *raison d'être* with the transfer of control of the RSS from MI 8 to the SIS.*

□

If Swinton had been abrasive in his insistence on reforming the management of MI 5, he had been a tower of strength in ensuring that its essential responsibilities were safeguarded within the expanded security machinery that was set up in the wake of the Fifth Column panic; and he was so again in the autumn of 1940, when further administrative measures were called for by the first phase of the Abwehr's attack on the United Kingdom.†

The capture of spies arriving by air and sea at that time raised questions about their custody. It had been laid down in July that MI 5 must be consulted about them, but by September the Service authorities were inclined to feel that as the United Kingdom had become a theatre of operations, they should have first claim on them. The Security Executive ensured, however, that they should all pass into the custody of MI 5 and be taken to Latchmere House.[10] Latchmere House had been opened as an interrogation centre for suspect Fifth Columnists in July,‡ but in October MI 5 decided that it should be used only for more serious cases among aliens, for example where espionage was suspected, and that British subjects should be taken there only in very exceptional circumstances. And from early in November the place was entirely reserved for captured agents, including some of the double-cross agents, arrangements being made by which MI 5 reported to the Home Office every month the names of those detained, the reason for their detention, and the length of time they had been there.

Once Latchmere House had been reserved for persons known

---

* See below, p 73ff.
† See Chapter 6.
‡ See above, p 67.

to be spies, or gravely suspected of being spies, it could not be used for short-term detention in view of the need to avoid leakage of information about the fate of agents and the methods used for interrogating them. From early in 1941 aliens who did not have to be kept there were sent to another camp and detained for the duration with the minimum of contact with the outside world. But as even this course was soon judged to be insecure, it became the policy to admit to Latchmere House, which was known as Camp 020 from December 1941, only such people as seemed to qualify for permanent detention.

Meanwhile, it also became necessary to institute new measures for the control of refugees and other apparently innocent arrivals. Until the autumn of 1940 the huge influxes of refugees had been processed hastily at improvised centres, and while under the Aliens Orders enemy alien visitors were normally interned, a visiting non-enemy alien had had only to satisfy the immigration officers and MI 5's representatives, the security control officers, that he had an adequate reason for his visit and that his presence would not be detrimental; and if refused leave to land, he had been sent in custody to a police station for interrogation.

In October 1940 the Security Executive insisted that all such arrivals must be interrogated at a central point by MI 5 for security purposes and by the SIS in the interests of intelligence.[11] In January 1941 a reception and examination centre was opened at the Royal Victoria Patriotic Schools in Wandsworth to which immigration officers were instructed to send eight categories of aliens, including refugees from territory under enemy control and those claiming to want to join the armed forces of the Allies. The Home Office accepted ministerial responsibility for the centre, the War Office provided the guard and the staff and MI 5 undertook the responsibility for the interrogation.[12]

Cases of friction between immigration officers and the security control officers, which had not been uncommon before, increased under the new system, MI 5 interpreting it as requiring that all aliens be sent to the Reception Centre except those whose bona fides could be established unequivocally. At the request of the Security Executive, and on its advice, the Home Office settled this problem in March by instructing the Immigration Service that leave to land or embark must be refused to any alien with respect to whom the security control officer so decided. The SCO was to give his reasons whenever possible; if he was unable to, MI 5 was required to make a report to the Home Office.[13]

The new policy was distasteful, also, to the Allied governments-in-exile, the more so as the atmosphere at the Reception Centre was to begin with that of an internment camp. Because of their complaints some 300 Norwegians brought back by the Royal Navy from the Lofoten raid in March 1941 were exempted; they were processed in circumstances which were still less comfortable and did not make for efficiency. As a result of this experience, however, the Security Executive, prompted by MI 5, insisted that while steps should be taken to improve conditions at Wandsworth, there should be no further exception to the rule that all aliens who could not show that their entry had been approved must be examined at the Centre, where visits and communications were at the discretion of MI 5. This rule and the rigorous conditions relating to outside contacts were reaffirmed by the Security Executive following a conference in October 1941 with the Home Office, the Prisoners of War Directorate and MI 5.[14]*

The intake at the Centre had by then risen from 155 in January to an average of 700 a month. It became known as the London Reception Centre (LRC) a year later, in October 1942.

□

A further organisational difficulty remained to be dealt with – that of settling, in so far as the complexity of the problem allowed a settlement, where to place administrative and operational responsibility for the RSS.

By the autumn of 1940 the work of the RSS, originally limited to the monitoring of illicit wireless activity in the United Kingdom, had been extended to the coverage of the communications of the Abwehr and associated enemy intelligence and security agencies anywhere in the world. But arrangements for its administrative and operational control remained unsatisfactory. Supervised by three staff officers in MI 8, it now consisted of a Headquarters staff of 20 officers and other ranks provided by the Army, of about 1,000 interception and technical staff provided, not entirely to the satisfaction of MI 8, by the GPO, and of another 1,000 part-time voluntary interceptors.

In October 1940 MI 8 proposed that administrative control of the RSS should be transferred to MI 5 on the grounds that MI 8 should concentrate on wireless intelligence of military importance whereas the RSS's activities were exclusively of interest to the security authorities. MI 5 resisted the suggestion; it argued that, whether or not the RSS's failure to intercept any illicit wireless in the United Kingdom cast doubt on its efficiency, its relevance to MI 5's responsibilities was marginal, almost all of its work having

---

* An unavoidable exception was that of alien merchant seamen. They were an accessible target for the Abwehr, but for obvious reasons could not be processed at the LRC. To deal with this problem MI 5 developed from the spring of 1941 a pool of 'useful contacts' among seamen to act as observers of the aliens.

so far been concerned with communications between enemy stations located abroad. It was perhaps on this account, as well as from the wish to avoid adding to the already formidable organisational problems in MI 5, that in January 1941, on the advice of Petrie, Swinton decided that the RSS should be taken over 'lock, stock and barrel' by the SIS. The DMI objected to this solution on the ground that while SIS's communications section was expert in the handling of communications with SIS's agents, it had no experience in the search for and interception of enemy and suspect transmissions. Swinton swept the objection aside with the argument that by virtue of his executive responsibility both for MI 5 and for the operations of the SIS in the United Kingdom, the two organizations should have no difficulty in working together to secure the effective direction of the RSS and the best use of its output. The transfer was effected in May 1941.

On the technical side great improvements were made in the resources provided for the RSS from the beginning of 1941. The GPO's agency for the provision of personnel and equipment was terminated. The best of the operators from the Post Office staff and the voluntary interceptors were enlisted into the Royal Signals. Better equipment was obtained, some of it from the United States, and new intercept stations established. These improvements were less a consequence of the decision to transfer control from MI 8 than of the increased volume and value of the work of the RSS that followed from GC and CS's solution of the main Abwehr hand cypher at the end of 1940.* As a result of this development, however, MI 5 ceased to take the view that RSS was of little value to it, and far from having no difficulty in co-operating to secure the best use of the RSS's output, as Swinton had expected, MI 5 and SIS were soon to be engaged in a running quarrel about it.†

□

By the summer of 1941 the Security Executive had completed its primary task of ensuring that the security defences were thoroughly re-organised. Thanks largely to Swinton's drive and authority, and to his understanding and judicious use of the machinery of government, it had overhauled the management of MI 5, made a firm decision about the control of the RSS, persuaded the Home Office to bring the Police fully into the security structure and secured the establishment of Camp 020 and the

---

* See below, p 88.
† See below, p 131ff.

LRC, and had taken the first step towards the creation of an efficient system of security within government departments. In June 1941 it set up a committee to review, improve and co-ordinate security measures within the government departments involved in secret business. Arrangements for this had been elementary at the outbreak of war and had subsequently been developed by individual departments at their own discretion. This committee's enquiry led to the establishment of a permanent committee responsible to the Lord President to act as a forum for all questions of security in government departments and to ensure that agreed measures were implemented.[15]* As we shall see, the Security Executive had also laid down the policy to be followed on the interrogation and prosecution of enemy agents† and put its authority behind measures to strengthen security arrangements overseas.‡ But if the Executive's main work was done by the summer of 1941 – if it had by then held more than a half of its total of 109 meetings – it had acquired the momentum and the recognition which enabled it to carry out until the end of the war without friction or further administrative upheaval the essential function of ensuring that the security system remained efficient.

This function was set out in a memorandum to the principal government departments in October 1942 after Swinton had been succeeded by Mr Duff Cooper, Chancellor of the Duchy of Lancaster, who as chairman continued to consult as necessary the Lord President of the Council. As we have seen§ the memorandum defined security as 'the defence of national interests against hostile elements other than the armed forces of the enemy', and emphasised that the role of the Security Executive extended to British territories overseas and to British ships and cargoes in foreign ports. It explained that the title of the Security Executive was somewhat misleading in that it was a co-ordinating and not an executive body. Responsibility for achieving security rested with a large number of departments and services; the Executive's function was 'to see that Security problems are properly envisaged, that the best practical measures are framed to meet them, and that responsibility for action is accepted by the appropriate departments', while at the same time maintaining 'a just balance between Security and other vital interests'. It went on to say that the Executive summoned *ad hoc* conferences as and when necessary, and assigned problems requiring continuous and detailed over-

---

* For this committee, which was to become known as the Bridges Panel, see below, pp 247–248.
† See below, p 96ff.
‡ See Chapters 9 and 10.
§ See above, p 3.

sight to standing committees representing the departments immediately concerned under its chairmanship. And it annexed a list of subjects considered by the Executive, as an illustration of the scope of its work.[16]*

---

* See Appendix 4 for this annex. The Security Executive had by then established five standing committees: the Liaison Officers Conference; the Committee on Communism; the Seamen and Overseas Shipping Committee; the Control at Ports Committee; the Shipping Information and Home Shipping Committee.

CHAPTER 4: REFERENCES

1. CAB 93/2, HD(S)E 7th Meeting, 10 June 1940.
2. CAB 93/5, SIC 1st Meeting, 15 June 1940.
3. CAB 66/10, WP(40) 271 of 19 July.
4. Hansard, Vol 364, Col 957.
5. CAB 93/4 for the records of the Liaison Officers Conference.
6. CAB 93/5, SIC 10 of 25 July 1940.
7. Hansard, Vol 365, Cols 103, 375–376.
8. CAB 93/5, SIC 1st and 2nd Meetings, 15 and 19 June 1940.
9. PREM 3/418/1.
10. CAB 93/5, SIC/A/91 of 10 September 1940.
11. CAB 93/2, HD(S)E 16th Meeting, 24 October 1940.
12. CAB 93/7, SIC Conference, 3 January 1941.
13. CAB 93/2, HD(S)E 27th Meeting, 27 January 1941.
14. ibid, HD(S)E 30th Meeting, 26 March 1941; CAB 93/3, HD(S)E 59 and 61 of 18 and 22 March 1941; CAB 93/7, HD(S)E (RPS) 8th (Special) Meeting, 16 October 1941.
15. CAB 93/6, HD(S)E (GD) 1st Meeting, 13 June 1941.
16. CAB 93/3, HD(S)E 218 of 26 October 1942.

PART II

CHAPTER 5

The Decline of the Threat from Subversion to the End of 1942

MI 5 had no reason to modify its assessment of September 1940 that the British Union and other pro-Nazi groups were unlikely to cause further trouble.* Organised Fascism did not survive the detentions of the summer of 1940. The political conviction of some of the detainees hardened and after their release some of them continued to associate with other sympathisers in small discussion groups that were chiefly distinguishable for virulent anti-semitism and admiration for Hitler. But their lack of following made it extremely unlikely that they would present any serious threat even in the conditions of public discontent that might accompany military set-backs or follow the end of hostilities. In relation to the Communist Party, on the other hand, the security authorities could not exclude this possibility. While there was only one case before the end of 1942 in which proceedings were taken against a member of the CPGB,† the Party's political propaganda continued to cause anxiety both before and after the German attack on Russia in June 1941 and was closely watched.

In August 1940, when the production drive after Dunkirk was calling for long hours and drastic changes in industrial conditions and air raids were producing war weariness and shortening tempers, the CPGB formed People's Vigilance Committees which promoted throughout the autumn a good deal of criticism about bomb shelters, rationing and the cost of living, under the central direction of a People's Convention and with the slogan 'For a People's Government and a People's Peace'. In November this activity was brought to the attention of the War Cabinet, which had not considered questions of subversion since its meetings in July.‡

The War Cabinet was then asked to decide what should be done about a libellous cartoon in the *Daily Worker* which implied that the Minister of Labour had taken bribes from capitalist organisations.[1]

---

* See above, pp 61–62, and Appendix 5(i) for the few cases in which proceedings were taken against members of the BU.

† See Appendix 5(ii).

‡ See above, p 56.

79

It accepted the Prime Minister's advice that this should be ignored as a vulgar insult, but the meeting was followed by discussions between the Prime Minister and the Home Secretary, and between Swinton, the Home Office and MI 5, and by the submission by the Home Secretary to the War Cabinet on 23 December of a memorandum on whether the *Daily Worker* should be suppressed.[2]

The memorandum explained that there were sufficient grounds under DR 2D for action against the *Daily Worker* and against *The Week*, a roneoed sheet published by Claud Cockburn which advocated similar views. It then set out the arguments for and against suppressing them. On the one hand, it could be argued that the steady reiteration of their propaganda must be having a bad effect on moral, and that the toleration of the Communist Party was inconsistent with the action taken against the British Union. On the other hand, there was no evidence that the propaganda was having any appreciable effect on morale even in the bombed areas or in industry, and its suppression would have awkward repercussions. Suppression would raise the question of proscribing the Party itself and detaining its leaders – a course of action that should be avoided unless it became essential on security grounds. It might rally support for the *Daily Worker* from the rest of the Press, which was sensitive about the danger of government interference, and from others who objected to the curtailment of free expression. It might also offend public opinion abroad, particularly in the United States. And it would undoubtedly be followed by a spate of pamphlets which would be more difficult to suppress than a daily paper.

On 27 December the War Cabinet decided to defer a decision for three weeks, but was practically unanimous in favour of suppressing the *Daily Worker*.[3] At a meeting of the Security Executive on 9 January 1941 Wall and a senior official representing the Ministry of Labour expressed serious misgivings about the confidence and growing effectiveness of Communist propaganda. They argued that the Trades Union leadership was being dangerously undermined by allegations that it was betraying the workers by co-operating with the government, and that the government was coming into disrepute as the feeling grew that it was afraid to take action against Communists. On the other side, Maxwell from the Home Office insisted that there was no point in taking action unless it was effective action, and doubted whether even the proscription of the Communist Party and the detention of its leaders would put a stop to its activities. MI 5 believed that the suppression of the *Daily Worker* and the detention of about 100 leaders would hamstring the Party for a few months, but that action might then have to be taken against new leaders.[4]

At the end of this meeting the Security Executive accepted that the Communist Party sought to destroy the authority of the government and the Trades Unions and to impede the war effort, and was in no doubt that its propaganda campaign was making sufficient progess to constitute a considerable risk.* But it made no recommendation on the question of suppressing the *Daily Worker* and it was divided as to whether it would be advisable to proscribe the Party and detain a few of its leaders. The Home Office remained determined that suppression of the *Daily Worker* and *The Week*, if it was decided on, should not be followed by the suppression of the Party or general action against Communist propaganda; these steps were undesirable. It made the point in another memorandum to the War Cabinet on 11 January 1941.[5]

On 13 January the War Cabinet approved the suppression of the two papers under DR 2D† and appointed a ministerial committee under Sir John Anderson, the Lord President, to consider what further action, if any, might be taken.[7] The committee reported on 10 February that it was not yet necessary to ban the CPGB or detain its leaders, and the War Cabinet accepted its recommendation.[8] During its deliberations the committee had heard from Ernest Bevin, the Minister of Labour that he was not impressed by claims that the Communists were having a great impact on industry, and that he believed that, if it came to detention, action should be directed against the intelligentsia rather than against working class members.[9] MI 5 had suggested that the government should publish the minutes of the Central Committee meetings leading to the Communist change of line in October 1939 as proof that the CPGB was subject to foreign control and dedicated to the defeat of Britain; but Swinton had not approved the idea.‡

The suppression of the *Daily Worker* was a heavy blow to the cohesion of the CPGB. The publication of illegal, roneoed copies was a short-lived gesture of defiance which could not sustain the momentum of its propaganda, and the lifting of the ban became a prime objective of the Communist leaders. In the spring of 1941, however, they derived encouragement from British adversities in Greece and north Africa, making use of them in April in a new

---

* This assessment was shared by the Communist Party. One of its leaders told a private meeting at the beginning of January that Britain was only one stage removed from a revolutionary situation. The People's Convention Movement must be the focal point of continuing pressure.

† The Home Secretary made the order on 21 January. A week after he had informed the House of Commons, Mr Aneurin Bevan moved a resolution expressing detestation of the *Daily Worker*'s propaganda, but regretting that the paper had been suppressed under Defence Regulations which the House had understood were for use only in circumstances of direct peril arising from invasion. The resolution was defeated by 323 votes to six.[6]

‡ For these minutes see above, p 36 and Appendix 2.

manifesto – 'The Truth Must be Told' – to reinforce the campaign against the imperialist war and in favour of a People's Government and a People's Peace.

The German invasion of Russia on 22 June took the CPGB by surprise, and it was no less surprised by the response of the British government. It instinctively assumed that the British government had been privy to the German plans – that this explained the mystery of Rudolf Hess's arrival on 10–11 May – and expected Britain to join Hitler against the Soviet Union.[10] And it remained unconvinced by Churchill's undertaking to support Russia until Stalin welcomed British assistance in his speech on 3 July. This was accepted as a clear intimation to Communists everywhere that the war had now become a genuine People's War, and that it was their duty to see that inefficiency, or 'friends of Fascism' in high places, did not deprive the USSR of the utmost assistance she could be given.[11] On 8 July Pollitt, who now resumed his post as General Secretary, informed Party branches that Churchill's speech and Stalin's reply had created a new situation in which the CPGB would give wholehearted support to the government and work to achieve a united national front.

For the leaders of the CPGB this change of policy was purely tactical. In confidential briefings they made it clear to members that in view of the revolutionary objectives of the Party, collaboration with the authorities would be temporary and should be exploited to its advantage. Any Russian successes were to be attributed to the superiority of the Communist system; any German successes to the failure of Great Britain to provide Russia with adequate assistance. The Party was to strengthen its position by using the new public sympathy for the USSR to obtain recognition as a responsible leader of labour, while continuing to undermine management and the Trades Union leaders, and to secure the removal of the ban on the *Daily Worker* as being unjustifiable now that the Party was enthusiastically supporting the British war effort.[12]

The CPGB derived some benefit from the new situation. By June 1941 the damage done by the embarrassing policy of revolutionary defeatism had reduced its membership to some 15,000, 25 per cent less than it had been in the spring of 1940. By the end of the year it had increased the membership to 23,000 without making any special effort. But it did not succeed in concealing its tactics from the security authorities. On 21 July the War Cabinet took note of a Home Office report on the Party's policy since the attack on Russia and re-affirmed the ban on the *Daily Worker*.[13] Pressed about the ban in the Commons on 2 October, the Home Secretary defended it on the ground that 'the Communist Party is not loyal to this country'.[14] In a detailed report on its tactics later in October the Security Executive concluded that, in Swinton's words, 'the Communist game is still the same, but it is being played on a much better wicket'.[15] Even less than before the German invasion of Russia, on the other hand, did its activities call for security counter-measures over and above the banning of the *Daily Worker*.

In April, before the German invasion of Russia, MI 5 had appreciated that while sophisticated Communists, realising that the British Empire was the greatest obstacle to the victory of the Communist International, were prepared to see Hitler defeat the British at the expense of the temporary set-back of their own ideals, they were nevertheless not pro-Hitler and would not assist a German invasion of the United Kingdom; there was accordingly no case for detaining them.[16] After the invasion the case for detaining them was no longer considered. Their overt propaganda ceased to be disturbing and it was sufficient to oppose their new tactics with discreet obstruction.

As it seemed to the authorities, the main planks in the Party's public propaganda after Russia's entry into the war were designed to serve both its long-term and its short-term objectives. It campaigned in support of maximum war production, but did so in the interests of the USSR as the champion of the working class. This was most obvious from the fact that, except for a brief lull following the Allied invasion of north Africa, it also campaigned for a Second Front in virulent attacks on the government which conflicted with its support for the war effort but which also exploited popular sympathy and admiration for Russia's sufferings and achievements. It had to be expected that it would use its patriotic stance to acquire respectability and gain positions from which to pursue its unchanged revolutionary objectives. Nor were these apprehensions contradicted by what was known about its less overt activities. The switch to energetic support for the war effort was accompanied by an important change of organisation, the factory group replacing the local branch as the basic unit in order to facilitate recruitment and political education. And the cadres, the politically conscious élite responsible for political education, were themselves taught that the alliance of the proletariat with the ruling class was a transient expedient and that the Party must remain ready to exploit any revolutionary situation.[17]

Despite the Party's new public position the Security Executive sharpened its watch on the Party's new tactics. It was advised by a Committee on Communism which, under Wall's chairmanship and with representatives from the Home Office, the Ministry of Labour, MI 5, the Metropolitan Police and (from December 1941) the Ministry of Information, met weekly until the middle of 1942 and fortnightly thereafter.[18] The Committee's chief concern was to block Communist attempts to use the Party's producion campaign as a means of undermining Trades Union leadership and promoting workers' control. The movement for establishing joint production committees was given official blessing but steps were taken to keep it under Trades Union control. Political meetings in government-controlled factories were forbidden, and private firms were encouraged to follow suit. In April 1942 the Wall Committee was satisfied that these measures had been entirely successful, but it advised that it was still necessary to counter Communist attempts to exploit 'non-political' meetings at factories by limiting speakers at such meetings to members of the armed forces in uniform and people selected by the Ministry of Information. The War Cabinet adopted this recommendation for government factories and informed the TUC, the Employers Federation and private firms of its decision.[19]

Another preoccupation was to prevent Communists from exploiting the Anglo-Soviet friendship movement. From November 1941 the Ministry of Information was countering any proposals for Anglo-Soviet friendship activities that appeared to be Communist-inspired by turning them into functions organised by the local civic authorities, and it was itself taking the initiative in encouraging local information committees to organise Anglo-Soviet demonstrations. In March 1942 it reported that it had had considerable success with this policy, which relied on advice from the Home Office and MI 5 as to which organisations were suspected of being under Communist influence. But difficulties continued to arise from the fact that while it was generally understood that official recognition was not to be given to Communist-influenced activities, this had not been formally laid down. In June 1942, for example, the Wall Committee decided that no government encouragement should be given to a demonstration organised by the Joint Committee for Soviet Aid to celebrate the anniversary of Russia's entry into the war, but then discovered that Sir Stafford Cripps, the Lord Privy Seal, was to address it.[20]

These measures may have checked the influence of the Party outside its own followers, but they did not prevent a considerable increase in its membership. A recruiting campaign in the first three months of 1942 brought in 25,000 new members. The Party was claiming a membership of 64,000 by December, and though the true figure was about 50,000, this still represented a marked increase over the 15,000 of the middle of 1941 and the 23,000 at the end of that year. The growth in following, as in influence, had been especially marked in the industrial Trades Unions; the number of factory groups, about 1,000 in April 1942, had doubled by the spring of 1943. But clerical, scientific and professional workers and intellectuals were also being drawn into the fold by sympathy and admiration for Russia.[21]

The main effect of the increase in the Party's following was that it at first strengthened and ultimately undermined the government's determination to maintain the ban on the *Daily Worker*. Until May 1942, when the lifting of the ban was supported by the Labour Party conference, the War Cabinet rejected the Party's repeated appeals against it. But the Home Secretary then advised that pressure for lifting it was growing and would become increasingly difficult to resist so long as the Party supported the war effort and refrained from the open profession of revolutionary aims. Two months later he informed the War Cabinet that the removal of the ban was being advocated in wider and wider quarters; and after he had reminded the Cabinet that it was government policy to make the least possible use of powers under the Defence Regulations which limited traditional freedoms, the Cabinet agreed that he should remove it before the Trades Union Congress in September. He did so on 7 September.[22]

CHAPTER 5: REFERENCES

1. CAB 65/10, WM(40) 295 and 296 of 25 and 27 November.
2. CAB 66/10. WP(40) 482 of 23 December.
3. CAB 65/10, WM(40) 310 of 27 December.
4. CAB 93/2, HD(S)E 22nd Meeting of 9 January 1941; HO 45/2552/832463/295.
5. CAB 66/14, WP(41) 7 of 11 January.
6. Hansard, Vol 368, Cols 185, 465.
7. CAB 65/17, WM(41) 5 of 13 January.
8. ibid, WM(41) 18 of 17 February; CAB 66/14, WP(41) 27 of 10 February.
9. CAB 98/18, CA(41) 3rd Meeting of 5 February.
10. CAB 93/3, HD(S)E 93 of 11 July 1941; CAB 66/35, WP(43) 109 of 13 March.
11. CAB 66/19, WP(41) 244 of 19 October.
12. ibid.
13. CAB 65/19, WM(41) 72 of 21 July; CAB 66/17, WP(41) 169 of 18 July.
14. Hansard, Vol 374, Cols 712–713.
15. CAB 66/19, WP(41) 244 of 19 October.
16. HO 45/2552/832463/320a.
17. CAB 66/35, WP(43) 109 of 13 March; CAB 93/3, SE 173 of 27 April 1942.
18. CAB 66/19, WP(41) 244 of 19 October; CAB 93/5 for the records of the Wall Committee.
19. CAB 65/26, WM(42) 49 of 15 April; CAB 66/23, WP(42) 150 of 7 April; CAB 93/3, SE 154 of 13 February, 157 of 6 March 1942.
20. CAB 65/30, WM(42) 70 CA of 1 June; CAB 66/25, WP(42) 240 of 5 June.
21. JIC(46) 101(o) of 18 November.
22. CAB 65/30, WM(42) 70 CA of 1 June; CAB 65/31, WM(42) 101 of 1 August; CAB 66/25, WP(42) 230 of 29 May; CAB 66/27, WP(42) 323 of 1 August.

CHAPTER 6

The Defeat of the Abwehr's Offensive, June 1940 to the Autumn of 1941, and the Consolidation of the Double-Cross System

SUCCESS in the conduct of counter-espionage operations was by no means delayed until the re-organisation of the security machine was completed in the spring of 1941.* Greater efficiency in the field developed independently of structural reform on foundations that were laid in the summer and autumn of 1940 when the direction, the morale and the reputation of MI 5 were at their lowest ebb. The foundations – the evolution of the double-cross system and progress against the enemy's cyphers – were also laid in time to ensure that the Abwehr's first concerted offensive against the United Kingdom was comprehensively thwarted. But that is not all. Though not without some assistance from the incompetence of the Abwehr, it was mainly on these foundations that in the next twelve months MI 5 progressed from a state of almost total ignorance about the Abwehr's capacities and intentions to the position in which the influence it could exert over the Abwehr's activities was so great that, far from constituting a threat to Great Britain, the Abwehr's activities were a serious handicap to Germany for the rest of the war.

The double-cross system had its origins, as already noted, in the early activities of *Snow*.† But his case remained on a precarious footing and the potentialities remained imperfectly understood before the summer of 1940, as may be seen from the briefest account of *Snow's* activities in the spring of that year.

In April 1940 *Snow's* German controller suggested that *Snow* should effect the introduction of a new agent at a rendezvous in the North Sea – presumably because he was aware of the possibility that meetings in Antwerp and Brussels might at any time be ruled out by Germany's offensive in the west. *Snow* went along with the idea in May, MI 5 producing both a trawler for him and sub-agent, alias *Biscuit*. The operation was a fiasco. *Biscuit* became

---

* See above, Chapter 4.
† See above, p 41ff.

convinced that *Snow* was actually a German agent who was double-crossing the British; *Snow* claimed under later interrogation that he had spoken and acted as if he was a German agent because he had suspected that *Biscuit* was a German agent who was leading him into a trap. Whether or not *Snow's* misunderstanding was genuine, *Biscuit* certainly acted on his conviction; when a seaplane circled over the trawler two days before the agreed rendezvous time and gave the agreed recognition signal, he ordered the skipper to make for port and had *Snow* tied up. Perhaps from the wish to have revenge for the Venlo incident,* MI 5 then piled folly on fiasco by sending the trawler back to the rendezvous on the correct day, but with a naval crew and a shadowing submarine, in an attempt to capture *Snow's* controller. Fortunately, it was saved by the elements from the consequences of its bravado: a rendezvous was made impossible by fog.

By July MI 5 had had wiser thoughts. In that month it contrived to introduce *Biscuit* to the Abwehr by sending him to meet *Snow's* controller and other Abwehr officers in Lisbon. At the meeting he stoutly defended *Snow* against charges of inefficiency. The Germans, accepting his explanation that fog had prevented the rendezvous, gave him a wireless set, a new questionnaire and 3,000 dollars in cash. He handed over to them his identity card and a traveller's ration book. The Germans rose to the bait. In August, at the Abwehr's request, *Snow* supplied it with specimen names and numbers for a dozen forged identity cards; in November the Abwehr asked for, and was sent, four more. They were to contribute to the capture of spies – and to the securing of new recruits to the double-cross system – when in the unexpected circumstances following the fall of France the Abwehr hastily despatched agents on short missions to the United Kingdom in support of the projected German invasion. The fact that the Germans were preparing to despatch some of these agents was disclosed in August. The RSS identified in that month traffic on a local network in northern France which was using one of the several simple cyphers solved by the RSS and GC and CS in the spring of 1940,† and the decrypts showed that the stations had been set up to work with new contacts in the United Kingdom. Traffic in another readable cypher was identified in the autumn of 1940 between Germany and a station in Oslo; its signals disclosed plans for establishing weather stations in Greenland and Jan Mayen Island‡ and they were used to enable HMS *Naiad* to

---

* See Appendix 1(ii) and Hinsley et al, *British Intelligence in the Second World War*, Vol 1 (1979), pp 56–57 for this incident.

† For some of these cyphers see above, p 44. Others that were solved carried traffic to north America and in the Balkans.

‡ See Hinsley et al, op cit, Vol II (1981) Appendix 7.

intercept a German trawler and capture 22 meteorologists of the German Air Force on 17 November. But a much more important advance was to be made at the end of the year.

Traffic on a far more extensive link than these others, between a control in Berlin and out-stations in Holland, Belgium, Yugo-slavia, Switzerland, Spain, Norway and Sweden, had been inter-cepted since the spring. It used more sophisticated cyphers and was assumed to be the Abwehr's main wireless network. In June, when the cyphers remained unbroken, the Y Committee* had decided that, in order to release operators who were desperately needed for the interception of the Enigma traffic of the German Air Force, the RSS should cease to intercept the Abwehr link, and the objections of the RSS were over-ridden in September. In October, however, the RSS and GC and CS had obtained permis-sion to resume the interception, and in December GC and CS broke one of the cyphers.

As expected, it proved to be the hand cypher used by the Abwehr and its chief stations abroad.† It yielded only a few hundred decrypts a week throughout 1941 but it was of immense value not only in transforming the Allied understanding of the Abwehr's order of battle‡ but also in combating the Abwehr's continued efforts to establish a network in the United Kingdom. During 1941 it was exclusively responsible for the capture of five of the 23 agents despatched to the United Kingdom, it identified two others and it was invaluable for the direction of the activities of six of MI 5's double-cross agents.

□

Until the summer of 1940 the Abwehr, apart from developing its contacts with *Snow*, had confined itself to plans for operating in Eire in conjunction with the IRA. In the spring it was about to send a liaison officer to the IRA, a man named Goertz, who after being educated in Edinburgh and serving in the German Air Force had been sentenced for espionage in England in 1936 and deported to Germany in February 1939, and who had met members of the IRA while in prison. He was on the point of leaving for Eire when Stephen Held, the treasurer of the IRA, arrived in Berlin with a proposal that Germany should land arms

---

* See Hinsley et al, op cit, Vol I, pp 23, 91, 267.

† The other traffic on this link was cyphered in the Enigma and remained unbroken for a further year.

‡ The first picture of the Abwehr's order of battle in Germany, the Low Countries, France, the Iberian peninsula and south-east Europe was constructed by MI 5 in December 1940. It was based on information from double-cross operations, captured agents and, most importantly, the RSS's study of Abwehr communications.

and carry out an attack in the Londonderry area with IRA support. The Abwehr thought the proposal amateur and over-ambitious but decided that Goertz could convert it into a practical programme of espionage and sabotage in Ulster. He landed in Eire by parachute on 5 May.

On 23 May the British High Commissioner reported from Dublin that, following up reports of a parachutist landing, the Police had raided Held's step-father's house, arrested Held and found a parachute, a large transmitter, a code book, 20,000 dollars and papers relating to German collaboration with the IRA in plans for attacks in Northern Ireland (Plan *Kathleen*).*

When this news was received the British authorities were already taking measures to introduce the censorship of mail between the UK and Ireland, and they now extended them. Telegrams were censored from 31 May; telephone calls, which had been monitored since November 1939, were made liable to interruption and disconnection; and from 21 June all persons travelling from Ireland were required to obtain a visa in Dublin or an exit permit in Belfast. The Eire government also adopted a vigorous security programme. In June the Emergency Powers (Amendment) Act authorised the internment of Eire citizens without trial and set up a military court for the trial of certain offences. Closer relations were established with the Royal Ulster Constabulary. And in the next few months the IRA was demoral-ised by police raids, arrests and internments.

In these circumstances the Abwehr's next attempt to increase its offensive was to despatch agents to Eire independently of the IRA.† H W Simon – an Abwehr agent who had been sentenced in England in 1938 for failure to register as an alien and subsequent-ly deported – and Wilhelm Preetz – a German who had married an Irish girl – were landed clandestinely in June. Simon was arrested within 24 hours of his arrival. Preetz was arrested in Dublin on 26 August with the assistance of decrypts of German illicit signals from Eire.‡ Their mission had been to report on weather condi-tions, shipping movements and troop dispositions in Northern Ireland, but Preetz had also recruited an Irishman to report on air raid damage in England. On 7 July three men who had been trained in sabotage were landed by U-boat, an Indian named

---

* Goertz was out when the house was raided and remained on the run in Eire until he was caught in November 1941.

† They also sent Sean Russell, the IRA Chief of Staff who had returned from the USA to Berlin, and Frank Ryan, who had held command in the International Brigade, back to Eire by U-boat. But they were not returning as agents; they were to have a free hand to 'make use of Ireland's opportunities'. Their mission was also ill-fated. Russell died en route and Ryan returned to Germany.

‡ See above, p 42.

Obed Hussein, who was a known German agent, and two Germans who had been born in South West Africa. They were arrested the day they landed.

□

The first attempts to infiltrate agents into the United Kingdom followed from the beginning of September. Between then and 12 November ten agents landed from four dinghies and four landed by parachute; in addition a fishing boat carrying Germans surrendered to a Royal Navy patrol boat in the Channel and another put in at Fishguard and gave itself up. Five of the total of 21 were Germans, five Dutchmen, three Cubans, two Danes, two Swedes, two Norwegians, a Swiss and a Belgian. Five of them had been on the books of the Abwehr and the remainder had been hastily recruited, several of them under pressure of one kind or another. They had had little or no training and were poorly briefed. Their identity cards and ration books, constructed from the information provided by *Snow*, were incriminating. Only one of those who did not give themselves up escaped immediate capture. The exception, a Dutchman, committed suicide in Cambridge when he ran out of money in the spring of 1941; the fact that the Germans had made no attempt to put him in touch with *Snow* strongly suggested that he had failed to establish contact with them.*

Of the remaining 20, five were tried under the Treachery Act† and executed, twelve were interned and three saved their lives by agreeing to work for MI 5. One of these three, to be known as *Summer*, was a Swede who had made two trips to England for the Abwehr in 1939, ostensibly as a journalist representing Swedish newspapers. His wireless set (transmitter and receiver), a code and materials for secret writing were captured with him. After agreeing to work for MI 5 he contacted the Abwehr, which instructed *Snow* to arrange accommodation for him and ordered him to cover the area London-Colchester-Southend; he reported back on 23 October that he was established near Cambridge. The second double agent was a Dane, alias *Tate*. On 16 October he told the Abwehr that he was established near Barnet; thereafter he maintained contact with Hamburg until the day before the city fell in May 1945 and was highly prized by his German controllers. The third, alias *Gander*, was a German; as he had been supplied with a transmitter but not with a receiver, MI 5 was able to use him only for a few weeks until his mission was exhausted, and he was thereafter detained.

---

* See Appendix 6 for an account of these cases.
† See above, p 47 and below, p 96.

Between January and July 1941 the Abwehr sent four more agents by parachute, two to England and two to Eire, and another party by dinghy to Scotland. The first of the parachutists, Joseph Jakobs, a German with reasonably good English and an innocent contact in England, broke his ankle on landing in Huntingdonshire in January and was arrested at once; his identity card was based on information provided by *Snow* and the Germans had asked *Snow* to contact him. Unsuitable as a double agent because of the publicity surrounding his capture, he was convicted and executed under the Treachery Act. The second parachutist to arrive in England, Karel Richter, met the same fate. A Sudeten German, he was sent in May to deliver some money and a spare wireless crystal to *Tate* and check that *Tate* was not under British control – important tasks for which his qualifications and equipment were lamentably inadequate.* Of the parachutists despatched to Eire, Günther Schutz was sent to deliver money to Unland† and then cross to England with a wireless set for *Rainbow* whom Schutz had been instrumental in recruiting;‡ he was arrested almost at once, as was Unland whose photograph he carried. The other, an Eire citizen called *Basket* by MI 5, landed in July. He had been in Jersey when the Germans occupied the island. Attempting to escape in a stolen boat, he was driven ashore in France by a gale, arrested and invited to return to Eire as a German spy. He was trained in Paris and after an abortive attempt in January 1941 was finally despatched from The Hague. He at once made his way to Belfast and gave himself up. He provided valuable information about the Abwehr, in Paris and the Netherlands, but could not be used as a double agent since his primary assignment for the Abwehr had been to transmit weather reports.§ The dinghy party, two Norwegians who were put into the dinghy from a seaplane off the west coast of Scotland in April, had been sent to carry out sabotage and to report by wireless on troop movements and civilian morale, and also, apparently, in the hope that they would find employment with the Norwegian forces in the United Kingdom. They surrendered on getting ashore and were enrolled as double-cross agents, aliases *Mutt* and *Jeff.*

---

* He spoke broken English and was an incompetent wireless operator. He carried not only an imperfectly forged identity card with particulars supplied by *Snow* but also a Czech passport in his own name. The spare wireless crystal did not fit *Tate*'s set. His own wireless could be operated only after he had purchased additional equipment in England. For the secret writing in which he had received instructions he had been told he had also to buy in England a substance, amidopyrine, for which he would have had to sign the poison book.

† See above, p 43.

‡ See above, p 43.

§ His story led to the imposition of special censorship on correspondence to and from Irishmen on the continent. This yielded information about another agent who landed in Eire by parachute in December 1943, (see below, p 194).

In all the operations described so far the agents were to be introduced without going through the normal travel controls. An alternative course was for agents to gain admission openly, posing either as refugees from occupied territory or as visitors with legitimate business in Britain. From the autumn of 1940 onwards, numerous agents were despatched by the Abwehr under one or other of these disguises. The first such case that came to light occurred in September 1940 with the arrival of a former member of the Czech Legion in France. He had been recruited in Lisbon by an Abwehr agent, who was also working for the SIS, and provided with secret writing materials and cover addresses. His sole object had been to get to England, and he at once gave himself up. He worked briefly as a double agent, alias *Giraffe*, before joining the Free French Forces. In June and July 1941 the Abwehr sent three more agents by this route, but they too, had accepted recruitment only as a means of getting to the United Kingdom. All three – a Belgian pilot, a Polish pilot and a Yugoslav woman – reported themselves before or upon their arrival and were added to the double-cross team as *Father, Careless* and *The Snark.**

Father, a pilot in the Belgian Air Force, arrived from Lisbon at the end of June 1941. He had returned to Brussels after the fall of France and was determined to escape. He obtained an introduction to an Abwehr officer and, posing as strongly pro-German, volunteered to join the German Air Force, intending to steal an aeroplane and fly it to England. He was told that he could not enlist but was invited to go to the USA as an Abwehr agent, to obtain work there as a test pilot, and report by wireless and secret writing. He agreed, and, after some training, travelled in December 1940 via Spain to Lisbon where he spent several months trying unsuccessfully to obtain a visa for the USA. When it became plain that this would not be forthcoming, he suggested to his Abwehr contact that he should go to England instead. His contact agreed and suggested that he should steal an RAF plane and fly it back to France, thus reversing *Father*'s original idea. In the event he left Lisbon without receiving any further instructions from the Germans. During his prolonged stay in Lisbon he had called on the Belgian Military Attaché and confided his story. He was therefore in a position to join the double-cross team as soon as he arrived – indeed he wrote his first letter, under MI 5 instruction, the following day.

Careless was a pilot in the Polish Air Force. He had been shot down just before the collapse of the Polish Army. Although

---

* Between July and December 1941, three more supposed refugees with Abwehr assignments arrived from Lisbon. One abandoned his mission, and the other two were arrested and interned.

wounded, he managed to escape and eventually reached France where he was in hospital for some weeks. After an unsuccessful attempt to get to England by boat, he crossed into Spain illegally at the end of April 1941. In Barcelona he was approached by a fellow Pole who suggested that he should work for the Abwehr. *Careless* agreed to this proposition and was passed on to Madrid, where he was given a questionnaire on Air Force matters, secret writing materials and cover addresses, and told to go to England and join the RAF. While waiting for transport in Lisbon he was financed by the German embassy. This contact became known to the Polish authorities. Moreover, he made friends with three Polish refugees, with whom he shared an apartment and who travelled to England with him. En route he told one of them something about his contacts with the Germans and on arrival his fellow refugees denounced him. Fortunately during the voyage he had also made a brief report to the ship's captain about the Abwehr approach. After thorough interrogation, *Careless* was judged to be trustworthy and it was decided to run him as a double-cross agent.

The Snark was a Yugoslav who had come to England in 1938 as a domestic servant. At the end of 1940 she decided to return home. She arrived in Lisbon in January 1941, but had difficulty in obtaining the necessary visas and moved on to Madrid in March. She was still in Spain when the Germans over-ran Yugoslavia. By then she was very short of money and was blackmailed into agreeing to return to England to report in secret writing on air raid damage, rationing and morale among the poorer classes of the population. She reported her contacts with the Abwehr to various British and Yugoslav authorities in Madrid, Lisbon and later in Gibraltar, and landed back in England on 23 July as a ready-made MI 5 double agent.

Meanwhile, the first agent purporting to be a bona fide visitor had also arrived in September 1940, and had since posed considerable problems. A Spaniard named Del Pozo, his visit as a special observer for the Spanish Institute of Political Studies was backed by the British Council and the embassy in Madrid. He was taken on a British Council tour of Scotland and the Ministry of Information allowed him to use its bag for sending his reports to his Institute; it was later discovered that he had taken advantage of this facility to send his espionage reports in secret ink on the back of his Press articles. But the SIS had learned that he was a German agent and this was confirmed when, ten days after his arrival, he wrote to *Snow's* sub-agent *GW* and gave a pass-word previously agreed between *GW* and the Abwehr. *Snow* queried his bona fides with the Abwehr and was told that Del Pozo was indeed bringing money which *Snow* had asked for. When *GW* met him in London he was given about £4,000 in notes and instructions to provide weekly reports on the Welsh Nationalist Party and on armaments factories in Wales. The two men had twelve other meetings before Del Pozo was recalled early in 1941. MI 5, which was able to curtail his opportunities for spying, secured his recall by having *Snow* report to the Abwehr that his dissolute behaviour and openly pro-Nazi sentiments had brought him to the notice of the British Press.

The next supposedly innocent visitor to come to MI 5's attention arrived via Lisbon at the end of December 1940. He was a Yugoslav commercial lawyer who had taken a degree in Germany. He was recruited for the Abwehr by a German with whom he had made friends at the University and who would later be known as *Artist* by the British. He reported the approach and, acting under British instructions, agreed to visit London to collect on behalf of the Germans reports from a notional friend in the Yugoslav embassy. His personality and attitude – he said that he was being well paid by the Germans and did not want money from the British – made an excellent impression in London and he returned to Lisbon at the beginning of January 1941 supplied with suitable information. Thereafter, well-established with the Germans and with excellent business cover for frequent journeys between London and Lisbon and other neutral countries, he was to have a distinguished career as a double agent under the alias *Tricycle*.

The Abwehr was also recruiting from the most numerous class of visitors to Britain, merchant seamen in ships docking at neutral ports. Several were caught.* Others may have escaped detection. But seamen, though easily accessible, were of limited value as spies. A more serious threat arose from another Abwehr undertaking in the spring and summer of 1941 – the inclusion of agents among genuine refugees in some of the small ships arriving from Norway. The Abwehr attempted this with six of the ships which sailed from Norway between March and September and although arrangements for screening refugees were by now in place they were still being perfected and these spies were extremely difficult to detect. Fortunately in five of the six cases ISOS decrypts disclosed the enemy's involvement and led to the arrest of several Norwegians sent over in the hope that they would get posted to Allied ships or as Allied agents in Norway. Thus three were taken from a ship which arrived in Lerwick in July and one from a ship which arrived in Iceland in August. In one of the five cases, however, the decrypts which disclosed the Abwehr's association with the sailing were not obtained for several months. The *Olav*

---

* See Appendix 7 for an account of two such cases.

arrived in the Shetlands in March, but the decrypts did not establish until the end of November that three of the Norwegians on board had been sent by the Abwehr. In the meantime they had not merely escaped suspicion; they had been taken on by the SOE for duties in Norway. And while two of them were then detained, the decrypts also disclosed that the third, who had been ferrying SOE agents to Norway, had been arrested by the Germans in September. But he did not betray the SOE's trust. No disturbance to SOE's operations followed his arrest.

□

With the capture of the spies who arrived from September 1940 several problems, ethical, legal and procedural, arose from the fact that under the Treachery Act spies were liable to the death penalty. The alternative of using them for counter-espionage purposes was discussed at the Security Intelligence Centre on 10 September 1940. Swinton outlined a procedure agreed with the Director of Public Prosecutions to representatives from the Home Office, the Service Departments, GHQ Home Forces, MI 5 and the SIS. The capture of a spy was to be reported to MI 5; MI 5 would decide whether the spy was to be invited to make a statement to the Police under caution or was to be interrogated by MI 5; if interrogation was decided on, the prisoner was to be given an opportunity later to make a statement under caution for use as evidence in a prosecution, and it was essential that no form of inducement should be held out to him. In the course of the discussion, however, all the Service Directors of Intelligence thought that agents should always be interrogated and Swinton 'confirmed that it was completely within the discretion of the Services whether they would forego prosecution and use the agent in any particular case for their own purposes'.[1]

MI 5 clearly assumed that this assurance empowered it to disregard in suitable cases the rule against offering an inducement. Two days previously it had told *Summer* that he could save his life – be treated as a prisoner of war and not as a spy – if he would collaborate in the transmission of messages to Germany. A little later it used words amounting to an inducement when interrogating *Gander*. It was accordingly surprised to learn on 7 October that in future no spy was to be offered his life without Swinton's authority. The ruling appears to have come after the Prime Minister had asked why none of the captured spies had been shot; and in a memorandum to MI 5 in March 1941 Swinton was to record that 'the Prime Minister has laid it down as a matter of policy that in all suitable cases spies should be brought to trial'. This memorandum insisted that 'in all suitable cases, every step must be taken, provided it does not conflict in any serious manner with the interests of intelligence, so to arrange matters that ... nothing should be done or omitted which could in any way jeopardise a successful prosecution'. It was Swinton's reply to a request from MI 5, supported by the SIS, for reconsideration of the October ruling. Six of the fifteen spies caught in September and October 1940 had by then been tried under the Treachery Act, of whom five were executed. MI 5 regarded executions as wasteful: 'intelligence should have precedence over blood-letting'. It was also fearful of the damage to security that might follow from the fact that, as was inevitable when a spy was put on trial, the Press demanded maximum publicity about the case.

Despite MI 5's discontent with the ruling of March 1941, Swinton continued to insist on it. As he wrote on 17 June, 'I have given my undertaking that any spy or enemy agent whom we no longer require ... for intelligence purposes shall be brought to justice if the case against him will lie. The right man to decide whether any case can be brought is the DPP, and we should certainly have the insurance of his opinion and advice in every case'. In November 1941, however, in discussions held between Swinton, MI 5, the DPP and the Attorney General about *Summer* and *Gander*, whose careers as double agents had come to an end, it was agreed that no question of prosecution could arise if MI 5 had used an agent or given him a promise: the risk that the agent's double-cross work would be revealed in court had to be considered; and a promise once given had to be honoured. It was also agreed that in the event of proceedings being taken against an agent, MI 5, to avoid undue publicity, should prepare a statement to be approved by the Home Office before release to the Press through the Ministry of Information.* But for the remainder of the war it rested with the DPP to decide whether or not proceedings should be taken where a prima facie case was made out that a criminal offence had been committed; and the policy, under which the number of spies executed finally totalled sixteen, nine of them between December 1940 and December 1941, was subject to only two qualifications.

---

* This issue arose in an acute form in two cases. After the execution of Jakobs in August 1941 the Press carried certain articles giving information about his capture and the way in which spies were handled when captured. This led to a re-assertion at a meeting of the Security Executive on 28 August 1941 of the principle that MI 5 was to be the sole judge of what was released to the Press.[2] The second case was that of Karel Richter, who had been sent to the United Kingdom to pay *Tate* and check on his activities, and it was feared that any announcement about his execution might arouse German suspicions about *Tate*. In November 1941, after he had been tried in camera and sentenced to death, MI 5 accordingly urged his reprieve. This request was refused and the agreed procedure for limiting publicity was followed.

In the first place, MI 5 could make representations to the DPP in exceptional cases about either the desirability of giving an inducement to an agent or the undesirability of prejudicing security by prosecution. In the second place, the DPP was not consulted if there was no prima facie case; and his ruling that no proceedings could be taken against non-British subjects in respect of acts committed outside the territorial jurisdiction of British courts meant that a considerable proportion of the agents handled by MI 5 did not have to be referred to him.

□

The need for some machinery for supervising the delicate operation of double agents had meanwhile exercised MI 5 since the capture of the first spies. Early in September 1940 it discussed with the DMI 'policy regarding communications sent to the enemy through our various agents', asking in particular for advice as to whether the aim should be to encourage invasion by denigrating British defences or to discourage it by exaggerating them. At the beginning of October a meeting attended by the Service Directors of Intelligence, the Chairman of the JIC, 'C' and a representative of MI 5 decided to establish a new committee – the W Committee – to supervise the use of double agents for 'the dissemination of false information'. At a meeting of this committee on 18 November MI 5 defined the objectives as being:

'(i)   To keep our agents sufficiently well fed with accurate information so as not to lose the confidence of the enemy;

(ii)   To control as many of the agents in this country as we can, in order to make [the enemy] feel that the ground is covered and they need not send any more of whose arrival we might not be aware;

(iii) By careful manoeuvring of these agents and a careful study of the questionnaires [submitted to them from Germany], to mislead the enemy on a big scale at the appropriate moment'.

In the next few weeks a sub-committee – the Twenty (XX) Committee – evolved for the day-to-day operation of the system. Its members represented the SIS, the Service Intelligence Directorates, GHQ Home Forces, the Home Defence Executive and MI 5, which provided the chairman, Mr J C Masterman, and the secretary. There was much discussion by the Directors of Intelligence and the chairman of the JIC as to whether the Twenty Committee should remain under the W Committee or be placed under the JIC, a course which was finally rejected in order to avoid the need to keep formal records and also to preserve the maximum secrecy about operations of high 'gossip value'. The Directors of Intelligence 'took the responsibility of running the double-cross agents on their own shoulders' and though each of them is believed to have informed his Chief of Staff in the most general terms about the work, the Chiefs of Staff collectively never formally approved it.

The Twenty Committee held its first meeting on 2 January 1941 to consider a memorandum from MI 5. This pointed out that there was a real danger that the double-cross system would collapse; the system could be kept in being only by constant advance planning and the maintenance of a flow of consistent and plausible reports to the enemy. It recognised that the provision of plausible reports involved taking risks, but argued that these would be more than off-set by the advantages that would accrue for counter-intelligence, for cryptanalytical work on the Abwehr cyphers and for the purpose of operations. Counter-espionage would obtain an insight into the enemy's espionage network and lead to the discovery of new agents. The enemy's confidence in the double agents would encourage him to believe that his cyphers were secure when that was not the case, and so might contribute to the solution of new Abwehr cyphers. Operationally, the question-naires he supplied to the double agents would yield valuable intelligence, and 'more important still is the fact that if, and only if, confidence on the enemy's side has been established . . . it will be possible . . . to mislead the enemy by false information with regard to large-scale military operations'. The meeting approved this statement of policy and referred to the W Committee a series of questions about its implementation. They arose from the fact that the Abwehr questionnaires requested information on a wide range of subjects – Army order of battle, weapons and tactical develop-ments, especially in the RAF, British defences, warship construc-tion, convoy movements, industrial output and the location of factories, food supplies and rationing, air raid damage, public morale. They had to be answered plausibly, having regard to Germany's other sources, which might include reports from agents who had escaped control,* if her confidence in her agents was to be maintained, but they had to be answered without betraying information of crucial importance.

The W Committee, which had adjusted to the new structure by re-naming itself the W Board, answered these questions on 8 January. It decided that such accounts as were provided for double agents about air raid damage and public morale should be reasonably accurate, but that no information should be supplied about the comparative effects of bombing on morale in rich and

---

* At the end of July 1941 MI 5 ventured to claim for the first time that it controlled 'the main portion of the German [espionage] system in this country' through the double-cross agents.

poor areas. The general objective should be to ensure that bomb damage was widely spread. It further decided that since the aim should be to discourage invasion, the reports of double agents should stress that the anti-invasion defences were powerful.

The posing and the answering of these questions raised doubts about the propriety of the new initiative. At the meeting of the W Board the DMI was critical of the Home Defence Executive's membership of the Twenty Committee, and the Board decided that Sir Findlater Stewart, the senior civil servant on the HDE, should be invited to attend the committee in his personal capacity. At the next meeting of the Twenty Committee on 9 January, however, Stewart questioned whether it ought to implement rulings from the W Board without reference to the civil authorities; and he pursued the point on 10 February at the next meeting of the W Board. He felt that the operation of the double-cross system might well have repercussions on matters for which ministers were responsible to Parliament; they might, for example, influence the consequences of Germany's bombing policy for industry and the civil population. And while he recognised that the need for secrecy made it impossible to get ministerial directions, he believed that authority should be obtained from the Lord President (Sir John Anderson), who might want to get approval for acting in this role from the Prime Minister. The W Board accepted this advice and asked Stewart to approach the Lord President.

The Directors of Intelligence, 'C', a representative of MI 5 and Sir Findlater Stewart met the Lord President on 18 February to explain the double-cross system. According to a later acccount by the secretary of the W Board, the Lord President explained that although neither he nor the Prime Minister could properly authorise Stewart to deal with matters appertaining to other ministers, they 'unofficially approved' of his acting as adviser to the W Board and urged him to continue. Stewart attended all subsequent meetings of the Board 'as representing all the civilian ministries'. Later in 1941, when it became necessary to obtain approval for the passing via double agents of material on political and international issues, it was arranged that the chairman of the JIC, himself a Foreign Office official, should act as an additional adviser to the W Board, but he did not attend its meetings.

The Twenty Committee met weekly from January 1941 to May 1945 to receive an account of the double-cross activities, consider new problems and take decisions on proposals for new initiatives. To this extent it can be said to have supervised the double-cross work. But it was MI 5 which rendered the accounts, posed the problems and suggested most of the initiatives, the primary responsibility for the detailed control and development of the double-cross system being with its section B1A. Indeed MI 5 continued to regard the agents as 'theirs' and from time to time asserted a claim to have the last word on how they should be used. Fortunately, any serious dispute was avoided by the good sense of all concerned.

The problem of what information could safely be purveyed to the enemy through the double agents continued to exercise the W Board till September 1941. In April it agreed on representations from Findlater Stewart that he should not approve detailed reports on air raid damage. In July, when *Tate* was requested by the Germans to supply a report on air raid damage in Coventry, he objected that the draft drawn up with *Tate* amounted to 'providing the enemy with a valuable bombing plan', and insisted on its revision.* In September the W Board had to rule on an associated question: should double agents be permitted to carry out acts of sabotage when they were requested to do so? It decided that the balance of advantage lay in permitting them to a limited extent, in that this would help to build up the enemy's confidence in the agents and provide information about his choice of targets. An arranged sabotage attack on a food dump at Wealdstone was carried out in November.†

In October 1941 new developments prompted discussion on the relative importance of counter-espionage and deception as the objectives of the double-cross system. At the end of July MI 5 had repeated its view that the advantages to be derived from the system included the opportunity to supply the enemy with mis-information as well as to improve counter-espionage, advance the attack on the enemy's espionage cyphers and obtain intelligence about the enemy's intentions. The government subsequently established a deception organisation in the UK, initially under Colonel Oliver Stanley as Controlling Officer, and an officer from the Middle East raised with the Twenty Committee the suggestion that double agents in the United Kingdom should be used to support deception operations in that theatre. In response to these developments MI 5 submitted a memorandum to the W Board which emphasised that while the use of double-cross agents for deception had been envisaged from the start, it must not be allowed to jeopardise the primary purposes of counter-espionage, and which insisted that MI 5 and SIS must therefore remain 'the sole judges as to how the machine under their control can be put in motion to the best advantage'. On the principle of 'the need to know' the W Board accepted on 29

---

* See in Appendix 8 the draft message submitted for approval and the message finally approved.

† See below p 105.

October that the new Controlling Officer for Deception should be told only that the Service Directors of Intelligence had means of conveying information to the enemy. It resisted the claim that SIS and MI 5 must be 'the sole judges', but agreed that they would 'normally be the best judges' in what was clearly going to become an important conflict of interest between the claims of counter-espionage and those of deception.

Even as the W Board reached this conclusion, the issue was already creating dissension within MI 5 itself as it debated whether or not to take action against the abuse of diplomatic privileges by the Spanish Embassy in London.*

□

Of the double agents under control at the end of December 1940 – *Snow* and his sub-agents (*GW, Charlie* and *Biscuit*), *Summer, Tate, Giraffe, Tricycle* and *Rainbow* – *Summer* was the first casualty. He escaped from his lodgings in January 1941 and, although he was recaptured after a few hours, his case had to be closed down. *Snow* informed the Germans that he had decided to try to get back to Europe because he had come under suspicion and that he had left his wireless set at the cloakroom in Cambridge station. The Germans instructed *Biscuit* to retrieve it. *Giraffe* was the next loss. He was re-supplied with money and secret writing materials by *Tricycle* in February, but the Germans became increasingly restive about the poverty of his reports. The loss of *Snow* and most of his team, a serious set-back to the British authorities, followed in the spring of 1941.

The occasion was the decision, which had been approved by the W Board, to introduce to the Germans a new sub-agent. This was *Celery*, an Englishman with fluent German who had been commissioned in the First World War but had since acquired a criminal record. He met *Snow* by chance in 1940, became suspicious of him and reported him to the authorities as being pro-German and an inveterate liar. MI 5 decided that the prudent course was to recruit him into *Snow*'s team. Arrangements were made for *Snow* to introduce him to the Germans in Lisbon in February 1941, MI 5 hoping that he might be accepted by them for training in Germany before returning to the United Kingdom, and that he might then perhaps even replace *Snow* as the principal German contact. The meeting in Lisbon appeared to go well; *Celery* spent three weeks in Germany before rejoining *Snow* and both returned to England in March with £10,000 and some sabotage material. But the SIS

---

* See below, p 107ff.

representative in Lisbon then reported that *Snow* had belatedly disclosed that on his arrival in Lisbon the Germans had accused him of working for the British and that he had admitted doing so.

This report could be reconciled with *Snow's* return to England with *Celery* only on the assumption that both were working for Germany, or on the assumption that *Snow* had not been unmasked but had invented the story out of jealousy of *Celery* or because the complications of his position were getting too much for him. Interrogation of the two, separately and together, failed to elicit the truth but, either way, it was felt that *Snow* could no longer be employed. He was detained for the duration under DR 18B on 21 April, and in messages purporting to come from him the Germans were told that he was too ill to carry on and that he had hidden his wireless set. He maintained to the end that he had under pressure admitted to the Germans that he had, again under pressure, worked for the British for the past two or three months, but had convinced them that he remained a loyal German agent. Developments after the collapse of *Snow* indicate that the Abwehr believed that he had been loyal to them but that *Celery* had betrayed him to the British. *Biscuit* and *Charlie* as well as *Celery* fell into oblivion with him, but *GW* and *Tate* escaped German suspicion or survived it in spite of their connection with him, as did *Tricycle*, who could have been connected with *Tate*, and *Rainbow*. *Rainbow*, now a pianist in a dance band at Weston-super-Mare who had heard nothing from the Germans since his recruitment in April 1940, received money and a new cover address from them in January 1941. In August he received from Portugal a message on a micro-dot disguised as a full stop – a highly sophisticated refinement of the technique of micro-photography now used by the Abwehr for the first time. At the end of the year the Germans agreed to pay him £1,000 a year to enable him to move to London. *Tate* was in May 1941 told by the Germans that he had been specially naturalised and awarded the Iron Cross; he had been supplying them with reports of high quality, mainly about the RAF. In July he was given an address from which to collect £20,000; he had previously received small sums from *Snow* and at a rendezvous with the Japanese Assistant Naval Attaché. The Germans no doubt hoped that his new-found affluence would enable him to move freely about the country, but it created for MI 5 the problem that he would have great difficulty in dodging embarrassing questions from his German controllers. He accordingly reported to Germany that he had been questioned by the Police about his failure to register for military service and had solved his problem by getting a job on a farm. Thereafter, apart from daily weather reports, his communications with Germany were for some time largely concerned with agriculture and rationing. *Tricycle* had meanwhile developed excellent relations with his controller, the head of the Abwehr in Lisbon, with whom he agreed in January 1941 to recruit two sub-agents in England before leaving for the USA to set up a network there. In February he persuaded the Germans to accept *Balloon*, an ex-Army officer of character and enterprise who had been obliged to resign his commission when he got into financial difficulties, and *Gelatine*, a woman born in Austria who had contacts in political circles. He also set up the arrangements which enabled the Germans to finance *Tate*.

In August 1941, *Tricycle* left for the USA where he came under the control of the FBI. The Germans had given him his instructions in a long questionnaire concealed in six micro-dots stuck on a telegram. The SIS in Lisbon also obtained a copy of the questionnaire and sent it to MI 5 and the FBI in August. It included detailed questions about ammunition dumps in Hawaii and the US naval base at Pearl Harbour. *Tricycle* later complained* that the FBI ignored not only this obvious warning of the forthcoming attack on Pearl Harbour but also the additional information, which he claimed to have obtained from his friend *Artist* in Lisbon and passed to the FBI on his arrival in the US, that at the request of the Japanese *Artist* had accompanied the German Military Attaché in Tokyo on a mission to Italy to obtain details about the British naval-air attack on Taranto. There is no record in the MI 5 and SIS files that *Tricycle* reported this additional information to the authorities in London, or that he took up the matter with them on his return to the United Kingdom in the autumn of 1942. There is no evidence, either, that MI 5 or the SIS took steps to draw the special attention of the operational authorities in London and Washington to the reference to Pearl Harbour in *Tricycle*'s questionnaire.

GW retained his special value as a contact with Spanish visitors. After Del Pozo's departure† *GW* was out of touch with the Abwehr till May 1941. MI 5 then instructed him to approach the porter at the Spanish embassy who had been the cover address for his correspondence with Del Pozo. The porter put him in touch with Luis Calvo, the London correspondent of a Madrid newspaper. Calvo advised him that he would be contacted before long by Alcazar de Valesco. Alcazar, a friend of Suñer, the Spanish Foreign Minister, had recently been in England with the title of Press Attaché at the Spanish embassy, but had been reported to the SIS as being a high level and dangerous agent. On another visit

---

* See D Popov, *Spy/Counter Spy* (1974), pp 117–119, 123–124, 131, 132, 138.
† See above, pp 94–95.

to London between July and September 1941 he saw *GW* several times. Thereafter *GW* continued to deal with Calvo ·– in all they had 15 meetings before Calvo returned to Spain in January 1942.

The loss of *Snow's* services was also off-set by the enlistment of new agents. *Mutt* and *Jeff, Father, Careless* and *The Snark* have already been mentioned.* *Dragonfly* had been born and brought up in England but his parents were German. He set up in business in Germany in the 1930s and left hurriedly just before the outbreak of war. He reported to the British authorities in April 1940 that the Abwehr had contacted him. In November, acting on MI 5's instructions, he had been recruited by the Abwehr while visiting Lisbon under business cover. He had returned to England in January 1941 with a wireless set disguised as a gramophone, a cover address in Lisbon and instructions to report on the RAF. In March he began transmitting under MI 5's control to an Abwehr station in Paris which valued him for his daily weather reports. *Mutt* and *Jeff's* primary mission for the Abwehr had been sabotage and it was supposedly by them that the Wealdstone sabotage attack was carried out in November to boost German confidence in them. They also reported to Germany on troop movements and civilian morale, *Mutt* having ostensibly joined the Army and *Jeff* being presented as being employed as an interpreter at interrogations of refugees from Norway. The Germans had wanted *Father* to go to the USA and had given him times and frequencies for receiving their instructions which were unsuitable for use in the UK. He had also been given secret ink for his reports but no developer. The Abwehr solved the resulting communications problem by supplying a new set of frequencies through *Dragonfly* and telling *Father* to use *Dragonfly's* radio link in an emergency. He normally reported in secret writing. His traffic presented some difficulty because the enemy knew that he was capable of reporting on technical developments in the RAF in a way which was very acceptable to them but not to the approving British authority. However, his case developed satisfactorily. *Careless*, who was notionally serving in the balloon barrage, was used to build up the strength of the anti-aircraft defences in German eyes; and *The Snark* reported on rationing and civilian morale.

---

* Above, p 92ff.

CHAPTER 6: REFERENCES

1. CAB 93/5, SIC/A/91 of 10 September 1940.
2. CAB 93/7, HD(S) (PRA) 1st Meeting of 28 August 1941.

CHAPTER 7

Counter-Espionage Operations and the Development of Deception from the Autumn of 1941 to the End of 1942

B Y THE summer of 1941, when *GW's* dealings with del Pozo, Calvo and Alcazar had established that the diplomatic privileges of the Spanish embassy were being abused in the interests of the Abwehr, MI 5 had taken steps against the threat to security from the diplomatic missions. As part of the programme, by which action through the Security Executive limited the number and scope of official visits sponsored by foreign governments and the JIC imposed restrictions on the movements of Service Attachés, it had established contacts with the Spanish embassy's staff and with the staff at other suspect embassies.* These contacts had produced further evidence incriminating Spaniards: a statement from Calvo that Lojendio, the Vice-Consul until his recall in the summer, had been involved in espionage partly on Germany's account, and a statement from Jose Brugada, a career diplomat serving as Assistant Press Attaché, that he had been asked in September 1940 to report on the effects of German bombing. In these circumstances, the senior staff in MI 5, learning that Calvo was returning to Spain, considered the advantages of having him arrested. Action against Calvo would be a salutary lesson to the Spanish authorities, and he might under questioning produce valuable information about the Abwehr.

MI 5's section responsible for the double-cross operations strongly objected. It feared that any action against Calvo might betray *GW*, who was the sole channel for passing seemingly authentic documents back to the Axis, and that if he was compromised the Germans might conclude that *Snow*† who had introduced him, *Tate* who had received money from *Snow*, and *Tricycle* who had set up the arrangements through which money

---

* Evidence was also obtained implicating the Japanese and Hungarian embassies. The Japanese Assistant Naval Attaché passed money to *Tate* (see above p 103). Until the rupture of diplomatic relations in May 1941 the Hungarian Military Attaché, Lt Col Utassy, sent out intelligence for Germany's benefit. But there is no truth in the suggestion that Utassy became a British double agent. (See Farago, *Game of the Foxes*, (1972) p 233.)

† See above, p 104.

was sent to *Tate* were all double agents. The Twenty Committee upheld these objections on 23 October 1941, and on 6 November it decided that no action should be taken without reference to the W Board.

In the next few weeks MI 5's contacts with the Spanish embassy obtained further evidence against Alcazar and Brugada, and also cast suspicion on the Military Attaché, Colonel Barra. But the decisive evidence was obtained from Signals Intelligence (Sigint) in January 1942. The decrypt of a telegram from the Japanese Minister in Madrid disclosed that he had learned that Alcazar controlled an espionage network in the United Kingdom involving 21 people, of whom two were Spaniards – one of them Calvo.* At the same time ISOS signals were decrypted from an Abwehr station in Madrid purporting to be reports from agents in the UK. These ISOS decrypts were the first fruits of a recent advance – the most fundamental of the war – in the supply of Sigint to the security authorities. In December 1941 Mr A D Knox's section at GC and CS had broken the Enigma key† which the Abwehr used in preference to the hand cypher (which, as we have seen, had been read by GC and CS throughout 1941) for most of the traffic between its headquarters and its controlling stations in occupied and neutral countries.

The Sigint convinced the senior officers in MI 5 that Calvo, who had by then left for Madrid, should be arrested on his return – the more so as they believed the risks had been exaggerated. Many people in London and Madrid knew that Calvo, who had behaved indiscreetly, was a German agent; there was thus good cover for his arrest. It would not necessarily blow *GW*, and the other dire consequences apprehended for the double-cross system were only a remote possibility. After consulting the Foreign Office, they recommended the action to the Home Office on 11 February 1942 and Calvo was arrested the following day.

MI 5 had avoided referring the matter to a formal meeting of the W Board for fear that it would be obstructive. MI 5 had recognized that the Service Directors of Intelligence must be consulted because *GW* had been used for passing military information for deception purposes and because it was 'desirable to carry the Ds of I with us since we are to a large extent dependent on the

---

* Later in 1942 further Japanese decrypts indicated that Alcazar, subsidized by Germany, was claiming to have recruited five Welshmen, two Irishmen, eleven Scots and two Spaniards in the UK. These decrypts also revealed that the Japanese Ambassador to Madrid had agreed to support a network run by Alcazar in the USA; from June 1942 he was sending on to Tokyo reports purporting to come from these agents.

† The Enigma decrypts were circulated under the name ISK to distinguish them from the hand cypher decrypts issued by the Strachey section at GC and CS as ISOS. For security reasons the difference between the two was known to very few of the recipients and ISOS was used to cover all decrypts of German secret intelligence services traffic.

information they supply for keeping our agents in position'; but it had chosen to consult them separately to obtain their approval. It had also ignored opposition in the Twenty Committee, which was at first inclined to send a deputation to a meeting of the W Board to protest and demand the issue of a new directive. Nor is there any doubt as to why it acted so high-handedly; in the course of preparing its case for the Home Office it referred again to its conviction that the primary purpose of the double-cross system was to prevent espionage and that the contribution it might make to deception was only a bonus.

In the event, Calvo's arrest did lead to the loss of *GW's* services. But the dire consequences for the whole double-cross system which had been feared did not materialise, and the cause of counter-espionage derived some benefit. Under interrogation Calvo admitted that he had acted as intermediary and interpreter for Alcazar with *GW*; that he had heard that del Pozo had sent reports in secret writing to Madrid, and a map of London marking bomb damage; and that Lojendio had told him he had sent reports in secret writing through the diplomatic bag. He added that he had had meetings with Alcazar during his recent visit to Madrid and that Brugada, who was also in Madrid but who was due to return, had been constantly in Alcazar's company. On this evidence, which justified holding Calvo for further questioning, the Foreign Office informed the Spanish embassy that there were grounds for thinking that its bag had been misused and requested that the Ambassador would personally investigate the bag that was about to be brought in by Brugada. Spain threatened reprisals, and in the further questioning Calvo turned out to be unexpectedly unforthcoming, the interrogators being handicapped by the need to protect their sources. Eventually, however, when ISOS decrypts had disclosed that he had met Abwehr officers while in Madrid, it proved possible to use this information without compromising its source and Calvo told all early in March.

Lojendio had sent espionage reports in secret writing by the diplomatic bag since the spring of 1940. Alcazar worked for the Germans with Suñer's approval. Calvo had acted for Alcazar with *GW* and had sent information to Madrid for which *GW* had been paid large sums; and in his recent meetings with the Abwehr Calvo had agreed to send military and naval intelligence by secret writing and by wireless. A questionnaire, instructions regarding communications, and money for agents were to be brought in the diplomatic bag by Brugada on 14 February; Brugada had himself met Abwehr officers while in Madrid.

These admissions added little to the information MI 5 already possessed; and Calvo threw no light on the claim made by Alcazar, and apparently supported by decrypts from the Abwehr station in

Madrid, to have a substantial network of (as yet unidentified) spies. Over the next two months, as persistent attempts to extract information on this subject from him proved fruitless, it came to be accepted that the claim to be running a large network was a product of Alcazar's vanity. But Calvo's confession at least prevented the development of such a network. It was conveyed to the Spanish Ambassador at the Foreign Office on 7 March, and while he subsequently informed the Foreign Office that Brugada's bag had contained nothing improper, he also took steps to prevent further abuse of the diplomatic bag. MI 5 learned of the measures taken by the Ambassador from a member of his staff in the embassy. Madrid did not take the threatened reprisals.

☐

Another enemy attempt to carry out espionage under cover of a neutral embassy was brought to light, again by Sigint, in the summer of 1942. When Rogerio Magalhaes de Menezes arrived in London in July 1942 to take up a minor clerical post at the Portuguese legation, ISOS decrypts had already revealed that he had been approached in Lisbon by a member of a Portuguese spy network that was working for the German and Italian intelligence services. The close watch that was kept on him in London established before long that he was passing out information of little or no importance, and he was considered unsuitable for recruitment as a double agent. MI 5 and the SIS arranged for his case to be taken up with the Portuguese government, whose response to repeated complaints about Axis intelligence activity in Portugal they regarded as unsatisfactory.* In February 1943 the Foreign Office gave the Portuguese Ambassador an SIS memorandum on this activity together with evidence incriminating Menezes – a letter allegedly obtained from an Axis traitor in Portugal in which the secret writing had been partly developed. The Foreign Office suggested that Menezes should be confronted with it in the Ambassador's presence; his diplomatic immunity should then be withdrawn and he should be handed over to the British authorities. The Ambassador agreed to this course of 'action after consulting his government.

Menezes confessed. He had been recruited by two officers of the SD before leaving Lisbon, taught secret writing and told to send his reports under cover of letters to his sister. He had accepted a similar assignment from the Italians. He had written once or twice a month to the Germans and received two replies with further instructions and his salary. He had written only two or three times to the Italians and received no reply.

---

* For enemy activities in Spain and Portugal see below, p 159ff.

Menezes was tried and sentenced to death in April. His appeal having been dismissed and his execution fixed for 28 May, the Portuguese government appealed for clemency. The Foreign Office intimated in May that it might be prepared to recommend a reprieve if it was satisfied that Portugal was doing all she could to eliminate Axis espionage against the Allies on her territory. She had already in April arrested a number of the agents named in the SIS memorandum, including the head of the SD, and on 25 May she gave further assurances and arrested a notorious Abwehr officer in Lisbon. The death sentence on Menezes was then commuted to life imprisonment.

☐

Menezes was one of a score of agents sent to the United Kingdom by the Abwehr during 1942. Only two of these agents landed illegally, one by U-boat in Iceland and the other by parachute near Ely; only two, including Menezes, came as visitors with legitimate business in England; and only two were merchant seamen. The majority were, or purported to be, refugees or escapers. All were arrested or placed under surveillance as soon as they arrived. None produced any evidence of the use of new methods or initiatives on the part of the enemy. So far as was known, no new arrival escaped detection, and MI 5 was virtually certain from July 1942 that all the agents operating in the country were under its control. But one case illustrated that close surveillance of a suspect person could not guarantee complete knowledge of his movements.* One agent, who arrived in the United Kingdom en route for South Africa, would have escaped suspicion under interrogation if Sigint had not identified him.† And three cases testified that German penetration of Allied clandestine organisations in occupied Europe now constituted a threat to security from enemy double agents.‡ For these reasons MI 5, which by now was well informed about the Abwehr, was not disposed to under-estimate it. In a joint report with Section V in August, it described the Abwehr's organisation and its deployment in the Reich, in occupied Europe and in neutral countries and with the armies in the field, and judged it to be 'a flexible and dynamic organisation'. It emphasised that the Abwehr was an organ of the Wehrmacht and drew attention to the SD as the secret intelligence service of the Nazi Party and the state.

Four of the new arrivals were tried and sentenced to death,

---

* See Appendix 9 (ii).
† This was Boyd, see p 168.
‡ These were Pelletier, *Victoire* and Tor Gulbrandsen, see Appendix 9 (i).

three being executed and Menezes reprieved.* Of the remainder, all but two were detained for the duration. These two, to be known as *Zigzag* and *Cobweb*, became double agents. Four other people offered their services as double agents: *Garbo*, *Brutus*, *Bronx* and *Hamlet*.

Garbo was a Spaniard who was anti-Republican but who had become disillusioned with the Franco regime.† He decided to leave Spain and to throw in his lot with the Allies as it seemed to him that only an Allied victory could bring about a change in the regime. His first attempts to offer his services to the British having met with no success, he conceived the bolder plan of offering himself to the Germans and then double-crossing them. In February 1941 he approached the German embassy in Madrid, and, after some complicated manoeuvres which included forging a Spanish diplomatic document, persuaded Abwehr representatives that he had arranged to visit the United Kingdom on an official mission. He left Madrid in July 1941, ostensibly en route for the United Kingdom, taking with him secret ink, questionnaires, money, cover addresses, and instructions to recruit sub-agents who could continue his work if he had to return to Spain.

In fact *Garbo* stopped in Lisbon where he again tried unsuccessfully to get a hearing from the British. However, he told the Germans that he had reached England safely and would send his reports by an airline employee who would post them in Lisbon; he invited the Germans to send their replies to 'Mr Smith-Jones' at a post box in Lisbon where they would be picked up by the courier. The Germans confirmed these arrangements at the end of July, whereupon *Garbo* again approached the British, offering to provide his secret ink and questionnaires. He was again rebuffed.

Garbo spent most of the next nine months in Lisbon, writing long and colourful letters, supposedly from England and posted in Portugal by the notional courier. Equipped with the most meagre aids – a Blue Guide to England, a map of Great Britain, a Portuguese publication on the British fleet, and reference books and magazines in Lisbon libraries – and despite knowing so little about England that he was unable, when submitting his 'expenses' to the Germans, correctly to convert pence into shillings, or shillings into pounds, and even remarked in one letter that 'there were men here [in Glasgow] who would do anything for a litre of wine', he succeeded in composing reports, based entirely on his own imagination and a careful reading of the Press, which convinced the Abwehr that in him they had a trustworthy agent

---

* See Appendix 9 (iii).
† For *Garbo's* own account of his activities before reaching the United Kingdom see J Pujol, *Garbo* (1986).

actually established in the United Kingdom. To help him in his work *Garbo* created three imaginary sub-agents: Agent No 1, supposedly a Portuguese named Carvalo, was in the Bristol area; Agent No 2, a Swiss names Gerbers, in the Liverpool area; and Agent No 3, an un-named Venezuelan, in Glasgow.

In the autumn of 1941 *Garbo* made another unsuccessful attempt to offer his services to the British in Madrid. However, in November his wife aroused the interest of a member of another embassy in Lisbon and was seen by him and an SIS representative. British representatives met *Garbo* for the first time in January 1942.

MI 5 first heard of *Garbo* towards the end of February 1942 in the course of a general discussion of the situation in Lisbon between an SIS officer and B1A. At this time B Division was puzzling about the source of reports 'of superb inaccuracy', allegedly from German agents in England controlled by the Abwehr station in Madrid, about convoy movements from the British Isles. These had appeared in ISOS and it seemed possible that they might emanate from *Garbo*. For this reason, and others, B Division was annoyed at not having been told of his existence earlier. On 3 March Liddell, its head, wrote to the SIS asking for a full report. He pointed out that *Garbo* might be the source of the convoy reports; he was ostensibly operating in England; he had received questionnaires which might be of great interest; and unless his case was co-ordinated with other double-cross operations he might be inadvertently blown.*

A struggle developed for the control of *Garbo*. B Division wanted him brought to England to have his story checked: it could then be decided whether he should stay in Britain – when control would pass to MI 5 – or return to Lisbon where he would be run by the SIS. B Division believed that he was potentially very valuable and was sure to be discovered if he continued to operate from Lisbon. Morover, it was essential that the work of all the double-cross agents reporting on the United Kingdom should be brought to a single focus. The SIS was reluctant to surrender control. MI 5 was asked for an assurance that if *Garbo* were brought to Britain he would continue to be handled by the SIS and allowed to return to Lisbon. B Division refused this assurance and complained that information was being withheld from it about *Garbo* and other double-cross agents (in particular *Tricycle* who was in the USA), while the SIS protested that B Division appeared to be making the unwarranted assumption that it had some kind of

---

* MI 5 had been on the point of taking action through *Balloon* to discredit the source(s) of the convoy reports.

supervisory authority over all double-cross agents in all parts of the world. Petrie observed that this correspondence bore out the general case for the unified handling of counter-espionage work which led him at this time to propose the amalgamation of the SIS counter-espionage section with B Division.*

Garbo arrived in the United Kingdom, where he was to remain until the end of the war, on 24 April 1942. The question whether to operate him as a double-cross agent was then considered by the Twenty Committee. Here a difficulty arose. His story was fantastic, but ISOS provided convincing evidence (in particular a message from Madrid to Berlin on 2 April about an alleged convoy from Liverpool to Malta which was based entirely on a report from *Garbo* and led to operational moves by the enemy) that the Germans believed him to be operating on their behalf in England. At this stage not all the members of the Twenty Committee had access to ISOS and one of them, the representative of GHQ Home Forces, felt unable to approve traffic for *Garbo* unless he was in possession of all the relevant data. The chairman accordingly requested and received 'C''s agreement that all members of the committee should be indoctrinated, and that 'all information relevant to double-cross work . . . be conveyed to the committee in the exact form in which it is available . . . since . . . decisions must often depend on the exact interpretation given to a few words'. *Garbo* was duly accepted as a double agent. His wife and small son were brought to London.

The case developed steadily. While he had been operating on his own in Lisbon *Garbo* had stamped it indelibly with his own personality. His supposed motivation was that he was a fanatical National Socialist prepared to risk his life for the New World Order. He had shown the Germans that he possessed great initiative and resource, and had adopted a highly idiosyncratic style of reporting, verbose, colourful and adorned with his own comments on the information supposedly acquired by him or his notional agents. Now that he had come under the control of MI 5 the task was to ensure that these characteristics were maintained, and that the brilliant imagination which he had displayed was further exploited. Fortunately, the case officer selected by MI 5 was well suited to the task: he and *Garbo* formed an ideal partnership jointly developing the unique and fanciful espionage organisation which had been the creation of *Garbo's* imagination. Fortunately, too, ISOS continued to confirm that the case remained viable.

Garbo had notionally come to England on a mission for the

---

* See below, Chapter 8.

Spanish Seguridad in connection with currency fiddles. He now explained to the Germans that he was being allowed to stay for an indefinite period as a political refugee, and had undertaken free-lance work in the propaganda field for the BBC and the Ministry of Information, thus providing himself with an entrée into official circles. He had been instructed to build up a network of sub-agents and, while still in Lisbon, had notionally acquired three, as we have seen. After his arrival here it was decided to expand the imaginary network. At the end of May he told the Germans that he had recruited a Gibraltarian waiter, Agent No 4, whom he had been cultivating for some time and who was one hundred per cent loyal to the German cause. This was quickly followed by two other recruitments: Agent No 5, who was No 3's brother, and Agent No 6, a South African who was violently anti-Russian and a first-class linguist with contacts in the Ministry of Information and other government departments. At the end of the year a seamen agent (Agent No 7), a friend of Agent No 4, was recruited. It transpired later that he was a Welsh Nationalist. *Garbo* himself developed two useful unconscious sources, an RAF officer, given the symbol J(2), and a high-ranking official, symbol J(3), in the Spanish department of the Ministry of Information. The latter was represented as a perfectly loyal British subject who, believing that *Garbo* was a refugee Spanish Republican entirely sympathetic to Britain, was prepared to discuss current affairs with him. The character was represented as becoming increasingly indiscreet as his liking for *Garbo* grew, and he developed into the most important of all *Garbo's* contacts.

However, the network also suffered one casualty. With the approach of Operation *Torch* in November, the presence of Agent No 2 (the Swiss named Gerbers) in the Liverpool area became embarrassing. The Germans were therefore told that he was ill and about to undergo an operation. After three months, during which he was unable to work but with German permission continued to draw pay, he 'died' on 19 November. An obituary notice in the *Liverpool Daily Post* was sent to the Germans who expressed their sympathy for the widow.

Much attention was devoted to the network's communications. In September *Garbo* was authorised to give his agents secret ink so that they could correspond direct with addresses in the Iberian peninsula. The notional airline official who posted *Garbo's* reports in Lisbon and collected German letters to *Garbo* from his post box there, or (later) arranged for friends in the airline to do so, was the Achilles heel of the organisation. Not only was this fictitious character barely credible, but after *Garbo's* move to London the problem of co-ordinating his imaginary movements with the actual means of getting the letters to Lisbon which was, through force of circumstances, very irregular, became extremely difficult. Dependence on the courier was substantially reduced when the Germans decided that, with certain precautions, the regular air mail could be used for *Garbo's* secret letters, but the courier had to be kept alive to enable *Garbo* to receive German letters and funds, and as a channel for delivering documents or bulky objects, such as crystals from *Garbo's* gas mask (requested by the Germans and despatched in a tin of Andrews liver salts), which could not be sent by air mail.

In the same tin *Garbo* enclosed a long letter giving a picture of his life and problems, and suggesting the establishment of a radio link. He reported that he had discovered that a transmitter which had belonged to an unlicensed radio ham could be acquired through a friend of Agent No 4. The friend, a radio technician employed at a factory on the outskirts of London, had strong left-wing sympathies and he believed that Agent No 4 wanted to acquire the set on behalf of exiled Spanish Republicans in order to establish a link with their organisation in Spain. *Garbo* concluded with a typical flourish, 'I do not wish to end this letter without sending a Viva Victorioso for our brave troops who fight in Russia, annihilating the Bolshevik beast . . . I am proud to be able to contribute from here, by informing you on matters which may contribute to hasten the defeat of our enemy'.

It was of course essential that the Germans should keep *Garbo* provided with adequate funds to finance the expanding network. They were unwilling to use banking channels and preferred to send remittances via the courier. MI 5 learnt that some fruit merchants in London had money available which they were prepared to sell to a buyer in the United Kingdom against payment in pesetas, or escudos, in Spain or Portugal. A buyer claiming to represent a large British insurance company which had frozen funds in Spain, got in touch with them through a third party. A bargain was struck (at a rate very favourable to the fruit merchants) and Plan *Dream*, as it was called, became a continuing, though very costly, operation.

During 1942 the case was exploited for counter-espionage intelligence by inducing the Germans to reveal cover addresses and secret writing techniques, and discovering where they wanted new agents placed. But a lot of the traffic was concerned with the development of the notional organisation. The financial loyalty and untiring energy of its chief were impressed on the Germans. The character of each agent was built up and a clear but (with an eye to maintaining freedom of action) not too precise picture of his personality and scope was conveyed to them. A good deal of accurate information was passed to build up the agents.

In the autumn advantage was taken of Operation *Torch* to give a dramatic demonstration of the organisation's potential. On 29 October *Garbo* reported the sailing of one of the principal convoys for the operation, which had left the Clyde on 26 October. The letter was sent to Lisbon (by 'the courier') with instructions that it was not to be posted until the Admiralty had confirmed that the enemy had seen the convoy. It was actually mailed on 4 November. On 1 November *Garbo* forwarded another report from Agent No 3 that troop transports had left the Clyde with battleships camouflaged in Mediterranean colours, adding that he himself had got a glimpse of a Ministry of Information directive which would come into force in the event of Allied action against French Morocco or Algeria. This letter was postmarked 2 November, and actually despatched by air mail on 7 November, the day the landing took place. Thus, the Germans had evidence that *Garbo* had reported the sailing of one of the main convoys in a letter written eight days before, and mailed in Lisbon by the courier three days before the landings, and that he had pointed to the target of *Torch* in a letter despatched five days before the attack. They could only blame themselves for not having acted more quickly to establish a radio link as *Garbo* had suggested in August. They wrote to him on 26 November saying 'your last reports are all magnificent but we are sorry they arrived late, especially those relating to the Anglo-Yankee disembarkation in Africa'.

Garbo finished the year by supporting an Admiralty deception plan designed to make the enemy believe that there were two British aircraft carriers in the Indian Ocean when in fact there were none.

Brutus was a Polish fighter pilot. After the defeat of Poland he escaped to France where he became an officer with a Polish division. He stayed in France after the armistice and from the autumn of 1940 built up an intelligence network. In October 1941 he was brought out to England by air and decorated for his achievements. Soon after his return to France his network was broken up and he was arrested. Eight months later he reappeared in Madrid explaining that he had escaped from Fresnes prison. He arrived in England on 2 October 1942.

As he had been a Polish agent, and was still on the books of the Polish Deuxième Bureau, it was arranged that he should be examined first by the Poles and afterwards by the British. The former carried out a thorough and painstaking investigation. *Brutus*'s story confirmed in every important respect what was already known about the break-up of his network. His account of his treatment and interrogation was somewhat surprising in that he had apparently been treated with severity but without brutality, and had not been interrogated very intensively. The story of his escape and journey to safety was amazing but credible. The Polish examiners were not altogether happy about him, but they felt that it was impossible that a man with his record could have accepted a German mission and were prepared to vouch for him.

On 20 November, three days before he was due to be questioned by the British, *Brutus* produced a manuscript entitled 'The Great Game'. In this he revealed that his 'escape' had been deliberately arranged after he had accepted a German proposal that he should return to England as their agent, provided with wireless crystals (which he produced from the heels of his shoes) and codes. He was to report military information of all kinds, but his primary task was to develop a pro-German party in Polish military circles by exploiting anti-Communist and anti-Russian sentiments. In return, the Germans would spare the lives of his colleagues in his network; they, his mother in Poland and his brother, who was a prisoner of war, would be hostages for his loyalty. *Brutus* explained that he had withheld this story when first examined because he feared the Polish Intelligence Service might have been penetrated by the Germans. He was most anxious to play the 'Great Game' and double-cross them.

Brutus was then examined by MI 5 who concluded that he had told the truth about his mission, but not about its origin, the initiative having come from him rather than the Germans.* His explanation of the delay in revealing it was acceptable. He had an intensely dramatic and egotistical nature and those characteristics had been accentuated by his success as head of his network. Although some doubt was felt about the wisdom and practicability of doing so, MI 5 recommended that *Brutus* should be run as a double-cross agent, primarily for political purposes as it would be very difficult to supply military intelligence of the standard the Germans would expect from a man with his record. Radio communication with the Abwehr in Paris was established on 20 December.

The Twenty Committee was informed of the case on the last day of 1942. The Committee thought that W Board approval ought to be obtained for running it, because it was known to the Poles, who could probably find out what traffic *Brutus* was passing, if they wanted to, and might be able to deduce what the real intentions were if he was used for deception. A note on *Brutus* by MI 5 was considered by the W Board on 13 January 1943. The Board was told that shortly after his arrest 'approaches were made either by him or to him' which resulted in his escape being facilitated. The nature of his mission and the events after his arrival were described. After considerable discussion the W Board agreed 'that *Brutus* should be played carefully, being run separately from other

---

* This was confirmed by a post-war interrogation.

agents* and used as little as possible for operational matters, and that he should be dropped if it became necessary'.

In mid-December 1942 the only parachutist to arrive during the year landed near Ely. A good deal (including his name) was already known about him from ISOS: more than 160 messages concerning him had been recorded between April and December. The first intercept was dated 27 April 1942. After several more messages he was given the code-name *Fritz* or *Fritzchen* and almost daily reports on his training and particulars were noted. It was learned that he had connections with Jersey; that he was being trained in sabotage and radio; that he needed extensive dental treatment; that he would carry two identity cards on his mission (one for an Englishman and one for an Irishman); that, in July, he was learning the preliminary ground exercises for parachute jumping and also practising codes; that on 27 August he signed his V-Mann contract;† etc. In addition, from July onwards, his practice traffic was being monitored in the United Kingdom (the RSS referred to him as 'The Three F man' from his call sign FFF) and it was clear that there would be no difficulty in recognising his style in any messages intercepted. Further details were that he would probably carry a captured English radio set, adapted with German parts; that his parachute harness might be of Russian make; that he was trained in secret writing; and that he would be wearing ankle bandages under his boots. Details of his questionnaire were also to hand, and it was known that an act of sabotage was his primary task.

While awaiting his arrival MI 5 had unsuccessfully investigated several candidates with his name – and set up an elaborate arrangement with the Police and RSLOs for him to be rounded up and handed over immediately upon capture without publicity. The Air Ministry was alerted to keep watch for an enemy aircraft on a special flight. This was expected to take place on 15 September. However, a delay occurred, due it was thought to a lull in GAF activity over the British Isles. It was known from ISOS that *Fritzchen* was standing by, but only six ISOS messages about him were read between the end of October and the second week of December, when Nantes signalled Paris, that 'F [was] visibly

---

* In theory and, it is believed, very largely in practice, double-cross agents were strictly segregated. It is true that *Tricycle's* account of his war-time activities (Dusko Popov, *Spy/Counter Spy* (1975)) conveys a different impression. As one of the early recruits, and a very astute òperator with much charm, he may have got to know more than he should have done about cases not associated with his own group, but his account owes a good deal to information acquired since the end of the war.

The W Board was probably anxious both that *Brutus* himself should not learn about other double-cross agents, and also that his case should not become involved in German eyes with other double-cross cases which would be compromised if he was disloyal or was blown.

† V-Mann = Vertrauungsmann or confidential agent.

relieved and very confident at news of his imminent departure'. He landed in a ploughed field, concealed his parachute, carried his radio set with him to the nearest farm house, and asked to be allowed to telephone the Police. He told the Police that he had just arrived from France and wanted to get in touch with the British Intelligence Service.

The same day, 16 December, he made a full statement at the LRC. His account of his career with the Abwehr coincided exactly with the story revealed by ISOS, and he cheerfully confessed that he had a British police record. He was sent to Camp 020 for debriefing and supplied a great deal of valuable information. His loyalty no longer being in question, he was taken over by B1A as a double agent under the cover name *Zigzag*.

Zigzag had had a varied career. He had been arrested several times and was serving a prison sentence in Jersey when the Germans invaded the Channel Islands. He was released in the autumn of 1940 and went to stay with a friend. At the end of November both men were arrested on suspicion of sabotage and taken to Paris where they were lodged in a camp for hostages and suspect spies. There *Zigzag* was recruited by the Abwehr about January 1942. He was released in April and taken to Nantes. His progess thereafter was charted in ISOS.

Besides his radio set *Zigzag* had brought with him explosives and £1,000. His mission included sending daily weather reports, particulars about US troops, and reports on shipbuilding. But his principal task was to sabotage the de Havilland works at Hatfield where the Mosquito light bomber was being built; for this he had been promised £15,000. His work in the United Kingdom was to last only a few weeks, after which he was to return to his controllers, either by ship as a seaman to Portugal, or via Eire. If all else failed a submarine would be sent for him.

Although *Zigzag's* behaviour and candid account of his mission and training convinced MI5 of his loyalty, the case presented difficult problems. The time element was all important; once accepted as a double-cross agent he had to be put on the air as soon as possible. Indeed, he sent his first message – during his stay at Camp 020 – four days after his arrival. The German reaction was excellent; a message of the same date (20 December) recorded his signal, and noted that his 'style' was recognised – ie that he was certainly operating the set himself. So far so good. But it was clear that if full advantage was to be taken of the case he would (ostensibly at least) have to carry out his act of sabotage and then return to Germany. The story of how this was accomplished belongs to a later chapter.*

---

* See below, pp 219–220.

Bronx made a less dramatic entry, but was to become a valuable double-cross agent. The daughter of a south American diplomat, she had been living in England since September 1939 and held an SIS brief when she visited her parents in Vichy in July 1942. While there she was introduced to the Abwehr by a French collaborator, and recruited to report by secret writing on economic affairs. Her first letter was despatched in November. In German eyes her motivation was partly affection for her Abwehr contact, and partly mercenary; she would be paid £100 a month, ostensibly as alimony from her husband whom she was divorcing. *Bronx*, who was a cosmopolitan socialite, was genuinely in touch with a number of prominent people.

1942 saw the establishment of two double-cross agents operating outside the United Kingdom but forming part of what could now fairly be described as the United Kingdom system. The first case, that of *Cobweb*, was uncomplicated. The second, that of *Hamlet*, was decidedly tortuous.

Cobweb, 'a good type of merchant service officer', was landed in Iceland from a submarine on 6 April. He gave himself up immediately and quickly convinced his interrogators that he had had no intention of working against Britain. An effective channel was opened from the Admiral's house. His arrival coincided with the arrest of the Icelandic ship *Arctic*. ISOS, and detective work by SIS, had established that the master and radio operator had been suborned to send radio reports to the Germans while on passage from Vigo. Confessions were later obtained from both. A plan was developed involving *Cobweb* and the *Arctic* to draw German heavy ships into contact with the Home Fleet, but this was not pursued. Another, to divert the enemy from the convoys to Russia, had some success.

Hamlet was an Austrian half-Jew who had property in Germany. In 1936 his property was confiscated and he was imprisoned for a short time. On release he moved to Italy and set up a business. He sent his children to England to be educated and himself moved to Belgium in 1939. In 1941 he went to Lisbon on behalf of the Abwehr to establish business cover for espionage. According to one account he undertook this task in return for being extricated from the clutches of the Gestapo. In Lisbon in the autumn of 1941 he became friendly with an Englishman who was given the alias *Mullet*. The latter had been in the insurance business in Belgium, had escaped to unoccupied France in 1940, had got himself certified unfit for military service and was en route for England. In the course of numerous meetings in October–November (which *Mullet* reported at the time) *Hamlet* asked him to take some valuables to England for his children; to act as his business representative there; and to seek contacts with elements which would respond sympathetically to approaches from moderate Germans anxious to overthrow Nazi domination.

In August 1942 *Mullet* returned to Lisbon, taking letters from the Ministry of Food expressing interest in one of *Hamlet's* patents and from contacts in the City who were said to be sympathetic to his political views. During their discussions *Hamlet* said that, having met his children in England, *Mullet* must realise that he was a Jew and had good grounds for hating the Nazis. He told *Mullet* that he had set up an organisation to obtain information on politics, morale and production in Great Britain and the USA. He was prepared to use this organisation to convince the German generals that the war was lost and they should make peace. He claimed that his information went direct to Admiral Canaris, the head of the Abwehr, and that he had a line to General von Falkenhausen, the Military Governor of Belgium, through a friend and business associate who was later given the alias of *Puppet*. *Mullet* returned to England in September with a full power of attorney to handle *Hamlet's* patents.

These developments were considered by B Division and the SIS. It was noted that, rather than being a channel for others, *Hamlet* now wanted help in putting across his own views, and that an espionage element had been introduced into the affair, but after consultation with the Foreign Office and PWE it was decided to keep the case alive.

Mullet went to Lisbon again in December, accompanied by an SIS officer. From *Mullet*, discussions with *Hamlet*, and from ISOS, it became clear that *Hamlet's* claims to represent a group of German officers who wanted to make peace, and to report direct to Admiral Canaris, were unfounded, and that the intelligence network (known as the Kolberg organisation) which he was supposed to have set up in the United Kingdom and the western hemisphere was also imaginary; *Hamlet's* reports to Brussels, a large number of which appeared in ISOS, were based on extensive newspaper coverage and conversations with contacts in Lisbon. On the other hand his friend (*Puppet*) was genuinely friendly with von Falkenhausen. It was judged that *Hamlet's* bona fides were reasonably established. His motivation was credible, his children were in the United Kingdom; and he had put himself into British power by giving evidence of his treachery.

□

While these recruits were being added, with varying degrees of difficulty, to the existing double-cross stable, the operation of the agents already under control encountered few problems if an exception is made – but it is a massive exception – of *Tricycle*.

Tate was on the air daily with weather reports from his farm. But notionally he also had a flat in London which he could visit from time to time, and increasingly during 1942 he made use of the story that he had met a girl, a cypher clerk in a government department, who was introducing him to British and US naval officers. These contacts were the alleged source of the misleading information he passed at the end of the year about British minefields. It encouraged the Germans to ask him to obtain specified navigational charts – an embarrassing request but one which he had no difficulty in rejecting as being too dangerous.

On German instructions, *Tate* made a payment to *Rainbow*, who continued to report on war production and economic affairs, and two payments to *Mutt*, who was allowed to stage a second sabotage operation with *Jeff* – this time in Hampshire – and report on its success.

Dragonfly, notionally a middle class suburbanite in Wembley who was employed in a local food office, reported from his own observation and casual contacts on airfields near London and troop movements in southern England. He tactfully obtained a period of silence in November, while the *Torch* sailings continued, by informing the Abwehr, following a series of complaints about having had no pay since September 1941, that he would send nothing except weather reports until he was paid. The Germans were only too willing to pay him, but found it difficult to get money to him.

Thanks to *Dragonfly's* intervention, *Father* received regular radio messages from the Germans after December 1941. They came to place a high value on the reports on technical developments in the RAF which he sent in secret writing to cover addresses in Spain and Portugal; when he was posted to a Coastal Command squadron in the Shetlands in May his German control station moved with him, from Brussels to Norway. He was the vehicle for very misleading accounts of such matters as radar and detector apparatus in night-fighters. Though actually in the Pioneer Corps, from which he was frequently absent without leave, *Careless* was notionally in the balloon barrage and the Abwehr valued him for his information on anti-aircraft defences. Despite his wayward and dissolute behaviour, he wrote forty reports for the Germans in 1942 and received about a dozen questionnaires. The questionnaires were useful in London as illustrating the limited nature of the enemy's information in his field.

Balloon was the source of a temporary alarm in the spring of 1942. Recruited by *Tricycle*, the Abwehr had taken him up with enthusiasm but in April it complained to *Tricycle* that his work was poor and asked *Tricycle* to put pressure on him. But *Balloon* responded vigorously on receiving the complaint, protesting his indignation that his control should have gone behind his back, suggesting that some of his letters had failed to get through and insisting that he would write no more until he was reassured about his lines of communication. He began reporting again in July and as he now supplied a great deal of the technical information for which he had been asked, his case again proceeded smoothly.

Tricycle himself, however, was then beset by grave difficulties. Under pressure from the Abwehr to move to the USA, he had arrived in New York in August 1941, ostensibly on a semi-official mission to report to the British authorities on the effect of British propaganda on Yugoslavs in the United States. He had there come under the control of the FBI, though the SIS, which took over his case from MI 5, had expected the FBI to leave the work of supervising his contacts with the Abwehr in the hands of British Security Co-ordination (BSC). But the FBI had proved unco-operative, not least because it had little faith in the value of double agents as a source of information about the enemy's interests, organisation and methods, let alone for the purposes of deception. In its view their sole function was to provide leads to other spies, who could be arrested and prosecuted with full publicity. A puritanically minded organisation under Hoover in his prime, it was shocked, moreover, by *Tricycle's* life-style – which was that of a playboy with a penthouse in New York, a country house, a large car, a ski-ing holiday and the company of a well-known film actress. The outcome was that, although arrangements had been made for the FBI to devise traffic for his replies to the Abwehr's questionnaire, it had produced nothing by the end of October; he had had no replies from the Abwehr to his own flimsy reports; and there was some danger that his case would end in disaster. But *Tricycle* was then told by the Abwehr to go to Rio de Janeiro for further orders.

In November the Abwehr representative in Rio gave him a large sum in dollars and asked him to establish a radio link with Rio and Lisbon for the communication of reports on war production, the composition and destination of convoys and technological innova-tions, particularly in anti-submarine warfare. He established the link in February 1942 with a transmitter which was supplied notionally by a disaffected Croat but actually by the FBI. But the FBI, while refusing to allow him any say in the traffic that was passed, continued to produce it with great reluctance and only under pressure from BSC, and in March there was another alarming development. The SIS informed MI 5 and the Twenty Committee that the Abwehr had become suspicious of him.

If relations between BSC and the FBI were by then distinctly cool, those between MI 5 and the SIS had also been deteriorating for some time. On the ground that it was responsible for liaison through BSC and on the principle that *Tricycle* was now operating beyond the three-mile limit, the SIS had controlled the case since his arrival in the USA; and it had not welcomed requests for information about it. On the same principle it had always withheld the special category of ISOS decrypts (ISBA) – those relating to the activities of the SIS's agents – which was the source of its knowledge that the Germans were suspicious of him. MI 5 learned of their existence for the first time when it pressed the SIS for details, and when it eventually obtained the texts of the decrypts in May 1942 it discovered that they included a signal from Berlin to Rio of 20 March to the effect that *Tricycle* was suspected of working for both sides, a signal of 21 March instructing Lisbon to send *Tricycle* a message about his salary that was designed to test his bona fides, and a signal of 5 May from Berlin to Lisbon to the effect that the Abwehr's air intelligence division had good reasons for suspecting that he had become an Allied agent since his arrival in the USA.

The Abwehr's suspicions, which had stemmed mainly from the poor quality of *Tricycle's* reports, were lulled in due course, but not before another difficulty had been surmounted. By June he was in severe financial straits, the FBI refusing to finance what it regarded as his useless extravagance, and while it was clear from ISOS decrypts that the Germans were trying to respond to his request for more money, plans were already being made to bring him back to London when the FBI insisted at the beginning of August that it wanted to be rid of him. It was accordingly decided that he should plead his financial difficulties to the Abwehr as an excuse for his return to the United Kingdom, via Lisbon, and in the hope that they would be accepted as explaining why he had not been more effective. He was not told that the Germans suspected him, but was advised that there was a grave risk that they would not accept his story, which BSC and MI 5 particularly rehearsed with him before his departure, and 'he offered, and persuaded us to allow him, to take the risk . . .'.

He arrived in Lisbon in October. As ISOS decrypts disclosed, the Abwehr representatives there had been told that they were to handle him with great care and break off contact if he could not give a satisfactory account of himself and guarantee to deliver in future 'precise reports of military importance' by radio and secret writing. Though he was helped by the fact that they did not share Berlin's doubts about him – and were pocketing some of the money supplied for his remuneration – it was thus a remarkable achievement on his part that his story was accepted. This was that he had genuinely been doing his best for the Abwehr and that the poor quality of his reports had been solely due to its failure to keep him in funds; that he was unlikely to be able to return to the USA, the mission he was supposed to be doing there for the Ministry of Information having come to an end; but that he would find it relatively easy to carry out another mission in England – provided he was well supplied with money. On 17 October the Abwehr in Lisbon informed Berlin that though severe precautions had been taken, no suspicious circumstances pointing to 'double work' had arisen in the course of several interviews.

The outcome of the meetings was that *Tricycle* was given another 26,000 dollars and 75,000 escudos – most of it to enable him to repay debts which he argued he had had to incur – and urged to try to return to the United States, but was in the meantime sent to London on a new assignment. It was impressed on him that Berlin did not want statistics or political appreciations, but intelligence of immediate value for operational purposes. He was to receive a questionnaire on micro-dots in a private letter addressed to the Savoy Hotel. He was to report in secret writing using five treated matches, each capable of writing 200 letters, which were sewn into the shoulders of one of his coats.

Back in London, he reported fully on his exchanges with the Abwehr; though he had absurdly exaggerated ideas of his import-ance, there was no question about his loyalty. And while he still refused to go on the British payroll – though determined to extract as much money as possible from the Germans – he was anxious to get on with his new assignment in collaboration with MI 5. This was cleared with the Yugoslav Prime Minister, as the Yugoslav government-in-exile had the right to claim his services, and he advised the Abwehr that he had failed to make arrange-ments to return to the United States but had found employment with a large commercial group as adviser on plans for post-war business developments in Yugoslavia.

☐

In the spring of 1942 the displeasure of some members of the Twenty Committee over the slowness of the SIS to report the facts about *Garbo* and *Tricycle*, joined forces with their conviction that the double agents should be used more offensively, in other words for the purposes of deception. Findlater Stewart and an MI 5 representative complained about SIS's delay to 'C', the Director General of MI 5 and the head of SOE (Sir Frank Nelson) at an informal meeting on 12 March. On 28 March they repeated their complaints at a meeting of the W Board at which Petrie and Nelson were present by invitation. But they also pressed at this meeting that the Service Directors of Intelligence should arrange for them to receive earlier information about Allied operations so that deception could be undertaken more effectively.

Some deception measures had been taken during the second half of 1941. Rumours had been passed on behalf of GHQ Home Forces about defences in Kent and on Salisbury Plain and, on behalf of the Admiralty, about convoy defences and the new battleship *Anson*. False documents had been forwarded via *GW* and the Spanish embassy about convoys and the proceedings of the Air Raid Review Committee. At the request of the War Office, several of the double-cross agents had been used in an attempt (Operation *Omnibus*) to raise the threat of an Allied invasion of Norway. These undertakings had introduced an element of excitement into the increasingly pedestrian process of keeping the double agents in being in the interest of counter-espionage. *Garbo's* case had now shown, moreover, that an agent could not only survive while supplying the Germans with wildly inaccurate information but could thrive on doing so, and this discovery was producing in MI 5 the first stirrings of discontent with the guide-lines which had hitherto restricted the operation of the double-cross system.

In April 1942 another development reinforced its view that the Twenty Committee was unduly concerned with preventing double agents from purveying undesirable information, and that instead of functioning as a body of censors, it should be converted into a body of planners. As already mentioned, the Germans complained to *Tricycle* that *Balloon* was submitting poor reports and asked for some improvement. An examination of *Balloon's* traffic confirmed that the quality of his reports had deteriorated until they were largely composed of political tittle-tattle and general information that would have been already known to the enemy, the approving authorities having disallowed most of the detailed intelligence he had submitted.

The representatives of the operational authorities were not enthusiastic about the case for adopting a bolder policy. In response to the request for operational information for use in deception the Directors of Intelligence had replied on 28 March that it could not be provided in the existing state of operational planning. At a W Board meeting on 20 May the suggestion was made by its secretary (Commander Montagu) and welcomed by the Board that the Twenty Committee might be able to carry out useful deception if GHQ Home Forces would nominate 'a deception target' in France; but the representative of GHQ Home Forces said that nothing could be done at present. And in June he was positively hostile when MI 5 circulated a memorandum on the subject to the members of the Twenty Committee.

The memorandum reiterated the two main arguments for a change of course: *Garbo* had shown that a double-cross agent could get away with false information in generous quantities, and while, on the other hand, the agent had to supply some accurate information, there was no case for censoring this merely because it might give the enemy a bombing target, or encourage him to invade, since agents' reports were unlikely to have much influence on the enemy's decisions in such matters. The arguments were strongly supported by Montagu. He pointed out that while the practice of cutting out anything that was conceivably dangerous on security grounds from the double-cross reports was reducing them to 'a dull sort of bowdlerised Baedeker', which involved risks for the agents, little had been done to exploit the great opportunity they offered for supplying the enemy with inaccurate intelligence both generally and in support of Allied operations. But GHQ Home Forces commented that there was no point in 'trying to control the enemy's espionage system by paying the Danegeld of good information'; if the double-cross agents could not otherwise be maintained, it was for consideration whether the system was worthwhile.

The Director General of MI 5 was scarcely more enthusiastic. His response to the June memorandum was to remind his officers of their own earlier insistence that the chief purpose of double-cross operations was not to deceive the enemy but to substitute an espionage organisation controlled by the British authorities for one controlled by him, and thus limit the mischief he could do to British security. But they, and especially those in Section B1A, were confident that this purpose had now been achieved, and were anxious to take on the wider responsibility. The main burden of their next memorandum, written in July and entitled 'MI 5 Double-Agents: their Status and the Potential Value of their Work', was that all German agents in the country belonged to the network which MI 5 controlled. Censorship had uncovered only one agent who had not been detected by other means. A major test in recent months had found no uncontrolled secret writing in outgoing mail to the Iberian Peninsula, where most of the cover addresses provided for German spies were located. Payments to the United Kingdom through Spanish and Portuguese banks were closely scrutinised, but except for those made to a controlled agent, no suspicious payments had been traced. The RSS had rapidly detected the transmissions made by the controlled agents even when they had made them without prior warning from areas distant from their normal locations, and it had intercepted no unexplained transmissions. It was 'inconceivable that there should exist . . . any network of agents so carefully concealed, so different in nature . . . and so wholly divorced from the network which we control that it is able to operate without colliding at any point' with one or other of the security procedures. Moreover, the possibility that the controlled agents were decoys to distract attention from the activities of genuine spies was also untenable in the light of the evidence that they enjoyed the Abwehr's confidence.

This memorandum, which concluded by urging that the double-cross system was a powerful weapon for influencing the German High Command and recommended the creation of an inter-Service section which could devote its full time to the preparation of the necessary traffic, was considered by the W Board on 15 July. The head of B1A attended the meeting and repeated the case for the expansion of deception: whereas nearly all double-cross traffic had so far been prepared by MI 5 and then censored by the approving authorities on security grounds, the Service Departments ought to reverse the process and prepare material which they wanted to put over for the purpose of deceiving the enemy. The Service Directors of Intelligence were by now not uninterested, but they made the logical suggestion that the Controlling Officer for Deception, who was awaiting a directive from the Chiefs of Staff, should be involved in the exploitation of the double-cross system for the purposes of deception. The outcome was that the Controlling Officer and, at MI 5's suggestion, the Chief of Combined Operations were invited to appoint representatives to the Twenty Committee.

This development was, in itself, perhaps not unwelcome to MI 5. But MI 5 was soon to be alarmed by the potential consequences. In August, when the DNI suggested that the Controlling Officer for Deception should become the chairman of the Twenty Committee, it at once appealed to the DMI, the chairman of the W Board, with the argument that such a step would result in the placing of undue emphasis on deception in the use of double agents, who had been recruited for counter-espionage purposes, and warned him that the Director General of MI 5 could not agree to any arrangement under which he did not have the final say as to how they were used. The DMI obliged by advising the members of the Board that the DNI's suggestion must be rejected on two grounds. The Committee 'has other work to consider besides deception, notably counter-espionage . . . as to which it is responsible to the Director General of MI 5, who appoints the Chairman'; and the Controlling Officer had in any case reported that he did not think he would have the time to be chairman, if indeed it would be proper for him to be so having regard to the terms of his directive. But the fact remained that his directive, which had made him formally responsible for all deception, had not mentioned the W Board either from ignorance of its existence or from regard for the secrecy and the informality which still surrounded its activities. And what was equally embarrassing, other members of the W Board took issue with the statement that the Twenty Committee was responsible to MI 5 and the implication that MI 5 had created it to supervise agents over whom MI 5 retained ultimate control. They believed that ultimate responsibility for the double-cross system belonged to the W Board, which would necessarily have to resolve any conflict of interest that might arise between counter-espionage and deception.

'C' made these points at a meeting of the W Board on 24 September. But he and the MI 5 representative quickly agreed not to pursue the matter of principle and the meeting accepted at their suggestion the practical formula that, while the Board or the Committee was responsible for deciding which material the agents should convey to the enemy for what purposes, MI 5 or the SIS must be free to decline to use agents to convey it if they believed that to do so would endanger the system and that, on the other hand, the final decision as to whether an agent should be sacrificed in the interests of security must lie with the Director General of MI 5. The Controlling Officer for Deception was equally co-operative; he would be content to explain what he wanted the enemy to believe and leave the Twenty Committee to supervise the detailed work involved in carrying out his briefs. On this note, and after agreeing not to pursue a suggestion that the Twenty Committee should be given formal terms of reference or a charter defining its responsibilities, the W Board recorded its confidence in the Committee and approved the adoption of a more ambitious use of the double-cross system. Every effort should be made to make the agents' reports more realistic by allowing the inclusion of accurate information about troops, weapons and aircraft, and this should be balanced, though with due restraint, by the inclusion of inaccurate information designed to deceive the enemy.

A further problem had by then been solved. In July, following the Anglo-American decision to carry out Operation *Torch* in 1942, the W Board had recognised that it would be essential to have the co-operation of the Americans in answering German questions to the controlled agents about US forces in the United Kingdom, and had agreed to invite General Eisenhower, who was about to be appointed C-in-C Allied Expeditionary Force, to add US representatives to the team which approved the double-cross traffic, and eventually to the Twenty Committee. At the meeting of 24 September the DMI reported that arrangements had been completed for clearing traffic relating to US forces. In the event no American joined the Twenty Committee, but these arrangements worked effectively for the rest of the war.*

---

* For the deception carried out in support of Operation *Torch* see Howard, *British Intelligence in the Second World War*, Vol V, (1990), Chapter 4.

CHAPTER 8

Disputes about Responsibility for Counter-Espionage from June 1941 to the End of 1942

THE friction which had arisen between MI 5 and the SIS on account of the SIS's secretiveness about counter-espionage operations overseas, particularly the cases of *Garbo* and *Tricycle*,* had meanwhile brought to a head the discontent which had developed in MI 5 with the situation in which the two bodies shared responsibility for counter-espionage.

MI 5's grievances stemmed from the operation of the agreement about handling the product of the RSS which was made in March 1941, when the control of the RSS was about to be transferred to the SIS,† and which laid it down that the SIS would be solely responsible for analysis, collation and distribution of the ISOS decrypts, but would issue directions to the RSS on interception priorities only on the advice of a committee representing itself, the RSS and MI 5. These terms reflected not only the fact that the SIS was assuming control of the RSS, but also the fact that MI 5 and the SIS continued to accept the long-established geographical division of responsibility for counter-espionage; and that division was re-affirmed in April 1941. Following discussions to demarcate the areas in which the two organisations were to record and index information, and thus avoid duplication, the SIS drew up and MI 5 approved the following memorandum:

'1.   The Director General of MI 5 has asked me to emphasise once more the division of responsibility between MI 5 and SIS.

2.   MI 5 are responsible only for the security of this country and in various parts of the British Empire, but have an additional responsibility for the security of Palestine and Egypt.

3.   SIS are responsible for the collection and collation of all counter-espionage intelligence in foreign countries.

4.   In order that MI 5 may be able to fulfil their responsibility it is essential that they should not be flooded with extraneous matter.

5.   In future, therefore, unless the particular paper under consideration, or connected papers, show that there is a likelihood that the

---

* See above, Chapter 7. In addition MI 5 believed that it should have been given a full account of the Sebold case, see below, p 157.

† See above, pp 72–73.

case in hand will require executive action in this country, or a part
of the Empire, in the fairly immediate future, it should NOT be
sent to MI 5'.

But two developments began to put a strain on these arrangements from the time they were made or re-affirmed.

On the one hand there was a large expansion in the counter-
espionage work of the SIS. As a result of the growing volume of
the ISOS output, the SIS section responsible for processing it
(Section V) came under heavy pressure, the more so as it was also
embarking on the establishment of counter-espionage representatives abroad.* On the other hand MI 5 came to believe that, as
espionage against British territory originated outside the three-
mile limit, it must see all intelligence about the enemy's activity and
participate fully in the direction of counter-espionage operations
overseas in order to discharge properly its responsibility for
British territory. It was fundamentally for these reasons that
though the joint committee for the direction of the RSS met
frequently from May 1941, it did so to the accompaniment of
continuous disputes.

The first sign of strain appeared in June 1941. Agreeing in that
month to a request to release officers and secretaries to reinforce
Section V, MI 5 commented that 'its work is so essential to our
Service that . . . we are fully justified in making this sacrifice. At
present [Section V] is grossly under-staffed and the work in Lisbon
and elsewhere is suffering'. In the same month MI 5 brought
pressure on the SIS to persuade it to increase its expenditure on
counter-espionage. Thereafter, contention increasingly focused
on the handling of the ISOS traffic. MI 5 complained that it was
denied an equal voice in the control of the RSS, forbidden to have
direct contact with GC and CS and given only restricted access to
the ISOS decrypts, with the result that full advantage was not
being taken of the intelligence. The SIS insisted that MI 5 attached
too little importance to the overriding need to maintain the
security of the source, circulating the decrypts too widely and
being careless in the use that was made of them.

One dispute arose when, after taking over the RSS, the SIS
ceased to circulate the intelligence summaries which the RSS's
Analysis Bureau, the experts in appreciating the Abwehr's wireless
traffic, had previously issued to MI 5 and other departments. Only
after months of pressure was the circulation resumed. Another
concerned the distribution of the decrypts of the Sicherheitsdienst's hand cypher. MI 5 had received these when the SD's
traffic was first read – as it was from time to time from early in

* See Chapter 9 for details.

1941 – but they too were withheld by the SIS from the end of May,* so that it was only 'unofficially' that MI 5 learned in June that they contained intelligence relevant to counter-intelligence in the United Kingdom. It was not till August that the SIS complied with MI 5's demand that it should receive them. The SIS's restrictiveness, on the other hand, received support from the use MI 5 made of decrypts at Latchmere House. In February 1941 it had assured the SIS that the interrogators there would not be shown decrypts or be informed of the source of such intelligence from them as they were allowed to see. But it subsequently became dissatisfied with or lax about this undertaking, and cases came to the SIS's notice in which the interrogators were given the full texts of decrypts.

By the autumn of 1941 MI 5 had become convinced that all these problems illustrated that the geographical division of responsibility for counter-espionage was out-moded and dangerous. When the head of the MI 5 registry complained that the existing rules regarding the division of labour between MI 5 and the SIS in recording and indexing did not make it clear whether he should keep records on people abroad who might come to the United Kingdom and suggested that MI 5 should be responsible for recording and collating all counter-intelligence and that the SIS should confine itself to collecting information for MI 5, his proposal was accordingly followed up with enthusiasm by MI 5's counter-espionage B Division. The proposal was submitted to the SIS at the beginning of September.

The SIS's rejection of the proposal was prompt and brusque. On receiving it, Petrie investigated the problem at some length for himself and came to the conclusion that while MI 5 must index and collate whatever intelligence it needed for its own purposes, even at the expense of overlapping with Section V, 'there need be no tearing up of boundary pillars'. The SIS could not be reduced to 'the status of a mere getter of information'. It must continue to be responsible for obtaining, evaluating and circulating counter-intelligence information, and if it was not doing so to MI 5's satisfaction, 'the remedy is the provision of an adequate staff, not a transfer of functions'. At the same time, having reassured the SIS on this point, he called for a meeting between 'C' and himself and their senior advisers to discuss the extent to which changes were required in the amount of intelligence MI 5 received from the SIS and in the use MI 5 made of it.

At this meeting, which took place on 18 November, there was no

---

* This was when a new series was introduced for the SD's decrypts with the cover-name ISOSICLE.

attempt at compromise on the issues which had soured relations for nearly six months. The SIS rejected MI 5's plea for the full distribution of intelligence; it insisted that Section V was fully acquainted with MI 5's duties and fully able to select whatever intelligence was relevant to them. MI 5 rejected the SIS criticism of the standards it applied in indexing, circulating and making use of the intelligence obtained from ISOS; it insisted that no more of its officers were indoctrinated than in the SIS.

The sole outcome, after a brief lull, was that the two organisations set up at the end of 1941 a small planning committee which would meet at least once a month to solve any future problems. But neither the planning committee nor the existence of continuous informal contacts averted the anger created in MI 5 by its discovery that the SIS had been withholding information about *Garbo* and *Tricycle*. In March 1942 it decided to return to the attack by claiming total responsibility not only for the assessment of counter-espionage intelligence but also for directing and advising on counter-espionage operations.

On 17 April Petrie sent 'C' a memorandum proposing that Section V should be incorporated in MI 5's B Division. In support of the proposal the memorandum argued that it was essential to overcome the difficulties arising from the fact that responsibility was divided on a geographical basis, which bore no relation to the facts of espionage, and from the divergent views to which this led. Responsibility for meeting the Abwehr's attack against the United Kingdom and British possessions overseas, and against the armed forces operating in and from them, ultimately rested with MI 5. Undivided responsibility carried with it the need for an undivided right of direction, and the simplest method of securing this was that the SIS should cease to handle counter-espionage. It should confine itself to acting as 'a getting agency for counter-espionage as it does for operational intelligence'. All the counter-espionage intelligence it collected should be passed to the new unified counter-intelligence division through an MI 5 liaison section at SIS, which should also be the channel through which the new division sent its instructions to the SIS's counter-espionage representatives abroad. The new division should scrutinise all ISOS material in direct liaison with GC and CS and, subject only to such veto as 'C' might impose for the protection of the source, should prepare the directives for all action based on it. It should also be responsible for the intelligence direction of the RSS and for the control of all double-cross agents.

The attractions which MI 5 claimed for the scheme – that it would offer the SIS and SOE better protection for their offensive operations, as well as making MI 5 more efficient in its defensive task, and that the elimination of duplication would release manpower which could be used to strengthen the SIS's counter-espionage intelligence gathering abroad* – did not make it accept-able to 'C'. He replied that it was based on 'a series of mis-apprehensions which have led to mistaken deductions'. Outside Great Britain the responsibility to inform and advise those con-cerned about defence against the Abwehr lay with the SIS, which alone had the necessary knowledge of local conditions, and counter-action lay with the Foreign Office, the Services, the Ministry of Economic Warfare and SOE. As head of the SIS he could not surrender control of double agents abroad. As Director of GC and CS he could not relinquish responsibility for the handling of any part of its output and for preserving the secrecy of its work as a whole. Some duplication of work was unavoidable, and too much emphasis should not be placed on the few instances where human error or pressure of work had led to mistakes.

Petrie stuck to his case, suggesting that it should be submitted to Swinton; and Swinton, who had already advised MI 5 that it was unlikely to succeed, but might extract important concessions from the SIS, suggested to 'C' and Petrie at a meeting at the end of June that they should jointly set up a single intelligence and planning centre for the appreciation and distribution of counter-espionage intelligence. And 'C' had by then decided to offer a similar solution. In a letter handed to Petrie at the meeting he 'accepted the principle that there should be a single unified body responsible to both of them for studying the activities of the enemy Secret Services, and for co-ordinating and directing action to counter them'. But far from conceding that the new body, a department of counter-espionage, should be incorporated in MI 5, he insisted that, as the work it would do was clearly related to other intelli-gence work and had a direct bearing on the SIS's offensive operations, it must be located with the SIS's central registry and Section V at St Albans. MI 5 would be responsible for taking decisions on the use of the intelligence in the United Kingdom. The SIS would establish at its London HQ a new section to control the use of the intelligence abroad and give directions to SIS counter-intelligence representatives abroad.

Meeting as they did MI 5's complaints about control of the RSS and access to ISOS, these were indeed important concessions. But MI 5 still hoped that the principle of joint responsibility could be extended beyond the collection and processing of intelligence to the field of operational decisions. In another long letter it objected that, the more so in view of the SIS's proposal to set up a new

---

* The expansion of counter-espionage work by the SIS, allegedly at the expense of operational intelligence, was now coming under attack – see below, p 176ff.

directing section in London, the new department would be merely a joint study group if located at St Albans. At another meeting on 22 July Petrie and 'C' and their advisers refused to yield on the question of its location, MI 5, whose B Division was in London, protesting that the department could not be effectively responsible for taking action on intelligence unless it was in London, the SIS insisting that it must be with Section V at St Albans and that MI 5 would realise this if it were more familiar with Section V's work.

The outcome was a visit to Section V by MI 5 officers. They found, as they reported in August, that MI 5 had indeed been under some misapprehension. MI 5 had been inclined to assume that action against Axis agents was necessary and feasible only on British territory. In fact, there was more Axis espionage and sabotage against British interests, particularly shipping, outside British territory than within it; and counter-intelligence operations on foreign territory in conjunction with the Services, the Foreign Office and SOE, as distinct from intelligence gathering, was a central feature of Section V's work. But they also felt that Section V was ill-equipped for this immense responsibility. It was understaffed at home, and while it now maintained full-time counter-espionage representatives abroad, they were handicapped by the fact that SIS's overseas agencies regarded counter-espionage as being less important than their other activities. The report recommended that MI 5 should accept the proposal for a new joint department, while continuing to press for its location in London, in the belief that, as well as giving MI 5 a voice in counter-espionage operations abroad and access to all counter-espionage intelligence, it would go a long way towards overcoming Section V's problems.

This advice was not acceptable to MI 5's senior staff. Not on the ground that the disagreement about the location of the department might remain unbridgeable, but with the argument that dual control would be unworkable, and in the belief that the SIS would eventually come round to the view that MI 5 should absorb Section V, Petrie proposed to 'C' on 21 August that Section V should move to MI 5's London offices, where it and B Division would have access to each other's records and B Division would acquire a share in the planning of counter-espionage operations abroad, and that the B Division/Section V planning committee, which had met briefly to no effect early in 1942, should be revived. 'C' replied that while he sympathised with MI 5's wish to be associated with the planning and direction of SIS's counter-espionage work and to receive all counter-espionage intelligence without the interposition of Section V, and was anxious to meet it provided there was no damage to the work or the constitutional position of the two departments, he would not move Section V to MI 5 or anywhere else in London. The most he could do was to offer MI 5 the services of the small liaison party from Section V which he was in any case intending to set up in London.

MI 5 now referred the deadlock to the Lord President and Mr Duff Cooper, who had suceeded Swinton as Chairman of the Security Executive in July, and Duff Cooper eventually, on 22 October, met 'C' and Petrie. According to the only formal record of the meeting – a letter from Petrie to 'C' of 23 October which was endorsed by 'C' – the discussion centred on two points. 'C' and Petrie agreed that relations had improved in recent months and accepted that regular meetings of the Section V/B Division planning committee would bring about such further improvements as were still needed. And in response to criticism of the SIS's conduct of counter-espionage, 'C' reported that he was undertaking the overhaul of Section V and Petrie offered to lend him every assistance.

No substantial changes were to follow from these agreements. The revised planning committee died quietly after a few months. Responsibility for counter-espionage continued to be divided at the three mile limit. Continued friction* and duplication of effort reflected the difficulties inherent in this division and the gulf which still separated the two Services. Nevertheless, relations between them improved greatly during the remainder of the war, particularly after the move of Section V to London in July 1943 made personal contact much easier.

---

* Notably over the organisation and support of counter-espionage with the Allied armies in the field, (see below, Chapter 14).

PART III

CHAPTER 9

The Development of Security Organisation Overseas to the End of 1942

THE links which MI 5 had established for counter-espionage purposes throughout the British Empire in the First World War had been maintained during the inter-war period, when subversion, not espionage, was the primary threat to security. The security authorities in the Dominions, in all cases the Police, corresponded directly with MI 5; in colonial territories the MI 5 correspondent was normally the Chief of Police, sometimes the Governor; where there were substantial British garrisons MI 5 posted officers of its own* to undertake defence security work, and in particular the co-ordination of counter-sabotage measures, on behalf of the Services. On the eve of the war there were Defence Security Officers (DSOs) in Gibraltar, Malta, Cairo, Aden, Singapore and Hong Kong. Through these links MI 5's information about suspect organisations and individuals could be made available to the civil and military authorities throughout the Empire, who in return contributed to MI 5's records. However, these arrangements were more impressive on paper than in practice. At the beginning of the Second World War there was no more than the skeleton of an imperial organisation for security. Executive responsibility rested with dominion and colonial authorities of varying competence. It was not until 1941 that, with vigorous support from Lord Swinton, effective steps were initiated to develop the organisation of security in British overseas territories.

In the autumn of 1937 the SIS reminded its stations abroad of their responsibility for counter-espionage outside the three-mile limit of the Empire,† but during the next two years it took only modest steps to strengthen its counter-espionage capability. In July 1940 'C' told Swinton, who had been given operational control of the SIS in respect of all its activities in Great Britain and Eire,[1] that in the circumstances much of the counter-espionage work which would normally be performed abroad would be done in the United Kingdom and the organisation for this purpose had

---

* Or officers seconded to it.
† See above, pp 4, 8–9.

been established in his Section V. No large expansion of the SIS's counter-espionage effort overseas took place until 1941, except in the western hemisphere.

□

The vital dependence of the British war effort on the political support and the material resources of the western hemisphere aroused understandable anxiety about British security arrangements for the area from the early months of the war. The Axis powers would obviously attempt to impede the production and delivery of munitions and essential supplies and to foster a climate of public opinion that was hostile to Great Britain, or at least indifferent to her fate. There was no lack of opportunities for them to exploit. Canada had accepted some 100,000 Germans by 1936, and the Auslands Organisation and its subsidiary, the German-American Bund, were active among them. In the United States the government had refused to tolerate the establishment of the AO, but it was known to be functioning covertly, and over and above the existence of large German and Italian speaking communities, Irish, Communist and pacifist opinion gave additional support to isolationism. In south America there were large German colonies in many countries, and several governments, such as those of the Argentine and Chile, were strongly pro-German. But until the spring of 1940 MI 5 had only tenuous links with the Commissioner of the Royal Canadian Mounted Police (RCMP) and the local Police forces in Bermuda and the Caribbean colonies, and the SIS was represented by only two officers in the whole of south and central America, one in Panama and one in Montevideo, and a small office in New York.

Out of deference to US susceptibilities, the SIS's New York office was forbidden to operate except through the FBI, and had to conduct its liaison with the FBI through the State Department. Since early in 1938 when, with the help of information supplied by MI 5,* the FBI had arrested Günter Rumrich, a deserter from the US Army who belonged to an extensive German espionage network, it had been anxious for closer collaboration with the British security authorities. But it remained under strict instructions from the State Department to enter into no arrangements which could be interpreted as infringing US neutrality until, early in 1940, 'C' sent Colonel (later Sir) William Stephenson to

---

* Rumrich's correspondence with Hamburg via a woman in Dundee came to MI 5's notice in July 1937. After his arrest in February 1938 he provided the FBI with information leading to the identification of several other agents operating in the USA. He and three others stood trial at the end of 1938 in a case which attracted a good deal of publicity.

Washington to explore the situation. Stephenson, a wealthy Canadian businessman with wide contacts in north America and Europe, arranged with the head of the FBI, Mr J Edgar Hoover, that the question of liaison should be laid before the President. The President immediately agreed that 'there should be the closest possible marriage between the FBI and British Intelligence'.[2]

This decision did not lead to any rapid co-operation in counter-espionage. Before December 1940, indeed, when FBI officers first visited London for discussions with the SIS and MI 5, the two countries had next to no counter-espionage intelligence that they could usefully exchange. But Stephenson at once saw the need to establish in the US with the agreement of the FBI – and indeed with Hoover's cordial support – a security organisation to undertake secretly what was not being done, and could not be done, by overt means to mobilise support for Britain and protect her interests. In June 1940 the SIS put him in charge of it. He was given no formal terms of reference, but it was understood that he would investigate enemy activities, organise public opinion in favour of aid to Britain, institute measures for the protection of British property and use his personal efforts to obtain desperately needed supplies, particularly destroyers, aircraft and rifles. In January 1941, when it could be publicly avowed that Great Britain had a legitimate interest in the protection of the war material supplies, the organisation was registered with the State Department as British Security Co-ordination (BSC), and recognised as being responsible for 'co-ordinating the liaison between various British missions and the US authorities in all security matters arising from the present abnormal circumstances'.[3]

The various British missions by then included the Imperial Censorship. The Censorship Regulations envisaged the establishment of independent censorships in all countries in the Empire which would be co-ordinated as to their policy by the Controller of Postal and Telegraphic Censorship in the United Kingdom. Sir Edwin Herbert, who became joint Director of the United Kingdom Censorship in April 1940 and took sole charge of it from January 1941, sought to bring all the censorships into one integrated system and, as far as possible, to develop co-operation between this system and Allied censorship organisations.[4] By May 1940, when responsibility for his department was transferred from the War Office to the Ministry of Information, it had, as 'The Imperial Censorship', taken on the Anglo-Egyptian Censorship from the War Office. By November 1940 the Censorship had assumed control at Bermuda and Trinidad and had, with the assistance of BSC, secured the co-operation of the US authorities in concentrating all trans-Atlantic mail (with the exception of that on a service between Rome and Brazil) so that is passed through these censorship posts.[5] In December it opened a Western Area Office in New York. In return for the co-operation of the US authorities there was an informal arrangement by which they would receive any interesting information derived from British censorship operations in the western hemisphere. Some 75,000 intercepts were passed to the American authorities in the next twelve months, and this period of informal co-operation culminated in December 1941 in an agreement between the United Kingdom, the United States of America and Canada which secured 'as much co-ordination as could be practically effective'.[6]*

BSC had by the end of 1940 established three divisions – for secret intelligence, special operations and security – and its work necessitated close relations not only with the US authorities, but also with authorities in the United Kingdom other than the SIS. Stephenson was thus appointed to represent the SOE in December 1940 and the Security Executive in January 1941. But all correspondence with the Security Executive and MI 5 regarding the activities of BSC's Security Division continued to be channelled through the SIS until March 1942, when the Division was subordinated directly to the Security Executive.

The Security Division was responsible for protecting British property and British and Allied shipping, vetting the companies working on Britain's account and individuals proceeding to British territory or joining the British and Allied Services, supervising the execution of anti-sabotage measures for factories, railways and docks and investigating suspected sabotage and subversion among labour unions and merchant seamen. To help it to carry out these functions it had appointed Consular Security Officers (CSOs) at all the major ports in the United States by March 1941; they were British citizens with wide experience of merchant shipping and extensive local knowledge. In July 1941 the Security Executive requested Stephenson to extend the appointment of CSOs to south America; 26 were established in the autumn of 1941 and there were 45 by the summer of 1942.[8]

After the entry of the United States into the war in December 1941 most of the security supervision which had previously been undertaken by BSC's Security Division was taken over by the

---

* The main steps in the further development of the network may be mentioned now. In May 1941 arrangements made with South Africa established Cape Town as the centre for the censorship of communications between Portugal and Mozambique and Angola. The Anglo-Iraqi Censorship was established after the failure of Rashid Ali's coup in June 1941. The Anglo-Soviet-Persian Censorship was established in February 1942. In May 1942 the Imperial Censorship established a Middle East office. In June 1942, after reporting to the Combined Chiefs of Staff that the mail carried by Pan-American Airways between Europe and Brazil was being used for espionage purposes, it succeeded in bringing that link under censorship control.[7]

appropriate US authorities. At their request, however, BSC continued to be responsible through its network of CSOs for the protection of British shipping in US ports, as well as in south America; in 1943 it maintained CSOs at 14 ports in the USA. And in the summer of 1942 it was authorised by the Chiefs of Staff, in agreement with the US authorities, to extend its overt security measures to the protection of the movement within south America of strategic raw materials from the place of production to the port of embarkation. During the next few months it appointed a network of Industrial Security Officers (ISOs) to carry out this work in co-operation with the FBI, training them in Canada. They numbered 61 by the middle of 1943.

On matters relating to counter-espionage and counter-subversion in the United States and south America, BSC was responsible solely to the SIS. For some time up to the autumn of 1941 it was also involved in these matters in the British West Indies, properly the preserve of MI 5. In January 1941 two counter-intelligence officers jointly representing the SIS and MI 5, one for Trinidad, the Barbados, British Guiana and the Windward and Leeward Islands, the other for Jamaica, the Bahamas and British Honduras, were made responsible to Stephenson at the insistence of Sir Edwin Herbert, whose examination of the censorship arrangements had convinced him of the urgent need to improve security in the area.* Their appointment did not go far to meet the growing uneasiness of the authorities in London. In the summer of 1941 representatives from MI 5 and NID made another examination of the provisions made for naval intelligence and security in the Caribbean. They found that, with the exception of Jamaica, neither the governors nor their governments had 'the least conception of what security is about'; and they recommended that MI 5 should send out additional DSOs to Bermuda, Jamaica and Trinidad, who would work with the officers already working under BSC, and a travelling Inspecting Officer based on Jamaica and also responsible to Stephenson. MI 5 agreed to make the appointments, but objected to its officers being placed under Stephenson who, as 'no more than the SIS representative in America', should not exercise executive functions on British soil. In September the Security Executive accepted that while maintaining a full exchange of information with BSC, the MI 5 representatives must advise the colonial governors direct, be responsible for co-ordinating all security intelligence and be answerable to MI 5's headquarters.[9] This decision settled the division of responsibility

---

* Another officer was to be sent to Bermuda but this appointment was obstructed by the colonial government.

between MI 5 and BSC (acting on behalf of the SIS) in the West Indies till the end of the war.*

The same division of responsibility was upheld in relation to Canada. After visiting the Caribbean the MI 5/NID mission had proceeded to Ottawa for talks with the Canadian authorities, and had pressed on them the need for appointing SCOs and declaring Protected Places on the British model. In September 1941, at the request of the Security Executive, the Prime Minister asked the Canadian Prime Minister to give these recommendations his personal attention, and offered to lend him experts. Mr Mackenzie King declined assistance but replied that the recommendations were being followed up.[10] During these exchanges Stephenson suggested the establishment of a BSC office in Ottawa but, with the concurrence of the SIS, Swinton decided that the proposal was unacceptable. 'We must deal with the Canadian Government through our High Commissioner, or Prime Minister to Prime Minister. If we can get our own liaison officers in Canada they must be sent from here and be responsible to MI 5'.

It was on this footing that MI 5 developed closer ties with the Canadian security and counter-intelligence authorities. In May 1942 an MI 5 representative visited St John's and Halifax and joined the Canadian Service departments in bringing pressure to bear for the establishment within the Royal Canadian Mounted Police (RCMP) of a Port Control Service, the acceptance of an MI 5 training mission and the appointment of an MI 5 DSO in Newfoundland. In November the RCMP decided to operate the first German spy captured in Canada as a double-cross agent† and invited MI 5 to send an officer to act as adviser. MI 5's representative arrived in December; he remained in Canada for the rest of the war and besides assisting the RMCP became an important liaison link between MI 5 and the FBI.‡

From the autumn of 1941 there had meanwhile been a large expansion of the SIS's counter-espionage activities in the United States and south America. New stations were opened in south America; in November 1941 the head of Section V visited the USA to prepare the way for the establishment of a counter-espionage section within BSC; and in January 1942 the SIS attached an RSS officer to BSC to promote the exchange of intelligence on illicit

---

* In the summer of 1942, when the U-boat campaign off the American coast was at its height, the United States authorities were critical of the state of security in the British Caribbean. It was partly for this reason that MI 5 made an abortive proposal that Stephenson should become its representative in the western hemisphere (see below, pp 147–148)

† See below, pp 201, 227–228.

‡ See below, p 187.

wireless traffic with the US and Canadian authorities.* After Pearl Harbour BSC regarded collaboration on counter-espionage with the FBI, which was the responsible agency in south America as well as in the USA, as one of its major tasks. Unfortunately relations between BSC and the FBI, once so cordial, were steadily deteriorating. In his determination to retain a monopoly of contacts with the British secret services, which had first been threatened by the appointment of Colonel Donovan as the Co-ordinator of Information in July 1941, Hoover resented Stephenson's efforts to cultivate co-operation with Donovan on behalf of the SIS. By June 1942, when Donovan's organisation became the Office of Strategic Services (OSS), relations between BSC and the FBI were very bad.

If relations between BSC and the FBI were deteriorating, so were those between the SIS and MI 5. In the spring of 1942 several months of increasing friction between the SIS's Section V and MI 5 about responsibilities for counter-intelligence culminated in a determined attempt by the latter to achieve far-reaching changes.† MI 5's catalogue of grievances included complaints that because of an alleged Section V 'bottleneck' MI 5 had been told little or nothing about *Tricycle's* activities in the USA‡ and other FBI investigations, and that important intelligence available in London was not reaching BSC, and its demands accordingly came to include the wish to be represented directly by the BSC. In August 1942 Petrie proposed that Stephenson should represent MI 5 in the United States and that MI 5 should appoint an officer to BSC's counter-espionage section, whence he would also assist the RCMP. After a good deal of argument it was agreed that Stephenson should become MI 5's representative and that MI 5 should communicate direct with BSC and appoint an officer to participate in liaison with the FBI and handle liaison with Canada

---

* The Canadian authorities readily agreed that BSC should be the channel through which their interception programme was co-ordinated with those of the UK and the USA. Arrangements with the latter presented more difficulty. In the United States the interception and exploitation of illicit wireless traffic was shared between the Federal Communications Commission, which roughly corresponded with the RSS, the Coastguard, which worked for the Office of Naval Intelligence, and the FBI, which had a small cryptanalysis section but no adequate interception facilities. Antipathy between these agencies was compounded by the wish of the FBI to be the sole intermediary for co-operation with BSC. Co-operation was also limited by British anxiety about the low standards of security which the US agencies applied to the use of the Sigint product. These problems were eventually solved early in 1943, when representatives of the FBI, the OSS and the US Service Departments were attached to the SIS in London to select ISOS decrypts bearing on their interests and BSC was permitted to negotiate separately with all three of the US illicit wireless agencies for the transfer of their intercepts and decrypts to London.

† See above, Chapter 8.

‡ See above, pp 124–125.

on MI 5 business. However, as we shall see, this was not to be the arrangement finally adopted.*

□

After the fall of France the Iberian peninsula provided a favourable environment for covert operations by the Axis powers. This was particularly the case in Spain where the government was under heavy obligations for help in the Civil War and the head of the Abwehr, Admiral Canaris, had friendly links with leading figures of the regime. The formal neutrality which Spain proclaimed in September 1939 became 'non-belligerence' in July 1940 and in the latter half of 1940 and throughout 1941, though German pressure to declare war and join in the capture of Gibraltar was resisted, the Spanish government not only raised no obstacle to Axis operations but allowed its diplomatic, consular, Service, Police and coastguard officials to give them active help. By contrast, Portugal was sympathetic towards Britain. In January 1943 the British Ambassador claimed that the majority of Portuguese had always been pro-British and had given 'many signs of fidelity during our darkest hours'.[11] However, the Portuguese government had to deal with realities, the likelihood of German victory and the close threat of German arms, and it, too, allowed Axis covert activities free rein throughout 1940–1941. Both countries were freely used for despatching and thereafter controlling agents sent to operate in the United Kingdom, the western hemisphere and Africa, and also as bases for the surveillance of British shipping, for sabotage attacks on British shipping in Spanish ports and for espionage and sabotage operations against Gibraltar.

Gibraltar in British hands was a standing offence to Spain and, as the key to the British position in the western Mediterranean, was a prime target for the Axis. It was extremely vulnerable to surveillance. Every ship in Admiralty Harbour and the commercial anchorage in Algeciras Bay could be seen from Spanish territory. La Linea almost adjoined the new airfield. Sabotage prospects were also good. Gibraltar's population indeed was loyal, except perhaps for a few Falangists, some of whom were interned in 1940, but the Fortress depended for labour on a daily invasion of some 8,000 people entering from La Linea and by water from Algeciras. Entry was of course controlled; an identity card system was introduced in 1938 and gradually strengthened; and the names of Spaniards seeking work (and in possession of the

---

* See below, p 187.

necessary Spanish passes, the acquisition of which might provide an opening for the enemy) were forwarded by British vice-consuls in La Linea and Algeciras for vetting. But in the circumstances vetting could not possibly be relied on, while the requirement for labour had to over-ride vague security misgivings. Moreover, smuggling was a major industry which could easily be exploited for the introduction of sabotage devices. Given the co-operation of Spanish officials in the Campo,* Gibraltar was thus an inviting sabotage target.

The SIS was weakly represented in both Spain and Portugal at the outbreak of war. It was not until after the Abwehr's hand cypher was broken in December 1940 that counter-espionage officers were posted to Lisbon and Madrid in March and April 1941 and began to lay the foundations of what became very large-scale penetration operations against enemy espionage and sabotage activities. This task was made the more difficult because, being in receipt of ISOS information, they operated separately from their colleagues and to begin with were not well received by them, and because political considerations in Spain made the British Ambassador extremely chary of activities likely to be objectionable to the Spanish government.

MI 5 had been represented in Gibraltar by a DSO since 1938. In June 1940 he took over responsibility for security intelligence in the Campo from the SIS and was given an MI 5 assistant. But the Services and the colonial government were reluctant to concede authority to the DSO. It was not until September 1941 that he was made responsible for frontier control and the direction of counter-sabotage, with the Gibraltar Security Police and Field Security Sections (as they became available) at his disposal. The SIS posted an officer to Gibraltar in July 1942 and resumed general responsibility for intelligence outside the Fortress. However, the DSO retained responsibility for obtaining counter-sabotage intelligence by agent operations and his organisation was strengthened by the appointment of a security intelligence officer.

□

In so far as there was any central direction of security in the Middle East at the outbreak of war, it was exercised by the DSO for Egypt. This post had been created in 1937 and filled by an officer seconded to MI 5. It took over the functions previously carried out by the European Department of the Ministry of the Interior;

---

* The Campo de Gibraltar is the area of lower Andalusia adjoining the Rock. It covers most of Cadiz province (but not Cadiz itself) and a small part of the neighbouring province of Malaga.

largely with British staff, this had supervised the security apparatus of the Egyptian government, including the Police, but had
been abolished, to the great satisfaction of the Egyptian government, by the Anglo-Egyptian Treaty of 1936. Unlike the SIS in
Cairo, which continued to collect covert intelligence on Egypt's
internal politics and diplomatic relations as well as on any subversive activities, the DSO worked both officially and privately in close
collaboration with the Egyptian Ministry of the Interior and the
Police. He also maintained close contact with the security authorities in Iraq and Palestine, with the DSOs in Aden, Malta and
Gibraltar and with MI 5's correspondents in Cyprus, Kenya,
Tanganyika, British Somaliland and the Sudan.

With the approach of war the DSO's staff was reinforced and
the planning of additional security measures for Egypt followed
the pattern adopted in the United Kingdom. Selected enemy
aliens were listed for internment. Preparations were made for the
establishment of a censorship organisation and the introduction of
travel control and other counter-espionage and counter-sabotage
measures. They included the training of naval officers by MI 5 to
work alongside the DSO's staff and with Egyptian officials as Fleet
Base Security Officers at Alexandria and in the Canal Zone. At the
outbreak of war, when Egypt severed relations with Germany and
declared a state of siege, these measures were brought into force
with reasonable efficiency.*

The situation in Egypt gave no cause for alarm for the next nine
months. But the need to provide for stronger defences against
Axis subversion throughout the Middle East provoked much
discussion. In September 1939 the War Office instructed the
C-in-C Middle East to set up a central authority to control the
existing security services, and the C-in-C proposed that all the
essential activities – the collection and collation of intelligence, the
study of subversion, censorship, the management of British
propaganda – should be co-ordinated by a security section in the
recently established inter-Service Middle East Intelligence Centre
(MEIC).† He also invited the DSO Egypt to take charge of the
section. MI 5 raised no objection provided the DSO retained his
responsibilities in Egypt and was given additional staff. But the
Foreign Office rejected the transfer of propaganda and censorship from civilian to military control, and the SIS objected to
control by the MEIC over operations in Persia and other non-

---

* There was, however, some confusion about the detention of the German suspect aliens.
47 managed to leave, and though 39 were interned, 17 were missing in the middle of
September 1939.

† For the MEIC see Hinsley et al, *British Intelligence in the Second World War*, Vol 1 (1979),
pp 13, 40–42, 191–195.

British territory where it was responsible for counter-intelligence. The C-in-C, on the other hand, insisted on the need for local control, and the outcome was a compromise. The new Security Section, set up in December 1939 and soon to be known as Security Intelligence Middle East (SIME), was placed on the staff of GHQ Middle East and entrusted with the following tasks on behalf of the Commanders-in-Chief of the three Services:

(a)   to watch the activities of hostile agents in the Middle East;
(b)   to maintain liaison with the Government of India's Intelligence Bureau and GHQ India about agents working against India;
(c)   to organise security intelligence services in the Middle East where they did not already exist, and to co-ordinate and improve the existing machinery;
(d)   to co-ordinate measures to counteract the activities of enemy agents;
(e)   to report periodically on hostile activities and counter-action.

It was required to obtain the approval of MI 5 or the SIS when discharging functions (c) and (d) in territory covered by them, and an SIS representative was attached to the Section to watch over the SIS's interests.

SIME remained closely associated with DSO Egypt's organisation. It shared the DSO's offices and records, and made use of his contacts with MI 5's out-stations and correspondents. Its head, the former DSO, frequently proposed that it should be financed and officered by MI 5 as 'the MI 5 of the Middle East'. This proposal was not pressed by MI 5 itself and was always resisted by the Services in Cairo, who eventually secured SIME's subordination as GSI(z) to MEIC in July 1941. It remained there until July 1943, when MEIC became the Middle East Political Intelligence Centre and SIME was made directly responsible to the Middle East Defence Committee.[12]*

SIME's position as part of GHQ Middle East meant that, as its jurisdiction was co-extensive with that of the Middle East Command, it was able to establish representatives in countries from which it would have been excluded if it had been a dependency of MI 5. Beginning with only three out-stations taken over from MI 5 – the DSOs at Malta,† Cairo and Aden – it established DSOs in Palestine in June 1940 and in Istanbul in December 1940. In November 1940 the Anglo-Turkish Security Bureau was set up by SIME and the Turkish Secret Service. It was supported by a Travel Control and Records Bureau, run by the Turks but

---

* See below, p 189.
† But the Malta DSO was only nominally under SIME and was soon restored to an independent post reporting directly to MI 5 in London.

financed by the SIS, which provided full details of all travellers between Turkey and the Balkans. By the end of 1941 these arrangements were working well. They continued to improve through all changes in the temperature of diplomatic relations between Turkey and the western Allies, despite the fact that some sections of the Turkish Police were in the pay of Germany until late in 1943 and the fact that the Turkish authorities maintained contact with the Abwehr about Russian activities. The Turks hoped, indeed, that Anglo-Turkish security co-operation would eventually be extended against Soviet Russia; MI 5 and the SIS discouraged all such overtures to avoid the risk of damaging Anglo-Soviet relations. In June and July 1941, after the collapse of Rashid Ali's coup, SIME set up a Combined Intelligence Centre in Iraq (CICI)* and sent a security mission to Syria to assist the Free French, and in October of that year it appointed a DSO in Beirut. By the autumn of 1941 the CICI's responsibilities had been extended to cover Persia[13] and SIME employed in all 90 officers and 100 other ranks, mostly drawn from the Army.

In view of its responsibility for counter-intelligence throughout the Middle East, SIME's expansion involved considerable duplication of effort with the SIS, which had established a regional headquarters (known as the Inter-Service Liaison Department) and had not abandoned its claim to be responsible for all counter-intelligence operations outside British territory. During 1940–1941 relations between the two organisations were close and amicable, but the posting in November 1941 of an SIS officer to Cairo to take charge of all SIS counter-espionage operations in the theatre – and to be solely responsible for receiving and distributing relevant ISOS material and for authorising action on it – might well have been followed by the extension to the Middle East of the jurisdictional quarrels which were preoccupying MI 5 and the SIS in London.† Fortunately, good sense and good personal relations in Cairo opened the way to arrangements which were acceptable to all the parties concerned there.

MI 5's contacts with SIME were tenuous throughout 1940 and 1941. In September 1941 the head of SIME invited Petrie to reconsider the suggestion first made in the spring of 1940 that SIME should be fathered by MI 5. Petrie replied that he doubted this being practical politics during the war. However, in the spring

---

* See Hinsley et al, op cit, Vol 1, p 411.

† In the spring of 1942 the SIS did in fact ask for extracts from the MI 5 charter defining its counter-espionage and security duties in the Middle East, hinting at its belief that the head of SIME had 'wandered a good long way from his original charter'. Petrie replied brusquely that the head of SIME derived his charter from the C-in-C who would probably not welcome any limitations being placed on SIME's activities 'in deference to any distinction we ourselves make in regard to the SIS and MI 5 fields'.

of 1942 MI 5 established a new section to service the security authorities in the Middle East and despatched an officer on a liaison visit to SIME. He reported that SIME suffered from staff shortages and lack of experience and the kind of support from MI 5 which it needed for its counter-espionage work. He was very favourably impressed, however, by its coverage of Egyptian affairs and by the excellent relations between SIME and the SIS. These had borne fruit during his visit in the establishment of a combined Special Section in SIME to deal with counter-espionage.

Besides SIME and the SIS there was another organisation with a direct interest in the conduct of counter-espionage in the Middle East. This was 'A' Force, which had been established at the end of 1940 by the C-in-C to carry out deception operations in connection with the offensive in the Western Desert.* As we have seen,† the head of 'A' Force had visited London in the autumn to discuss his plans for Operation *Crusader* with the Twenty Committee, and SIME's Special Section was designed to meet the requirement for similar machinery in Cairo, SIME and the SIS agreeing that the Special Section should be headed by the Section V representative and should contain an ISOS sub-section staffed by the SIS and an agent sub-section staffed by SIME. 'A' Force would appoint a liaison officer and keep in very close touch with the Special Section's work.

In June 1942 the head of SIME resumed his efforts to have his organisation removed from the control of GHQ Middle East and placed under MI 5 for staffing and finance and under the Middle East Defence Committee for operational purposes. He claimed that 'SIME represents MI 5 in the Middle East' and 'receives direction from the Director of MI 5' and that, being responsible on behalf of the three Services for counter-espionage, counter-sabotage, vetting and the control of travel permits and passes and also responsible to the civil power for civil security, it did not properly form part of the GHQ. MI 5 judged it inopportune to press for such a change while the General Staff was preoccupied with Rommel's threat to Egypt. It was no doubt also rendered wary by the thought that the proposal would extend to the Middle East the quarrels that it was waging with the SIS in London. It contented itself with providing SIME with some experienced registry staff and giving energetic support to obtaining a much expanded War Establishment for SIME which received War Office approval in August.

□

---

* For further details see Howard *British Intelligence in the Second World War*, Vol V (1990), Chapter 2.

† See above, p 101.

In the colonies in west and east Africa security arrangements remained on a peace-time basis until the spring of 1941. Even though the Cape route became of vital importance after the fall of France and the entry of Italy into the war, there had been no evidence of enemy interest in these areas when a SCO was appointed to Freetown in the spring of 1941. After the summer of 1941, when a DSO and an SIS officer were established at Lagos and a DSO attached to the East African Governors' Conference, there was still no evidence of any German attempt to send agents, though in 1942 several were directed unsuccessfully to the Belgian Congo.* Swinton's appointment in August 1942 as Minister Resident in west Africa gave a new impetus to security in what MI 5 described as 'this very sluggish area'.

In the Union of South Africa, where MI 5 had only a tenuous connection with the Police, the opportunities for German sabotage, subversion and espionage were more obvious. The border with Portuguese East Africa was easily crossed. The German consulate in Lourenço Marques provided a base for operations. Its staff had been reinforced by the Consul General in Pretoria, Dr L Werz, who had been withdrawn from South Africa on the outbreak of war. It was reported by January 1940 that Werz was cabling to Germany not only political and economic information about South Africa but also shipping intelligence acquired through agents in Portuguese East Africa, and was acting as a link between the Abwehr and its contacts in the Union. The South African Broederbond, anti-British and with extreme elements that were pro-German, had penetrated deeply into the Police and the Civil Service, while the Ossewa Brandwag (OB), a still more extreme organisation with a National Socialist ideology and a para-military framework, was known to be helping German internees to escape and to be planning sabotage at the ports.[14] In April 1941 the Abwehr despatched a well-known South African boxer, Robey Liebrandt, to join the OB in raising a rebellion; he fell out with the OB but until his arrest at the end of 1941 he was recruiting for his own organisation, the Nasionaal Socialistiese Rebelle, throughout the Transvaal and using it for various acts of sabotage.[15]

Action to overcome the lack of intelligence about German espionage activities in South Africa was precipitated by Japan's entry into the war at the end of 1941. In January 1942, at the prompting of the Security Executive, the British government invited the South African authorities to accept the appointment of a British Security Liaison Officer and possibly an expert in port

---

* See below, pp 167–168.

security.[16] The offer was accepted and in March MI 5 posted two men to Cape Town. At the same time the SIS sent a representative to Lourenço Marques to investigate Axis activities in the ports in east Africa and obtain intelligence about Madagascar. No counter-measures had proved possible, however, by the end of the year.

CHAPTER 9: REFERENCES

1. CAB 66/10, WP(40) 271 of 19 July.
2. H Montgomery Hyde, *The Quiet Canadian* (1962), pp 22–26.
3. ibid, pp 58–59.
4. DEFE 1/334, *History of the Postal and Telegraph Censorship Department 1938–1946*, Appendix 20.
5. ibid; DEFE 1/333, *History of the Postal and Telegraph Department*, paras 259–261, 1224, 1445, 1500–1514.
6. DEFE 1/333, paras 182–191; DEFE 1/334, Appendix 20.
7. DEFE 1/333, paras 206, 246–248, 259–261, 1500–1513; DEFE 1/334, Appendix 20.
8. CAB 93/7, HD(S)E(SSA) 1st Meeting of 23 July 1941. See also Hyde, op cit, p 6 ff.
9. CAB 93/7, HDSE(SC) 1, 2, 4 and 5 of 11 and 15 September 1941.
10. CAB 93/6, HDSE(CS) 1st Meeting of 11 September, HDSE(CS) 1, 2 and 3 of 10 and 18 September, 15 October 1941.
11. FO 271/34611.
12. E E Mockler-Ferryman, *Military Intelligence Organisation*, Appendix H.
13. ibid, Appendix G.
14. J C Smuts, *Jan Christian Smuts* (1952), p 386.
15. Leverkühn, *German Military Intelligence* (1954), pp 124–128.
16. CAB 93/7, SE(SAS) 1st Meeting of 27 January 1942.

CHAPTER 10

Counter-Espionage and Deception Operations Overseas To the End of 1942

THE THREAT of a German sabotage campaign in north and south America, which had caused the British security authorities so much anxiety since the spring of 1940, had failed to materialise. Up to the summer of 1941 this was not due to the existence of good intelligence or to the efficiency of the British precautions. The fact is that Hitler had vetoed the Abwehr's plans for a sabotage campaign in the United States in April 1940, and that after the failure through incompetence of its attempt to organise sabotage from Mexico in the winter of 1940–1941 it was again instructed to desist from such activities.[1] After the entry of the United States into the war the Abwehr's plans for sabotage operations were frustrated by Allied intelligence. ISOS, the Imperial Censorship and the travel control system in the Caribbean all played a part. From January 1941, moreover, when the Pan-American conference recommended the breaking of diplomatic relations with the Axis by all the American states, the German position came under increasing pressure and by the end of 1942 there was no serious threat to security in the western hemisphere from Germany – or, for that matter, from Italy.

In the field of espionage, one of the most damaging blows suffered by the Abwehr occurred in the summer of 1941. William Sebold (*Tramp*) was a naturalised American who returned to Germany in February 1939 to visit his family. He was approached by the Abwehr to become an agent, reported the approach to the US embassy and was instructed to accept it. After training as a radio operator and in codes and micro-photography, he returned to the USA, where he was given a large number of important German agents to service, some of whom had been working for several years. Guided by the FBI, who actually operated his set from Long Island, he proved so efficient in his role that he became the main channel of communication between the Abwehr and its agents in the US. The FBI struck in June–July 1941. Thirty-three agents were brought to trial, 19 pleaded guilty and all were duly convicted.

By the time of these arrests the Imperial Censorship was making an important contribution to security in the western hemisphere. Evidence leading to 27 convictions was provided by the Bermuda station, the peak year being 1942 when 63 agent communications were intercepted in the first six months.[2] Three important cases were those of Kurt Frederick Ludwig, Heinz Luning and Frederick Lehmitz.

Kurt Frederick Ludwig, alias *Joe K*, was born in the US. He was taken to Germany at the age of two, and brought up as a German, but retained his US citizenship and travelled on a US passport. Having been recruited by the Abwehr, and trained in Berlin, he was despatched from Spain to New York in March 1940 by his case-officer, Major Ulrich von der Osten. His instructions were to recruit from members of the German-American Bund, and obtain information on the US Army, aircraft production and shipping movements between the US and Britain. He was to report in secret writing by air mail to cover addresses in Lisbon and Madrid, and was also to establish radio communication. Ludwig quickly recruited eight sub-agents, one of whom, Borchardt, a Jewish ex-officer of the German Army, was already employed by the Abwehr. Ludwig failed to set up a wireless transmitter, but was an industrious correspondent, writing several times a week, ostensibly about the export of leather, to his 'customers' in Lisbon and Madrid.

By January 1941 Bermuda had become suspicious of the *Joe K* letters and had managed to develop the secret ink which Ludwig was using. The FBI was alerted through BSC. Further intercepts showed that at least two agents were involved, one of whom was known as *Phil*, alias *Konrad*, alias *Julio*. The investigation made little progress until the end of March. On 25 March Bermuda intercepted a *Joe K* letter, dated 20 March, the open text of which referred to a motor accident in which *Phil* had been killed, while the secret text gave more details of the tragedy, including the number of the car which caused *Phil's* fatal injuries.

The dead man had at first been identified as Julio Lopez Lido with a Spanish passport, but a telephone call (made by Ludwig to the hotel where he had been staying) enquiring about his luggage aroused suspicions. The FBI was brought in and concluded, after examining his documents, that he was probably a spy. Bermuda's information clinched the matter. *Julio/Phil's* effects included letters from Dinnies Carl Wilhelm von der Osten living in Denver, Colorado, who was interrogated and admitted that the dead man was his brother, Ulrich von der Osten, attached to German military intelligence.

Joe K had often referred in his letters to 'Uncle Dave' and 'Aunt Loni'. Ulrich von der Osten's papers provided a telephone number which led the FBI to a couple named Dave and Loni Harris, and an address which proved to be that of their nephew Fred Ludwig, whose handwriting was identical to that of *Joe K*. He was arrested on 23 August 1941 and brought to trial with his associates in March 1942. Ludwig and Borchardt were sentenced to 20 years' imprisonment; the others received sentences totalling more than 60 years.[3]

Luning's case began in October 1941 when a letter from Havana was found to contain a report in secret writing on aerodromes, shipping and other matters of military interest in the US. A long series of messages followed, one of which contained an address for reply enabling the agent to be identified. Luning was executed in November 1942.[4] In February 1942 Bermuda intercepted a letter containing a message in secret writing from the USA to a cover address being used by Luning, but obviously from a different agent. A long series of messages followed before the FBI managed to identify the writer as Frederick Lehmitz of Staten Island. He, and an accomplice, Irwin Harry de Spretter, were both sentenced to 30 years' imprisonment in September 1943.[5]

□

Until about the middle of 1941 intelligence about the organisation and the activities of the Axis in Spain and Portugal was sketchy and the scope for effective action to restrict them extremely limited. During the next 18 months the situation was transformed by the copious flow of Sigint (swollen by the breaking of the Abwehr's Enigma cypher in December 1941), the development by the SIS of large-scale agent operations to penetrate German waterfront networks and its acquisition of sources able to report on German intelligence personnel.

By the spring of 1942 the SIS and MI 5 had acquired an encyclopaedic knowledge of the Abwehr's order of battle and its operational preoccupations in the Iberian peninsula. The HQ in Madrid had some 20 officers supervising out-stations at San Sebastian, Bilbao, Vigo, Huelva, Cadiz, Algeciras, La Linea, Cartagena, Barcelona and Tetuan. Algeciras, overlooking shipping in and out of Gibraltar, was the most important of these. San Sebastian organised frontier crossings, legal and illegal, and investigated Allied crossings. Barcelona was believed to run a training school for agents, staffed by German instructors. La Linea was manned entirely by Spaniards and many of the other stations received regular shipping reports from Spanish coastguards and light-houses. Tetuan controlled sub-stations at Tangier and Ceuta, which maintained watch from the southern shores of the Straits on convoy movements, and at Melilla, which organised sabotage against Allied shipping loading iron ore. In Portugal a smaller organisation had its operational HQ in Lisbon with out-stations in the Azores, the Canaries, Portuguese Guinea and Portuguese East Africa. The Abwehr supplemented its direct observations of shipping by recruiting agents in the Spanish and Portuguese fishing fleets and among merchant seamen, some of whom also served as couriers across the Atlantic and supplied weather reports. In July 1942 the Royal Navy arrested two Spanish trawlers after ISOS revealed that these boats had been reporting shipping and weather information to the Germans. The radio operator made a confession at Camp 020. Another radio operator, a Portuguese, who had passed shipping information, was arrested on the high seas on 1 November when his trawler was on a course which would have met a large *Torch* convoy. In order to supplement its day-time observations of the Straits of Gibraltar the Abwehr had also installed there an ambitious system of detection of shipping at night and in bad weather which used infra-red apparatus and special telescopes. ISOS gave full details about this undertaking (Operation *Bodden*) from the time the Abwehr embarked on it in the autumn of 1941.*

From the same date the decrypts produced increasing information about the involvement or the acquiescence of the Spanish authorities in the Abwehr's mounting sabotage activities, as did agent services, which were now improving. Particularly with the assistance of a reserve lieutenant in the Spanish Army, who volunteered to act as a double agent and was run by the DSO Gibraltar, it became clear that sabotage operations against shipping, the dockyard and the airfield at Gibraltar were being carried out under the general direction of a colonel attached to the Spanish General Staff at Algeciras by a group led by a Falangist former captain. In February 1941 there was a serious explosion in the North Tunnel. In April a bomb exploded near oxygen cylinders on the airfield. In October the DSO's staff discovered the hiding place of mines intended for use against shipping. In December an Admiralty trawler sank at sea after an explosion and a bomb was found on a Hurricane about to be embarked on an aircraft carrier. In January 1942 another Admiralty trawler was destroyed in dock and other trawlers damaged. Airfield petrol dumps, the dockyard ammunition tunnel and two capital ships were the targets of abortive projects.

Attempted espionage against the Fortress led to the arrest in February 1942 of a Gibraltarian, Jose Estrella Key, who was subsequently tried and executed in England.

---

* See Hinsley et al, *British Intelligence in the Second World War*, Vol II (1981), Appendix 15, p 719ff.

In the absence of any equivalent of ISOS less was known about Italian covert activities, though from time to time ISOS contained some reflection of them and by May 1942 had established that they included a large-scale ship-reporting service working closely with the Abwehr and the Spanish authorities. Agents reported that some of the men who took part in a successful attack by Italian human torpedoes launched by a submarine against shipping at Gibraltar in September 1941 had been helped by Spanish Carabinieri and handed over to an Italian consular official at Algeciras, and that similar successful attacks in July and September 1942 had been launched from the Spanish shore of the Bay with Spanish complicity. An operation in December against HMS *Nelson* and the aircraft carriers *Furious* and *Formidable* in Admiralty Harbour was frustrated.

During 1941 arrangements were established for warnings, received from ISOS, of sabotage attacks on shipping in Spanish ports to be passed by the Naval Attaché to the consular officers in the ports concerned. These arrangements worked well, but a successful attack in December 1941 on a ship which had loaded ore at Melilla led the Security Executive to authorise the recruitment of merchant seamen to act under the supervision of DSO Gibraltar as guards on ships calling at Melilla or any other port where they were needed.[6]

The struggle with the Axis in the Iberian peninsula illustrates the complementary roles of the clandestine services and the conventional machinery of government in the field of security. So long as the enemy was allowed to operate with the support or the tacit acquiescence of the Spanish or Portuguese authorities defensive measures were unlikely to be wholly effective. The fundamental requirement was to move these governments from their positions of non-belligerence or embarrassed neutrality and persuade them to take action to control and eventually to eliminate Axis covert operations from their territory. This was a task for the Foreign Office, briefed by the SIS and MI 5.

Diplomatic action began early in 1942. In March, when the Foreign Office was taking up Calvo's case with the Spanish Ambassador,* it retaliated to a Portuguese complaint against the SOE's activities in Portugal by submitting to Salazar some of the SIS's evidence about the Abwehr's activities there. The dossier named the head of the Abwehr's Lisbon office and several of his subordinates, complained of their attempts to employ Portuguese stevedores in sabotage operations and also named Portuguese police officers who were under German influence and other

---

* See above, p 109.

Portuguese who were reporting for the Abwehr in the Portuguese colonies.[7]* Salazar recognised that it was Portugal's duty to proceed against Portuguese citizens known to be working for any of the belligerents, but he professed to regard the evidence as falling short of proof. At the end of September, when the Portuguese government had taken no action, the Foreign Office supplied him with copies of correspondence, obtained by the SIS, that had been carried between the Abwehr and agents in Angola, Madeira and the Azores by a courier system organised by a Portuguese named Raposo. He accepted that this material was of an 'altogether different category' from the evidence submitted to him in the spring, and Raposo and several of his associates were arrested in December. But at the end of the year he was still refusing to take action against the Abwehr itself.[9]

Meanwhile, however, a first substantial check to the Abwehr in the Iberian peninsula had been achieved through diplomatic pressure on Spain. Although the intelligence about Operation *Bodden* was mainly from ISOS, that undertaking was on so large a scale that there was no difficulty in supporting a protest against it with evidence supposedly obtained from less sensitive sources. In May 1942 the British Ambassador in Madrid made strong representations which led to the withdrawal of much of the special equipment and some of the personnel.† But Spain moved even more slowly and reluctantly than Portugal to withdraw her support for or toleration of Axis activities on her territory.

□

In Egypt and the Middle East, operationally and strategically the most crucial areas after the United Kingdom itself, next to nothing had been known about the Axis intelligence services before the war, and little was learned of them before the autumn of 1941. It was believed that the Germans had handed some of their agents in Egypt over to the Italians on the outbreak of hostilities, but none was detected. Italy had excellent opportunities for espionage and sabotage in Egypt, but no sabotage occurred after her entry into the war and no trace of a stay-behind network of agents was discovered. SIME assumed that the internment of Italians in considerable numbers had disrupted her operations. Since it has subsequently emerged that Italy was well informed

---

*   The detailed nature of the dossier surprised the Foreign Office where a senior official minuted: 'It is an astonishing piece of work . . . I had no idea we were going to be so explicit', and wondered whether it would stimulate vigorous Portuguese action against both sides. 'C' replied that the Germans had much more to lose than the British.[8]

†   See Hinsley et al, op cit, Vol II, Appendix 15, p 720ff.

about Britain's naval movements and the state of her land forces, this may have been an optimistic assessment. It is not known how much of her intelligence came from other sources than agents – from a Sigint attack on Allied communications and the Japanese diplomatic service – but there was firm evidence that Japanese diplomatic and consular posts in Cairo, Alexandria and Port Said were active in procuring military and shipping intelligence both for the Germans and for the Italians.

In Malta the evidence was that Italy had abandoned subversion and espionage after the middle of 1936, when her Consul-General was expelled for organising it. Following the internment of Italians and of some pro-Italian Maltese on Italy's entry into the war there was no Fifth Column activity, and no sign that she had resumed espionage arose until May 1942. In the only known war-time attempt at espionage, Carmelo Borg, a Maltese, was then arrested on landing from the sea with a W/T set, maps, money and instructions to report to Italian naval intelligence on operational movements, morale and food supplies. He was executed in November 1942.

It was known after the fall of France and Italy's entry into the war that the Axis powers were active and influential in the Levant, the Arab world and Persia. Nothing reliable was learned, however, about the nature and sources of their intelligence in these countries before the crushing of Rashid Ali's coup in the summer of 1941.* In September 1941 SIME believed that the entry of Allied forces into Iraq, Syria and Persia had 'disorganised what organisation existed' for Axis espionage. It recognised, however, that the enemy was making strenuous efforts to reconstitute an organisation that would operate in these countries from Turkey, Greece and the Balkans, and it owed this knowledge to two developments which were at last providing reliable sources of counter-intelligence.

The first was the increase in the flow of ISOS decrypts of the Abwehr's hand cypher which had provided some reliable information about the Abwehr's order of battle in Turkey during 1941. After the breaking of the Abwehr's Enigma in December 1941 Sigint became an even more valuable source of intelligence. The decrypts of the SD hand cypher – broken early in 1941 but read less regularly than the Abwehr's – threw light on the activities of Amt VI, the foreign section of the SD which was interested in the scope for political subversion and propaganda in the Middle East. From the end of 1941 the decrypts were providing reports from two

---

* For the intelligence obtained before and after this operation, see Hinsley et al, op cit, Vol I, pp 366–368; 409–415; Vol II pp 81–83.

competing stations in Ankara, one working to Hamburg and the other to Berlin, and from an Abwehr station in Istanbul under Paul Leverkühn. They disclosed that at that stage the Germans were depending on Turkish officials for much of their information from all countries in the Middle East. No doubt because these officials were becoming less co-operative towards Germany, it was noticed that the quality of the reports began to decline from early in 1942. From the autumn of 1941, on the other hand, liaison between SIME and the Turkish Secret Service through the Anglo-Turkish Security Bureau became steadily closer, and from the end of the year was second in importance only to ISOS among the sources which enabled the British security authorities to penetrate the German and Italian intelligence services in Turkey and check their activities throughout the Middle East.*

Between September 1941 and the autumn of 1942 they succeeded in arresting 25 agents who arrived in the Middle East by parachute, boat or overland from Axis posts in Turkey, Greece or Rhodes.† The first to be captured, two Armenians recruited by the Italians, landed by parachute near Aleppo in September 1941 with a W/T set, a simple code, a cover address in Switzerland and orders to report on the British order of battle in Syria. In October a German Jew, Paul Fackenheim, was dropped near Haifa; he claimed on being captured that he had accepted an Abwehr mission only as a means of getting to Palestine, but was detained for the duration. An entire German spy ring – seven young Palestinians, Lebanese and Syrians organised by a student named Latifi to collect information in their countries – was rounded up at the end of 1941 after being betrayed by one of its members. In April 1942 the Italians parachuted two agents into Egypt and one into Cyprus; all three were captured, as were two others dropped near Aleppo in July.

In June 1942 Sobhy Hannah, an Egyptian lawyer who had built up a successful practice in France, was arrested at Dar es Salaam on the strength of intelligence from ISOS. The Abwehr had despatched him back to Egypt via Lisbon with a W/T set, materials for secret writing and a considerable sum of money, and with instructions to contact anti-British circles in Cairo. Another operation against Cairo of which ISOS gave early warning was an expedition led by Count Ladislas Almassy, a well-known desert

---

* For the Anglo-Turkish Security Bureau see above, p 151.

† These successes led SIME to claim in October 1942 that the information which the enemy was obtaining was low grade and small in volume. So far as agent operations were concerned this was true, but in 1941 and until June 1942 Rommel obtained very valuable information about British operations from the intercepted traffic of the US Military Attaché in Cairo and the lax signals security of the British forces, (see Hinsley et al, op cit, Vol II, pp 298, 331, 361, 389).

explorer. It left Tripoli in March 1942 and infiltrated two German agents into Egypt at Assiut in May. ISOS reported that the agents, Johann Eppler and Heinrich Sanstede,* had reached Assiut and that their mission was to collect military intelligence and pass it by radio to an Abwehr detachment with the field Sigint unit at Rommel's headquarters. Perhaps because this unit was captured near Bir Hacheim on 27 May,† they failed to establish contact with Rommel's HQ, and nothing more was heard of them until the DSO Egypt learned from an agent that Victor Hauer, an Austrian employed at the Swedish embassy to look after the affairs of interned Germans, had been asked to help two Germans. Hauer was taken into custody on 21 July, and his confession led to the arrest and the internment of the Germans and several contacts in the Egyptian Army.

At the end of July 1942 ISOS disclosed that a U-boat from Salamis was to land an agent south of Beirut. The U-boat was attacked and disabled off Haifa on 4 August and the agent, a Lebanese student named Hamada, was among the survivors who were taken prisoner. Later in August, after ISOS had reported the departure from Greece of three agents bound for Syria, an ex-officer of the Royal Hellenic Air Force and two companions were intercepted in a small boat off Latakia. The ex-officer, who had accepted the assignment in order to get out of Greece, was taken on as a double-cross agent; he established W/T contact with the Germans in September and maintained it for two years under the alias *Quicksilver*. Another party of three Greeks was caught with the assistance of ISOS on arrival in northern Syria by boat in October; one of them, who had been in contact with the SIS in Athens, also became a double agent under the alias *Pessimist*.

Quicksilver and *Pessimist* joined two other double-cross agents already in service with SIME, *Doleful*, a Wagon Lits attendant on the Taurus Express, who had been acquired through the good offices of the Turkish Secret Service and was used for deception purposes from the spring of 1942, and *Cheese*.

The founder of the *Cheese* network was a man of Italian Jewish origin, who was intelligent and resourceful and had travelled widely. He was in Italy when the war began and in December 1939 told the British authorities that he had been asked to work for the Abwehr. He was instructed to accept the invitation and carried out Abwehr missions to France. After the fall of France the Abwehr transferred him to Italian military intelligence, which sent him to

---

* Eppler, the son of a German woman who had subsequently married an Egyptian judge, had spent several years in Cairo before the war. Sanstede, who had worked for many years in east Africa, had been repatriated from Tanganyika on an exchange in January 1940.

† See Hinsley et al, op cit, Vol II, p 404 and note.

Cairo with a W/T operator in October 1940 via Istanbul. The Turks arrested them for trafficking in counterfeit money, but the SIS got *Cheese* to Cairo without the operator in February 1941. Under SIME's control he established communication with the Italians, who promised, but failed, to furnish him with a W/T set and reliable contacts. He provided them with the story that he had managed to find a set and an operator – a wholly fictitious Syrian of Slav origin called *Nicossof* – and arranged that the operator would begin transmitting towards the end of May while he himself returned to Italy to discuss his mission. Back in Rome the Italians greeted him with deep suspicion – in November, a development unknown to SIME, they imprisoned him for five years for black market activities – but *Nicossof* had finally established regular W/T contact with Italy by mid-July, and in October 1941, when the enemy was showing increasing interest in the information he provided, 'A' Force decided to use the *Cheese* link for deception in support of the forthcoming Allied offensive in north Africa (Operation *Crusader*). For this purpose another notional agent was added to the network, an anti-British South African NCO called *Piet*, who was supposedly working as confidential secretary to an unnamed general. ISOS decrypts disclosed that the Abwehr accepted that *Piet* was a well-placed source.

It was thought that *Crusader* had achieved tactical surprise and that the *Cheese* messages had played an important part in this success.* By all the rules *Cheese* should therefore have been discredited. It was in fact clear that the enemy had become suspicious and the case was in the doldrums for several months. During the first half of 1942 sporadic messages were exchanged, mostly about money matters, but with Rommel's arrival at El Alamein at the end of June the case acquired a new lease of life and control was resumed by the Abwehr, which throughout had taken a more favourable view of its originator than the Italians had done. On 4 July it was learnt from ISOS that *Cheese* was considered 'credible', and on 12 July that he was rated as 'trustworthy'. This was followed by a request for daily instead of twice weekly transmissions, and the Abwehr arranged to pass *Cheese* reports direct to the HQ of the Panzer Army. In response the notional *Cheese* network was re-furbished. *Nicossof* was provided with an 'amie', supposedly a Greek girl (cover name *Misanthrope*) who was reputedly intelligent, well educated, witty, brave and animated by hatred of the British. Besides sustaining *Nicossof* she assisted the work by forming friendships with Allied officers, from whom she extracted information, and by learning to operate the radio in case

---

* See Howard, *British Intelligence in the Second World War*, Vol V, (1990), Chapter 2.

Nicossof was ill.* Thus satisfactorily re-established, *Cheese* played an important part in the deception plan for the battle of El Alamein.†

□

Firm intelligence about Axis espionage activities in Africa south of the Sahara remained scanty up to the end of 1942. Three Portuguese subjects who had accepted Abwehr missions in southern Africa were arrested in Freetown in the autumn of 1942. Four other German agents en route for the Belgian Congo and one destined for South Africa were arrested in transit through the United Kingdom. The most important of those aimed at the Congo were Hilaire Anton Westerlinck and Gabriel Pry. Westerlinck was a Belgian who had been a ship's doctor. In the autumn of 1940 he was reported to be working for the German Consul in Lisbon, persuading Belgian seamen to desert their ships and get themselves repatriated. When he applied for a visa to go to the Congo it was accordingly arranged to route him via the United Kingdom, where he arrived early in May 1942. At Camp 020 he admitted his earlier activities and confessed that (as was known from ISOS) he had accepted an Abwehr mission to the Congo, the reward for which would be a comfortable administrative post there after Germany's victory. He also said that when it was known that he would have to travel via the United Kingdom he had been briefed to obtain information there too. As he had been well trained in radio and secret writing, an attempt was made to run him as a double-cross agent, but his letters remained unanswered and it was suspected that he had contrived to warn the Germans that he was under control. In January 1948 Westerlinck was sentenced to ten years imprisonment for bearing arms against Belgium and her allies and attempted espionage.[10]

Gabriel Pry, a Belgian subject born in 1917, arrived in the United Kingdom from Lisbon in October 1942. He had sought the help of the Belgian authorities in Lisbon to get to the Congo, telling them that he had left Belgium at the request of the President of the Association des Intérêts Coloniaux Belges, who had given him letters for the Governor-General of the Congo and the Colonial Minister of the Belgian government in London. The Belgian authorities were suspicious and sent him to the United Kingdom. At the LRC, Pry disclosed for the first time that he had volunteered his services to the Abwehr in Brussels in order, as he

---

* An ATS officer in the British Army was employed as substitute operator, and a Greek girl was selected and briefed to play the part of *Misanthrope* in case she was needed to meet a courier bringing money for *Cheese*.

† See Howard, op cit, Vol V, Chapter 4.

said, to escape, and had accepted an espionage mission to the Congo. The LRC examiner thought that he was withholding material information and he was sent to Camp 020.

Pry had served with the Belgian Army in 1940. He was demobilised after the Belgian surrender and joined an insurance company which shortly afterwards came under German control. In 1941 he spent several months in Hamburg on business and on returning to Brussels in December wrote to a German acquaintance volunteering to do secret work for Germany. Having accepted a mission to the Congo, he was introduced to the President of the Colonial Association as a member of the British intelligence service who was about to go to Lisbon and would act as a courier. He was to gather information about military and economic matters in the Congo and the Germans hoped to use him for liaison between Leopoldville and London.

Pry claimed that he had all along intended to deceive the Germans. MI 5 thought that his behaviour was inconsistent with his claim and that he was a thoroughly dangerous spy. The DPP was of the opinion that proceedings could not be taken under the Treachery Act as Pry had done nothing that could be proved to indicate beyond reasonable doubt an intention to assist the enemy. Pry was detained at Camp 020. He was deported to Belgium in February 1945, and in 1947 was sentenced to three years' imprisonment, perpetual banishment and deprivation of civic rights. The sentence was reduced on appeal to deprivation of civic rights for 20 years.

The man aimed at South Africa was Charles Oliver Boyd, a young South African who had been captured on the high seas in 1940 and interned in France. He was a highly impressionable character and after some mild brain-washing during internment decided to become a National Socialist and offered his services to the Abwehr. His release was engineered, and after several months' training in radio, coding and secret writing he set out to return to South Africa via Spain and Portugal. After crossing the Spanish frontier he surrendered to the Spanish authorities and spent some weeks in internment. He was then released to the British and reached the United Kingdom by way of Gibraltar. His cover story – that he had escaped into the Paris Metro while being transferred from one internment camp to another and made his way clandestinely into Spain – stood up at every point, but while final arrangements were being made for his repatriation ISOS information pinpointed him as an Abwehr agent. At Camp 020 he made a full and prompt confession.

CHAPTER 10: REFERENCES

1. Leverkühn, *German Military Intelligence* (1954), pp 58–59; L de Jong, *The German Fifth Column in the Second World War* (1956), pp 214–215.
2. DEFE 1/334, *History of the Postal and Telegraph Censorship Department 1938–1946*, Appendix 22.
3. ibid. See also Hyde, *The Quiet Canadian* (1962), pp 79–87.
4. DEFE 1/334, Appendix 22.
5. ibid.
6. CAB 93/7, SE(SNP) 1st and 2nd Meetings of 23 December 1941, 16 January 1942; SE(SNP)1 of 17 December 1941.
7. FO 371/31113.
8. ibid.
9. FO 371/31113, 31115, 30961.
10. Masterman, *The Double-Cross System in the War of 1939 to 1945* (1972), p 117.

PART IV

CHAPTER 11

Security Organisation in the United Kingdom and Overseas after 1942

THE SETTLEMENT of October 1942 between MI 5 and the SIS,* such as it was, did not put an end to discussion either of what might be their proper relationship or of what might be their proper position within the wider structure of government. All further discussion proved inconclusive, however, and the security organisation that had evolved by the end of 1942 remained essentially unchanged till the end of the war, except that the Security Executive declined in importance and over-all responsibility for security was moved away from the Lord President.

The chairman of the Security Executive continued to be responsible to the Lord President until Sir John Anderson was succeeded in that office by Mr Attlee in September 1943, and it was understood that, with the chairman acting as his agent, the Lord President was ultimately responsible for any aspects of MI 5's work which did not fall within the jurisdiction of another minister, notably the Home Secretary. When Duff Cooper left the Security Executive in November 1943 he felt that there was no longer any need for the chairman to refer MI 5's affairs to the Lord President, and recommended that it would be sufficient if the Director General could refer directly to a senior minister if he required support. Eden at the Foreign Office acted as this minister for the rest of the war. At the same time, beginning with the discussion of security measures for Operation *Overlord*,† the Prime Minister himself took over from the Lord President and the Security Executive the leading role in the direction of over-all security policy. The importance of the Security Executive in co-ordinating security measures declined rapidly in the last eighteen months of the war, though the Prime Minister's responsibility for the co-ordination of security arrangements was not yet explicitly recognised.‡

In March 1943, after nine months' experience as chairman of the Security Executive, Duff Cooper sent a memorandum on 'The Future of the Secret Service' to the Prime Minister. He argued the case for unity of control. Under existing arrangements responsi-

---

* See above, Chapter 8.
† See below, Chapter 14.
‡ On the initiative of Duff Cooper, MI 5 submitted monthly reports on its activities to the Prime Minister from the spring of 1943.

bility was dispersed between no fewer than five ministers – the Foreign Secretary, the Home Secretary, the Minister of Economic Warfare, the Lord President and the Chancellor of the Duchy in his capacity as chairman of the Security Executive. The SIS, MI 5 and SOE were housed separately and there was a great deal of overlapping and squabbling, not least because of the indefensible division of responsibility for counter-espionage at the three-mile limit. There ought to be a single Secret Service with three branches – information, security and operations – the head being responsible to the Foreign Secretary and the Home Secretary and assisted by a Board representing the Foreign Office, the Home Office, the Service Departments and the Treasury. Duff Cooper recognised that the temporary dislocation resulting from attempts at reform during war-time might outweigh the advantages to be gained from long-term improvement, but he felt that 'if the reform is postponed until the Utopia of normal conditions is restored it may well be postponed until it is unnecessary'. He made the additional point that proper terms of service would have to be worked out if MI 5 were to be able to retain 'the services of the many brilliant and experienced officers' it had recruited since the beginning of the war.[1]

Desmond Morton, the Prime Minister's personal assistant for intelligence and security matters, advised him that the memorandum was 'largely inspired by Sir David Petrie', expressing as it did the views held by MI 5 in its disputes with the SIS, and that friction between the two bodies was not necessarily harmful. And the Prime Minister's reply to Duff Cooper of 4 April was decidedly unsympathetic. On the suggestion about the need for proper terms of service he remarked that: 'Every Department which has waxed during the war is now considering how it can quarter its officials on the public indefinitely when peace returns. The less we encourage these illusions the better . . .'. As for the need for re-organisation, he picked up Duff Cooper's remark about risking 'attempts at reform during the emergency of war . . .' and said 'I have a feeling that it would be a mistake at the present time to stir up all these pools . . .'. He concluded by suggesting that Duff Cooper should hold a monthly meeting of the heads of the SIS, MI 5 and SOE, with Morton representing the Prime Minister, at which 'cases of friction could be smoothed out and common action promoted'.[2]

This suggestion led to the creation of the Secret Service Co-ordinating Committee. Its first meeting on 9 April discussed the question of representation in the United States.* It met for the

---

* See below, p 187.

second and last time in July to consider the same subject, Duff Cooper having previously told the Prime Minister that there would not be sufficient business for regular meetings.[3]

Criticism in other quarters had meanwhile focused on MI 5. In the spring of 1943 Bridges, the Secretary of the Cabinet, asked the chief security adviser to the Bridges Panel,* a Foreign Office official, for an aide memoire on the 'disquiets and anxieties which we feel about the present functioning of MI 5'. The resulting document was highly critical. It questioned whether MI 5 was under proper ministerial control and suggested that its wide powers were being improperly used, producing 'injustices to the public', particularly in the process of vetting and the treatment of aliens at the LRC and Camp 020. It also argued that there was considerable duplication between MI 5 and the Metropolitan Police, and between MI 5 and other authorities with regard to port control, and that it was MI 5 that was superfluous. 'Indeed it may be argued with some force that the collection of information about a suspected crime, such as espionage, the apprehension of the suspect, and the preparation of the case against him, would be better entrusted to professional police officers, trained to deal with all forms of criminal activity'.[4] In July 1943 Sir Norman Kendal, a senior officer at Scotland Yard, put this view in a letter to Bridges in even stronger terms.

Kendal claimed that 'the root cause of the appalling overlap between Special Branch and MI 5' lay in the fact that since 1931 MI 5 had 'stretched their writ to cover subversive activities wherever they occurred'. 'Government departments have got the idea that MI 5 is in sole charge of everything connected with Security . . . the result is interference by amateurs in what is in effect criminal investigation'. All work against subversion outside the armed forces ought to be done by the Metropolitan Police, and the interrogation of spies should also be a matter for the Police, who were much better qualified for the work, in close co-operation with the SIS.[5]

No doubt because he was aware that they did not recognise the complexity of what he called 'a pretty thorny and difficult business',[6] Bridges did not follow up these criticisms. In June 1944, however, he sent a memorandum on the Secret Service to the Principal Private Secretary to the Foreign Secretary. This paper suggested, tentatively, that there should be a single Secret Service combining the functions of SIS with the counter-espionage and counter-sabotage function of MI 5, and that responsibility for counter-subversion should be returned to the Police. The Private

---

* See below, pp 247–248.

Secretary pointed out in reply that in this case 'C' would have to owe allegiance to the Home Secretary as well as the Foreign Secretary, and that the unified Secret Service would have to take a very close interest in the study of subversive movements in the United Kingdom which were inspired by foreign governments or agencies. A better solution might be to set up an organisation comprising Section V and the MI 5 sections dealing with counter-espionage, counter-sabotage and counter-subversion, staffed by a mixed team from MI 5 and SIS and jointly responsible to 'C' and the Director General of MI 5. The Permanent Under-Secretary at the Home Office, Sir Alexander Maxwell, echoed the comment about ministerial responsibility when he saw the Bridges memorandum in October. The Home Secretary would have to be kept informed of the measures taken to counteract the activities of spies and sabotage agents in the United Kingdom, and have a say in regard to them. 'As regards subversive organisations', Maxwell added, 'on the whole I think experience during the war has shown that the work has been done satisfactorily by MI 5, and whatever arguments there may be for taking it away from them, I don't think they are Home Office arguments'.[7]*

A committee established by the Foreign Office to consider the future organisation of SIS reported at about the same time. It noted that there was much duplication and overlapping in the field of counter-espionage. Accepting that 'C' must remain responsible to the Foreign Secretary, and that 'any action taken in this country must equally remain with the Home Secretary', the committee considered that it was grossly wasteful to have two separate bodies covering much the same ground, and that there should be an inquiry into the division of responsibilities between MI 5 and SIS. In a report by the chairman and secretary of the JIC in January 1945 they recognised that intelligence affecting the internal security of the country was on a special footing; subject to this they doubted whether any case could be made for the retention of the system under which responsibility for counter-

---

* Cf a minute of February 1945 by a Home Office official following a visit to the division of MI 5 which was responsible for the surveillance of subversive activities. Noting that this division was very well informed, particularly on the Communist side, the minute continued: 'There is certainly no blimpishness and the attitude is one of almost scientific detachment. They have a problem, and a series of specimens, and they study them without animus. They do not, however, lose sight of the fact that they are dealing with human beings, and that any interference in their personal lives involves a heavy responsibility'. There was great insistence on accuracy, and officers were realistic about the true importance of their targets. The minute proceeded: 'I found the general attitude very different from that which one associated with MI 5 in the earlier part of the war . . . They have arrived by different routes at a belief very like our own, namely that any interference with personal or political liberty must on grounds both of principle and expediency be regarded as an exceptional course . . .'.

espionage was divided between two authorities with no better basis of division than that of geography. They suggested that experience had shown that 'an attempt to draw a distinction between military and civil security must fail' and that a single authority – the JIC itself – should in future be the co-ordinating authority for both. They conceded that 'as the JIC was subordinated to the Chiefs of Staff it might be thought that it would give excessive weight to military considerations, but believed it should be possible to give satisfactory guarantees to avoid this criticism.

'C' and Petrie of course had their own strong views. 'C' was opposed to any suggestion that MI 5 should be permitted to run a foreign intelligence service parallel to, or in conjunction with, SIS, or should be given sole responsibility for collecting counter-espionage or counter-subversion intelligence, since both related to a multitude of British interests abroad, including the security of SIS itself. But he was anxious that SIS should not be associated with the idea of an internal Gestapo, and accordingly did not want to take over MI 5's responsibilities in the field of counter-subversion.[8]

Petrie had to meet a two-pronged argument – that there should be a single Secret Service which would be responsible for counter-espionage; and that counter-subversion should be returned to Scotland Yard. In a paper[9] written at the end of 1944, entitled 'Readjustment in the Functions of MI 5 and SIS', he argued that while the differences between them had been exaggerated by personalities and the situation had improved, there was nevertheless an underlying problem which arose from treating the two services as parallel rather than complementary. Counter-espionage had to be seen as a whole, but that was not to say that it must all be handled by one organisation, or that each organisation should counterpart all the work done by the other. There were objections to a unified Secret Service, including the difficulty of finding a suitable head and then preventing him from becoming indispensable, and the possibility that if no independent check existed mistakes might be covered up. The right solution was to make the division between MI 5 and SIS functional but not geographical, 'or in other words defensive and offensive'. It should be automatic that all information required by MI 5 should be passed to it without reservation; Section V's claim to exercise a sort of proprietary right on information from SIS had been substantially modified during the last two years but had been largely responsible for earlier difficulties. Touching on other particularly sore spots in MI 5/SIS relations, Petrie argued that control of GC and CS and of the RSS (which must act as the technical tool of both SIS and MI 5) should be taken out of 'C''s hands, and that the links which had developed between MI 5 and the Security Services of the Allied governments should be maintained after the war.*

The suggestion that the task of keeping a watch on Communist and other subversive activities should revert to the Police was dealt with in a letter to Maxwell in February 1945. Petrie argued that this arrangement had not proved satisfactory in the past; the work required people of higher intellectual calibre than were generally available in the Police; Police security was not good enough for the protection of information about subversion from delicate sources, including SIS; and the Police should be kept out of politics.

□

If these discussions remained inconclusive it was partly because of the constitutional difficulties that stood in the way of any fundamental revision. But it was also due to the fact that from the end of 1942 the security organisation as a whole was operating smoothly and with great efficiency.

Within the United Kingdom MI 5 was under-pinned by the complex machinery of security controls – control of travel in and out of the country, vetting, the physical protection of government departments, munitions factories and other important targets, the control of aliens and suspected persons, the censorship of communications and guidance to the Press – which were designed to prevent espionage, sabotage, subversion and the leakage of information to the enemy. This comprehensive system was operated by government departments, the Police, public utilities and industry, guided and helped by MI 5 which had itself recommended the establishment of many of the controls. Although it was directly responsible for the capture of very few of the agents despatched to the United Kingdom, it provided the indispensable foundation for B Division's work. 'The really great asset of a security system', Petrie told the Home Office in 1943, 'is the fact that it exists and not what it does'. The British and the Germans had both built up the same sort of very extensive security control system: this seldom caught spies but it compelled the opposition 'to work round and through the inevitable gaps'.

Within MI 5, Petrie's re-organisation in the spring of 1941 had freed B Division to concentrate on counter-espionage. C Division was responsible for vetting, D for travel control and munitions security and E for the control of aliens. F Division studied Fascist and Communist activities. The main operational sections of B Division were grouped in B1. They were supported by sections

---

* See below, p 188.

handling peripheral counter-espionage enquiries and liaison with the RSS and the censorship authorities, and B1 had facilities, some of which were outside B Division, for the physical surveillance of suspects, the investigation of suspicious incidents in co-operation with the Police, and the operation of agents.

Section B1A was responsible, as we have seen, for the double-cross operations and for MI 5's participation in their by-product, the management of deception. The primary role of the double-cross agents in the deception programme, and the publicity it has received, should not obscure the fact that the double-cross system was originally set up for counter-espionage purposes – or the fact that the system's contribution to counter-espionage was immense and continuous from 1941 to the end of the war. It enabled MI 5 to be increasingly confident from that date that it controlled all German agents in the United Kingdom. It limited the Abwehr's attacks not only by frustrating the enemy's actual undertakings, but also by persuading him that he had a good espionage network in Britain when none actually existed. It threw much light on the Abwehr's order of battle and communications, including its cyphers, and gave some guidance about the enemy's intentions.

Section B1B received, analysed and exploited for counter-intelligence purposes information from all sources, including that obtained by B1A. The other sources were the interrogations at the LRC and Camp 020, Censorship, the SIS and, most valuable of all, Sigint in the shape of the ISOS traffic. In view of its centralising function, B1B was the steering section for the whole of B Division. It superintended all espionage investigations, briefed and guided the interrogators, decided in conjunction with B1A whether or not a spy was to be used as a double-cross agent, and arranged with the Home Office and, when appropriate, the Director of Public Prosecutions whether spies were to be detained or put on trial. But it delegated these responsibilities in three particular areas to specialised sections set up in 1941 to counter the Abwehr's activities: the Iberian peninsula and among the Spanish, Portuguese and Latin American communities in the United Kingdom (B1G); Eire (B1H); alien merchant seamen and, later, the staff of civil airlines (B1L).*

Section B1C collated all information and experience relating to the methods and aims of the Abwehr in its sabotage operations. It distributed this intelligence to the appropriate authorities in co-operation with the MI 5 section concerned with munitions security. It also used its specialist knowledge to help the Police to

---

* The work of B1L proved unrewarding – it did not lead to the detention of any agents – and it was greatly reduced during 1943.

carry out their formal duty of investigating cases of suspected sabotage and to advise the RSLOs, who were responsible for reporting all suspected cases in the United Kingdom to MI 5. It was responsible beyond the United Kingdom for training guards for ships in Spanish ports and for advising the security authorities in Gibraltar. From 1942 it collaborated with the FBI and the Canadian authorities in countering the threat of sabotage in north America, and thereafter extended its advice to other theatres.

To meet the reliance of its sections on information which had to be handled under strict precautions – the files of captured spies and double-cross agents and the ISOS material – B Division established a special registry, separate from MI 5's central registry, and an associated research section (B1 Information). In the second half of the war these came to be recognised in the intelligence community as providing the most comprehensive and best organised of all records on German intelligence in western Europe. The SIS, however, continued to regard MI 5's efforts in these directions as excessively meticulous.

SIS's Section V, which had consisted of three officers at headquarters and two overseas at the outbreak of war, had increased only slowly to 12 at headquarters and 12 overseas by the summer of 1942; and even this expansion had incurred the criticism that the SIS was developing counter-espionage at the expense of its work on obtaining operational intelligence for the Services. But Section V expanded rapidly thereafter. It had some 60 officers at home and about the same number abroad in 1944.

Its headquarters staff was distributed between six geographical sub-sections and sub-sections dealing with the double-cross agents and deception, enemy espionage communications, Soviet espionage and Communism,* the protection of the SIS itself against penetration and, from the end of 1943 in conjunction with BSC, German trans-Atlantic smuggling of strategic materials. The overseas staff in Europe was confined to Portugal, Spain, Turkey and Sweden – Switzerland, the only other country open for operations, being left untouched.

□

Of the several sources of information on which MI 5 and the SIS were both dependent, Sigint surpassed all others in the importance of its contribution. The SIS controlled the production of ISOS and, through Section V, the elucidation and distribution of the decrypts.

---

* This sub-section had become a separate Section IX by March 1944.

The shared interest of MI 5 and the SIS in the work of the RSS, the source of much friction until the middle of 1942, produced little disagreement after that date. The MI 5/SIS Wireless Committee set up in 1941 had been a far from unanimous body.* In December 1942, however, the SIS and MI 5 agreed that it should be replaced by two new committees, a high-level committee to decide major questions affecting RSS policy and a committee at working level. The former, the Radio Security Committee, was established in March 1943 as a standing committee of the Security Executive responsible for co-ordinating the interests of the SIS and MI 5 in the RSS and for supervising radio security. It met only twice before the end of the war because the new working level committee proved to be effective in solving most problems that arose. Known as the Radio Security Intelligence Conference, chaired by B Division and with representatives from Section V of the SIS, GC and CS, the RSS and the Service intelligence departments, the working level committee met fortnightly to settle interception priorities and discuss any question relating to the production and use of the ISOS material.

Within this framework the administrative and technical development of the RSS, which had made great strides from the time it was transferred to the SIS in May 1941, encountered few difficulties. At the peak of its expansion it had a staff of 2,094: 98 officers, 1,317 operators, 83 engineers and 471 administrative personnel on a War Establishment, and 125 civilian clerks. In addition, it employed some 1,200 voluntary interceptors in the United Kingdom. It maintained intercept units in the Middle East and, to cover traffic in Latin America, in the United States under the auspices of the BSC. Almost half of the resources were engaged on the interception of known German intelligence and security service traffic. The remainder were divided between general search staff, responsible for recording unidentified traffic, and the Discrimination Section, which used its elaborate records to distinguish between suspicious and innocent intercepts. In all its activities the RSS achieved a high and continuingly increasing degree of efficiency.

At the level of decryption the policy of concentrating all the work at GC and CS caused no dissension, and the arrangements made there presented few problems. From the time when GC and CS broke the Abwehr's hand cypher at the end of 1940, and even more so from the end of 1941, when GC and CS broke the Enigma used by the Abwehr for communications between Berlin and the control stations in occupied and neutral countries, the volume and

---

* See above, pp 131–132.

the value of its contribution were enormous.

The number of ISOS decrypts circulated by GC and CS, which had risen from 30 to 70 a day during 1941, increased steadily to over 200 by December 1942 and was 282 at its peak in May 1944. In all, some 268,000 decrypts were issued during the war, 97,000 from the Abwehr's hand cypher (ISOS) which was used by its local networks, 140,000 from the Enigma (ISK), 13,000 from the SD (ISOSICLE)* and the remainder from minor sources. The decrypts were being obtained from the traffic of 78 German stations by the end of 1941, and of 147 stations by the end of 1942. They constituted a very large proportion of the total German traffic, especially of the most important part of it that used the Enigma, from the beginning of 1942 to the end of the war.

GC and CS did not achieve this output without interruptions. From time to time, especially from May 1943, the Germans brought in new security measures which reduced and delayed decryption. But the interruptions were not prolonged, not least because of help received from double-cross agents on cyphers used in the Iberian peninsula (*Garbo* May 1943), in France (*Brutus* and *Treasure* autumn 1944) and by the mobile intelligence and security units attached to German field armies in early 1945.†

ISOS repaid its debt to the double-cross organisation by yielding a considerable amount of intelligence about other means of communication used by the enemy's espionage system – secret inks, cover addresses – and about its radio procedures.

With this invaluable assistance the information from double-cross and other captured agents and defectors about every aspect of German espionage came to rival in bulk and comprehensiveness the product of ISOS itself. But ISOS remained the principal source of the comprehensive knowledge of the personnel, the organisation, the order of battle and the objectives of the Abwehr which was the key to the success of the Allies in defeating the enemy's efforts, and particularly to their ability to conduct double-cross operations on a large scale over so long a period of time. It was from the decrypts that they obtained advance warning of the enemy's undertakings, such as those for observing shipping move-

---

* The SD did not make much use of the Enigma before the middle of 1943, and very little of the traffic was read. All the traffic between Berlin and Rome was read from that date until the SD brought a new machine into force from early in 1944. As the traffic remained slight, virtually none of it was readable for the rest of the war except, irregularly, on the link with Turkey. Most SD decrypts were thus obtained from the SD's hand cyphers. These were more difficult than those of the Abwehr, so that the supply of SD decrypts was always less than that of Abwehr decrypts.

† For further information on the assistance to GC and CS against the new security measures given by double agents and the mobile intelligence and security agents see below, pp 226, 235, 266–267, 274, 383.

ments in the Straits of Gibraltar and sabotaging ships in Gibraltar and Spanish and north African ports, and advance notice of his plans for acting against Allied agents or establishing stay-behind networks as he withdrew from Italy and western Europe. And it was the decrypts which provided checks on the loyalty and veracity of the double agents who were in direct touch with the Germans, such as *Tricycle* and *Zigzag*, and evidence of the reception the Germans were giving to the intelligence they received from the double-cross system, including that which was sent to them for deception purposes. At the W Board's last meeting in May 1945 the chairman of the Twenty Committee told it that, but for ISOS, 'none of this work . . . would have been possible . . . It was vital to double-cross work'.

Notwithstanding the comprehensiveness and the continuity of the ISOS traffic, the elucidation and interpretation of the contents of the decrypts frequently encountered difficulties. Over and above the facts that individual texts might be corrupt or form only part of a wider exchange of which the remainder was not available, the German intelligence services made extensive use of code names for individuals, countries, towns, organisations, projects and even pieces of equipment; and their elucidation called not only for the maintenance of a meticulous ISOS index but also for collation with other sources of information.* With the transfer of the RSS to the SIS in 1941 the RSS's Analysis Bureau, which had been set up to deal with these problems, was placed under Section V, though remaining geographically distant from it, as Section V(W). Its unhappy relations with Section V represented the only serious exception to the smooth conduct of Sigint operations after the autumn of 1942. In its search for assistance with the elucidation of the ISOS material and its anxiety to ensure that maximum circulation was given to the results, it thereafter fought a running battle against Section V's determination to deny it contacts with GC and CS, MI 5, the Service intelligence departments and other bodies outside the SIS – a battle sustained by personal animosities which was brought to an end only with the removal of the Analysis Bureau from Section V and its establishment as a separate section of the SIS (the Radio Intelligence Section) in the summer of 1943.

☐

---

* To give one example. On 7 August 1942 the Abwehr in Lisbon signalled Berlin that the agent *Palmolive* had reported meeting the *Queen Elizabeth* on 3 August at position 18°E, 34°S. A reference to the Admiralty showed that the only ship near the *Queen Elizabeth* at that position was the SS *Lourenço Marques*. On 3 June 1943 Lisbon informed Hamburg that SS *Ambriz* with *Palmolive* was among the Red Cross ships working for the Abwehr. The only name common to the crew lists of the *Lourenço Marques* in 1942 and the *Ambriz* in 1943 was that of the first officer.

The intelligence about the Abwehr's procedures and plans derived from the decryption and analysis of ISOS material and the traffic of the double agents contributed enormously to the efficiency of the LRC and Camp 020 as obstacles to the enemy's attempts to infiltrate agents into the United Kingdom, while they added yet more information about the enemy's organisation from their detection and interrogation of suspects.*

The LRC saw all aliens arriving as bona fide visitors or escapers.† They numbered between 7,000 and 9,000 a year from 1941, the bulk being Norwegian escapers and arrivals from the French colonies that had adhered to de Gaulle and from liberated north Africa, but with an increasing flow of French, Dutch, Belgian and Polish escapers from western Europe after 1942. In these circumstances the screening could not be absolutely reliable; and many of those detained for close examination had been identified as agents by ISOS or the double-cross system before their arrival. But only three agents are known to have escaped scrutiny. Of those detained, on the other hand, more than 50 confessed. Over and above the intelligence obtained from them, the LRC collected from the multitude of innocent visitors a steady supply of information about occupied Europe for the SIS, which maintained officers at the LRC, and for the Services and government departments which were represented by officers from MI 19. Most suspects detained for close examination were sent to Camp 020.‡ Between the autumn of 1940 and the end of the war 390 people suspected of espionage were sent there, as compared with the 70 taken before that date who were made up of the British and foreign Fifth Column internees and of suspects detained by the French and brought to the United Kingdom at the time of Dunkirk. Of the 390, 50 of them were released as innocent. About 100 were agents aimed at the United Kingdom, 120 were agents aimed at overseas targets,§ and 120 were persons captured in Europe after D-day and suspected of association with the enemy's espionage and security services. Only five undoubted agents resisted making any kind of confession, and in only the same small number of cases was it impossible to reach a firm conclusion.

□

* See Appendix 10 for the techniques employed at the LRC and Camp 020.

† But from November 1944 only aliens arriving direct from enemy territory, or via Sweden, Switzerland and the Iberian peninsula, were sent to the LRC as a matter of course. Before that date the only exemptions were for certain specified categories – aliens travelling on diplomatic passports; aliens arriving under the auspices of government departments; Allied military personnel; accredited agents of the SIS and, until early in 1943, of the SOE.

‡ Women were not detained at Camp 020 but several were interrogated there or at Holloway Prison by Camp 020 officers.

§ In June 1942, at MI 5's insistence, powers were taken to enable suspects to be detained on colonial territory and brought to Camp 020 for examination.

The primary function of the Censorship was preventive: to stop all communications which might disclose valuable information to enemy states. Its secondary function was to collect any information that might be of value to the Allied powers. In exercising both functions, however, the Censorship naturally gave priority to detecting communications that might be related to enemy espionage. It early developed a method of sorting the mails which enabled it to make a systematic examination of the most suspect categories of correspondence, and was soon subjecting a small part of every day's mail to random testing for secret writing. But its labours in these directions remained unproductive until early in 1941 for lack of co-operation from MI 5.

Despite its initial scepticism about the benefits it might obtain from the work of the RSS,* MI 5 believed in the early months of the war that enemy agents would use wireless as their principal means of communication, and that the interception of secret writing, if that was used at all, was unlikely to be of much importance for counter-intelligence purposes.[10] Partly on this account, and partly because it was reluctant to impart sensitive information to the Postal and Telegraph Censorship Department, its relations with the censorship authorities were distant until evidence from captured agents and ISOS showed conclusively from early in 1941 that the Germans were relying heavily on secret writing. It was this evidence which persuaded MI 5 of the need to take the censorship authorities into its confidence and establish close collaboration with them. In March 1941 it finally accepted an invitation from them to appoint an MI 5 representative at Censorship Headquarters to be responsible for making available all secret information and for selecting censored material for distribution to MI 5 and, through MI 5, to the SIS.

The discovery through the double agents *Tricycle* and *Rainbow* in the summer of 1941 that the Abwehr was using micro-dots for its communications further emphasised the importance of close relations between the Censorship and MI 5, and from that date MI 5 made every effort to ensure that all intelligence obtained from captured agents, double agents and ISOS was used to maintain the efficiency of the censorship system.

The contribution of the Censorship to counter-espionage was comparatively small in the United Kingdom, where MI 5 was so well served by GC and CS, the RSS, the double-cross system, the LRC and Camp 020. Only one agent there (Laureyssens)† was detected and captured solely as a result of censorship. But the

---

* See above, pp 72–73.
† For Laureyssens see above, p 95 and Appendix 7.

work of its chemists played an important part in the case of de Menezes* and it helped to frustrate German plans to use POW mail for espionage purposes.

There was more scope for its assistance overseas. The censorship of mail between Eire and the continent led to the identification of some of the agents who were being prepared for operations in Ireland. Censorship provided leads to more than a score of the agents who were convicted in the United States. It was largely on its evidence that the Allies were able in June 1942 to establish checks on the mail carried between Brazil and Europe by the Pan-American Airways 'Lati – substitute' service,† and it played a large part in unmasking the German espionage organisation in the Argentine, Brazil, Mexico and elsewhere in Latin America.[11]‡ The Anglo-Iraqi censorship was similarly effective in the Middle East, especially in the investigation of the Ratl organisation.§ The South African censorship was instrumental in securing the capture of an agent who had landed in Angola.[12]

The value of this work was recognised in August 1943 when representatives of the Imperial Censorship and the US, Canadian and South African Censorships met in Miami to discuss 'the development ... of a better appreciation of censorship as a counter-espionage weapon'. As a result of this conference the British and US authorities established counter-intelligence officers for the first time at a number of their censorship stations. In September 1944 the Australian Censorship joined the other censorship authorities at a conference in Quebec to consider the improvement of their counter-intelligence arrangements against Japan.[13]

□

During 1943 even the tortuous problem of relations between MI 5 and the SIS with BSC and the US authorities on security matters was resolved. We have seen‖ that in the autumn of 1942 MI 5 persuaded 'C' and the Chairman of the Security Executive that BSC should represent MI 5 in the United States and that an MI 5 officer should be attached to BSC to participate in liaison with the FBI on counter-espionage and to handle liaison with Canada. However, at the beginning of December Hoover appointed an FBI officer as an attaché to the US embassy in

---

* See above, pp 110–111.
† See above, p 144n.
‡ See above, pp 158–159 and below, pp 202–203.
§ See below, p 210.
‖ See above, pp 147–148.

London 'to assist in maintaining the liaison that is being established between the FBI and MI 5'. Thereupon Petrie proposed acceding to the FBI's wish for direct and exclusive liaison with MI 5 by posting its own representative to Washington.

The question was discussed in April 1943 at the first meeting of the new Secret Service Co-ordinating Committee.[14]* It was then decided that, while it appeared to be desirable for MI 5 to establish direct liaison with the FBI by appointing a representative to Washington, the SIS should first send an officer to the USA to review BSC's counter-espionage activities. That officer returned with a favourable report on BSC's work. He argued, with strong support from Sir Edwin Herbert who had also been in Washington, that it was most undesirable to divide the representation there of the British clandestine services, and in July the Secret Service Co-ordinating Committee accordingly decided at its second, and final, meeting to suspend the decision to appoint an MI 5 representative while a compromise was worked out.[15] The compromise eventually arrived at in September 1943 was that MI 5 should be represented in Washington neither by BSC nor by an MI 5 appointment. Its liaison with the FBI was to be through the FBI's representative in London – this to be supplemented by visits to the United States made with the agreement of BSC, particularly by the MI 5 officer posted to Canada in December 1942.† Hoover, 'although somewhat disappointed' that no MI 5 officer was to be stationed in Washington, acquiesced. An active liaison was maintained in London and the MI 5 representative in Canada made frequent visits to Washington. The business handled through these channels was predominantly concerned with counter-espionage. BSC's Security Division continued to transact a substantial volume of routine work, particularly vetting, on behalf of MI 5.

Meanwhile an agreement had been reached in December 1942 between the SIS and the newly established Office of Strategic Services (OSS) for full co-operation on counter-espionage between Section V and OSS's counter-espionage division, X2, in London and at overseas stations. Representatives of X2 joined Section V in March 1943 and a mutually profitable liaison developed.

Section V also had important liaisons with the intelligence and security services of the European Allies and with the Turks in the Middle East. In addition, considerations of convenience and efficiency led to direct contacts between MI 5 and these services on such matters as the examination and disposal of spies and visitors

---

* See above, pp 172–173.
† See above, p 146.

at the LRC and on administrative problems in the handling of double-cross agents, for example *Brutus*. A suggestion that an attempt should be made by MI 5 to establish liaison with the Russian security authorities was not pursued after 'C' had advised that it would be 'a waste of effort and an embarrassment', the Russians being 'more interested in penetrating our intelligence than in helping'. This was borne out when informal contacts were developed in Tehran between the DSO Persia and Russian security officers. Some practical collaboration was achieved while hostilities lasted, but blatant attempts were made to recruit members of the DSO's staff as agents.

□

By the beginning of 1943 the SIS had appointed counter-intelligence representatives in all the countries to which SIME had expanded except Cyrenaica and Tripolitania. Relations between the two networks remained good, both in Cairo and at the out-stations. But SIME persisted with its campaign for amalgamation with MI 5. In February 1943 it formally requested MI 5 to press for the change despite having been advised that, since MI 5 had a charter for security work only within British territory and the SIS was responsible for security intelligence in foreign countries, its staff should 'count it as a considerable blessing that they were not territorially limited, and had been enabled, owing to their responsibility to the Commander-in-Chief, Middle East, to establish their representatives in such territories as Turkey, Syria, Persia and Iraq'. Its arguments were that its DSOs regarded themselves as MI 5 representatives – a position which in fact belonged only to the DSOs in Egypt, Aden and Malta* – and that it should look ahead to the time when, after the war, Britain would be in de facto control of most of the Middle East and MI 5 would be the appropriate security authority. But Petrie again refused to take the initiative; he remained reluctant to disturb arrangements that were working tolerably well, apprehensive of the constitutional, financial and personnel difficulties that would be encountered by any attempt to change them and – with respect to SIME's post-war ambitions – unable to see how MI 5 could 'survive on foreign soil after the war'.

In July 1943, following the transmutation of MEIC into the Middle East Political Intelligence Centre, SIME at last achieved its

---

* Except for a brief period when he was nominally under SIME the DSO Malta reported directly to MI 5. In addition to his normal responsibilities to the Services, he was Secretary for Public Security with responsibility for the Police.

transfer from GHQ to the Middle East Defence Committee and recognition of its special relationship with MI 5.* A charter approved by the MEDC described it as 'an inter-Service body responsible to the Defence Committee for all Civil Security and Counter-Intelligence work in the Middle East with the exception of operational theatres', noting that civil security comprised 'the provision of intelligence on political, tribal and minority activities and approved executive action thereon', and that counter-intelligence included 'the investigation, detection, penetration and prosecution . . . of enemy espionage, sabotage and propaganda organisations'. The charter added that 'SIME, although not administered by MI 5, acts on their behalf . . . and receives directions as to general security matters and policy from the Director General'.[16] At the same time, a charter imposing similar responsibilities on CICI† stated that in view of the need for co-ordination between the Middle East and Persia and Iraq Commands, CICI would receive directions on policy and methods from SIME.[17] Like SIME, the CICI thereafter became more closely associated with MI 5. Except that in March 1944 the membership and terms of reference of the JIC (Middle East), which had hitherto confined itself to operational intelligence, were extended to enable it to supervise the work of SIME and some other non-operational bodies, the charters of July 1943 fixed the security arrangements in the Middle East for the remainder of the war.[18]

The establishment of deception channels for 'A' Force had been by no means the only reason for establishing SIME's Special Section in April 1942.‡ Increasingly from that date, however, deception had absorbed SIME's attention. In December 1942 the head of 'A' Force persuaded SIME and the SIS to agree to the establishment of 'Thirty Committees' in Cairo, Beirut and at other centres to control 'special agents' – defined as real or notional agents that were to be used primarily for deceiving the enemy rather than for penetrating his intelligence organisation. These committees consisted of representatives of 'A' Force (chairman), SIME and the SIS, and policy control rested with the head of 'A' Force, subject to the provisos that SIME must be consulted about the counter-espionage implications of any operation and that SIME and the SIS must decide whether any agent was used for deception purposes.

By the beginning of 1943 MI 5 was critical of SIME for subordinating its counter-espionage activities not only to the collection of political and tribal intelligence but also to deception

---

* See above, pp 151–153.
† See above, p 152.
‡ See above, p 153.

operations; it believed that the deception programme had been of scarcely any value for counter-espionage purposes, and that it had induced SIME to neglect the development of adequate machinery for extracting security intelligence from the examination of new arrivals in the occupied Middle East from enemy or neutral territory (about 1,000 a month, mainly through Turkey) and the interrogation of captured agents and major suspects.* In the spring MI 5 took measures to rectify these short-comings, sending the head of the LRC temporarily to the Middle East, appointing an officer from Camp 020 to be SIME's chief interrogation officer and persuading SIME to post examination staff to the refugee camps run by the Armed Forces Intelligence Organisation in Syria and Cyprus and to the Middle East CSDIC at Maadi. It took time for these measures to take effect; examination and interrogation were not fully organised until the spring of 1944.

---

* The examination of travellers was still being carried out by the Armed Forces Intelligence Organisation, which had little interest, and no expertise, in security questions.

CHAPTER 11: REFERENCES

1. Future of the Secret Services, May 1943 – January 1945 (Unregistered file held in Private Office of the Secretary of the Cabinet).
2. CAB 101/243, PM Minute 231/3 of 4 April 1943.
3. Future of the Secret Services.
4. ibid.
5. ibid.
6. ibid.
7. ibid.
8. ibid.
9. ibid.
10. DEFE 1/333, *History of the Postal and Telegraph Censorship Department 1938–1946*, paras 1055, 1063.
11. ibid, paras 206, 246–248.
12. DEFE 1/334, *History of the Postal and Telegraph Censorship Department*, Appendix 22.
13. DEFE 1/333, paras 794–797.
14. Future of the Secret Services.
15. ibid.
16. Mockler-Ferryman, *Military Intelligence Organisation*, Appendix H.
17. ibid, Appendix G.
18. ibid, p 160.

CHAPTER 12

Counter-Espionage Operations in the United Kingdom and Overseas from the Beginning of 1943 to Mid-1944

T HE ABWEHR persisted in its attempts to introduce new agents into the United Kingdom, Eire and Iceland until the middle of 1944. But there were no innovations in the methods it employed and there was no improvement in the results it obtained. Except that in the spring of 1944 a special effort was made to penetrate Iceland, seven agents in three separate parties being despatched there by sea,* the agents all arrived in the guise of escapers from occupied territory or were dropped by parachute. So far as could be judged at the time – and no subsequent evidence has cast serious doubt on this conclusion – only one of them evaded early detection.

The exception was Pierre Neukermans, a Belgian and one of the ostensible escapers.† He arrived at Poole by air from Lisbon in July 1943; he had been sent on to Lisbon after reporting to the British Consul at Barcelona that he had escaped across the Pyrenees with two other Belgians. He made a good impression on the Immigration Officer and the SCO, and the examiners at the LRC accepted his story. He was accordingly released to the Belgian authorities and given employment in their Ministry of Agriculture in London. In December, however, when the SIS had reported from Lisbon that another Belgian using the same escape route had claimed that every group using the route contained one German agent, he was taken into custody and interrogated at Camp 020. On 8 February 1944 he made a partial confession. He had been recruited by the Abwehr early in 1941, trained in radio and secret writing and eventually driven across the Spanish frontier by the Abwehr, which had briefed him on the escape route he was to say he had followed and provided him with matches for secret writing and cover addresses in Lisbon and

---

* A single agent had been landed by U-boat in Iceland in September 1943. He had at once given himself up and was recruited to the double-cross system as *Beetle*. See below, pp 196, 218.

† See Appendix 11(i) for details of some of the other agents in this category who were intercepted in this period.

Belgium. He admitted that since arriving in England he had written two letters to a Lisbon address, but had sent no secret messages; claimed that he had had no intention of helping the Germans; and offered to do all he could to help the British authorities.

Unfortunately for him, the details of this confession identified him as an agent who had figured in ISOS decrypts in the summer of 1942 under the cover-name *Fred*, and the decrypt of an ISOS message sent from Madrid to Berlin in December 1943 indicated that his two letters had been sent not to Lisbon, but to Barcelona. When interrogated again he admitted that he had also been given a cover address in Barcelona, to which he had sent eight or nine letters in secret writing with information either obtained from Belgian contacts or the newspapers, or invented by himself, about the location of Belgian troops, the numbers of French and US troops, the sailing of convoys and public morale. He thought the information was of no importance and, as he had been unable to carry out instructions to obtain a radio set, he had had no replies from the Germans.* He was convicted under the Treachery Act and hanged in June 1944.

Of the agents who were dropped by parachute – four in all – the first was Nicolay Hansen, a Norwegian coalminer, who landed in Aberdeenshire on the night of 30 September 1943.† The fourth, who was also the last German agent to arrive during the war, landed in June 1944. This was *Zigzag*; he had returned to Germany in April 1943 after carrying out his notionally successful sabotage attack on the de Havilland factory at Hatfield.‡ In between these arrivals two Eire nationals with IRA connections, who had been in the Channel Islands at the time of the German occupation, were dropped by parachute in Eire with two radio sets on the nights of 15 and 16 December 1943 – John Francis O'Reilly, who had worked for the Irish section of the Berlin radio station since September 1941 and had been recruited by the Abwehr the following June, and John Kenny, who had been working for the Germans in the Channel Islands as a driver. Both were arrested almost at once. Their arrival had not been entirely unexpected. O'Reilly had corresponded freely with Eire and a special censorship watch on mail to and from Irishmen on the continent had been maintained since July 1941, when *Basket* (also an Eire citizen

---

* Interrogated after the war, his Abwehr controller stated that he had been employed since 1939, if not earlier, had been very pro-German and had pressed to be given a mission in England. About 12 letters had been received from him in England; with the exception of one letter, rated good, the information in them had been assessed as bad to satisfactory.

† For details see Appendix 11(ii).

‡ See above, p 120, and below, pp 219–220.

recruited in Jersey) had given the British authorities a full account of himself.*

It turned out that O'Reilly had been taken over from the Abwehr by the SD, and that, in addition to collecting naval and military information, he had the political mission of reporting on the state of the British political scene. In particular he was to try to infiltrate the Independent Labour Party in Glasgow, which the SD believed was supporting an underground movement to overthrow the government, and to obtain information about the Scottish and Welsh nationalists.

The arrival of O'Reilly and Kenny coincided with a British request to the Eire government that it should require the German legation in Dublin to surrender its radio transmitter, and their capture strengthened the British case. In the middle of 1941, when it was established that the German legation in Dublin was in regular radio contact with Germany, British representations had persuaded the Eire government to tell the German Minister that he could not be allowed to use his transmitter. The legation had not been heard on the air again until February 1942, when it transmitted what were assumed to be weather reports during the passage of the *Scharnhorst* and the *Gneisenau* from Brest through the Channel. The Eire government had then warned the Minister that further use of his set would bring British and American pressure for its surrender, and perhaps for the expulsion of the legation, and the set had since been silent. In January 1943, however, the Allies broke the German diplomatic cypher and the decrypts of the traffic between the legation and Berlin had disclosed that in October 1942, while refusing requests from Berlin to resume transmissions, the Minister had undertaken to do so if he obtained any vital operational intelligence. This exchange had taken place during the Allied preparations for Operation *Torch*, and anxiety about the transmitter increased with the progress of planning for *Overlord* from October 1943 – the more so as the decrypts revealed that Berlin was pressing the legation for information about Allied intentions. The capture of O'Reilly and Kenny on 16 and 19 December occurred when the authorities were considering how to approach the Eire government, and it helped to persuade the Dublin authorities to accede to the request that the legation should be required to hand over the transmitter. It was later learned that the Minister complained to the German Foreign Office, begging that no more agents should be sent, and that the SD was severely reprimanded for undertaking O'Reilly's disastrous mission.

---

* See above, p 92.

In April 1944, prompted no doubt by their anxieties about *Overlord* and their suspicion that the Allied invasion plans included a diversionary attack on Norway, the Germans made an equally ineffective attempt to infiltrate agents into Iceland. Two Icelanders, trained radio operators who had instructions to report on the weather and on military and shipping movements, landed from a motor-boat on 17 April. They at once gave themselves up, having dumped their transmitters overboard before landing. Two others followed suit as soon as they were landed from a U-boat on 25 April; they had been given the same mission. A third party – a German and two Icelanders – came ashore from a U-boat on 30 April. They were captured within a few days and sent to Camp 020, where they were at first unco-operative but eventually made confessions. They had arrived with radio sets, codes and a large sum of money, which they concealed on landing, and with instructions to report on airfields and other army, navy and air installations, on shipping and on the weather. Two of them had been trained in sabotage by a man who spoke German with an English accent; and from their description and with the help of photographs he was identified as *Zigzag*.

☐

The successful interception of these new arrivals supported the conclusion that there was no serious penetration of the home base (the United Kingdom with Eire and Iceland), as did the even more significant evidence supplied by the continuing availability of ISOS decrypts and the flow of communications between the double agents and their controls in Germany. But apart from the fact that, in the nature of things, the confidence of the security authorities could not be unqualified, there remained two particular grounds for anxiety. The first was the threat to security in the United Kingdom, no less than to the activities of the Resistance movements in Europe, from the penetration of Allied clandestine networks in Europe by or with the assistance of double agents working for the enemy. The second – and for this the evidence came from ISOS itself – was the fact that a number of German agents were transmitting reports which appeared on investigation to be fictitious or concocted, but which raised the lingering suspicion that some spies had evaded the security net.

The threat from enemy double agents had been emphasised by the cases of Pelletier, *Victoire*, *Brutus* and Gulbrandsen in 1942.* They were followed by evidence of extensive German penetration

---

* See above, p 113, 117ff and Appendix 9.

of the Resistance organisations which prompted MI 5 early in 1943 to insist that accredited agents of SOE, who were exempted from interrogation at the LRC when they returned to the United Kingdom,* must be examined by an MI 5 officer as well as by SOE's security section if there was the slightest reason for suspecting that they had been in touch with the enemy. This additional precaution was activated in the case of Henri Déricourt at the end of 1943.

Déricourt, an airline pilot who had served with the French Air Force in 1939–1940, had escaped to England in 1942 and been recruited by the SOE. In 1943 he was dropped by parachute to take charge, under the alias *Gilbert*, of the organisation of clandestine landings in northern France, and a large number of successful landings were made under his management in the next ten months. Suspicions about his loyalty, or at least his security, were first raised in June 1943 but they were vigorously contested by the French section of SOE and it was only after prolonged argument that he was ordered to return to England. He arrived in February 1944 and was interrogated by the SOE security section and the attached MI 5 officer. The case against him rested mainly on statements supported by circumstantial evidence to the effect that *Gilbert* was one of the Gestapo's principal informants. MI 5 reported that interrogation had been very difficult because little of the adverse information could be used. Déricourt's antecedents seemed to be unexceptionable; he had made a good impression and had been firm in his denials. Nevertheless, serious suspicion remained. If SOE decided to take 'the considerable risk' of sending him back to the field any other department concerned should be warned that he was under suspicion and if there was any question of using him or his organisation in connection with D-day activities the Chiefs of Staff would have to be informed. SOE decided not to send him back to France.†

Meanwhile, the knowledge that MI 5's double agents were not alone in supplying the Abwehr with concocted reports from fictitious sources had become a source of grave anxiety. Time, labour and a considerable depth of material were required before it could be determined that the reports from these uncontrolled sources, which were drawn up with some skill and were usually at least plausible, were not the work of genuine agents. Even when it had been established that they were bogus, there was the continual risk that, either by contradicting what the Germans were learning

---

* See above, p 184 note †.
† For a fuller account of the Déricourt case see M R D Foot, *SOE in France* (1966), pp 290–305. In 1947 a French court martial acquitted him of intelligence with the enemy. However, his case has continued to be the subject of controversy.

from the controlled agents or by fortuitously hitting the truth, they would endanger the controlled agents and prejudice the Allied deception operations.

In the winter of 1941–1942 ISOS had revealed that an Abwehr out-station at Sofia known as the Dienststelle Klatt was forwarding daily to Vienna operational intelligence reports about the Russian front and on British dispositions in the Mediterranean and the Middle East. The reports on Russian matters were known as *Max*, those on British as *Moritz*. In 1942 *Max* reports had come in a steady, copious and increasing flow. In the four months ending in March 1942 between 260 and 300 such reports had been received and it was believed that the total number was considerably higher. In the same period there were 40 *Moritz* reports.

The sources of the reports and the channels through which they reached Sofia were a mystery. Examining the problem in August 1942 Section V had noted that both series had a professional flavour, being up to date, terse, well arranged and definite. The localities covered by *Max* reports stretched from Leningrad to Persia, those by *Moritz* reports from Syria through Iraq and Persia to Egypt and Libya. The Germans seemed to regard the *Max* reports as valuable. Section V had rejected the hypothesis that the intelligence was secured by the interception of Russian and British military, naval and air force radio communications. It tended to think that the *Max* reports were supplied by high-grade, well-placed agents on Russian soil using camouflaged radio links with Bulgaria. There were no clues to the sources of the *Moritz* reports.

In view of the inherent improbability that a large espionage network of the kind predicated could operate undetected behind the Russian lines and, in the case of the *Moritz* reports, of the failure to identify any suspect radio transmissions, the theory gained ground that *Max/Moritz* was a Russian double-cross operation. The importance of the *Max* reports was discounted and it was noted that the most striking feature of the *Moritz* reports was that they were at the same time detailed and for the most part so inaccurate that they seemed to be reasonably explained either as a deliberate attempt to deceive the Germans or as a concoction put out for mercenary reasons.

In the spring and summer of 1943 the assessment of the *Max* reports was radically revised. Study of *Max* messages led MI 14 to conclude that they had clearly been useful to the Germans in predicting Russian moves and contained practically nothing to support the theory of deliberate deception. There was ample evidence that the Germans considered the reports to be of great value. It was decided to inform the Russians and in October the SIS representative in Moscow handed over a summary of information. There was no reaction from the Russians and the *Max* reports continued until February 1945.

No doubt as a corollary to the change of view about the *Max* reports, in the spring of 1943 special arrangements were made in Cairo for a systematic check of the *Moritz* reports, including the posting by MI 5 of an officer from London to collaborate with the Section V analyst in studying the decrypts. During the next six months the veracity check confirmed the general inaccuracy of *Moritz* reports. Out of 49 reports received in June and July only five were considered to be of any value (being classified as either 'probable' or 'partly true'); 33 were useless ('untrue', 'nonsense', 'incorrect', 'improbable'); 11 had not been checked. No *Moritz* reports were transmitted in September and towards the end of the year they ceased altogether. Post-war interrogation of members of the Dienststelle Klatt left little doubt that the *Max* reports were a Russian-controlled operation based on the penetration of the White Russian circles which purported to supply Klatt with his intelligence. Klatt's principal source himself admitted that the *Moritz* reports were 'pure smoke' concocted in Sofia as an additional lure for the Abwehr.

By the autumn of 1943 attention was concentrated on two operators, one in Portugal and the other in Sweden, purporting to report intelligence obtained by agents in the United Kingdom. Paul Fidrmuc, alias *Ostro*, was a Czech businessman who had been in touch with the Abwehr for some years before he became a German subject as a result of the Munich agreement. In July 1940, after working for the Abwehr in Denmark and Rome, he had settled in Portugal under business cover and begun reporting to the Abwehr's headquarters in Berlin through its station in Lisbon. Between January and October 1942 the RSS had intercepted 37 *Ostro* reports on this channel. They purported to come from Egypt, South Africa, India, the United States and the United Kingdom, but it was soon clear that those dealing with the United Kingdom were not only all inaccurate but also elaborate inventions carefully planned to give the impression that they came from a well-placed team of agents. Nor was it long before the decrypts showed that the Abwehr believed that *Ostro* had four or five agents in England, communicating with him in secret writing, and regarded him as one of their best sources.

In September 1943 the Twenty Committee discussed the threat from *Ostro's* activities to the Allied deception programme with the Controlling Officer for Deception, suggesting that some way should be found to eliminate or discredit him. No action had proved possible by February 1944 when MI 5, alarmed at the danger he presented in view of the approach of Operation *Overlord* – and aware that it would be extremely difficult to discredit him in view of his high reputation with the Abwehr –

believed that he might be eliminated or brought under control if a direct approach were made to him. But again nothing was done, and at the beginning of June MI 5's misgivings were vindicated by the receipt of a report from *Ostro* which contained among much erroneous detail the information that the cross-Channel attack favoured by the Allies was 'an assault on the Manche [Cherbourg] peninsula'. Although the report produced no detectable effect on Germany's appreciations, it created alarm in London.* Discussion about what to do about *Ostro* was resumed; it went on until 20 June, when it was decided to defer any action in view of the fact that the threat he presented was steadily declining.

Besides being the channel for *Ostro's* confections, the Abwehr station in Lisbon originated its own. Two series of fraudulent reports from it to Berlin were intercepted, one claiming to be obtained from Portuguese consulates in the United Kingdom and the other purporting to come from the British embassy in Lisbon. An officer attached to the station who worked semi-independently also sent fictitious messages, alleging that they were based on the work of Swiss agents in the United Kingdom. These reports were less troublesome than *Ostro's*, but others which in the end proved to be more so came to light in the autumn of 1943. OSS in Switzerland obtained copies of authentic telegrams sent to the German Foreign Office from the diplomatic mission in Stockholm. These were ascribed to agents named *Josephine* and *Hektor* who were apparently in England. *Josephine's* were about shipping and naval matters. *Hektor's* contained statements allegedly made by Sir Stafford Cripps, Minister of Aircraft Production, about the production of four-engined bombers and extracts from a discussion between Cripps, the CAS (Portal) and the AOC-in-C Bomber Command (Harris) about round-the-clock bombing. They were signed by Kraemer, an Abwehr officer who was known to have been posted to Stockholm under diplomatic cover towards the end of 1942 and who had been identified under three cover-names in the ISOS decrypts. Similar messages then appeared with increasing frequency among the ISOS decrypts.

The first impression that the messages represented an alarming leakage of information did not survive close scrutiny of them. Like *Ostro's* they were a mixture of speculation, which was not unintelligent, and factual statements, which were almost always either wrong or of low intelligence value. Exceptionally, some of their information about aircraft production figures was accurate, and Kraemer provided details of a contact he claimed to know in the

---

* See Hinsley et al, *British Intelligence in the Second World War*, Vol III Part 2 (1988), pp 43, 61.

Ministry of Aircraft Production. Like *Ostro* he caused anxiety during the run-up to *Overlord*, reporting in February 1944 that on account of Allied disagreements the second front had been postponed till June.* But rigorous enquiries failed to identify the source in the Ministry; the dates of the reports ruled out the use of the Swedish diplomatic bag or the Swedish airline; and the RSS was confident that it was missing no illicit transmissions. MI 5 accordingly concluded that the Kraemer network was fictitious, and that his habit of attributing items of intelligence to Cripps, Sir Archibald Sinclair, the Secretary of State for Air, Portal and Harris was his way of building up the reputation of his notional agents. The SIS was not so sure.†

□

The first spy caught in Canada, who was also the first double agent (alias *Watchdog*) to be operated there, was arrested at the end of 1942. Although he had earlier lived for some time in Canada, he had quickly attracted the attention of the Police. But there had been no warning of his arrival early in November; he had been landed by U-boat on the coast of the Gaspe peninsula in Quebec.‡ When Alfred Langbein gave himself up to the Canadian authorities in 1944 it turned out that he, too, had been landed by U-boat in the spring of 1942 without any warning. He had arrived with several thousand dollars and a radio set and instructions to report on shipping movements, but had buried the radio set, which he handed over unused, and had lived quietly in Ottawa until his money ran out. These two men had arrived in the period from February to December 1942 in which GC and CS was unable to read the U-boat Enigma. From the beginning of 1943, when the regular reading of the Enigma made it less likely that landings from U-boats would go undetected, no more were reported until August 1944. Enigma decrypts then disclosed that a U-boat had been detailed to land spies in Maine, but had been sunk before she could accomplish the mission. In November the decrypts reported that another U-boat had put spies ashore in the United States.§ Other agents may have succeeded in arriving by U-boat both before and after the end of 1942. If they did, neither the RSS nor the Censorship intercepted any messages from them.

With valuable help from the Censorship, successful security operations meanwhile continued against other German agents

---

* See Hinsley et al, op cit. Vol III Part 2, p 51.
† See below, pp 276–278.
‡ For further details of *Watchdog's* activities in Canada see below, p 228.
§ See Hinsley et al, op cit, Vol III Part 2, p 487.

deployed in north and south America. When Bermuda was closed to neutral shipping in 1942 Trinidad became the focal point for the censorship of all mail between Europe and north and south America and also for the control of passenger traffic. In 1943 the Censorship staff at Trinidad was more than 400 strong. Among the cases dealt with were those of *Max* and von Rautter.

In January 1942 Bermuda had detected micro-dots in a letter from Mexico to Sweden. A score of other spy letters, eastbound and westbound, followed, some of those from Mexico being signed *Max*. The flow suddenly stopped and it was soon realised that this was because the Mexican Police had arrested a number of Germans, including *Max*. The case seemed to be over, but in November 1942 the Censorship intercepted another letter from Mexico containing micro-dots. Further interceptions confirmed that the network had been re-organised under a new leader to whom there was one reference in the earlier *Max* correspondence. Collaboration between the Censorship, BSC and the FBI led eventually to the identification of the new leader and several other members of the network, but for political and operational reasons no arrests were made. By the autumn of 1944 the network was moribund.

Another case, which had begun in April 1942 with the interception of a message in secret writing numbered 6 in a letter to a known Abwehr cover address, was only concluded in 1944. Further messages numbered up to 14 passed at monthly intervals until March 1943, but it took a most laborious investigation by the FBI to identify the writer in January 1944 as the son by an English mother of a Prussian named von Rautter. The son, who had become a US citizen, had visited Germany in 1940 when he had been pressurised by threats of what might happen to his relations into accepting an Abwehr mission, in pursuit of which he had returned to the United States via Mexico in April 1941. He was sentenced to a long term of imprisonment in July 1944.

The control of passengers at Port of Spain was also of great value to security. Beginning in September 1941 numerous suspects on their way to or from the Americas were intercepted in transit. Under emergency legislation enacted by the government of Trinidad a score of important cases were sent to Camp 020 for interrogation; others were interned in Trinidad. Nearly all the important cases stemmed from ISOS. The DSO, who was responsible for initiating action, had to take the greatest care to disguise the real grounds for his suspicions.

A case which led to the arrest of five other agents was that of Andreas Blay Pigrau, the Paraguayan Consul General at Barcelona. As a result of ISOS information he was detained at Trinidad in September 1942, when travelling to Buenos Aires on a ship of the Spanish Ybarra line. A search revealed that he was carrying an incriminating letter from Joaquin Baticon (a steward on the same ship) to a known German agent. Baticon was arrested in February 1943 when he next touched at Trinidad. Although he was not an important agent, he had had numerous contacts with the Abwehr and knew quite a lot about German intelligence activities in Spain, Cuba and the Argentine. His information led to the arrest at Trinidad, between June and August 1943, of three other Ybarra line employees who were Abwehr couriers and of the Secret Police Attaché at the Spanish embassy in Buenos Aires.

Another case which had important consequences was that of Oscar Hellmuth. An Argentine national of German origin, he had been known since 1942 as a principal German agent in Buenos Aires. In October 1943 he was despatched to Europe carrying a diplomatic passport, with a view to acting as an unofficial ambassador in Germany in the event of the severance of diplomatic relations between the two countries. His arrest at Trinidad provided the SIS with a peg on which to hang evidence from many secret sources about German activities in Argentina, and thus to bring pressure to bear upon the Argentine government to join the Allies. The arrest was also a severe blow to the Abwehr and probably contributed to its absorption by the RSHA in the summer of 1944.*

In addition to using seamen as couriers the Abwehr recruited agents on Spanish and Portuguese ships to report on shipping movements in the Atlantic. Increasingly from the beginning of 1943 it also used them to smuggle from the Americas strategic materials of small bulk and high value. Against these activities the SIS employed large numbers of its own observers on the ships, and did so with some success. In November and December 1943, with assistance from ISOS, two Spanish radio operators were arrested on the high seas. By July 1944 the observers had secured, in co-operation with the British and Dutch contraband controls at Curaçao, Trinidad and Gibraltar, the dismissal from employment on Spanish and Portuguese ships of some 60 smugglers. But neither smuggling nor intelligence gathering could be eliminated entirely so long as the Abwehr benefited from the connivance of the Spanish and Portuguese authorities. As late as the summer of 1944, as the security authorities were aware, no large Spanish ship crossed the Atlantic without an agent recruited by the Abwehr in Barcelona or Bilbao.

□

---

* See Appendix 1(iii).

Despite continual protests to the Spanish and Portuguese governments, enemy intelligence gathering and sabotage operations in the Iberian peninsula were maintained at a high level throughout 1943.

With Spanish assistance the Abwehr's coverage of shipping in the Straits of Gibraltar was little affected by the restrictions imposed on the *Bodden* reporting system following the representations made to General Franco in May 1942.* In August 1943, regular protests on the subject having culminated in another approach by the British Ambassador to Franco, the Spanish authorities raided the Abwehr's posts at Tangier and Ceuta, but they warned it to move to other locations before they acted. They expelled the Germans from their post at Algeciras in October 1943, but they continued to provide the Abwehr with their own shipping reports from the area.[1] Following the reprieve of Menezes† the Portuguese government agreed to make espionage by foreigners on Portuguese soil against third countries a criminal offence. It took no action against the Abwehr, however, until October 1943 despite British complaints that the Germans were reporting convoy movements from the Cape Vincent area. Acting on information supplied by the SIS, the Portuguese Police then discovered radio sets in the St Vincent lighthouse and a villa adjoining property belonging to Hans Bendixen, one of the more important of the Abwehr's representatives. Even then, Bendixen remained at large; the British Ambassador was still demanding his expulsion in December 1943.[2]

In 1942 there had been several attacks on shipping in Gibraltar by Italian naval units.‡ In two further attacks in May and August 1943 six merchant ships totalling over 40,000 tons were sunk or damaged. The British authorities knew from agents' reports that these attacks were shore-based, and must have been made with Spanish complicity. But they remained ignorant of the Italian organisation on the shores of the Bay, including the use of an Italian tanker, the *Olterra*, which had been scuttled in the Bay at the outbreak of war and later refloated by the Spaniards and moved to Algeciras, until after the Italian surrender, when a member of the *Olterra's* crew provided a full account of the campaign, and of the assistance it had received from Spanish officials. There was better intelligence about the Abwehr's sabotage campaign, which was carried out with mounting intensity up to the autumn of 1943. On this account, and thanks to improvements in the British counter-measures organisation, the Abwehr's

---

* See above, p 162, and Hinsley et al, op cit, Vol II (1981), Appendix 15.

† See above, p 111.

‡ See above, p 161.

efforts were largely frustrated, especially those against Gibraltar.

The staff of the DSO at Gibraltar was increased from September 1942, when a Security Intelligence Officer was appointed to assist him. By 1944 the DSO's staff numbered 15 officers and 115 other ranks. The SIO, whose own staff was reinforced from the beginning of 1943, succeeded in recruiting double agents among the group of saboteurs employed against Gibraltar by the Abwehr. Between November 1942 and August 1943 these informers – some of them ruffians interested only in making money from both sides, others honest men who ran serious personal risks to help the British authorities – disclosed details of more than twenty projected Abwehr operations and handed over the bombs that had been provided for them. The targets thus safeguarded included the caissons of the two largest dry-docks, the Armaments Tunnel, HMS *Manxman*, HMS *King George V* and other important ships. During 1943, in contrast, there were only two successful Abwehr attacks against Gibraltar.* The first put Coaling Island – the dockyard's inflammable stores depot – out of action for several weeks at the end of June.† The second, the destruction by fire of an army launch at the end of July, was the last successful operation against the Fortress. In September 1943 the Spanish authorities closed down the sabotage organisation in the Campo. The number of attempts declined rapidly from that date and ceased entirely after April 1944.

The Abwehr's operations against ships in Spanish ports were also effectively countered. Its biggest success was an operation against a dozen Italian ships following the Italian surrender; most of them were damaged, some seriously. Towards the end of 1943, following British successes in removing mines attached to ships, ISOS decrypts revealed that the Abwehr was changing tactics and placing time-bombs in cargoes before shipment. The new tactics were difficult to counter; four such bombs exploded in two ships

---

* In order to preserve the credibility of the double agents, however, and to enable them to claim their rewards from the Abwehr, fake sabotage successes were staged on several occasions in the first half of 1943.

† The most enterprising, courageous and trustworthy of the double-cross agents had reported that this operation was being planned and a youth who had been the first choice to carry it out was removed from the depot as a result of the information. His place was taken by another dockyard employee, Martin Munoz, aged 19, who brought the bomb into the Fortress concealed on his body. Information obtained by the same double agent during the first few days of July pointed to Munoz as the likely culprit, and the identification was confirmed in the middle of the month when the agent met Munoz and learnt that he had hidden a second bomb in the Fortress intended for the dockyard power station. After some weeks spent in rapidly making his way through the 25,000 pesetas he had received from the Germans Munoz entered Gibraltar again on 29 July and was arrested. He was tried, sentenced to death and executed in January 1944, together with Lopez Cordon Cuenca who had been caught red-handed with sabotage equipment to be used for an attack on the Armaments Tunnel as a result of information from the double-cross group.

on passage to the United Kingdom at the end of December. But these incidents led to British protests which induced the Spanish authorities to impose further restrictions on the Abwehr.

In December 'C' sent a memorandum by Section V on German espionage and another by MI 5 on German sabotage to the Foreign Office suggesting that both should be presented to the Spanish government and that the British Ambassador should 'remind Franco sharply that it is not only the Axis satellites which have openly declared war on us that are required to work their passage home'. An aide memoire given to the Spanish government on 23 December regretted that in spite of repeated representations – and repeated assurances from the Spanish government – 'the illicit activities of German agents in Spain and Spanish controlled territory continued unabated'. On 24 January 1944 Mr Eden told the Spanish Ambassador that the bombs in British ships were an example of his government's utter failure to control German agents and that it was hard to imagine an instance where more political damage could be done by a few bombs. On 28 January, in an interview with General Franco, the British Ambassador demanded the closure of the German Consulate General's office in Tangier and the expulsion of 125 named German agents from Spanish Morocco and the mainland.[3] In February ISOS revealed that Berlin had prohibited sabotage against British ships until further notice following reports from the Abwehr representative in Madrid of increasing Spanish pressure on his organisation.[4] In May the Spanish government accepted the British Ambassador's demands, though it continued to defer carrying out its undertaking to expel the German agents.[5]

□

When Field Marshal Smuts visited the United Kingdom in the autumn of 1942 he suggested that representations should be made to the Portuguese government to suppress the activities of Axis agents in Portuguese East Africa. This was discussed at a meeting of ministers and officials on 24 December with the Prime Minister in the chair. The First Lord argued that the large number of sinkings by U-boats in the Mozambique Channel would not have been possible unless the U-boats were using bases in the area and getting help from agents. The Prime Minister said that there was no doubt whatever that agents in the colony were assisting the U-boats and strong pressure should be put on the Portuguese to stop them. The Foreign Secretary agreed that a protest could be made, but opposed precipitate action. However, it was decided that, in addition to the protest, SOE should take steps to stop the use by enemy agents of clandestine wireless sets.[6]

The Foreign Office and the SIS resisted the intervention of the SOE, and the War Cabinet agreed to postpone it in March 1943 after being informed that Portugal had responded co-operatively to the British protest and that it was in any case now known that, although the Axis consulates in east Africa were an important link in the enemy's espionage network, the main sources of enemy intelligence were in South Africa.[7] The SIS owed this information to the fact that after the end of 1942 there was a marked increase in its own intelligence about the German activities. This improvement owed something to the recruitment by the SIS officer in Lourenço Marques of a well-placed member of the German community there, but it was mainly due to Sigint. GC and CS had broken into the diplomatic cypher used between the German Consulate General and Berlin. The evidence from these sources threw some light on earlier developments and still more on current activities.

It emerged that the Abwehr had introduced three agents into South Africa by the spring of 1942. Hans Rooseboom, a naturalised South African of German or Dutch origin, had arrived in October 1939 to report by secret writing via an address in Holland on shipping movements in Durban and Cape Town; he had been briefly interned in October 1940 but had escaped, and by early in 1942 he was in close, but not amicable, contact with the Ossewa Brandwag (OB) and was reporting to Lourenço Marques on a secret transmitter. L J Elferink had arrived with a transmitter via Lourenço Marques in July 1941; a Dutch journalist and Professor of Literature, he had handed his radio and his code to the head of the OB, who had requested some form of communication with Germany, but had himself been inactive. Lothar Sittig (alias *Felix*), a German national who had lived in South Africa since 1925 and who had twice previously escaped from internment into Portuguese East Africa, had joined Rooseboom and the OB from Lourenço Marques in April 1942; in July he had received a new code by courier from Lourenço Marques and instructions to give all 'the information he collected to the OB for transmission to Germany'. In the spring of 1943 it was learned that these three were being reinforced by Nils Paasche, a German who had escaped from internment in 1940 to Lourenço Marques, where he had since worked for the German consulate on shipping intelligence. He joined *Felix* in March; in April Sigint disclosed that they were building another transmitter, and from June their transmissions direct to Berlin were intercepted.

The improved state of intelligence paved the way for countermeasures. In May 1943 British agents kidnapped Alfredo Manna, the head of the shipping intelligence network operated by the Italian consulate in Lourenço Marques in close collaboration with

Werz, the German Consul General there.* He was put across the Swaziland border, arrested and sent back to Camp 020, where he supplied a considerable amount of information about the Axis activities. In August Werz's own chief agent, a Greek named Basil Batos, was taken to Camp 020; he had been expelled by the Portuguese and arrested in Kenya while trying to fly back to Greece. Elferink was removed from South Africa with the co-operation of the Dutch authorities in the United Kingdom, who called him up to their armed forces in September; but he refused to talk when taken to Camp 020 in November.

South African attempts to locate *Felix's* transmitter by DF had by then come to nothing. Smuts agreed in November 1943 that further efforts would be made to find him, but was obviously apprehensive, in the light of the evidence implicating the OB, a semi-legal organisation, in espionage activities, that taking action against him might raise political difficulties. In March 1944 no progress had been made, not least because of lack of co-operation at the top of the South African Police. An associate of Rooseboom, who had been supplanted by *Felix* in the favours of the OB, then revealed that *Felix* was operating a transmitter from a farm belonging to van Rensburg, the OB leader; he also produced a statement by Rooseboom about his unhappy relations with van Rensburg. At the request of the MI 5/SIS representative in Pretoria,† Smuts authorised *Felix's* arrest, but insisted that van Rensburg must be left alone and that there must be no incident on his farm. A plan to arrest *Felix* on these conditions, together with Paasche and Rooseboom, proved abortive; Rooseboom and his associate disappeared and *Felix* and Paasche, who continued to transmit to Berlin till the end of 1944, were never caught.

In May 1944 MI 5 and SIS abandoned their efforts to have them silenced. Somewhat piqued, but without apprehension, they withdrew their representative from Pretoria. Petrie noted that 'it offends all one's professional instincts to leave the case in this untidy state, but the obstacles have been the unreliability . . . of the Police and the unwillingness of Field Marshal Smuts to drag van Rensburg and his fellow conspirators out into the open . . . Failure to liquidate is not, therefore, something that can be laid to our charge'. But MI 5 had known all along that the information reaching the Abwehr from the agents in South Africa was virtually worthless. It had consisted mainly of political gossip that could be

---

* See above, p 154.

† After the breaking of the diplomatic cypher, the MI 5 and SIS representation (see above, pp 154–155) in South Africa was re-adjusted. By September 1943 one of the MI 5 representatives had been withdrawn and the other transferred to Pretoria to act for both services.

obtained from newspapers and occasional inaccurate information about shipping movements; of the items supplied by *Felix* only two had been of possible value – a report from the Belgian Congo authorities to Pretoria on aviation fuel and a report on morale among South African troops. This was equally true of the output from Werz's network in Portuguese East Africa; examination of its shipping reports revealed a mass of inaccurate information, much of it invented. But pressure was kept up on the Portuguese government to expel him and his agents. It finally succeeded in October 1944, when he and five of his associates were sent to Germany under safe conduct.

□

Axis attempts to establish agents in Egypt and north Africa after the end of 1942 met with no success. The Germans sent two Egyptians to Egypt, Mohsen Fadl who had worked at the Egyptian embassy in Vichy, and Elie Haggar, the son of the head of the Egyptian Police, who had been a student in France at the out-break of war. Fadl returned to Cairo in November 1941 via Istanbul with the assistance of the SD, and with the understanding that he would report on political and economic matters. He had been given no means of communicating with Germany, but in August 1942 he was approached by another Egyptian who re-vealed that he had been charged with setting up a radio link with Berlin for Fadl and others. The DSO Egypt learned of the plot at that stage and, keeping it under close surveillance, knew that the efforts to establish the radio link had come to nothing by March 1943, when Fadl received a letter in secret ink complaining of his failure to make contact. He and a few of his associates were arrested in April. By that time ISOS and other sources had disclosed that Haggar had returned to Egypt with a mission to obtain military intelligence for the Abwehr. He was arrested in Palestine in February 1943. The stay-behind network which the Italians had tried to organise in Tripolitania had meanwhile been penetrated and broken up.

The efforts of the Italians to operate elsewhere in the Middle East appear to have stopped following the capture in December 1942 of three parachutists who had been dropped near Damascus with orders to set up a network for reporting military intelligence to Rhodes by W/T. The Germans, on the other hand, intensified their attempts to organise espionage and subversion in Syria, Iraq, and Persia after the Allied occupation of those territories, though they also encountered increasingly effective counter-measures.

In May 1943 the French authorities and DSO Syria rounded up a spy network that had been passing military information to

Jalal-ud-Din'uf, an agent working for Germany in Turkey. In the next three months four Greeks were arrested as they arrived via Turkey to carry out espionage and report on possible sabotage targets for the Abwehr. In the second half of 1943 the Turks arrested two men and handed them over to the authorities in Syria; it turned out that they had been used by the SD to penetrate the Polish underground and were now en route to join the Polish forces in the Middle East and seek to foment unrest among them.

In Iraq, where the occupation was followed by the establishment of the Anglo-Iraqi Security Board and the Iraqi Censorship, the internment and interrogation of subversive elements produced during 1942 evidence of the existence of the Ratl (the National Liberation Column). A close watch was kept on it through the head of the Iraqi Police in Mosul, alias *Zulu*, who was a member of it, and by the Censorship. They discovered that it was receiving instructions from Bay Quassia, an Iraqi in Istanbul, in secret writing and that Quassia was in league with Paul Leverkühn, the senior Abwehr officer in Turkey. In December 1942 it was asked to supply a weekly written report and a W/T set for the use of the group was also handed over to *Zulu* by the double agent *Doleful** on the Taurus express. It failed to open up radio communication for lack of operating instructions, but in the summer of 1943 *Zulu* met Quassia and Leverkühn in Istanbul to pick up further instructions and a large sum of money. The authorities then closed in; several Iraqis were arrested in September and interned. As late as June 1944, however, three more Iraqis were arrested on evidence that they were still passing military and political intelligence by secret writing to the Abwehr via a member of the Ratl living in Istanbul.

In the middle of June 1943 the Abwehr dropped three Germans and one Iraqi near Mosul with instructions to organise espionage, incite rebellion among the Kurds and arrange for the reception of a follow-up party. They landed about 200 km away from where their equipment was dropped – it included small arms, maps and two W/T sets – and were arrested at the end of the month. Under interrogation the Iraqi provided the names of two others whom he believed to be in the pay of the Germans. One of them, Louis Bakos, was arrested at once but released after interrogation. The other, Robert Bahoshy, was not arrested till October 1944. He confessed that he and Bakos had been trained by the Abwehr in wireless and secret writing, and that he was to have followed Bakos, who had arrived in Iraq in June 1943, but that with the arrest of Bakos the undertaking had been abandoned.

---

* See above, p 165.

In Persia, where the rail link with the USSR and the Abadan oil complex were of vital importance, the existence of tribal lawlessness, pro-Axis sympathies and nationalist resentment against the Allied occupation, and the` lack of co-operation from a weak central government, greatly delayed the establishment of adequate security. The CICI assumed responsibility in the autumn of 1941, but it had no effective organisation until the beginning of 1942 and counter-sabotage arrangements for the railway line and Abadan were still incomplete in February 1943. By the middle of 1942, on the other hand, the CICI knew that Franz Mayr, an agent of the SD, was active in building up a Fifth Column organisation among Persian politicians, officials and Army officers in readiness for the arrival of the German Army from Cairo or through the Caucasus, and that Berthold Schultze, an Abwehr agent who had been sent to Persia as German Vice-Consul in Tabriz, was with the disaffected Qashgai tribe in the north of the country. They had gone into hiding after the Anglo-Russian occupation, and it was later to transpire that they had received five W/T sets and cash from the Japanese embassy when the embassy staff was withdrawn from Persia in April 1942.

ISOS supplied sporadic information about them from the autumn of 1942, but following betrayal by an associate Mayr only narrowly escaped capture in November 1942. Papers were seized which enabled the security authorities to insist on the arrest of some 150 conspirators, including the Commanding Officer of the Isfahan area, General Zahedi. Nothing more was learned until August 1943, when the arrest of another Army officer led to the capture of Mayr and four wireless operators with W/T sets. Their interrogation revealed that, following suggestions made by Mayr in messages sent through the Japanese and by courier to the German embassy in Ankara, a joint Abwehr/SD mission of six Germans, including the four wireless operators, had landed by parachute at the end of the previous March to report on troop movements and the supplies on the railway to Russia – as they had done under elaborate precautions to avoid detection – and to carry out sabotage of the railway – which Mayr had deferred. They also disclosed that three SD agents and a Persian interpreter had been parachuted into Schultze's area towards the end of July.

The arrest of Mayr led to the internment of another 200 Persians. But Schultze and his reinforcement party remained at large until March 1944 when the Qashgai chiefs, pressurised by the central government, disillusioned by the failure of the Germans to supply arms and now convinced that Germany would lose the war, handed them over to the British authorities.

Meanwhile in February 1944 the Abwehr in the Middle East had suffered a major set-back through the defection of Erich Vermehren and his wife Elizabeth. Vermehren, a convert to Roman Catholicism who came from an anti-Nazi family, had served in the Army as an interpreter at POW camps for British officers. His wife, a cousin of von Papen, the German Ambassador in Ankara, belonged to a Catholic family with close contacts with Adam von Trott zu Solz, one of the leaders of the July Plot to assassinate Hitler, and with Freiherr von Bieberstein, who got him into the Abwehr in 1942. In October 1942 the Abwehr posted him to Leverkühn's Kriegsorganisation Nahe Orient in Istanbul. With support from von Papen and von Bieberstein, his wife was allowed to join him in November 1943 and they decided to defect after obtaining an introduction to the SIS representative. The Turks co-operated with the SIS in arranging for them to leave the country for Cairo. In Cairo in February 1944 they gave a Press conference to announce their belief that the only hope for 'the true Germany' lay in an Allied victory. By that time two of their Abwehr friends in Istanbul, Karl von Kleckowski and Wilhelm Hamburger, had approached the SIS on being ordered to return to Berlin under suspicion of complicity. They too, were smuggled out with Turkish assistance.

Vermehren proved to be a mine of information about the Abwehr's order of battle throughout the Middle East; he had had access to the files of all its agents and was familiar with their pseudonyms. Von Kleckowski was no less informative about the Abwehr's activities in the Balkans. Their defection thus had a traumatic effect on the Abwehr. Leverkühn was withdrawn from Istanbul and his successor was unable to restore morale before the Turks severed diplomatic relations with Germany in August 1944. Another defection from the Abwehr then disrupted Germany's plans for a stay-behind network in Turkey which had already ceased to be a viable base for enemy subversion and intelligence operations in the Middle East by the time the Turks expelled the Japanese in January 1945.*

The last German efforts in the theatre to come to light were aimed at organising Arab bands against the Jewish underground and the British authorities in Palestine, where the Jewish terrorist campaign had created increasingly serious security problems since the escape of members of the Stern Gang in November 1943. In November 1944 two Germans and an Arab were dropped by parachute near Jericho and four Iraqis at Tel Afar, 40 miles west of Mosul. All of the first party and two of the Iraqis were captured

---

* More generally the defections and the subsequent demoralisation of the Abwehr were an important contributory cause of the dismissal of Canaris and the absorption of the Abwehr into the RSHA. (See Appendix 1(iii)).

without delay but the other two Iraqis contrived to remain at large
for the remainder of the war.

□

Before dismissing enemy espionage and subversion in the
Middle East as being largely ineffective note must be taken of the
penetration in the winter of 1943–1944 by Amt VI of the SD of the
British embassy in Ankara – the notorious *Cicero* case. However,
this important coup did not involve major damage to the Allied
cause.

That there might be a breach of Allied security was first
suspected in December 1943, when the State Department learned
through the Hungarian legation in Stockholm that the Axis had
some information about the talks that had taken place between
Eden and the Turkish Foreign Minister in Cairo early in
November.[8] Then, early in January 1944 the Turkish Foreign
Minister told the British Ambassador in Ankara that von Papen,
the German Ambassador there, knew a good deal about arrangements recently made between the Turks and the Allies for
establishing radar stations at Turkish airfields.[9] The first instinct
was to assume that the source of the leakage was Turkish insecurity, but this belief was soon shattered. On 15 January 1944 the
President advised the Prime Minister that an OSS agent in the
German Foreign Ministry had produced copies of telegrams from
von Papen to Berlin giving the substance of documents assembled
in the British embassy for Eden's meeting with the Turks in Cairo
and of a minute of 6 December from the Prime Minister to the
Chiefs of Staff about Operation *Saturn* – a plan for the preparation of airfields in Turkey to receive Allied fighter squadrons. The
minute had stated that if the Turks agreed to the plan two
operations would go forward – Operations *Accolade* and *Anvil* –
and that British submarines might enter the Black Sea.[10]* The
President added that the Germans appeared to have acquired the
documents from a German agent.

An investigation was at once carried out by a Foreign Office
official and an SIS officer from Istanbul. It found that, while
access to the documents might have been obtained on the train
during the Ambassador's journeys to and from Cairo, the Ambassador's house was the most likely source of the leakage, and
security was strengthened there and in the embassy. It checked the

---

* Copies of this minute had been handed to the Turkish President and to the British
Ambassador in Ankara at the meetings of the Turkish President with President Roosevelt
and the Prime Minister in December 1943. *Accolade* was the plan for attack on Rhodes; *Anvil*
the plan for a landing in the south of France.

reliability of the Ambassador's personal servants and found nothing disturbing; in particular, it concluded that the personal valet was too stupid to be the culprit and in any case did not understand English. A secretary working in the Amt VI office in Ankara defected to the Americans in April 1944; she reported that the Germans had a valuable agent whose cover name was *Cicero*, but could supply no further information. There the matter rested till the end of the war.

At the end of the war a fuller account of the *Cicero* case was obtained from the interrogation of Walter Schellenberg, the head of Amt VI, Schuddekopf, of its British section, Ludwig Moyzisch, its representative in Ankara, and Maria Molkenteller, who had translated documents supplied by *Cicero* from November 1943 to April 1944.

At the end of October 1943 a man, first name Ilya, who had once been employed as a servant by a senior member of the German embassy staff, had called on him offering to provide important information from the British embassy in exchange for large sums of money. He had returned a few days later with two undeveloped films of documents as evidence of the kind of information he could supply in return for a monthly salary of £T15,000 plus £T5,000 per film. The films turning out to be copies of Most Secret political documents, von Papen had authorised an initial payment and sent them with Moyzisch to Berlin. Berlin had authorised acceptance of Ilya's terms, and from mid-November 1943 till early March 1944 Ilya, code-named *Cicero* by von Papen, had handed over films to Moyzisch at frequent rendez-vous. Moyzisch thought that he had received between 40 and 50 in return for about £T700,000 (some £150,000 sterling), which he paid in Turkish pounds by selling forged sterling notes supplied by Berlin. In December 1943 Ilya had handed over impressions of keys belonging to the British Ambassador for which he received an extra £T50,000. He had left the service of the Ambassador at the end of February 1944 and did no further work for the Germans, although he continued to receive his monthly salary. In August 1944 Moyzisch had put him in contact with the Japanese embassy in Ankara but nothing seems to have come of this introduction.

Beyond the fact that Ilya was Ilyas Bazna, who had become the Ambassador's valet in July 1943, Moyzisch's subsequent book on the subject added little that is reliable.[11] Bazna's own book is useless as evidence of anything not independently corroborated.[12] It is clear, however, that both books exaggerate *Cicero's* achievement. He photographed a vast amount of material, some of it of the highest secrecy, and so much so that the Germans in Berlin expressed considerable uneasiness (not shared by von Papen) that the material was being planted by the British. But the importance of the material was more limited than these books have claimed. Moyzisch admitted under interrogation that he rarely had time to do more than glance at the contents of the prints and the films. The translator, Maria Molkenteller, retained a good memory of their contents. From her interrogation and from the post-war capture of the telegrams to Berlin in which von Papen summarised some of the photographed papers, it appears that they consisted of briefing papers for, and reports on, the discussions in Cairo in November 1943 between Eden and the Turkish Foreign Minister and in December 1943 between the Prime Minister, Roosevelt and the Turkish President, and (probably) the meeting in January 1944 in Adana between the Prime Minister and the Turks, together with telegrams between the Ambassador and Whitehall about the subsequent negotiations, day to day business and reports from the embassy about Turkey's trade relations with Germany. According to Maria Molkenteller there were between 130 and 150 telegrams and they included one in which the Foreign Office warned the Ambassador that Berlin had copies of important documents from his embassy.

It is unlikely that the leakage of this material did any great damage to Allied interests. It was well known that the Allies were seeking to bring Turkey into the war. The leakage no doubt strengthened Germany's efforts to prevent Turkey from joining them, but the Turkish decision not to do so was reached independently of German pressure. Although not all the documents have been identified, it may be added that they did not include the proceedings of the Allied conferences at Casablanca, Moscow, Cairo and Tehran and of the military staff talks in Tehran, as Moyzisch's book implies, since only those parts of the proceedings that related to Turkey were sent to the Ambassador. The film entitled 'Five Fingers', which was based on Moyzisch's book, claimed that they included the plans for Operation *Overlord*, and this has often been stated since. But not even the broad outlines of military operations, let alone detailed plans, were distributed to ambassadors, and *Overlord* can have been compromised in Ankara only to the extent that passing references to it would have indicated that it was the code-word for a major Allied amphibious operation in the west. The claim made by both Moyzisch and Bazna[13] that *Cicero's* material enabled the Germans to break the Foreign Office cyphers is also without foundation.

'C' and Petrie agreed that, by good luck, the Allies had escaped 'the appalling national disasters' which might have accrued from this enemy penetration of a key embassy.

CHAPTER 12: REFERENCES

1.   FO 371/34858.
2.   FO 371/34641, 34642, 34643, 34645.
3.   Templewood, *Ambassador on Special Mission* (1946), p 255.
4.   FO 371/34769, 34858, 39665, 39666, 39684, 39687, 39716, 39717, 39718, 39862, 39863
5.   Templewood, op cit, p 263.
6.   CAB 78/4, Misc 38(42) 1st Meeting of 24 December; CAB 66/34, WP(43) 98 and 99, both of 9 March; FO 371/34646.
7.   CAB 65/37, WM(43) 41 Conf Annex of 16 March.
8.   FO 371/37477.
9.   ibid.
10. CAB 170/711, President's telegram 442 of 15 January and PM's reply 548 of 19 January 1944.
11. Moyzisch, *Operation Cicero* (1950).
12. Bazna, *I was Cicero* (1962).
13. Moyzisch, op cit, pp 55, 93, 113, 122, 149; Bazna, op cit, p 1.

CHAPTER 13

Double-Cross and Deception Operations in the United Kingdom and Overseas from the Beginning of 1943 to Mid-1944

SEVERAL agents arriving in the United Kingdom in these months were added to the double-cross network. With one exception – *Beetle*, who was intercepted in Iceland – they divulged their Abwehr mission to British authorities before their arrival and completed their passage to London under British auspices. In addition, *Garbo* introduced several entirely fictitious new agents, supposedly recruited in the United Kingdom, into his network.

A Croat naval officer (alias *Meteor*) and a Czech who had been living in Yugoslavia (*The Worm*) arrived in April and May 1943. ISOS had indicated that they had been introduced to the Abwehr in Belgrade by a relative of *Tricycle* (alias *Dreadnought*) when *Tricycle's* friend *Artist** had asked him to suggest recruits. *Dreadnought* had no contact with the British authorities and knew nothing of *Tricycle's* activities, but, as *Meteor* and *The Worm* later disclosed, he had nominated them in the knowledge that they would be likely to offer their services to the British if they got the opportunity.

The Worm had reported to the British authorities when he reached Switzerland in May 1942 on the first stage of his Abwehr mission to England; his onward journey had then been delayed and the Abwehr did not get him to Spain until the spring of 1943. *Meteor*, who had arranged with the Abwehr that he would make his 'escape' to England via Salonika and the Greek islands, had run into serious difficulties; his intention to work for the British had been betrayed by a companion and the Germans had arrested him and sentenced him to death. But *Artist* had secured his release by proposing an elaborate triple-cross plan. *Meteor* was now to present himself to the British as a genuine escaper and to hand over to them the cover address and the secret ink the Germans had supplied to him, but once accepted by the British as a double agent

---

* See above, p 104.

217

he was to write uncontrolled letters to different cover addresses in a different ink. He reported his triple-cross mission to the British authorities when he arrived in Madrid in March 1943 and began to write letters soon after he reached London. As we shall see, he was joined early in 1944 by another *Dreadnought* nominee, *Freak*.* *Hamlet's* friend *Puppet* arrived in April on a visit which had been approved by the Abwehr in Brussels. Under cover of attending to *Hamlet's* business interests he was to report intelligence supposed by the Abwehr to have been collected by an agent of *Hamlet's* fictitious organisation.† It was learnt after the war that the Abwehr regarded *Puppet's* reports as the first reliable account it had received of the processing of travellers at the LRC.

The next double-cross recruit was *Beetle*. A Norwegian who was put ashore by U-boat in Iceland in September 1943, he buried his radio and codes and presented himself to the US forces as an escaper. But he had confessed to his espionage mission when sent to Camp 020 and given much useful information. He returned to Iceland to work as a double-cross agent with *Cobweb*.

Beetle was followed by *Treasure*, a White Russian woman brought up in Paris. She had offered her services to the Germans in 1940, had been trained by the Abwehr, and had eventually been selected for a mission in England, where she had relatives. On her arrival in Madrid in June 1943 she disclosed her mission to the US embassy and the SIS; they got her to London via Gibraltar in November. The Abwehr had arranged to communicate with her by coded messages on public broadcasts, to which she would reply by secret writing. She began writing her letters in mid-November.

In that month *Sniper* also arrived from Gibraltar. He was a former member of the Belgian Air Force who had accepted recruitment by the Abwehr at the end of 1942 in the hope of getting to England and as a means of obtaining information for the Allies. The Abwehr had taken him to Spain in September 1943 with instructions to report himself as an escaper and he had at once disclosed his mission to the Belgian and British authorities there. At Camp 020 he proved to be eminently suitable for double-cross work and the nature of his mission for the Abwehr suggested that he would be especially valuable for scientific deception. He had been instructed to obtain technical intelligence on night-fighters, anti-submarine apparatus and the location of factories producing aircraft components, as well as information about the Allied invasion plans. As he had not been able to bring a transmitter – though the Abwehr had said it would try to deliver one, and told him to buy a radio receiver – he had been given

* See below, pp 223–224.
† See above, pp 121–122.

three cover addresses for letters in secret writing (all new to MI 5), a new formula secret ink (which MI 5 had already acquired through *Garbo*), three codes, three other addresses that he might contact in case of trouble, and a method of warning the Germans if he was under control. He at once began sending letters containing technical intelligence and references indicating that yet other letters he had written had gone astray. He also pressed the Germans to deliver his transmitter, and they named a site to which it would be sent, but the problem of getting it to him proved too much for them. His correspondence with them had ceased by the middle of 1944.*

The last of the new double agents reached Camp 020 in May 1944. This was *Rover*, a young Pole, who, after being held as prisoner first by the Germans and then by the Russians, was overtaken by the German assault on the USSR. In June 1942 he accepted recruitment by the Abwehr as a means of escaping to the Allies. He had been given an exceptionally thorough training in morse, secret writing and the construction of radio sets, and had recently contrived to reach Gibraltar after a long and arduous journey. In Gibraltar he gave a brief account of his Abwehr connections to the authorities, developing an impregnated hand-kerchief as evidence of his good faith. At Camp 020 he told the full story, producing a complicated code, cover addresses and micro-dots containing instructions for building and operating a transmitter, and was persuaded to become a double agent.

□

The newly acquired double agents off-set the loss of *Zigzag, Careless, Rainbow, Father, Dragonfly, Balloon* and *Mutt* and *Jeff*, whose operations were now closed down or suspended.

Zigzag, who reported to the Germans at the end of January 1943 that he had successfully carried out his sabotage attack on the de Havilland works,† was then anxious to return to Germany. He had provided a wealth of information not only about his contacts in the Abwehr, its training methods and its radio procedures (with most

---

* For *Sniper's* activities in the field after he was moved to Belgium late in 1944 see Appendix 15, p 384.

† See above, p 120. The most elaborate precautions were taken to conceal the notional nature of this attack by creating what would appear a scene of devastation if photographed from more than 2,000 feet. *Zigzag* having informed the Germans after reconnoitring the target that he would blow up the mains transformers, two wooden replicas of the transformers were placed on their sides as if they had been wrecked, the real transformers being camouflaged to look like a hole in the ground, and a chaos of rubble, smashed gates and blackened walls was simulated and tarpaulins laid out to suggest attempts to mask further damage.

of which MI 5 was already familiar) but also about its sabotage techniques (most of which was new); and as he was temperamentally unsuitable for service as a long-term agent, he was allowed to urge the Abwehr to arrange his return. In the end he had to arrange it himself; the Abwehr ruled out sending a U-boat for him, and its suggestion that he should book a passage to Lisbon was not practicable. To guard against the possibility that the Abwehr wanted to leave him in England, he indicated that he was in danger, first breaking off a message in the middle of a transmission and then, when the Germans failed to pick up this transmission, reporting that his notional accomplice in the sabotage attack had been arrested for possessing explosives and that he was trying to get to Lisbon. His journey to Lisbon in March – as an ex-convict who had got a job as a ship's steward with the help of the Prisoners' Aid Society – had to be arranged by MI 5, who thus had the satisfaction of confirming that it would have been virtually impossible without official assistance. The ISOS decrypts disclosed that he had duly deserted in Lisbon and was making his way to Germany.*

Meanwhile, the Germans had asked *Garbo* in January to provide *Careless* with a new cover address and a new method of secret writing. But *Careless* had refused to send more letters unless he was released from Camp 020, and his case had to be closed down by having *Brutus* inform the Abwehr that he had learned from the Polish Intelligence Service that *Careless* had been arrested as a spy. *Rainbow* retired without difficulty; the Germans had shown little interest in his activities for some time and he informed them in June 1943 that he was ceasing to operate. In the case of *Father* it was increasing German demands on him that forced a review; he received so many technical enquiries which he could not answer from early in 1943 that he had either to be closed down or transferred. As the former course might endanger his family in Belgium, he notified the Abwehr in April that he was being posted to India, but would continue to write to the cover address in Spain.† *Dragonfly*, who had confined himself to transmitting weather reports since the end of December until the Abwehr found some way of sending payments to him, was informed in September 1943 that jewellery was being delivered for him by a trustworthy courier to an address he had provided. With the arrest of the courier, Oswald Job, at the end of November and the

---

* They also indicated that the Germans were planning for *Zigzag* to sabotage the ship, but MI 5 had the further satisfaction of learning that he had handed over the sabotage device – a piece of incendiary coal – to the ship's master (who was privy to his real identity) as a parting present.

† See below, pp 231, 233–234 for *Father's* career in India.

decision to prosecute him,* *Dragonfly's* transmitter was closed down in the hope that the Germans would conclude that Job had compromised him. The possibility that they would conclude, rather, that Job had been compromised because *Dragonfly* was a double agent, was considered, but this risk was accepted.

Balloon, though not closed down, had ceased to operate by then. During a visit by *Tricycle* to Lisbon in July 1943† the Germans had indicated to him that they suspected that *Balloon's* recent reports had consisted of material planted by the British intelligence service. In the autumn, when they learned that the secret ink used by *Balloon*, among others, had been compromised,‡ they instructed him not to write again till he received a new one; but they rejected an offer by *Tricycle* to get a new ink and more money to him. *Tricycle* learned at that time from *Artist* that while the Germans did not think *Balloon* was a double agent, they did not greatly value his work; he was careless, lacking in judgment and never likely, as an Englishman, to provide intelligence of real importance. They never supplied him with a new ink.

Mutt and *Jeff* were supposedly engaged in sabotage, their main task for the Abwehr, during 1943. The Germans made no less than four parachute drops of supplies for them in Scotland, including two radio sets, sabotage material and £1,000 in cash; they repaid the Abwehr by carrying out a notional attack on a power station at Bury St Edmunds which involved a genuine explosion and achieved some newspaper publicity. They also supplied naval and military intelligence designed to sustain the deception threat to Norway, and the intention was to use them in the same way in 1944. At the end of 1943, however, MI 5 heard that the Germans might have learned they were double agents, and as the Abwehr ceased to show any interest in them, their case was allowed to expire.§

□

Tricycle had returned from the USA via Lisbon in October

---

* See Appendix 11, pp 344–345.
† See below, p 222.
‡ See below, p 226.
§ In September 1941 *Jeff* had been interned in the Isle of Man at Camp WX, which was used for detainees who had been at Camp 020. Camp WX was close to Camp L, which housed Nazi German internees, and such extensive illicit communications developed between the two that, until the WX detainees were moved to Dartmoor in September 1942, practically everything they knew was known at Camp L. In November 1943 it was reported that the WX detainees had heard that a Nazi from Camp L had been repatriated and were confident that he would have told the Germans that *Mutt* and *Jeff* and *Summer* and *Tate* had worked for British Intelligence.

1942.* During the winter of 1942–1943 he used a secret ink for his reports to the Abwehr. There were supposed to have been 36 of these but not all of them had been allowed to evade the Censorship. In April 1943 the Abwehr wrote to him complaining that his work was inadequate and urging him to try harder. *Tricycle* had been hoping for some time that he would be allowed to contact *Artist*, who served with the Abwehr, in the belief that *Artist* would collaborate with the British, and when *Meteor* confirmed that *Artist* had intervened to save him from imprisonment and despatched to Spain, *Tricycle* proposed an ingenious plan for renewing personal contact with the Abwehr, and possibly with *Artist*. The Yugoslav government wanted to arrange the escape of a number of officers marooned in Switzerland. *Tricycle* would go to Spain and Portugal and persuade the Abwehr to help him to set up an escape route for these men as a cover for his own espionage operations on Germany's behalf. The plan was approved in London and *Tricycle*, called up by the Yugoslav Army and provided with a diplomatic passport, informed the Abwehr that he would arrive in Lisbon in July. The Abwehr, which had continued to be dissatisfied with and suspicious of his reports, thereupon decided that *Artist* should meet him to assess his reliability.

In Lisbon the Abwehr representatives were again critical of the reports he took with him about Dover and areas on the south coast, and initially suspected that they were planted and that he was unsafe. On further reflection, however, and after *Artist* had reported on him, they informed Berlin that they were finally convinced that he was genuine – and fell in with his suggestion that, provided the Abwehr could include nominees of its own among the escapers, the escape route for the Yugoslavs in Switzerland should be organised. The detailed scheme, proposed by *Artist*, was that *Tricycle* should tell the Yugoslav authorities that an old friend (*Artist*), who worked in a branch of OKW but who wanted to ingratiate himself with the Allies because he believed Germany would lose the war, would use his official position to obtain passports for the Yugoslavs and get them to Spain; and that *Tricycle* would there meet and vouch for such Abwehr agents as were infiltrated into the escape operation, who were to be selected by *Dreadnought*, and obtain the help of the British in sending them on to the United Kingdom.

The Abwehr authorities in Berlin had meanwhile assessed as 'very valuable' some of the reports *Tricycle* had taken with him to Lisbon. Early in August they urged that he should go back to England as soon as possible as further reports from him, especially

---

* See above, pp 125–126.

on invasion preparations, shipping concentrations and plans for Allied air operations, were badly needed. He returned a month later with a transmitter in a forged Yugoslav diplomatic bag, the large remuneration which, as usual, he had extracted – and the conviction that *Artist*, who had indicated that he was living in some fear of the Gestapo, knew that he was working for the British and was himself co-operating with *Dreadnought*.

Tricycle's diagnosis of *Artist's* situation was soon confirmed. *Artist* went on from Lisbon to Madrid, made contact with an Abwehr officer (alias *Junior*)* who had made contact with the SIS, told him that he could not return to Germany because he was in trouble with the Gestapo and asked him to find out whether the British would evacuate him if his position became untenable. A deal was struck and for the next few months, while *Artist* supervised the Madrid end of the Yugoslav escape operation for the Abwehr, he was debriefed by the SIS. *Tricycle* returned to Lisbon and Madrid as a Yugoslav diplomatic courier in November 1943 to take over the first of the Abwehr-trained infiltrators from *Artist* and arrange his passage to England via Gibraltar. This was *Freak*, a former Yugoslav officer, who was to operate the transmitter which *Tricycle* had taken back to London.†

Whatever his motives – he claimed that he was in trouble with the Gestapo because he had anti-Nazi and defeatist views as well as because he had denounced Gestapo officers who had taken part with him in currency irregularities – *Artist* was a courageous man and he provided invaluable information about the organisation and operations of the Abwehr, its relations with the SD (then at a critical stage)‡ and also about political and economic conditions in Germany and occupied Europe. It had to be assumed that he would realise that Abwehr agents who continued to operate after he had given information about them – *Garbo* above all – were under British control, but no harm to them developed from *Artist*.

At the end of February 1944 *Tricycle* paid another visit to Lisbon, staying till the middle of April. One of the purposes of the

---

* *Junior* had met *Snow's* agent *Celery* when the latter was in Lisbon in February 1941 (see above, pp 102–103) and had made no secret of his anti-Nazi views. A year later he contacted the SIS but his offer to defect was not taken up for fear that it would blow some of the double-cross agents who had been handled by the Abwehr in Lisbon, particularly *Tricycle*. *Junior* moved to Spain in January 1943 and resumed contact with the SIS. After *Artist* was recruited there was anxiety that he would be compromised by his connection with *Junior* who was therefore evacuated to the United Kingdom in November 1943.

† He also took delivery of a new secret ink, a cover address, money and instructions for *Gelatine* – and of a further large instalment of salary and back pay for himself. The Abwehr told him that although she lacked discrimination and reported a lot of rubbish, *Gelatine's* work was satisfactory and that there was always the hope that she would come across intelligence of real importance.

‡ See Appendix 1(iii).

visit was to advance the programme of bringing out Abwehr-trained Yugoslav escapers; he prevailed on the Abwehr to bring *Dreadnought* to Lisbon as the agent responsible for selecting the escapers. There was much other evidence that, as *Artist* had reported, the Germans were now entirely satisfied with his work. He brought back to London two questionnaires from the Abwehr and one from the SD, as well as five reports from *Artist* and messages from Mihailovic to King Peter which he had received from *Dreadnought*. But disaster struck a fortnight after his return.

On 28 April *Artist* told his SIS contact that the OKW was convinced of *Tricycle's* loyalty to the Germans and that he himself had been decorated for his work for the Abwehr. Later the same day, however, he was kidnapped in a joint Abwehr/SD operation and taken back to Germany in the false bottom of a trunk. The operation, which had been carried out without the knowledge of the local Abwehr and SD officers, was brought to light by the ISOS decrypts. They could be interpreted as indicating that the Abwehr had feared that *Artist* was intending to defect, not that they thought that he was already a traitor and that *Tricycle* was under British control. But this was far from being certain and in any case it had to be feared that, under pressure, *Artist* would tell all he knew. Post-war enquiries did indeed establish that he had been arrested for currency swindles, and to prevent him defecting in order to escape punishment. There is no evidence that the Germans discovered the truth about his relations with *Tricycle*, *Dreadnought* and the SIS, and their confidence in *Tricycle* does not seem to have been shaken. But there could be no question of continuing *Tricycle's* double-cross career.

Tricycle's traffic on *Freak's* transmitter was continued until 19 May. *Tricycle* then informed the Germans by letter that the link had been closed down because rumours from Mihailovic sources that *Freak* was a German agent had given rise to enquiries about him. As the Germans continued to call *Freak*, he contacted them at the end of June referring to *Tricycle's* letter and reporting that he no longer seemed to be under suspicion, but adding that he was expecting to be sent abroad by the Yugoslav authorities. The Abwehr replied that it had not received the letter and was at a loss to understand 'the sudden unnotified interruption of work in the present critical time'.

Tricycle was later decorated for his services to the Allies, as were *Dreadnought*, who escaped to Italy in August 1944, and *Meteor*, *Freak* and *The Worm*.* *Artist* is believed to have perished in the

---

* *Meteor* and *Freak*, who were both naval officers, had been useful to the Admiralty for deception purposes. Perhaps because of his long delay in reaching England, *The Worm's* case was not developed.

concentration camp at Oranienburg.

□

Up to the spring of 1943 the communications sent from *Garbo's* network to the Germans consisted either of correspondence on administrative matters or of intelligence reports by observers in the areas where his notional agents were supposed to be located. Agent No 7, who was in the Merchant Navy, was busy setting up a new link for the carriage of mail and parcels by seamen couriers recruited from among his friends. In reality the material on this link went by SIS channels to Lisbon and was mailed there to correspond with the arrivals of ships from Britain. No 1, a commercial traveller, reported from the west country and also paid a visit to Northern Ireland. No 3, a Venezuelan, reported from Glasgow. His brother, No 5, who was also in Glasgow, announced in February that he intended to return home via Canada, where he was willing to continue working for *Garbo*. Before his departure *Garbo* sent him to reconnoitre the south coast, the Isle of Wight and south Wales. His success in getting to the Isle of Wight, where a visitors ban was in force, greatly impressed the Abwehr.* In March *Garbo* reported that he had been to Liverpool to see No 2's widow and recruited her as a home-help and a maid-of-all-work for his organisation.† No 4, a Gibraltarian who was directed to underground construction work in Chislehurst caves on account of his natural aptitude for tunnelling, was the chief source of reports, plans and drawings on the entirely fictitious development, in preparation for the opening of the second front, of a huge underground depot with a network of underground tunnels for the distribution of arms and ammunition to airfields and anti-aircraft defences in the London area. It was foreseen that the build-up of this project (Plan *Bodega*) might later be exploited for deception purposes in connection with Operation *Overlord* but in fact no use was made of it. No 6, who had been sent to north Africa with Operation *Torch*, was supposedly reporting from there on military and naval matters in secret writing both directly and via *Garbo*, *Garbo* sending his letters on to the Abwehr by seamen couriers. He was 'killed' in June when the MI 5 officer who wrote the letters died in an air crash.

On 7 March 1943 the *Garbo* network made its first radio

---

* See below, p 228 for his career in Canada as *Moonbeam*, and Chapter 14 for the visitors ban.

† Her usefulness was demonstrated by *Garbo* when No 3's friend in the RAF sold him an aircraft recognition book. This was put in a cake baked by her and iced by *Garbo* and delivered, disguised as a present from the seaman to a girl friend, to the Abwehr cover address in Lisbon by one of No 7's notional seamen couriers, actually by an SIS agent.

transmission, the operator at *Garbo's* end being the notional radio mechanic with strong left-wing sympathies who was delighted to do secret work on behalf of Spanish Republican exiles.* The regular exchange of signals with Madrid that was established after a trial period had the valuable consequence that in May the Germans sent *Garbo* a new cypher and a new transmitting plan. The cypher was related to one which had recently been brought into force on Abwehr circuits throughout the Iberian peninsula, and which GC and CS had not yet broken; it saved GC and CS from any further delay. The transmitting plan required *Garbo's* station to adopt military procedures while the Abwehr continued to use standard amateur procedure. This raised the problem that *Garbo's* signals would be masked by a mass of military traffic and difficult to connect with the station in Madrid, and in fact *Garbo's* transmissions were temporarily lost by the operators who had been intercepting them for the RSS from places as far apart as Scotland, Gibraltar and Canada. Fortunately it proved impossible for *Garbo* and his control to follow the plan without breaking into each other's transmissions. It was a tribute to the efficiency of the RSS's intercept network that after a few weeks it again reported *Garbo's* transmitter as a suspect station.

To begin with a large volume of material continued to pass by air mail and courier. From the end of August, however, almost all his messages were sent on his radio link. This followed from the need, in support of Allied deception plans, to force the Germans' correspondence with him on to the air and receive it with greater speed, and also from the fact that, to give verisimilitude to his network by indicating to the Germans that MI 5 was aware of its existence but could not track it down, steps were taken to show them that its air mail letters were being intercepted. On 11 August Agent No 1 reported that as he believed that a special military censorship had been imposed in Southampton,† he was posting his letter from Winchester, but the letter was still marked to show that it had been tested for secret writing by a re-agent that had failed to develop the ink. On 19 August an overt test for secret writing which did develop the ink that *Garbo's* network was using – ammonium vanadate – was applied to all mail to the Iberian peninsula, thus obliging the Abwehr to assume that the network's letters would now be stopped by the Censorship. The agents sent occasional letters by courier with numbers which reinforced the impression that letters they had sent by air mail had been intercepted. At the same time, to convince the Germans that the

---

* See above, p 116.
† In connection with the deception operation *Starkey*, see below, pp 236–237.

British authorities, while seeing the letters, had failed to identify the agents, the SIS interrogated all the cover addresses in Lisbon, offering bribes for information.

The German response was to instruct *Garbo* to cease all use of mail, to use his radio as little as possible and to reduce the network's activity. Although the use of air mail was never resumed, the use of radio was not restricted for long, and the Germans had constructed a new cover-address network in Lisbon for courier traffic by the end of 1943. For *Garbo*, far from reducing his activity, recruited new notional agents. Agent No 1 was paid off, having been badly shaken by being searched by the authorities in Southampton, and No 5 finally left for Canada, but *Garbo* had personally recruited a secretary at the War Office (J(5)) with whom he developed an amorous relationship, and his agents formed other new contacts. No 3 acquired a talkative lieutenant in the 49th Infantry Division (3(2)) and a Greek seaman with strong Communist sympathies who had deserted from the Merchant Navy (3(3)). No 4 became friendly with an American sergeant in the Service of Supply (4(3)). No 7 recruited a soldier in the 9th Armoured Division (7(1)), who faded out at the end of 1943, but also several agents from a weird organisation known as the Brothers in the Aryan World Order to which he had been introduced by a friend who, like himself, was a Welsh nationalist. The Abwehr responded cautiously to the idea of recruiting from this group, chiefly because it feared that by some extraordinary coincidence the Welsh nationalist might be *GW*, who had been blown by the arrest of Calvo.* But *Garbo* persuaded it that the group consisted of fanatical Fascist extremists, who were prepared to collect military intelligence for Germany, and No 7 took on no less than six of its members – a retired seaman who was sent to operate in the Dover area (7(2)); an English girl who was in the group as the mistress of an Indian member and was about to join the WRNS (7(3));† the Indian member, a poet, who was established in Brighton (7)4)); two men with jobs in Swansea (7(5) and 7(6)); and the treasurer of the Brotherhood, who was assigned to the Harwich area (7(7)).

□

In spite of the difficulties they had experienced over *Tricycle* MI 5 and the SIS were on the look-out for opportunities to collaborate with the FBI or the RCMP on double-cross operations. The first such operation in Canada was mounted from early in

---

* See above, pp 107–109.
† For her career in Ceylon, see below, p 234.

1943 with *Watchdog*,* an officer from MI 5 helping the authorities there to set up a system for approving the traffic and make the necessary arrangements with the Censorship and the illicit wireless interception service. *Watchdog* established radio contact with Hamburg in January and maintained it until August. In July he asked the Abwehr to send him assistants, and when he had received no reply after three weeks his transmissions were closed down. This may have been a premature decision, as his control station in Germany continued to call him for another six months. But his traffic had yielded no useful intelligence, his case had received some publicity in the Quebec Legislative Assembly and the Press, and he was truculent and difficult to handle. He was sent to Camp 020 and detained for the duration.

The attempt to establish another double agent in Canada was equally unproductive. A German (alias *Springbok*) who had lived in South Africa, and who had been recruited by the Abwehr to return there via south America, had offered his services to the SIS on reaching Rio de Janeiro and, on the SIS's advice, had suggested to the Abwehr that, as he could not get to South Africa, he should go to Canada. The Abwehr agreed, but the operation was abandoned when his subsequent attempts to make contact with Germany from Toronto had evoked no response by August.

The only successful double-cross operation in Canada centred on *Garbo's* fictitious Agent No 5.† MI 5 decided to transfer him notionally to Canada in the hope that he would contribute to Canadian security, and the Abwehr welcomed the plan with enthusiasm. Re-christened *Moonbeam*, he began writing letters in secret ink‡ in the autumn of 1943 and was soon claiming that he had acquired both conscious and unconscious sources. At the end of 1944 he was joined by another of *Garbo's* fictitious agents (No 4),§ equipped with a transmitter. Contact was established with the Abwehr in Madrid in January 1945 and continued until the middle of April. The Abwehr's final orders were that *Moonbeam* and his associates should divide any remaining funds between them, and take all necessary precautions for their own safety.

Following the return of *Tricycle* from the United States, the SIS embarked on another attempt to co-operate with the FBI in establishing double-cross agents in north and south America. The opportunity was provided by a Dutchman, known as *Pat J*, who arrived in Madrid early in 1942 en route for the United States with

---

* See above, pp 146, 201.
† See above, p 225.
‡ Before *Moonbeam* left England the Abwehr was given a sample of his handwriting – a message actually penned by the MI 5 representative in Canada.
§ See above, p 225.

a mission from the Abwehr. He disclosed his recruitment by the Abwehr to the Dutch consulate, and at SIS's suggestion the FBI agreed to receive him as a controlled agent. His radio transmissions to Germany, which began before the end of 1942, continued till the end of the war despite the problems the Germans encountered in financing him. It is believed that the US authorities made some use of them for strategic deception purposes. But the authorities in London were by no means well informed about his traffic. In January 1943 an Anglo-American Board was set up in Washington, the Joint Security Control, to supervise the release of strategic deception information to the enemy through US channels. It did not produce any meeting of minds between the FBI and the British authorities on the subject of deception. The FBI continued to regard double agents primarily as instruments for catching other spies.

□

In the United Kingdom after the beginning of 1943 double-cross operations continued to perform an immensely valuable counter-intelligence function despite the increased use of them for deception purposes. In the Middle East and the Mediterranean, a vast area in which it was impossible to establish the same nearly total control over access, their effectiveness as a counter-intelligence measure could not be so great, though they perhaps went some way towards persuading the Abwehr that its requirements were being met in Egypt and north Africa. But in view of the fact that this theatre was one in which the Allies were directly engaged with the enemy, and from which they would carry out such offensives as might be made against southern and south-eastern Europe, the use of double-cross agents for the purposes of operational deception continued to receive high priority.

In the deception plans associated with the invasion of Sicily and the Allied entry into Italy* and in those subsequently drawn up to sustain the threat of Allied offensives in the eastern Mediterranean the *Cheese* network was heavily used, as were *Doleful*, *Quicksilver* and *Pessimist*. In the second half of 1943 they were reinforced in 'A' Force's deception campaign by a Cypriot who notionally operated from Cairo and by two Greeks operating from Cyprus. The Cypriot, a member of an Abwehr party which was intercepted on its arrival in Cyprus in July (alias *The Savages*), reported to the Abwehr that he had moved to Cairo with his W/T set and obtained employment in the Allied Liaison Branch at GHQ. The Greeks

---

* See Howard, *British Intelligence in the Second World War*, Vol V (1990), Chapter 5.

(alias *The Lemons*) had been sent by the Abwehr to Syria, but had been captured when the skipper of their boat had lost his nerve and taken them to Cyprus.

Despite the heavy use that was made of them, these double-cross agents appeared to have escaped the enemy's suspicions. *Cheese* in particular retained the confidence of the Abwehr; ISOS disclosed that it had up-graded him to the status of 'Proven Agent' in the spring of 1944.* After the entry of British forces into Greece 'A' Force decided to transfer him to Athens and he made arrangements for the Abwehr to leave money and a W/T set for him in an Athens suburb. SIME was unable to locate them, but the *Cheese* network was closed down only when the Abwehr provided him with the name and address of a Greek contact who had already been arrested. The 432nd and final message from his network to the Abwehr announced that he was returning to Cairo. *Quicksilver* and *The Lemons* were closed down in the autumn of 1944. *Pessimist*, *Doleful* and *The Savages* maintained their W/T links with the Abwehr till the spring of 1945. SIME attempted to transfer *Doleful* to the service of the Japanese in Turkey but the plan was frustrated by the expulsion of Japan's representatives from Turkey in January 1945.

A number of other enemy agents were used for double-cross purposes after volunteering to work for the British authorities. They were valuable less for deception than for penetrating the enemy's organisations and throwing light on his plans.

From 1942 a businessman of Russian origin who had long lived in Istanbul (alias *Baroness*) offered his services to the SIS after being asked by the Germans and the Italians to provide them with military information during his visits to Syria and Palestine. The Abwehr subsequently proposed that he should open a café in Jerusalem as a meeting place for agents, that he should go to India and, in November 1943, that he should become the chief stay-behind agent in Turkey if Turkey joined the Allies. Nothing came of these plans, but he remained a valuable contact for SIS until he moved to Argentina for personal reasons early in 1944.

Another double agent, alias *Twist*, offered his services to the SIS in May 1942 while he was employed at the Italian consulate in Istanbul. For the next twelve months he supplied information about Arab nationalists in exile but revealed little or nothing about the Axis espionage organisation. In October 1943 ISOS disclosed that the Abwehr was recruiting him, its interest whetted by his

---

* The greatest test of SIME's ingenuity in his case was to find ways of enabling the Germans to supply him with the money he supposedly needed to pay some of his sub-agents. This was achieved through complicated black market arrangements in Istanbul in December 1943 and July 1944.

telling them that he had been recruited by the SIS. Over the winter the Abwehr and the SIS tried unsuccessfully to get answers from each other to questionnaires submitted through him. In April 1944 he reported that the SD had asked him to work for them without the knowledge of the Abwehr. He agreed, on instructions from the SIS, and in June he produced a questionnaire from the SD about Allied military intentions in the Balkans. 'A' Force supplied the replies to this and to supplementary questions until August, when Turkey broke off relations with Germany and interned all German nationals, including Abwehr and SD representatives, prior to repatriation. The SD's attempts to maintain contact with *Twist* through a Japanese intelligence officer had come to nothing by the time the Japanese were expelled from Turkey.

An Armenian working for the Abwehr in Istanbul offered his services to the SIS in May 1943. He lived up to the name given to him (*Infamous*) by passing unauthorised fabricated information to the Abwehr, as was learned when an Abwehr officer defected. On the other hand, a Persian who volunteered to work for the SIS in the autumn of 1943 belied his name (*Blackguard*). The Abwehr had sent him to Istanbul to recruit agents and despatch them to Persia, Egypt and India. In this capacity he became one of SIME's most important double-cross agents. He engineered the arrest at the end of 1943 of a Persian student who had been sent on an Abwehr mission to Tehran and who from March 1944, as double agent *Kiss* under Allied control, passed deception intelligence to the Germans about the political situation and about Soviet troop movements. In July 1944 he helped the Abwehr to send a radio transmitter to the double-cross agent *Father*, then operating in India.

All such volunteers had to be received and handled with caution. In only one case, however, were the necessary suspicions of the British authorities substantiated. In December 1942 the SIS in Istanbul recruited a Swiss citizen (alias *Odious*) after he had reported that the Abwehr station in Vienna wanted him to go to Syria but that he would prefer to work for the British. Although he was on the Security Black List because he was known to have been trained by the Germans in 1940, he was sent back to Vienna with a questionnaire and with authority to say that a trip to Syria could be arranged. He returned with answers to the questionnaire in March 1943 and was allowed into Syria in April. The DSO's organisation in Syria strongly suspected after interrogating him that he was a German spy. This was confirmed during a second permitted visit to Syria in October. He was arrested and interned after confessing that he had worked for the Abwehr in Spain, Morocco, Tangier and Vienna since 1941.

□

In July 1942 the MI 5 officer who had recently been in Cairo, where he had joined in discussions between SIME, SIS and 'A' Force on setting up machinery for controlling double-cross operations,* suggested that this might also need attention in India. A Controller of Deception had already been appointed there and he would need assistance in establishing channels through which to operate.

In December 1942 MI 5 learnt that a special section had been established in the Intelligence Bureau of the Indian government's Home Department 'to exploit existing opportunities and create new lines', and that the help of an officer with practical experience of double-cross work would be gratefully accepted. Indians returning through Burma with Japanese intelligence assignments might provide opportunities, and there were connections with Axis legations in Kabul.

The MI 5 officer, who arrived in Delhi in March 1943, found that 'double-cross was regarded as an aspect of deception and nothing else'. All the initiatives were being taken by the deception authorities. The tendency for the military to take control was aggravated by the Intelligence Bureau's lack of resources and by the fact that essential machinery for developing double-cross cases, such as facilities for the examination of refugees and the interrogation of suspected agents, insofar as they existed at all, were in Army hands. There seemed to be a grave danger that the security advantages to be derived from double-cross work would be entirely neglected. During the summer of 1943 MI 5 took advantage of a visit to London by the DMI India and the Controller of Deception to urge the need for a more balanced view of the functions of double-cross and for the establishment of more suitable machinery which would give effect to them. Arrangements agreed in the autumn gave the Intelligence Bureau the final word on whether a spy should be used for double-cross operations, and left to the Police the handling of such agents as were considered suitable for this role. For the rest of the war there was close contact between the Intelligence Bureau and B 1 A on double-cross matters.

In March 1943 the Indian authorities were already running one double-cross case that was valuable for counter-intelligence. *Silver* came from a middle class Hindu family and had graduated through the Congress Party and the Congress Socialist Party to the Kirti Communist group. He was introduced to Subhas Chandra Bose, the leader of the extreme anti-British Forward Bloc, and when Bose left India in 1941 en route to Germany via Kabul *Silver*

---

* See above, p 153.

became the link between the Axis legations there and sympathisers in India. At the same time he kept the Russians informed about these contacts. In 1942 *Silver* was arrested when visiting India to consult the Kirti leaders. He told his story and returned to Kabul to act as the main Axis link with India, keeping both the Russians and the British informed. But no effective German (or Italian) operations developed before the arrival of Bose in the Far East in June 1943, and by that time Japan was the main external threat to security in India. She developed agent operations on a considerable scale; in the spring of 1944 it was believed that some 1,500 persons had been despatched on various missions including espionage, sabotage, propaganda and the subversion of Indian troops in the forward areas. These so called JIFs (Japanese Inspired Fifth Columnists) achieved little. Very few of the 600 or so who had reached India were unaccounted for and it was rare for them to make any serious attempt to carry out their missions. However, one of their operations yielded important counter-intelligence dividends. In December 1943 eight agents were landed by submarine in Kathiawar. They were equipped with radio and had instructions to work in pairs, reporting through one pair which was to be located in Bengal and was to make contact with supporters of the Forward Bloc. In due course all these agents were caught and the expedition gave rise to a double-cross operation, known as *Pawnbroker*, through which radio contact was established with Bose and a dangerous group of revolutionaries, known as the Bengal Volunteer Group, was smashed.

As we have seen,* in June 1943 difficulty over the traffic of the double-cross agent *Father* made it necessary to post him away from England and India was chosen as his destination. He arrived in July and came under the control of the Intelligence Bureau. The Germans had been warned of the move and showed their intention to continue the case by advising *Father* of the frequencies on which he should listen for their messages. They were heard calling until October 1943 and it was noted that the station was the same as the one which was also trying (vainly at this time) to contact *Silver*. *Father's* first letters from India in secret writing, dated 1 and 2 September and purporting to be sent by air mail, were forwarded to his cover address in Barcelona in October. The Germans came on the air again on 22 December when they acknowledged receipt of his first three letters. By now he was supposed to be in Calcutta attached to a notional Spitfire squadron.

Father continued writing: his nineteenth letter was sent in May 1944 and a message reported in ISOS that month said that he was

---

* See above, p 220.

working well. He was, however, becoming extremely discontented in India and increasingly difficult to handle, and when the Germans mounted a plan to send him a transmitter MI 5 advised the Intelligence Bureau to co-operate. *Father*, MI 5 said, was no longer of much use as a letter-writing agent because of postal delays and he would have to be kept in India while he remained one. If he became a wireless agent someone else could operate the set in his name. In July a radio transmitter was notionally collected by *Father* with suitable precautions. Contact was made with the Germans on 6 August by an operator impersonating *Father*. He himself returned to England. The Germans were told that he expected to be re-posted at the end of the year and they asked him to find a replacement. He duly nominated a disaffected officer in the Indian Air Force (actually a sergeant in the Calcutta Police, code-name *Radja*) who was accepted by the Germans and enjoyed a brief double-cross career devoted to deception. The Germans hoped to resume contact with *Father* after his return to England but it was decided to close the case.

In August 1944 *Garbo's* imaginary sub-agent 7(3) who was supposed to have been called up to the WRNS* joined South East Asia Command HQ in Ceylon. No useful role had been found for her in the United Kingdom and the SEAC deception staff wanted another agent. She had been taught secret writing and given a suitable ink, a cover address in London and instructions on what to report: *Garbo* forwarded her first letter to his Lisbon post box in September. Her letters were actually written in London by an MI 5 scribe, the secret and cover texts being provided by the SEAC deception staff. The traffic was high-grade and in view of the long delays which were bound to occur in transit much of it could be accurate. The Germans passed it to the Japanese Military Attaché who sent it on to Tokyo by wireless.

In January 1945 an ISOS message from Berlin to Madrid expressing surprise that certain information in her reports was almost identical with that received through other channels led to the discovery that the SEAC deception staff had passed the same information through *Silver* and *Father*. B1A judged that this gave rise to an unacceptable risk of compromising her, and *Garbo* through her. She therefore met with a motor accident; her bottle of secret ink was smashed and she herself had to go before a medical board. She had not resumed work when the war with Germany ended.

□

---

* See above, p 227.

The most valuable work of the double-cross agents in the United Kingdom continued to lie in their contribution to counter-intelligence. Their traffic with the enemy yielded a wealth of information about the Abwehr's plans and preoccupations and sometimes greatly assisted GC and CS to maintain the supply of the other major source of counter-intelligence, the ISOS de-crypts.* It gave the security authorities the reasonable assurance that, despite the discovery that it had grounds for distrusting *Balloon, Mutt* and *Jeff*, the Abwehr regarded the double agents as forming a reliable and generally sufficient espionage network in the United Kingdom, and that, despite the delay in detecting Neukermans, the anxiety about Kraemer and *Ostro* and the risks incurred in letting *Zigzag* leave Britain and closing down *Dragonfly*, no uncontrolled agents were at large. The importance of this service can scarcely be exaggerated.

Any information from the double agents about the enemy's policy, strategy or military operations, as distinct from the activities of his Secret Services, was an uncovenanted bonus. Such intelligence was occasionally obtained from recent defectors like *Artist*.† But few attempts were made to acquire it through the established double agents, and the only attempt of any import-ance, which related to the V-weapons, added little to the informa-tion that was being obtained from other sources.

On his visit to Lisbon in July 1943 *Tricycle* was advised by his Abwehr controller to live outside London in view of the impend-ing V-weapon offensive. Before his visit in February 1944 he was briefed to find out what he could about the V-weapons, but he was unable to obtain any useful information. *Garbo* began to put questions to the Germans about the V-weapon threat in October 1943. There was no response until the following December, when they told him to make plans to set up a new headquarters outside London and build a reserve transmitter. In further correspond-ence about these plans he received no indication of the date when the threat might materialise, and in February 1944 the Germans told him that they would probably be unable to give him advance warning as to when the attacks would begin. Thereafter, his traffic contained some signs that the threat was imminent. In April the

---

* See above, p 182.

† See above, p 223. Another valuable defector, known as *Harlequin*, had been taken prisoner in Africa. The failure of the 1942 German offensive on the eastern front convinced him (and, he believed, many like him who, in order to shake off the shackles of the Versailles Treaty had been willing to go along with the Nazi regime, albeit disapproving of much of it) that Germany must lose the war and that in the interests of humanity the end should be accelerated. The wide-ranging and valuable information which he supplied included the fact that the insecurity of British Army radio communications in the field had enabled the Germans to build up the British order of battle in north Africa and the United Kingdom.

Germans discussed with him a plan (which came to nothing) by which he would receive a single code-word from an unknown agent three or four times a week and transmit it to Madrid. In May ISOS decrypts disclosed that they were arranging to send to Madrid, for onward transmission to *Garbo*, special questionnaires bearing the code-name *Stichling*; Madrid was to forward *Garbo's* answers in priority signals to Berlin and Arras, the HQ of the Abwehr units with the armies in France. As it happened the double-cross authorities did not recognise that these preparations were associated with the V-weapon offensive. But their oversight was of no consequence: the Abwehr signals added nothing to what was known about the threat from other sources.*

If the acquisition of intelligence, as distinct from counter-intelligence, was not among the purposes the double-cross system was intended to serve, it was otherwise with strategic deception. Concern to use the agents for deception had become prominent, as we have seen, from the middle of 1942, when the threat of espionage, sabotage and subversion to the security of the United Kingdom appeared to have been brought under control with their assistance.† Except in the Middle East‡ they were first used for strategic deception, though to little effect, in support of Operation *Torch*, for which *Father*, *Mutt* and *Jeff*, *Tate*, *Garbo*, *Dragonfly*, *Balloon* and *Gelatine* were employed.§ In August and September 1943 *Garbo's* network was used on a large scale to support Operation *Starkey*, the object of which was to persuade the Germans that a major landing was intended against the Pas de Calais and to force them to engage their fighter aircraft at times and places chosen by the Allies.‖ Reports of shipping concentrations, troop movements and assault preparations were submitted by *Garbo's* agents from the Southampton, Shoreham and Dover areas, while *Garbo* himself reconnoitred the Brighton area. Throughout the exercise ISOS decrypts disclosed the German reactions to these reports. On 6 September the Abwehr in Berlin appreciated that they had been 'particularly valuable' and on 13 September it informed *Garbo* that it was very satisfied; it also paid

---

* See Hinsley et al, *British Intelligence in the Second World War*, Vol III Part 2 (1988), pp 534–535. The first *Stichling* questionnaire, sent on 16 June, the day the V 1 bombardment opened, asked *Garbo* to report the time of fall of the V 1s and the location of impact. This was an embarrassing request since no plans had been made for conveying false information to Germany on these matters, but *Garbo* was able to delay responding to it because the Germans had asked him to use an obsolete map. It took him a fortnight to agree with the Abwehr that he would use Baedeker.

† See above, Chapter 7.

‡ See Chapter 10.

§ See Howard, op cit, Vol V, Chapter 5, and Masterman, *The Double-Cross System* (1972), pp 109–110.

‖ See Hinsley et al, op cit, Vol III Part 2, pp 4–5.

his agents a special bonus and increased their salaries by 50 per cent. As no landing took place, and the Allies announced that they had been carrying out large-scale exercises, the deception authorities feared that *Garbo* might be discredited. He characteristically off-set this risk by advising the Abwehr that the Allies were lying; they had changed their plans at the last minute as a result of the Italian armistice.

Encouraged by their experience during *Starkey*, the deception authorities looked to the opportunity of turning the double agents to still greater account in support of the Allied invasion of western Europe. The employment of them on some scale for deception in association with Operation *Overlord* was in any case unavoidable if their credibility – and thus their value for counter-intelligence purposes – was to be preserved. The Germans were asking them to pay particular attention to the Allied plans for a cross-Channel invasion from as early as August 1943, and did so with increasing urgency from the beginning of 1944.* It would have seemed strange to the Abwehr if, given the position they had built for themselves, the agents had had nothing to report on so vast an enterprise. At a meeting of the W Board at the end of September 1943 the Controlling Officer for Deception was co-opted as a member and the Chairman emphasised that the use of the double agents in support of *Overlord* should become a major element in the Twenty Committee's planning. He asked the MI 5 and SIS representatives whether all the German agents operating in the United Kingdom were under control. While they could give no absolute assurance, they stated that there was no trace of any others even in ISOS, which would, they believed, have reflected their existence. At the next meeting of the W Board, on 21 January 1944, the MI 5 representative reported that it was 98 per cent certain that the Germans trusted the agents, though absolute certainty was always impossible. The Board authorised the Twenty Committee 'to go ahead strongly with these agents to give all possible support to strategic deception plans in aid of *Overlord*', and agreed that a representative of SHAEF's deception staff (Ops B) should be invited to join the Committee.

The deception plans were then being drawn up. *Bodyguard*, the overall strategic plan approved by the Combined Chiefs of Staff in January, sought to induce the enemy to make faulty strategic dispositions by indicating that the Allies were ready to take advantage of a serious weakening of his position anywhere in north-west Europe, that there was to be an Anglo-American invasion of Norway in conjunction with the Russians and that,

---

* See above, p 218, and below, pp 239, 241.

while the scale of the eventual cross-Channel assault was to be greater than was in fact planned, its date was being deferred beyond the date that was in fact intended. Within this framework SHAEF drew up a two-part plan which was approved by the Combined Chiefs of Staff on 26 February. *Fortitude North* simulated preparations for a descent on Norway from a notional Fourth British Army based in Scotland and Northern Ireland. *Fortitude South*, to be implemented at a later date, aimed to persuade the enemy that the main invasion area was the Pas de Calais and that any attack in the Normandy area would be a diversionary operation to be followed by the main assault, carried out by a notional 1st United States Army Group (FUSAG), when he had committed his reserves. *Fortitude* was reinforced by Plan *Premium*, which drew attention to the threat to the Pas de Calais, the Low Countries and Norway, and Plan *Ironside*, designed to indicate a landing on the Biscay coast. Plan *Foynes* sought to conceal for as long as possible the transfer of eight divisions from Italy to the United Kingdom.

From early in 1944 material sent to the Germans by the double agents in support of these plans was concocted at daily meetings of their case-officers with SHAEF's Ops B, the approving authority, *Tricycle*, *Brutus* and *Garbo* being the main-stays of the deception programme.

In February 1944 *Tricycle* took with him to Lisbon a large number of observation reports bearing on the order of battle made up for the *Fortitude South* deception plan. *Freak*, who had established radio communication with Lisbon on behalf of *Tricycle* and himself in February, transmitted further deception material while *Tricycle* was in Lisbon; as well as supporting *Fortitude South*, he contributed to *Fortitude North* by reporting on visits that he was notionally able to make to Northern Ireland. But the contribution of these two was brought to an end by the arrest of *Artist* at the end of April. *Fortitude* deception material was immediately omitted from their traffic on *Freak's* transmitter and, as we have seen, the transmitter was closed down on 19 May.

The retirement of *Tricycle* and *Freak* was off-set by the fact that the ground had been laid for making greater use of *Brutus*. *Brutus* had been used as a double agent with great caution, and under strict surveillance, from the beginning of 1943. He was given a post with the Polish intelligence authorities, his work for the Germans being to report by radio to Paris on the state of the Polish armed forces and the possibility of forming a pro-German movement among them. He was allowed to visit Scotland and transmit a comprehensive account of Polish troops there – as also to note that they were unlikely to sympathise with Germany unless she meted out better treatment to the Poles – but was then arrested by the

Poles on a disciplinary charge. An operator imitating *Brutus's* transmissions warned the Germans that he expected to be arrested and was thus hiding his radio set; and he remained silent till late in August. He then advised the Abwehr that he had been released but was awaiting a court martial, and that it would be dangerous for him to transmit regularly; however, he would send written reports if given a cover-address. This signal provoked a message reported in ISOS describing *Brutus* as 'a hitherto very valuable wireless agent', and he received a cover-address. He used this while waiting for his court martial, sending in the last weeks of 1943 a long report on south-eastern England.

In December the Polish court martial sentenced him to two months' imprisonment; this was off-set by the weeks he had spent under arrest, and he was able to resume his radio transmissions. But MI 5 took the precaution of interposing its own radio operator; he was accepted by the Germans after *Brutus* had informed them that he was a fellow Pole recently retired from the Polish Air Force who had lost his family in Russia and was keen to help for ideological reasons.

Given this further safeguard, the fact that the Polish authorities had tactfully abstained from showing any curiosity about him and the knowledge that he was in good standing with the Germans, who at the beginning of 1944 were arranging to send him money, a new transmitter and a camera, *Brutus* now appeared to be eminently suitable for employment on deception. In April he told the Abwehr that he was visiting the Polish forces in Scotland. From there he built on the notional order of battle intelligence that had been conveyed to the enemy in connection with *Fortitude North* by reporting on 16 April that an attack on Norway must be expected early in May and, on 4 May, that a Russian military and naval mission was established in Edinburgh. A fortnight later he returned to London to support *Fortitude South* by being posted to FUSAG, as he informed the Abwehr, with effect from 27 May. He then passed to the Abwehr a series of messages disclosing the entire order of battle of this shadow Army Group in south-eastern England and, on D-day itself, the news that it was going into action independently of 21st Army Group at any moment.

At the beginning of 1944 the Germans had urged *Garbo* to concentrate on the Allied preparations for the invasion of Europe. He responded by re-deploying his agents and supplying a large part of the order of battle information required for the *Fortitude* deception programme. Between January 1944 and D-day more than 500 radio messages were exchanged between London and the Abwehr in Madrid, which re-transmitted the London reports immediately to Berlin. Reports from the south-west and south coast, the areas covered by Agents 7(5) and 7(6) from Swansea and

Agent 4, posted to a camp near Southampton, were few and disappointing in quality. Those from Agents 3 and 3(3), who covered the Forth and the Clyde, and from the south-east of England, where the majority of the agents were based, were designed to support a threat to Norway from the imaginary Fourth British Army in Scotland and to the Pas de Calais from the imaginary FUSAG under General Patton in the south-east. Many of the formations identified as belonging to these and other Allied Commands actually existed but their reported locations were largely inaccurate. *Garbo* stayed in London to be close to Agents J(3) in the Ministry of Information, J(5) in the War Office and 4(3), who supplied information on the US order of battle; and a fortnight before D-day, to add weight to the conclusions he freely offered the Germans on the intelligence that was being passed to them, he obtained the Abwehr's approval for himself to accept a part-time job in the Ministry of Information.

While *Garbo* and *Brutus* forwarded the bulk of the deception material after the withdrawal of *Tricycle*, the other double agents were pressed into service.

Tate had continued to make daily weather reports during 1943, but except for a minor contribution to Operation *Starkey*, had otherwise been inactive. It was difficult to make out what the Abwehr thought of him because he never appeared in the ISOS decrypts, his control station at Hamburg communicating with Berlin by land-line. In September, when he had received only 14 messages from Hamburg in the past six months, MI 5 considered closing him down as being of no further value for counter-intelligence purposes, but he was left alone in case he was needed for deception on behalf of the Admiralty.* In November 1943 there was some evidence to suggest that the Germans had learned that he was a double agent.† In March 1944, however, he was used to support *Fortitude North* by informing the Germans that the British Ambassador to Sweden was in London for special consultations, and he then contributed to Plan *Ironside*, which was devised to suggest that a landing was to take place on the Biscay coast.

Cobweb, like *Tate*, came near to being closed down in the autumn of 1943; although he was supporting a deception threat to Norway (Operation *Tindall*), he was tying down an SIS officer in Iceland to do no more than an hour's work a day. But he was reprieved, and in 1944, when he was joined by *Beetle*, the two made a minor contribution to *Fortitude North*.

The *Hamlet-Mullet-Puppet* network was used to draw German

---

* He was used for this purpose after D-day, see Hinsley et al, op cit, Vol III Part 2, pp 470–471n.

† See above, p 221, fn §.

attention to the threat to the Pas de Calais and the Low Countries. *Mullet*, who had been in business in Belgium, was notionally employed by a large British insurance company. Until April 1944, under Plan *Premium*, he supplied *Hamlet* with intelligence on requests his firm was supposed to be receiving from official quarters for industrial and economic information about the Low Countries. But MI 5 had no great faith in the plan. *Artist* had disclosed in 1943 that the Abwehr station in Brussels was keeping *Hamlet* in play from self-interest rather than from confidence in him, and *Mullet's* reports were perhaps forwarded chiefly to maintain credibility for *Hamlet*. If this was their object they had no effect; it was known by the middle of 1944 that the Germans actively distrusted him.

Bronx, on the other hand, had established herself as a highly trusted Abwehr agent by the end of 1943. She had written more than 60 letters to a Lisbon cover address by April 1944 when the Germans, who had already asked her to concentrate on enquiries into the Allied invasion plans, arranged that if she learned anything reliable about the target area and date of the invasion, she would notify them by a telegram using a plain language code and sent care of the Portuguese bank through which she received her regular monthly payments. She obliged on 15 May in a telegram which, to reinforce the activities of *Tate* and *Garbo* in support of Plan *Ironside*, reported that there would be a landing on the Biscay coast in the middle of June. *Gelatine*, to whom *Tricycle* had delivered a new secret ink and a cover address in November 1943, participated with *Brutus* and *Puppet* in Plan *Foynes*, the plan to conceal for as long as possible the transfer of eight divisions from Italy to the United Kingdom.

Treasure, who made only a small contribution to *Fortitude South*, came close to jeopardising the deception programme. She notionally worked in the film division of the Ministry of Information and in this role she visited Lisbon in February 1944 to meet her Abwehr controller and collect instructions and a transmitter from him. She returned at the end of March, the transmitter being forwarded for her by the British embassy, but did not open regular radio communication with Paris till 10 May. A week later she confessed to her MI 5 controller that she had concealed from him the special check in her transmission procedure which she could use if she wanted to warn the Abwehr that she was under control; distressed by the fact that her dog had been kept in quarantine in Gibraltar, and even more by the news that it had died there, she had intended to get the traffic going and then to take her revenge by alerting the Germans, but had changed her mind. MI 5 dispensed with her services but kept the traffic going with one of its own operators.

After D-day the task of the double-cross agents was to maintain the threat to the Pas de Calais for as long as possible by reporting on the strength and readiness of FUSAG in the hope of persuading the Germans that it would launch its assault when their reserves had been committed to Normandy. *Garbo* and his network took the lead. He first reported that a PWE directive issued on D-day had forbidden any reference to or speculation about further assaults, suggesting that this was a strong indication that other attacks were planned. On D+2, ostensibly after a conference with his principal agents, he sent an appreciation to the effect that no FUSAG formations had taken part in the Normandy landings, that two Armies, with Dutch and Belgian contingents attached, were still in their concentration areas in the south-east and that landing craft were being assembled on the east coast. A few days later he forwarded to Madrid a document purporting to be extracts from the minutes of a meeting of the Cabinet Committee on *Overlord* Preparations in May from which it could be deduced that *Overlord* comprised two major operations, one of them launched from south-eastern England.

Tate supplemented *Garbo's* efforts. From the beginning of June, making use of his involvement in farming, he supposedly installed himself with his transmitter in a prohibited zone in Kent and struck up an acquaintance with a railway guard. In signals sent on 8, 9 and 14 June he reported the arrangements that were being made to move FUSAG to Tilbury, Gravesend, Dover, Folkestone and Newhaven for embarkation.

An awkward problem faced the deception authorities at the beginning of July, when First Canadian and Third US Armies, which had belonged to FUSAG in the notional order of battle drawn up for *Fortitude South*, moved to Normandy. Some explanation had to be provided for their departure from FUSAG, and FUSAG had to be replenished if the threat to the Pas de Calais was to be maintained. The explanation adopted for the enemy's consumption (*Fortitude South II*), was that Montgomery had got into difficulties in Normandy and had demanded reinforcements; that while these could only be supplied from FUSAG at the expense of delaying its assault, FUSAG was receiving the notional Fourth British Army from Scotland, the notional Fourteenth US Army and the real Ninth US Army (which was destined for Normandy); and that Patton, who had bitterly opposed those decisions, had been demoted for insubordination. Information about the move of First Canadian and Third US Armies had still to be withheld from the enemy, however, until he had identified them in Normandy; and as it would look extremely suspicious if *Brutus* and *Garbo's* network failed to notice their departure, some way had to be found of silencing them for a period.

This presented no difficulty for *Brutus*: he was sent on a week's visit to Scotland in the middle of July. *Garbo*, who could not plausibly go absent, invented an ingenious if somewhat elaborate excuse. He told the Germans at the end of June that he was dissatisfied with the V 1 reports that were being provided by his agents and then sent two reports on bomb damage to show that he was running risks in making his own investigations. Agent No 3 followed up with reports that *Garbo* had been arrested and, after a few days, had been released. The Germans, who had instructed No 3 to close down the radio and do all he could to save the organisation, were reassured in a letter from *Garbo* dated 14 July that he had convinced the Police of his bona fides. But they decided that such a valuable source should no longer be risked on the V 1 operation, and on 29 July they informed him that the Führer had awarded him the Iron Cross, a decoration granted only to front-line combatants.* His radio had been off the air from 12 to 24 July.

On returning from Scotland *Brutus* conveyed to the Germans the substance of *Fortitude South II* in messages between 18 and 21 July. In a letter sent by courier on 22 July *Garbo* sent similar information, attributing it to his agent No 4. Letters from *Gelatine* and *Bronx* supplied the story about Patton's demotion. By the beginning of August there had ceased to be any need for deception to sustain the threat to the Pas de Calais. In the second half of that month *Brutus* and *Garbo* reported that while the Fourth British Army and a recently formed Allied Airborne Army were preparing for a large amphibious and airborne assault against the German right flank and rear, the Ninth US Army and Fourteenth US Army were being transferred to SHAEF's strategic reserve. During the autumn their messages gradually removed most of the remaining notional forces from the Allied order of battle in the United Kingdom.

□

This is not the place to attempt an assessment of the value of the contribution made by the double agents to the *Overlord* deception programme.† The double agents were only one among several resources on which it was based. As well as exploiting their contacts with the Abwehr so ingeniously manipulated by their controllers, it utilised radio deception, the construction of dummy

---

* They took the same view about *Brutus*, who had been instructed toward the end of June to report on the fall of V 1s. On 12 July he was told to confine himself to intelligence on the Allied order of battle.

† See Howard, op cit, Vol V and Hinsley et al, op cit, Vol III Part 2, for full accounts.

craft and installations, the massive intelligence available from Sigint relating to the German armed forces and operational movements and diversions designed to mislead the enemy as to the Allies' real intentions. It is impossible to isolate the work of the double agents and evaluate its effectiveness without regard for that of the other ingredients.

If not quite impossible, an attempt to compare the effectiveness of the agents with that of the other means of deception runs into serious problems. Among the channels available for conveying false information to the enemy about the Allied order of battle and Allied intentions, they surpassed the others in being able to convey it more explicitly, and they differed from the others in that they conveyed it in a dialogue with the enemy. There is thus some danger that their success will be judged by the enemy's evident interest in what they were transmitting or by the plausibility of what they were transmitting.

The need for caution in reaching conclusions applies not only to the influence of the double agents but to that of the deception programme as a whole. After allowing for all the difficulties, however, it may be said with some certainty that the total programme was of great importance in prolonging until the end of July the enemy's hesitation to move infantry divisions from the Pas de Calais to Normandy; and it may be added that by helping to build up the notional order of battle of the Allied forces, and by continuing to report so fully on their notional deployment after D-day, the agents probably made the chief contribution to this success.

At the same time, it should not be overlooked that, in this context at least, *suggestio falsi* was of less consequence than *suppressio veri*. Deception, whatever its contribution, could be instrumental to the success of *Overlord* only to the extent that, thanks in part to the shortcomings of the enemy's intelligence, in part to the success of their own counter-espionage operations and in part to the efficiency of their own security precautions, to which we now turn,* the Allies were able to conceal their true intentions from him.

---

* See Chapter 14. Not least of these precautions were the measures taken to ensure that Allied radio communications were secure (see Hinsley et al, op cit, Vol II, (1981), Appendix 1).

PART V

CHAPTER 14

Security Precautions for Operation *Overlord*

I N THE middle of 1943, when the planning of a cross-Channel invasion began in earnest, responsibility for devising and implementing the measures required for maintaining security during the preparation of British operations lay formally with the Inter-Services Security Board (ISSB). The ISSB had been set up by the JIC in February 1940, when operations were projected in support of Finland, to co-ordinate and improve both the provision of cover for British operations and the prevention of leakage of information about them. Consisting of representatives from the Service departments, MI 5 and the SIS, its terms of reference, as approved by the Chiefs of Staff, had included responsibility for 'measures designed to deceive the enemy as to our plans and intentions', and they had envisaged that it would remain in existence under the JIC for the duration of the war.

At the end of 1941, following the appointment of a Controlling Officer for Deception and the formation of the LCS, these terms of reference had been altered: the ISSB was now required only 'to assist in the preparation of schemes to deceive the enemy'. And in practice its work was limited to its security function and, within the security field, to such routine matters as the selection of code names, the maintenance of indoctrination lists, the control of the circulation of sensitive documents, the marking of stores and the printing and distribution of maps. This had been recognised in October 1942 when the LCS was made solely responsible for the planning and implementation of deception programmes.[1]

Even in the security field the work of the ISSB was to some extent overtaken from the spring of 1942. The enquiry launched by the Security Executive in June 1941 into the state of security within government departments involved in secret business had by then produced the decision to establish a standing committee – the Bridges Panel – under the Lord President to act as a forum for all questions of security in government departments and to be responsible for ensuring that agreed measures were implemented.[2]*

---

* The Bridges Panel was formed early in 1942. It had the Secretary of the Cabinet as chairman and representatives from the Prime Minister, the Treasury, the Foreign Office, the

In these circumstances it is perhaps not surprising that the ISSB was not consulted in advance of the Dieppe raid in August 1942, which was in any case the first substantial operation to be undertaken from the United Kingdom since the Board had been set up. The JIC learned of the omission from an enquiry which concluded that though the raid had not been compromised, there had been defects and indiscretions during the planning of it. It at once protested to the Chiefs of Staff that 'the more secret the operation, the more essential it is that the organisation which had been established for the preservation of secrecy should be informed about it'. The ISSB's charter was accordingly revised again, to emphasise its responsibility for the security of impending operations. At the same time, the Joint Planning Staff was instructed to inform it of all such operations and a representative of the Chief Security Adviser to the Bridges Panel was added to its membership.[3]

In the autumn of 1942 the ISSB, for the first time playing the security role for which it had been designed, co-ordinated the security precautions imposed during the planning of Operation *Torch*, the invasion of north-west Africa. It reported to the JIC in December that 'although there were certain bad lapses, the security arrangements made were on the whole satisfactory and remarkably successful for an operation of this magnitude'.[4] MI 5 carried out its own review and reached less confident conclusions. It advised the JIC in February 1943 that had the enemy been in a position to acquire and appreciate it, 'there was . . . in this country for some considerable period before the actual date of the operation enough material . . . to have informed him of the forthcoming events'.* The report pointed out that the information might well have reached Germany from neutral diplomats, as it was known that both the Turks and the Spaniards had expected Allied landings in north Africa; that the Russian Ambassador had mentioned the locality and the approximate date of the operation to contacts in Fleet Street; that there had been an uncomfortable amount of speculation among journalists, a number of whom had

---

Service departments and MI 5. It issued guidance on such matters as the security of documents and buildings and the selection and supervision of staff. In May 1943 it approved a four-tier system of classification – Most Secret, Secret, Confidential and Restricted. This was later modified by the substitution of Top Secret for Most Secret. After big reductions in 1940 (see above, p 32) the number of vetting submissions to MI 5 increased again to a weekly average of about 6,000 at the end of 1942. Advice from the Panel led to a fall of about 3,000 a week at the end of 1944.

* MI 5 had no doubt been impressed by the fact that on his own initiative *Balloon* had in October 1942 submitted the following for approval: 'From what I can gather there is a plan to attack Rommel from the rear in Africa, and it is possible that this may mean an Anglo/American landing in north Africa, using Gibraltar as a jumping-off place'. This was not, of course, forwarded to the Germans.

guessed the target; that there had been cases of indiscretion and of negligence in handling documents by British officers and the United States forces; and that confidential documents had also been carried by passengers who had been killed in an aircraft which had crashed off Cadiz.[5]*

Despite the work done by the ISSB for Operation *Torch*, and despite MI 5's call for still greater vigilance, the operational staffs and the planners again failed to alert and employ the ISSB during the planning of Operation *Starkey*, the series of deception operations carried out by COSSAC in 1943. The omission drew another protest from the JIC, and by the end of 1943 the ISSB had set up, with support from the JIC, a special committee consisting of itself and representatives from COSSAC, the Home Forces, 21st Army Group, the Naval Force Commander and Air Defence of Great Britain.

In the period up to D-day this committee supervised the adoption by the forces involved in *Overlord* of all the obvious security precautions. They included measures for the special protection of highly sensitive preparations, such as the building of the *Mulberry* harbours, as well as such routine precautions as the suspension of Service leave from 6 April and the segregation of troops in sealed camps after the briefing of the *Overlord* formations. In addition, the Bridges Panel issued instructions to departments to tighten up all security measures.[7] Further, extraordinary, measures were called for from the autumn of 1943, and as they aroused considerable opposition from the civilian authorities they had to be referred to ministers.

□

One such measure concerned access to the coastal areas. In the spring of 1943 the Home Office and the Ministry of Health had opposed the re-imposition of the ban on holiday and casual visitors to the coast between King's Lynn and Littlehampton which had been introduced in 1940 and renewed in the summers of 1941 and 1942, and which the Service departments and the Army Commands wished to retain. The War Cabinet had eventually decided that while local restrictions might be imposed at the discretion of the military within newly defined Regulated Areas, the ban should

---

* The body of one of the passengers was handed over by the Spaniards with assurances, supported by inspection of the documents, that it had not been searched. But ISOS later disclosed that documents carried by another passenger had come into German hands. This experience was turned to account before the invasion of Sicily a few months later, when deceptive documents on a body supposedly from a crashed aircraft were fed to the Germans (Operation *Mincemeat*).[6]

be restricted to the Isle of Wight and the Kent coast.[8] In October 1943, however, Home Forces Command and 21st Army Group requested the re-imposition of a visitors ban throughout the Regulated Areas, which comprised a coastal belt from the Humber to Penzance, the area between Milford Haven and Portishead and areas around the estuaries of the Forth, Tay and Clyde. They were supported by COSSAC, the War Office and MI 5 but opposed by the Home Office, the Ministry of Home Security* and the Ministry of Health. At the end of the year the Chiefs of Staff submitted the problem to the Prime Minister; their minute pointed out that the ban was an essential part of the deception plan, to which they attached great importance. They also suggested that he should consider ways and means of securing the collaboration of the Press in preventing dangerous speculation about the coming invasion.[9]

The Prime Minister, who was in north Africa, replied that all newspapers should be given the strictest injunction against discussion and speculation,† but that he was not in favour of 'sweeping restrictions . . . particularly the visitors ban . . . We must beware of handing out irksome for irksome's sake'. And on Ismay's advice that the ban was likely to be strongly opposed at ministerial level on the ground that it would not in practice contribute to security, the Chiefs of Staff agreed to see whether a compromise could be reached by an *ad hoc* committee under Sir Findlater Stewart, the Chairman of the Home Defence Committee.[10]

This committee, which had representatives from SHAEF, Home Forces, the Service departments, the Home Office, the Ministry of Home Security, the Ministry of Health, the Scottish Office and the Ministry of War Transport as well as from the Security Executive and MI 5, was unable to reach agreement. The Service departments, supported by MI 5, argued that a ban would facilitate the detection of agents and reduce the innocent spread of important information. SHAEF argued that it would limit the enemy's ability to appreciate where the Allies intended to strike and would also boost Allied morale. Opponents of the ban, led by the Home Office and the Ministry of Home Security, believed that its effect in increasing security would be trifling. With those two departments dissenting, however, the committee recommended at the beginning of February 1944 the introduction of the ban at the earliest possible moment, and the Chiefs of Staff sent its recommendation to the Prime Minister with the comment that 'even if, as

---

* An emanation from the Home Office, sharing a single minister and responsible for all civil defence activities.

† This step was taken in February 1944 without further debate, the Press being warned to avoid forecasting the month or the season for an invasion, discussing the desirability or likelihood of particular places for the landing or attempting to estimate the scale of the attacks. Similar warnings were given to the Press in the United States.

the Home Office suggests, the imposition of these restrictions would add little to the security of *Overlord*, we cannot in a matter of such vital importance afford to neglect any precautions however small'. They added that they believed 'that the Americans attach great importance to this point and are prepared to press hard for it'. The Prime Minister again expressed disapproval of the ban, but agreed to remit the question to the Committee on *Overlord* Preparations which had recently been set up under his own chairmanship to 'speed up and stimulate *Overlord* preparations in all aspects other than tactical and strategic and to review and adjust their impact on war programmes and the life of the community'.[11] In addition he asked for a list 'on one sheet of paper of the kind of things that you particularly do not wish visitors . . . to see'.*

Another problem had by then emerged; the Chiefs of Staff had asked Findlater Stewart to consult the Service departments about the likely effect on the morale of the Services of the imposition of a ban on leave to Ireland and as to the possibility of curtailing civilian traffic to and from Ireland. Although the British authorities had recently secured the closing down of the transmitter in the German legation in Dublin,† MI 5 had recommended early in January that these measures should be adopted from the middle of March in view of the fact that 150,000 Irish labourers were working in the United Kingdom, many of them in areas affected by *Overlord* preparations. Findlater Stewart advised the Chiefs of Staff early in February that there was no insuperable objection to the measures provided that they were applied to both Service and civilian traffic, and the Chiefs of Staff sent to the Committee on *Overlord* Preparations the recommendation that a ban should be applied at 24 hours' notice as soon as the necessary administrative steps were completed.[12]

The committee met on 9 February, seventeen ministers, the Chiefs of Staff and Findlater Stewart under the Prime Minister's chairmanship. It agreed without difficulty to a ban on travel to and from Ireland, but the visitors ban remained controversial. The Chiefs of Staff argued that, when thousands of lives were at stake, any precautions that might increase security must be taken. They had been informed on 7 February that SHAEF thought the ban vital to the success of *Overlord*: 'If the enemy obtains as much as 48 hours' warning of the location of the assault area the chances of success are small and any longer warning spells certain defeat'.[13] Findlater Stewart, who reported that the number of visitors to Brighton alone was 200,000 a month, also reported the views of

---

* See Appendix 12.

† See above, p 195.

MI 5: it feared that without the ban 'a large influx' of enemy agents might pick up information about the *Overlord* preparations, and about the dummy installations that supported the deception plan, from observation and listening to careless talk. The Home Secretary, opposed to interfering with public liberty without good reason, doubted whether the ban would serve any purpose, if only because it would be impossible to enforce. The Prime Minister broadened the debate. Pointing out that a ban would not cut off the enemy's access to the most dangerous sources of information – the export of newspapers; foreign diplomatic representatives; agents working in Eire – he suggested that the only effective way to achieve security would be to draw a cordon round the whole of the British Isles, including Eire, to censor all communications, including diplomatic communications, and to stop any air or sea traffic not under direct British control; and the committee concluded that a decision about the visitors ban should be deferred until it received a report on the practicability of these wider measures.[14]

This report was prepared by a sub-committee consisting of the Minister of Production (Lyttelton), the Minister of Aircraft Production (Stafford Cripps) and the Parliamentary Secretary to the Ministry of Supply (Duncan Sandys) on the basis of enquiries made by Findlater Stewart's staff of all relevant departments and organisations, which discussed them with him at a series of meetings attended by MI 5.[15] Completed by 28 February, it recommended a series of security measures additional to those already in force.[16] They included the imposition of the visitors ban, which would, it was estimated, exclude some 600,000 visitors a month from the coastal areas affected.* Of the other recommendations, the principal ones were:

The diplomatic representatives of all neutral governments, including the government of Eire, should be prohibited from sending or receiving uncensored communications whether by bag or cypher, and from leaving Great Britain. (The report stated that the Foreign Office was unable to agree to this recommendation and suggested as an alternative that all neutral outward communications should be stopped for about ten days before D-day).

The existing 50 per cent censorship of mail to Northern Ireland should

---

* In a memorandum for the sub-committee in support of the ban MI 5 accepted that 'the Germans have no single [uncontrolled] agent in this country' and that knowledge of the enemy's espionage system was so complete that 'any intensification of enemy activity . . . would be likely to be registered in a sort of seismographic fashion'. But MI 5 believed it possible, perhaps probable, that a number of spies would be dropped by parachute as D-day approached, and since the ban would make it easier to catch spies and reduce the danger of indiscreet talk, it regarded the ban as 'a precaution which on no consideration would [MI 5] be justified in neglecting'.

be increased to 100 per cent. Artificial delays to bring the period between despatch and receipt up to one month should be imposed on mail to foreign countries and Gibraltar. For mail to prisoners of war in Germany (which was thought to be a very easy way for an enemy agent to communicate in plain language code) the period should be three months. The strongest possible measures should be taken to prevent aircrews taking uncensored mail out of the country. Overseas telegrams should be paraphrased and artificially delayed.

The Aer Lingus service between Liverpool and Dublin should be discontinued. Only air services operated by BOAC should run to Eire. The Swedish AB air service between Aberdeen and Sweden should be interrupted for as long as possible before D-day.

Special precautions should be taken to ensure the reliability of the crews of ships sailing from the United Kingdom to continental ports including Gibraltar. The existing practice of bringing all ships sailing from Eire to foreign ports into British ports for examination should continue.

In order to make the infiltration of agents more difficult the transfer of Allied nationals to the United Kingdom should be kept to a minimum.

Every precaution should be taken to prevent leakage through secret agents sent from the United Kingdom to the Continent who might have operational knowledge which could be deliberately or inadvertently transmitted to the enemy.*

Government sponsored travel should be reduced to a minimum. The ban on travel to Ireland should be imposed as soon as possible.

A visitors ban would be justified if it would make a substantial additional contribution to security. It would reduce the number of visitors to the coastal areas involved by some 600,000 each month.

On 1 March the full committee approved these recommendations except for those relating to diplomatic communications and the visitors ban. With regard to the former the Foreign Office offered a new suggestion to the effect that the diplomatic communications of neutral states and of all Allied governments other than those of the United States and Soviet Russia should be banned from time to time for short periods. On the visitors ban the Prime Minister remained unhappy, asking the sub-committee to consider whether it could be restricted to selected areas of the coast. The sub-committee reported on these suggestions to a

---

* 'C' had made this point several times. He told the JIC on 15 February that he was satisfied as regards SIS agents, but was filled with alarm by what he knew of the activities of other agencies, including those of Allied authorities. MI 5 fully shared his misgivings.[17] Nor were these misgivings groundless. As the result of the penetration of an SOE circuit in France, messages broadcast by the BBC on 1 June were recognised by German counter-intelligence as calling a state of alert and others broadcast at 2100 hours on 5 June as action messages. Late on 5 June warnings that invasion was imminent were issued to Seventh and Fifteenth Armies. Fifteenth Army alerted its Corps, but Seventh Army, which was responsible for most of the assault area, took no action.[18]

further meeting on 8 March. It found the Foreign Office's suggestion impracticable, but agreed that a ban on diplomatic communications should apply to all the Allies except Russia and the United States, as well as to the neutrals. It also reported that it would be impracticable to limit the application of the visitors ban – on which subject General Eisenhower, prompted by General Montgomery, had written to the Chiefs of Staff on 6 March that 'it would go hard with our consciences if we were to feel . . . that by neglecting any security precaution we had compromised the success of these vital operations or needlessly squandered men's lives'. On 8 March the Prime Minister nevertheless reserved decisions on these two questions for the War Cabinet, but the committee authorised the implementation of the other recommendations.[19]

As already noted, the other recommendations included the ban on travel to and from Ireland, which came into force at once, and measures aimed at isolating Eire. The latter had assumed greater importance when, on 7 March, the Eire government rejected, as being incompatible with its neutrality, a request from the United States, supported by the British government, that it should sever relations with Germany and Japan, or at least procure the withdrawal of the German and Japanese diplomatic and consular missions, 'as constituting a danger to the lives of American soldiers and to the success of Allied military operations'.[20] Under pressure from the Prime Minister, the Chiefs of Staff asked Findlater Stewart for a further report on what else might be done to supplement the travel ban. On 18 March he advised that the British government should offer to charter Eire ships trafficking with the Iberian peninsula and to supply the imports they carried; should seek to immobilise the Aer Lingus service to the United Kingdom, which operated the only civil aircraft in Eire capable of flying to the Continent; and should withdraw until after D-day the concession by which Eire travellers were allowed to use the BOAC and American air lines operating from Shannon, these being the only air services from Eire to other overseas destinations. He pointed out, however, that should the Eire government resist these proposals and retaliate, the United Kingdom might suffer the loss of valuable concessions by Eire authorities, notably to the Royal Air Force.[21] In the event, the Eire authorities accepted the proposals at the beginning of April.

Meanwhile, on 10 March, the War Cabinet had decided that the visitors ban should be imposed from 1 April throughout the coastal area from The Wash to Cornwall and in the area round the Firth of Forth, the Prime Minister still doubting whether it would contribute materially to security but recognising that the *Overlord* forces must have the assurance that every possible precaution was being taken. But it had again postponed a decision as to the banning of diplomatic communications in deference to the concern of the Foreign Office. The Foreign Secretary had argued that a ban would cause considerable inconvenience and might lead to damaging retaliation.[22] On 13 April, however, after further consultations between ministers, SHAEF, the Chiefs of Staff and Findlater Stewart, the War Cabinet finally agreed that a ban on these communications, and on the movements of couriers and other diplomatic personnel, should be applied to neutral and Allied governments, other than the Russian and American governments, as soon as possible.[23]

These restrictions became effective at midnight on 17–18 April. On 19 April they were extended to the military communications and to the movement of the military personnel of Allied governments in the United Kingdom. The Allied governments were, however, permitted to send messages from 5 May provided they deposited copies of the cyphers they wished to use and submitted the messages in plain language to the British authorities, who would decide whether the messages were to be forwarded in the originator's cypher or in British cypher.[24]* A few exceptions were also made to the ban on movements of military personnel.†

□

Little evidence of serious leakage about the *Overlord* preparations came to light in the weeks before D-day. It is impossible to say how far this was due to the special precautions, but it may be noted that some of the more disturbing evidence surfaced before they came into force: MI 5 reported on 3 March that there had been more than a dozen cases of the communication or attempted

---

* With the exception of the French authorities, the Allied governments accepted these stringent measures with good grace. Largely as a result of the reluctance of Roosevelt and Churchill to recognise de Gaulle's Committee of National Liberation as the provisional government of France, relations with the French authorities were already bad when the measures were introduced, but General Koenig, de Gaulle's military representative in London, suspended contacts with SHAEF because they made it impossible for the CNL 'to communicate in French code with its diplomatic and military representatives in London'. Anxiety about the security of French cyphers and the possibility that information reaching Algiers and the Resistance movement would leak to the Germans had in any case led the Combined Chiefs of Staff to give orders on 1 April that no information that might compromise *Overlord* should be passed to the French authorities.[25]

† A Czech application for the despatch of some 100 officers to a Czech division being formed in Russia was declined; they were to travel via Egypt, 'a notoriously insecure spot'. But the transfer of 2,000 Norwegians from Sweden to the United Kingdom in United States bombers, which had been approved previously, was allowed to continue, the men being flown to the Isle of Man for examination by MI 5, and the Polish government, anxious to keep contact with its forces overseas, was permitted to send out a few officers after obtaining approval in each individual case.[26]

communication to unauthorised persons of information about *Mulberry* harbours and *Pluto* (Pipe Line under the Ocean), and that the organisation called 'Mass Observation' had invited its 1,400 observers to report, either from their own knowledge or by making enquiries, where and when the second front would be opened. In reports covering April and May MI 5 drew attention to further leakages, but none was of more than marginal importance. Just before D-day, as a result of errors in Press censorship, a practice message from Associated Press to the effect that the Allies had landed on the French coast was circulated in the United States, and articles from accredited correspondents with the expeditionary forces, which should have been embargoed until SHAEF had issued its first communiqué, were released to some newspapers and news agencies.[27] But these mistakes had no serious consequences. The only leakage that, on the evidence of Sigint, came to the notice of the Germans in fact emanated from the inspired guesswork of Kraemer and *Ostro*. In February Kraemer reported from Stockholm that the second front had been postponed till June, partly on account of disagreements between the Allied Expeditionary Air Force and the British and US strategic bomber forces.* As already noted *Ostro* informed the Abwehr at the beginning of June that the Allies favoured an assault on the Cherbourg peninsula.† Though they were disturbing for the Allies, these reports did not influence German appreciations.‡

It may be supposed that it was the absence of grounds for serious alarm which enabled the civilian authorities to contemplate, even before D-day, the early removal of the special precautions which they had in any case accepted with great reluctance, as being politically embarrassing and socially irksome. As early as 22 May the Chiefs of Staff learned that the Prime Minister was assuming that the ban on diplomatic communications would be lifted on D-day and that the CIGS, concerned that to end the ban at that stage would undermine the effectiveness of the *Overlord* deception plan, had arranged for SHAEF to be consulted and for the sub-committee on *Overlord* security to take the matter to the War Cabinet.[28]

On 25 May a memorandum from SHAEF urged that none of the special restrictions should be removed until at least D+30. On the same day, in an interview with the Foreign Secretary, General Eisenhower and his Chief of Staff, Bedell Smith, conceded that the

---

* See above, p 201, and Hinsley et al, *British Intelligence in the Second World War*, Vol III Part 2 (1988), p 51.

† See above, p 200, and Hinsley et al, op cit, Vol III Part 2, p 61.

‡ See Hinsley et al, op cit, Vol III Part 2, Chapter 44.

diplomatic ban might be lifted on D+7; but Eden, feeling unable to hold the position even for a week, proposed to announce the lifting on D+1 or D+2, while delaying the restoration of normal communications till D+7. The War Cabinet accepted this proposal, and on 31 May the Prime Minister told Eisenhower that the programme must be followed unless he could produce new arguments against it.[29]

SHAEF did not respond before D-day. On 11 June, however, Bedell Smith submitted to the Foreign Office high-grade Sigint decrypts attesting to 'the enemy's continuing belief that the present landings are soon to be followed by others, possibly in Norway, the Pas de Calais, the Low Countries and elsewhere in France'. On this evidence he urged that 'it was imperative that the enemy receives no scrap of information which might indicate to him the true nature of our plans', and reported that Eisenhower earnestly hoped that there would be no relaxation of the ban before 21 June (D+25).* The War Cabinet yielded to this appeal, fixing 19 June as the date for lifting the ban, but on 19 June it rejected a last-minute suggestion from the Home Secretary that the ban should be retained as a means of denying the enemy information about his V 1 offensive.[30]

SHAEF had by then been advised that all the other special *Overlord* precautions would be removed at the end of June unless good reasons were produced for the retention of any of them; it now made a case for maintaining the ban on visits to the coastal area. On 27 June the War Cabinet was advised that SHAEF thought that, at least in the area from The Wash to Southampton and in Scotland, this ban remained essential in support of the deception programme in view of the fact that the Germans continued to believe that attacks were planned in the Pas de Calais and Norway. On 28 June Eisenhower repeated this argument to the Chiefs of Staff and told them that Montgomery regarded retention of the ban as essential to the success of his operations. Influenced no doubt by the slow progress of the Allied forces in Normandy, the War Cabinet at once deferred action regarding all the special precautions other than those which could be withdrawn without public announcement; the latter would be cancelled on 1 July, but Findlater Stewart was requested to report on the others. On 7 July it accepted Findlater Stewart's recommendations: until a further review at the beginning of August the visitors ban should be retained except in the south-west, west of Southampton; the restrictions on overseas travel and travel to and from Ireland

---

* For full details of the Sigint evidence submitted to the Foreign Office see Hinsley et al, op cit, Vol III Part 2, p 176ff and for the deception programme after D-day see above, Chapter 13 and Howard, *British Intelligence in the Second World War*, Vol V (1990), Chapter 9.

should be retained, though they might be eased by granting exemptions on compassionate grounds; Service leave should continue to be suspended.[31]

On 21 July the Chiefs of Staff recommended that Service leave should be resumed from 1 August; it had been suspended since 6 April, and its resumption was highly desirable from the point of view of morale. They were dissuaded by Eisenhower, who insisted that the conjunction of the suspension of leave with the visitors ban had been decisive in supporting the credibility of the deception programme, and that the deception programme was still influencing the enemy's appreciations.[32] In the review carried out at the beginning of August, however, SHAEF accepted that Service leave should be re-opened from 15 August, and also that the Firth of Forth area could be released from the visitors ban and that the restrictions on overseas travel and travel to and from Ireland could be lifted. It still sought to retain the visitors ban between The Wash and Southampton for another month. But on 9 August the War Cabinet expressed the hope that, as the military situation in Normandy had shifted decisively in favour of the Allies, SHAEF would not persist with this request, and Eisenhower agreed that the visitors ban could be wholly withdrawn from 25 August provided no early public announcement was made.[33]

CHAPTER 14: REFERENCES

1. Mockler-Ferryman, *Military Intelligence Organisation*, p 11.
2. CAB 93/6, HD(S)E(GD) 1st Meeting 17 June 1941; CAB 98/48, S (42) Minutes and Memoranda.
3. CAB 79/24, COS(42) 355th Meeting of 23 December; JIC (42) 44th and 59th Meetings of 8 September and 8 December; JIC(42) 468(o) of 5 December.
4. JIC(42) 470(o) of 3 December.
5. JIC(43) 9th and 11th Meetings of 23 February and 2 March.
6. CAB 121/496, SIC file E/North Africa/3F, ISSB enquiry into accident of 26 September 1942, COS(42) 136th(o) Meeting of 3 October, C-in-C Gibraltar telegram to War Office 076450 of 4 October, Cabinet Office minute to Chiefs of Staff, 1 November 1942.
7. CAB 98/50, S(44)5, 6 and 7 of 12 April, 6 and 24 May 1944.
8. CAB 65/33, WM(43) 35 of 23 February, 46 of 29 March; CAB 66/34, WP(43) 74 of 20 February; CAB 66/35, WP(43) 112 and 116 of 21 and 23 March; CAB 93/7, SE(SO) 1st Meeting of 19 March 1943; CAB 71/11, LP(43) 18th Meeting of 24 March.
9. CAB 113/18, C-in-C Home Forces memorandum HF/2404/7(G1(b)) of 8 October 1943; CAB 93/7, SE(SO) 2nd Meeting of 6 December 1943; CAB 121/381, SIC file D/France/6/7, COS(43) 782(o) of 22 December, COS(44) 2(o) of 1 January.
10. CAB 121/381, FROZEN telegram 1087 of 4 January 1944, COS(44) 14(o) of 7 January, COS(44) 7th (o) Meeting of 10 January.
11. ibid, COS(44) 122(o) of 3 February, COS (44) 34th and 41st (o) Meetings of 4 and 9 February, Ismay minute to PM of 4 February, PM Directive D/35/4 of 5 February, Hollis to Findlater Stewart, 6 February; CAB 66/46, WP(44) 68 of 31 January.
12. CAB 121/381, COS(44) 26th and 33rd (o) Meetings of 27 January and 3 February, COS(44) 63(o) of 22 January, 118(o) of 2 February, 128(o) of 7 February.
13. ibid, COS(44) 128(o) of 7 February.
14. ibid, OP(44) 2nd Meeting of 9 February.
15. CAB 98/40, OP(S)(M)(44) series.
16. ibid, OP(44)9 of 28 February, OP(44) 4th Meeting of 1 March.
17. JIC(44) 6th and 7th Meetings of 8 and 15 February.
18. MRD Foot, *SOE in France* (1966), p 388; Hinsley et al, *British Intelligence in the Second World War*, Vol III Part 2, p 127 fn*.
19. CAB 121/381, OP(44) 4th and 5th Meetings of 1 and 8 March, Minutes of Conference of OP Committee also 8 March, OP(44) 11 of 7 March, Montgomery letter to Eisenhower 21 AGp/1001/C-in-C of 3 March and Eisenhower to COS SHAEF/5MX/INT of 6 March; CAB 98/40, OP(S)(M)(44) 4th Meeting of 6 March.
20. PREM 3/133/5; CAB 65/45, WM(44) 15 CA of 4 February; CAB 121/381, WP(44) 151, 156 and 160 of 7, 10 and 15 March.
21. CAB 121/381, COS(44) 269(o) of 18 March, PM Telegram T605/4 of 19 March, COS(44) 92nd(o) Meeting of 20 March, PM Minute M306/4 of 22 March, 'C' to PM 23 March, No 10 Downing Street to Cabinet Office 24 March.
22. ibid, WM(44) 31 of 10 March.
23. ibid, OP(44) 23 of 10 April, OP(44) 7th Meeting of 12 April, Ismay to PM 12 April, WM(44) 48 CA of 13 April, 51 of 15 April.
24. ibid, COS(44) 346(o), 349(o) of 17 and 18 April, COS(44) 128th(o) Meeting of 19 April; JIC(44) 169(o) of 1 May

25. ibid, FO to CIGS 16 March and COS reply 17 March, SHAEF to Hollis 27 March, COS(44) 104th (o) Meeting of 30 March, COS(W) 1243 of 30 March, FAN telegram 353 of 1 April, COS(44) 152nd, 155th, 156th and 163rd (o) Meetings of 10, 12, 13 and 18 May; Ehrman, *Grand Strategy* Vol V (1956), p 317ff; Woodward, *British Foreign Policy in the Second World War* Vol I (1962), p 264ff.

26. CAB 121/381, COS (44) 386(o) of 2 May, COS(44) 145th (o) Meeting of 4 May.

27. ibid, COS(44) 544(o) of 19 June; PREM 3/345/6.

28. CAB 121/381, COS(44) 166th(o) Meeting of 22 May.

29. ibid, COS(44) 166th(o) Meeting of 22 May, COS(44) 457(o) and PM Minute 44/371 both of 25 May, COS(44) 174th(o) Meeting of 27 May, 175th(o) Meeting of 30 May, WM(44) 69 of 30 May, 70 CA of 31 May, PM to Eisenhower, 31 May.

30. ibid, Bedell Smith to Eden, 11 June, Ismay to Bedell Smith 14 June and reply 16 June, WP(44) 319 of 12 June, WM(44) 77 and 77 CA of 13 June, COS(44) 191st(o) Meeting of 13 June, WM(44) 80 of 19 June, COS(44) 200th(o) Meeting of 19 June.

31. ibid, WP(44) 350 of 27 June, Note by Controlling Officer, 28 June, WM(44) 84 of 29 June, COS(44) 214th(o) Meeting of 29 June, WP(44) 374 of 5 July, WM(44) 88 of 7 July.

32. ibid, COS(44) 241st(o) Meeting of 19 July, COS(44) 252nd(o) Meeting of 29 July.

33. ibid, WP(44) 432 of 5 August, WM(44) 104 of 9 August, COS(44) 267th(o) Meeting of 9 August, Bedel Smith to Hollis, 9 August, Hollis to Attlee, 18 August, COS(44) 280th(o) Meeting of 18 August, WM(44) 109 of 21 August, WP(44) 468 of 25 August, WM(44) 111 of 28 August.

CHAPTER 15

Counter-Espionage Operations in the Field

AS WELL as providing security for the *Overlord* preparations that were taking place in the United Kingdom, it was necessary to expand the organisation that would be responsible for security in support of the operations of the Allied forces in the field. Pre-war regulations, set out in the Manual of Military Intelligence in the Field, had laid it down that the Intelligence Branch of the GHQ of an expeditionary force should contain a security section (Section Ib) under a GSO 2, with three sub-sections responsible for the collection of intelligence; for counter-espionage, counter-sabotage and the control of civilians; and for the security of military establishments and personnel.[1] But no effective field organisation had existed during the campaigns in western Europe in 1940 and there had been little opportunity to develop one before the planning of Operation *Torch*.

In preparation for *Torch*, Ib sections had been established under G-2 at AFHQ and at HQ First Army under a GSO 2. In addition, the SIS had supplied a mobile Special Intelligence (b) Unit to carry out covert counter-espionage operations and to be responsible for communicating ISOS information to the Ib sections and supervising the exploitation of it, and this unit was supported by a static SIS station staffed from SIS's Section V.[2] MI 5 had offered to contribute to this programme. Before the war the War Office War Book had required it to assist in completing the Ib establishments for the Field Force and in issuing such security intelligence hand-books and instructions as they might require. In 1942 MI 5 believed that while the SIS units should supply intelligence about the enemy's intelligence service, it lacked the expertise needed for many of the processes that were essential for effective counter-intelligence, particularly the examination of suspects, control of the civilian population, counter-sabotage and protective security measures, and that the experience gained in these matters in the United Kingdom should be brought to bear in the operational theatres by officers who had served with or been trained by MI 5. But its participation had been rejected by the SIS and AFHQ on the ground that north Africa was foreign territory in which MI 5 had no standing.

The field units supplied for *Torch* proved to be of little value in the event. If security and counter-intelligence operations in Tunisia were remarkably successful, as they were despite the large semi-hostile Arab population and the scope which had existed for Axis penetration, particularly through the Armistice Commissions set up after the fall of France, this was because staff from the HQ of the Service de Securité Militaire (SSM) escaped from Vichy to Algiers soon after the landings and offered their services to the Allied forces. It was largely due to their knowledge and experience that the territory had been effectively controlled and that all the German stay-behind agents had been rounded up.[3]

For the invasion of Sicily and southern Italy the field organisation was further expanded; a Field Security Section was allotted to each division and all higher Headquarters, and 15th Army Group was supplied with mobile units for the detection of illicit radio transmitters as well as with a Special Intelligence (b) Unit responsible for co-ordinating the recruitment and employment of informers and counter-intelligence agents. Steps were also taken to improve the transmission from the United Kingdom to the operational theatre of all available information about the activities of the enemy's secret services.[4] The effectiveness of these measures was not seriously tested, since neither the Abwehr nor the SD left stay-behind networks in Sicily or Calabria.

MI 5 had meanwhile continued to press on the War Office and the SIS the case for using its experience and its staff. Its persistence was rewarded in the summer of 1943 with the posting of three MI 5 officers to AFHQ and a request from COSSAC's intelligence branch, with the grudging agreement of the SIS, that MI 5 should provide an officer to undertake the planning of civil security for the *Overlord* forces. This officer encountered serious difficulties – notably the unfamiliarity with the subject of the American members of COSSAC's staff and the lack of agreement about how to divide responsibility between the Field Security Sections and the Special Intelligence (b) Units – and so little progress was made that in November 1943 MI 5 was asked to take charge of the programme. A senior MI 5 officer was appointed Adviser to COSSAC's I(b) staff, another was made GSO 2 I(b) for civil security at 21st Army Group and a third was loaned to the Theatre Intelligence Section (TIS).*

Through the last of these representatives MI 5 supervised the production of the hand-books summarising all the available information about the enemy's secret services and the political situation in the occupied countries that might be needed by the

---

* For the formation of the TIS see Hinsley et al, *British Intelligence in the Second World War*, Vol III Part 2 (1988), Appendix 1.

security and counter-intelligence units in the field.* The other two MI 5 appointees played a large part in drawing up the directives for the field units that were set out in SHAEF Intelligence Directive No 7 on Counter-Intelligence, which was issued in February 1944.† It laid down the duties of the Field Security staffs that were to be trained by MI 5‡ for service in the operational zones – these were primarily the investigation of cases of espionage and sabotage and the screening of refugees, of escaping civilian internees and of released or escaping prisoners of war and of any suspicious civilians to prevent the infiltration of enemy agents and saboteurs – and defined their relations with the Special Intelligence (b) Units that were to be supplied by the SIS to the British Army Group and Army HQs. The latter, now re-named Special Counter-Intelligence Units (SCIUs), would receive from the SIS on an independent communications link the latest information on known and suspected enemy agents and collaborators and on the location of documents, premises and other targets of importance to counter-intelligence. They would convey it to the security staffs and would be consulted on the use made of it, but executive action would be the responsibility of the security staffs. Those staffs, on the other hand, would inform the SCIUs of the capture of enemy agents and intelligence personnel and follow their advice about the interrogation of the agents, as also about the examination of captured documents of counter-intelligence value.[5] After preliminary interrogation in the field, important enemy agents would be sent to the United Kingdom for examination at Camp 020. Special arrangements were made for the information obtained there to be fed back to the SCIUs with the utmost despatch.

The SHAEF Intelligence Directive on Counter-Intelligence made no reference to the arrangements that had been made for carrying out deception and obtaining counter-intelligence by operating double agents in the operational zones. In January 1944, on MI 5's initiative, a meeting attended by representatives of the LCS, SHAEF, Ops B, the SIS and MI 5 had agreed that an experienced MI 5 officer should be attached to 21st Army Group HQ to be responsible for selecting double agents in consultation with its SCIU, and that case officers for handling them should be trained and held in readiness by MI 5. The meeting had decided that they should be attached to the SIS's SCIUs when sent into the

---

* The information was collected from no less than 12 authorities, including the TIS, the SIS, the RSS, MI 9, MI 14 and the SOE as well as MI 5.
† See Appendix 13.
‡ MI 5 put a considerable effort into training British and US personnel for I(b) duties. In addition, numerous MI 5 officers were transferred to counter-intelligence appointments.

field, but it was agreed in May that double agents in the field should be handled by two additional SCIUs, one at 21st Army Group and the other at SHAEF, to be staffed by MI 5. Another SCIU, to carry out this function in the American part of the theatre, was provided by the OSS.

The SIS accepted with some reluctance the growing encroachment of MI 5 in the area of counter-intelligence overseas. And it drew the line when MI 5, foreseeing problems in collating and distributing the mass of counter-intelligence data that was likely to be required by the Allied armies and anticipating the security requirements of the Anglo-American occupation of Germany, proposed the immediate establishment of a co-ordinating counter-intelligence staff at SHAEF which would be the nucleus for a Central Counter-Intelligence Bureau to be set up on the entry of the Allied armies into Germany. 'C' vetoed this proposal on the ground that in relation to Germany the SIS must remain solely responsible for the preparation of counter-intelligence data and the control of counter-intelligence operations. But in the end the arrangements made for the entry into Europe, which were completed by June 1944, included not only a new German section in the SIS but also a section at SHAEF under an officer from MI 5, to supervise the collection of intelligence about the Nazi Party and the German Police, and a joint SIS/OSS War Room, to service the SCIUs, to which MI 5 and the French SSM* attached representatives.

□

When the Allied armies landed in Normandy it was known from ISOS and from *Artist* that Canaris had been dismissed in February and that Hitler had signed an order for the creation of a unified intelligence service as a result of which the Abwehr was absorbed into the RSHA as the Militärisches Amt (Mil Amt).† Meanwhile the 1942 assessment of the Abwehr's competence‡ had been drastically revised. A manual on the German Secret Service, issued for the guidance of counter-intelligence officers in the field, rated the efficiency of the Gestapo and the SD as 'markedly greater than

---

* Agreement on the full co-operation of the SSM, which was essential for the efficiency of security and counter-intelligence in the liberated areas, was reached at the professional level in May on the basis of formally recognising French sovereignty while reserving essential rights for the Allied military authorities. But acute political difficulties between the Allies and de Gaulle held up the implementation of the agreement until after D-day.

† At this stage the arrangements preserved much of the Abwehr in its original form, but the July Plot in which its leaders and other members were implicated completed its ruin. (For further details see Appendix 1(iii).

‡ See above, p 113.

that of the Abwehr', where 'corruption, financial and professional', was common.[6] In June MI 5 and Section V reported to the JIC in similar vein.

It was also known by D-day that the Abwehr had been replacing its static stations in France and the Low Countries by mobile units.* ISOS had shown that the units were controlled operationally from Paris and administratively, according to whether they were to operate north or south of the Loire, from Stuttgart or Wiesbaden. Especially through the decrypts of practice messages used by the Abwehr to give training in radio technique, ISOS had, moreover, identified many of the members of these units together with the approximate locations and the names or cover-names of more than 100 stay-behind agents. Intelligence about the plans and dispositions of the SD was less complete, its cyphers being, as always, more secure than those of the Abwehr.

During June and July about a dozen stay-behind agents and line-crossers were sent to Camp 020 for interrogation. All but one were young Frenchmen. In August some 20 more were sent to 020; they were considerably more experienced, several of them having worked for the Abwehr for a long time, and twelve of them had been provided with radio links. From the middle of August the speed of the Allied advance through France both enlarged the opportunities for enemy agents and militated against systematic counter-intelligence work, and following the Allied entry into Belgium the over-stretched counter-intelligence authorities were hampered by delays in identifying Abwehr and SD operators among the large number of collaborators who were being arrested by the Belgian authorities. It was at this time that the enemy achieved what was, so far as is known, his only potentially dangerous penetration of Allied military security during the campaign in north-west Europe. Christian Lindemans, alias *King Kong*, who had carried out massive betrayals of Dutch, Belgian and French Resistance organisations before he was instructed to stay behind in Brussels for the Abwehr, and who had then succeeded in getting himself recruited by IS 9, the agency which worked under MI 9 in organising the escape of Allied prisoners of war, conveyed some information to the Germans in September about an impending airborne attack. The information does not appear to have included a mention of Arnhem, however, and it did not alert the Germans to the fact that Arnhem was the Allied objective.† Also in September, ISOS disclosed that some 20 radio agents were operating behind the Allied lines, most of them short-term

---

* For the Abwehr's mobile units see Appendix 1(iii).
† See Appendix 14 and Hinsley et al, op cit, Vol III Part 2, p 387n.

stay-behind agents concentrated near the French west coast, and the files of the HQ of the Abwehr's sabotage division, captured near Paris, revealed that preparations for sabotage had been made on a large scale, with nearly a thousand dumps of equipment dispersed throughout France. But with the assistance of ISOS and of these files, which contained details of the organisation and lists of agents, spies were rounded up in large numbers in October. Only twelve of those captured in October were of sufficient interest to be sent to Camp 020.

The Allies suffered a serious set-back in October: the temporary loss of the ISOS decrypts. As a result of changes in the cypher procedures of the Abwehr and the SD, the traffic to and from Berlin and other control stations in Germany ceased to be readable, except for that with Spain and Portugal, as did the traffic of the mobile units. But the latter was recovered in the middle of December, from which time it was decrypted, with the help of a double agent, regularly and currently till the end of the war.* In the interval the lack of Sigint was off-set by the fact that the stay-behind agents included people who had been blackmailed into working for Germany, and who quickly defected, and known collaborators, who were quickly arrested. Four of the principal SD agents in Brussels gave themselves up a few days after the Allies entered the city, and three more were arrested. Two Belgians who had served in the SD also went over to the Allies, bringing with them a mass of information about the enemy's stay-behind organisation. An Abwehr sabotage organisation in western Flanders collapsed as a result of the defection of its radio operator and eight of its sub-agents. Still more information came to light in November with the capture of a line-crosser who was familiar with the SD's archives in Berlin. By the end of 1944 about a hundred agents had been captured since the Allied entry into Belgium, and although thirty identified by ISOS or in interrogations had not been accounted for, the ISOS decrypts showed that the stay-behind agents still reporting to the Germans were all under Allied control.

The intention to use agents captured in the field as controlled agents for deception purposes had been abandoned by the middle of September.† From October however, SHAEF and its 212 Committee ‡ operated them for counter-intelligence purposes – to penetrate the enemy's networks as a means of improving security for the Allied forces, of checking any attempt to set up an

---

* It was unfortunate that this traffic was not being read in the weeks preceding the German offensive in the Ardennes. When the decrypts became available they disclosed a pronounced movement of the units into this sector of the front and a striking concentration of their effort there.

† See below, p 273.

‡ For the formation of the 212 Committee see below, p 273.

underground organisation for use after the end of hostilities and of assisting GC and CS to overcome the cypher changes which had recently made the Abwehr tràffic unreadable. Between July, when the first of them was recruited, and the end of November their number had grown to 17. Seven of the more important of them remained in contact with the Germans till the last days of the war.* Especially while the ISOS decrypts were in short supply, their traffic usefully supplemented the Sigint that was available about enemy espionage and sabotage behind the Allied lines.

This activity increasingly relied on parachutists and line-crossers as the uncontrolled stay-behind agents in France and the Low Countries were eliminated, and it was intensified from November, and especially during the Ardennes offensive. Early in November, when line-crossing was taking place along the whole front, it was known that eight parachute landings were being planned. By mid-December the newly recovered ISOS decrypts were providing detailed information about the distribution of Canadian and US uniforms and identity papers to line-crossers and the widespread dropping of parachutists on sabotage missions against pipe-lines, fuel stocks and the Paris Metro; two had landed at Lyons, eight at Blois, one at Montpellier, two at Boissy and five at Epinay. By the end of December 21 parachutists, most of them members of pro-German Fascist parties, had been captured and 11 were known to be still at large. From early in 1945, as well as giving advance notice of continuing parachutist and line-crossing missions and revealing that the enemy was attempting to establish new stay-behind agents in the liberated areas, ISOS decrypts gave the names, or cover-names, and often the locations of about 200 stay-behind agents who were to operate in western Germany. By April, however, it was virtually certain that the whole of the German network in the liberated areas was again under Allied control, and the speed of the Allied advance had meanwhile frustrated the plans for a stay-behind network in the Reich.

□

In the light of experience in the summer and autumn of 1944, changes in the arrangements for providing expert back-up for the counter-intelligence organisation in the field were discussed from November. It was clear by then on the one hand that the SIS/OSS War Room was inadequately staffed for this purpose and on the other hand that the SCIUs had been kept so busy circulating ISOS and other intelligence to the field units handling captured spies

---

* See Appendix 15.

and examining captured documents that they had been unable to carry out their special responsibility for running agents for counter-intelligence purposes. In November 1944, in preparation for the entry into Germany, SHAEF proposed that the War Room, enlarged in scope and supported by the special registry and staff of MI 5's B Division, should come entirely under SHAEF's control and should circulate its intelligence to the counter-intelligence staffs in the field direct instead of through the SCIUs.

Mainly because of his responsibility for the security of ISOS, 'C' opposed the suggestion that the SIS, MI 5 and the OSS should lose over-all control of the War Room to SHAEF, but on this point SHAEF had its way. As for the work of the War Room, SHAEF wanted its terms of reference to be extended to cover surveillance of any pro-Nazi organisations that might be operating in Germany, but the SIS and MI 5 argued that a body composed of staff provided by them and the OSS, and dependent principally on their records, should accept responsibility only for countering activities involving the enemy's intelligence services. SHAEF accepted this argument. The SHAEF G-2 Counter-Intelligence War Room became operational in London on 1 March 1945. Its Director, supplied by MI 5, and its Deputy Director, supplied by OSS, were posted to SHAEF, but its other staff remained under the administrative control of the SIS, MI 5 and the OSS. A French contingent from the Direction des Services de Documentation was attached to it from the outset and participated fully in its work. It was to deal direct with the counter-intelligence staffs in the field, and would serve those in Austria as well as those in Germany. Its terms of reference made it the central point for collecting and circulating all information from the field or from the SIS, MI 5 and the OSS on 'all secret and subversive functions, including the RSHA as it exists now or maybe in the future', but not on 'any new and locally inspired subversive and Resistance groups'.

The new War Room had no sooner begun to operate than it became clear that the enemy was abandoning any attempt to set up a stay-behind network in western Germany. From the beginning of April ISOS and the traffic of the double agents showed that the activities of the German mobile field units were rapidly declining as, together with their controlling stations, they moved almost daily in a general eastward withdrawal. In the last few weeks of the war the disintegration continued. All known intelligence personnel had been listed from the comprehensive files of MI 5 and the SIS for inclusion in the categories of Germans who would be subject to automatic arrest when Germany surrendered, and some 3,000 were taken in by the beginning of June. Their examination confirmed that the German Secret Service had lost all vestige of central control and had ceased to exist as an organisation.

□

Late in 1943 an SIS officer from Section V reported that Special Intelligence (b) work in Italy was still poorly organised with inefficient records and inadequate interrogation facilities. These deficiencies had been remedied by the spring of 1944 when three SCIUs were available and close collaboration had been established with the Italian Military Intelligence Service (SIM). This collaboration played a large part in enabling the Allies to contain a sustained German espionage and sabotage effort during the rest of the war in Italy.

Besides despatching line-crossers and parachutists in increasing numbers from early in 1944, the Abwehr and the SD were known to be positioning a formidable corps of agents in Rome for espionage and sabotage purposes; ISOS decrypts had disclosed the existence of no less than 150 by the time the Allies captured Rome at the beginning of June. But by 12 June a large number of the agents in Rome had defected or been captured, and the number of saboteurs captured grew to 50 by the beginning of August, all of them Italians who had been trained by the SD but whose morale was poor. A group of 25 was still at large at that date, but it was being penetrated by the Italian security forces and early capture of the agents was expected. Seventeen German radio links had meanwhile been identified and closed down or brought under control; one link escaped control for several months, but the information it transmitted was innocuous and sometimes misleading.

Despite these set-backs, there was little or no reduction in the scale of the German effort before the end of the year. The loss of ISOS in October, however, made it difficult to keep a check on the activities and the objectives of the line-crossers, but intelligence from other sources – interrogation of captured agents and defectors, the Italian Resistance, and double agents* – enabled the counter-intelligence authorities to avert a serious threat to the Allied forces. Twenty-three agents were captured between 15 and 20 November, eleven of them saboteurs. Of ten parachutists known to have been dropped in December, nine were rounded up before the end of the month, and 56 other agents were captured in December. At the end of the year AFHQ reported that 82 suspected agents had so far been tried since the beginning of the campaign, of whom 29 had been executed and 29 imprisoned.

In January 1945 a further 58 agents were captured. But Section V noted that in the absence of ISOS it was difficult to gauge the success of the enemy's line-crossing operations. Bad weather

---

* Several double agents were employed, of whom the most valuable were *Primo*, who was used in Naples for deception purposes during the offensive on Rome, *Addict*, who operated in Rome, and *Axe*, who was awarded the Iron Cross by the Germans for his work in Florence.

reduced the scale of German agent operations in January and February, but at the beginning of March activity was picking up. By then over 70 German intelligence stations, sub-stations and training schools in northern Italy had been identified; 27 were concerned with espionage, 22 with sabotage and eight with counter-espionage. The main weight of operations during March and April was on sabotage missions – mostly unsuccessful – by agents introduced by sea. It was not until some weeks after the German collapse at the beginning of May that it was possible to assess the effectiveness of Allied counter-intelligence. At the end of May Section V recorded that the rounding up of the German Intelligence Service was going smoothly; all the main towns in northern Italy had been covered by the SCIUs and not many of the major intelligence personalities had escaped; a mixed bag of some 150 agents – comprising stay-behind agents and agents under training or awaiting despatch – had been arrested. A month later it could be said that 'a cursory reading of a flood of intelligence reports' had indicated that knowledge of the enemy intelligence services in 1944–1945 had been sufficiently complete to enable their operations to be effectively neutralised.

CHAPTER 15: REFERENCES

1. Mockler-Ferryman, *Military Intelligence Organisation*, p 112; WO 33/1571B, War Office War Book 1939, paras 53–57.
2. Mockler-Ferryman, op cit, pp 169, 178.
3. ibid, pp 169, 179.
4. ibid, p 171 and Appendix J.
5. ibid, pp 138–139.
6. *A History of the German Secret Services and British Counter-measures* (Ogden, Utah 1986), pp 17, 32.

CHAPTER 16

Security against Germany in the United Kingdom to the End of the War

I T HAD been assumed that, whether or not the *Overlord* deception programme succeeded in misleading the Germans, it would have the result that the agents taking part in it, their reporting contradicted by events, would be fatally compromised. In fact they survived with their reputations in Germany unscathed; and while some of them were phased out at different dates for a variety of reasons, several were operated till the end of the war either as a means of keeping in touch with the intentions of the German Intelligence Service or in support of further deception operations.

Few opportunities arose for deception operations in support of SHAEF's campaign in north-west Europe. A project by which *Brutus* would volunteer to work for the Germans in that theatre was abandoned early in August 1944. Towards the end of August, to supervise the work of the three SCIUs which had been set up to run suitable agents captured in the field as double agents, 21st Army Group, 12th US Army Group and the naval and air components of the Expeditionary Force formed the 212 Committee at SHAEF. In view of the speed of the Allied advance from that time, however, successive deception plans became out-dated as soon as they were formulated. As early as the middle of September SHAEF had decided that the double agents in the field should be used only for counter-intelligence purposes and that any further strategic deception, should it be worth-while, would be best carried out by the established double agents in the United Kingdom. But there was no call for strategic deception on behalf of the armies in Europe even from the United Kingdom after September, when *Brutus* was used briefly to provide cover for the airborne attack at Arnhem; in two messages on 10 and 14 September he reported that an airborne attack was intended for 15 September, but that the target area was either in Denmark or in the Kiel-Bremen area.

From June 1944 *Tate* took part in a deception plan drawn up to provide the Germans with false information about the fall of the V-weapons, and from November 1944 to May 1945 he was the channel used by the Admiralty for passing to Germany bogus intelligence about the laying of a minefield to deter the U-boats operating in British inshore waters. German records obtained after the war showed that this information had been acted on despite some uncertainty in the Abwehr as to whether he could be trusted.* But he appears to have retained the confidence of his control in Hamburg, which maintained contact with him till a few hours before the fall of the city. *Treasure's* signals, continued by an MI 5 operator after her dismissal in June 1944, were also used in the V-weapons project, but their chief value lay in the assistance they gave to GC and CS; they were phased out in November 1944.

Rover was released to the Royal Navy in September 1944 after failing to make radio contact with Germany. But the Germans then began to call him and it was decided to re-establish communication using MI 5 operators. From early in October *Rover's* signals were an important channel for deception about the fall of V-weapons. They continued till the end of the war. *Gelatine* and *Bronx*, who also remained in contact with Germany till the end of the war, were used mainly as a possible source of information about German intelligence for the future. Because of her connections, *Gelatine* was also a possible channel for news about any peace feelers that might emanate from Germany. Though her last letter was dated 30 April 1945, she in fact received no intelligence of any importance. *Bronx*, who sent with her last letter on 3 May an offer to continue her collaboration with Germany, was asked early in 1945 to report in the plain language code devised in 1944† if she obtained any information about the attack on Norway which the Germans expected.

Zigzag, the last war-time spy to reach England, as already noted, had arrived in Cambridgeshire by parachute on the night of 27–28 June 1944 with two radio sets, cameras, a large sum of money and much useful information. Notice of his arrival had been given in an ISOS decrypt of 10 June and he now revealed that his mission was to collect information on ASDIC equipment, on anti-aircraft radar, on the bases and operational plans of the US Army Air Force, on the fall of V 1s and the damage they were inflicting and on a new radio frequency which, the Germans believed, might affect their operation of the V 2 weapon. He was soon in radio contact with the Germans and was used for deception about the V 1 offensive and in connection with the development of anti-submarine weapons. By October, however, he had become so much of an embarrassment that his contract was terminated on generous terms; it was known that he had disclosed details of his

---

* See Hinsley et al, *British Intelligence in the Second World War*, Vol III, Part 2 (1988), pp 470–471n.

† See above, p 241.

work to a wide circle of his criminal acquaintances, and there was a further problem. He had brought with him instructions as to how to contact another agent, whose identity he did not know but who was obviously *Brutus*, to hand over a camera and money. He had not been allowed to carry out his instructions, because of the risk that suspicion would be thrown on *Brutus* if the Germans began to distrust *Zigzag*. But if he continued to operate he could not be kept away from *Brutus* indefinitely.

In June the Germans had asked *Brutus*, who was then supposedly with FUSAG in Staines while keeping his transmitter in London, to report on the fall of V 1s as a matter of urgency. But in the middle of July they had instructed him to confine himself to reports on the Allied order of battle. Towards the end of August he had advised them that he was leaving his FUSAG appointment to rejoin the Polish Air HQ. His messages, which mainly related to the dispersal of the notional forces assembled for *Fortitude*, had then become much less frequent. He sent the last on 2 January 1945; it informed the Germans that he was being sent on a visit to Belgium. Some of his former associates, who knew that he had made a deal with the Germans before moving to the United Kingdom, had by then been arrested, and there was considerable risk that if the Germans learned of the arrests, and if *Brutus* continued to operate, they would assume that he was doing so under control.*

Garbo, also, greatly reduced his activity after August 1944. No sooner had he intervened personally in sending reports on the V 1 offensive† than a Spanish agent of the Abwehr told the SIS in Madrid that the chief German agent in England was communicating by radio to Spain and offered to divulge his name in return for money. As this offer could not be refused, *Garbo* took evasive action by informing the Germans that he had heard through his courier that he was about to be betrayed and that he was taking refuge in a hide-out in Wales. In German eyes he remained there till the end of the war, leaving his organisation in charge of Agent No 3 and keeping in touch with it by courier and occasional meetings. The Germans co-operated zealously in various measures designed to convince the British authorities that *Garbo* had escaped to Spain, and in the discussion of various plans to effect his actual escape from Britain, and they assured him that they continued to value the work of the organisation. But the organisa-

---

* A senior German intelligence officer, questioned in the summer of 1945, claimed that he had often suspected that *Brutus* was under control, but that there was no firm evidence of deception and the Operations Staff had valued his reports. At the end of the war *Brutus* was awarded an OBE

† See above, p 243.

tion was gradually run down,* the Germans being informed that No 4 was being sent to Canada in October and that other members were resigning or being paid off during the winter, and on 1 May 1945 the Germans advised *Garbo* to wind it up.

Garbo carried out one more mission. On 8 May, in their last message to him, the Germans hoped that he would be able to make his way to Madrid and instructed him to frequent a cafe there every Monday evening from 4 June; they warned him that it might be impossible for them to keep the rendezvous. Although *Garbo* turned up, MI 5 being anxious to maintain contact in case the Germans had plans to continue their activities after the end of hostilities, the rendezvous was not kept. But he succeeded in tracking down his case-officer, to whom he explained how he had succeeded in getting to Spain via south America and expressed his wish to work for the Germans in any plans they might have for the future. The case-officer knew of no such plans, but he was full of praise for *Garbo's* past services and promised that the balance of what was owed to him would be paid. The money, 35,000 pesetas, was subsequently handed over in cash to Mrs *Garbo* by an anonymous intermediary.†

□

In July 1944 a new source of information on Kraemer's activities became available: the decrypts of signals from the Japanese Military Attaché in Stockholm, who was also head of the Japanese Intelligence Service in western Europe, were found to contain reports described as 'K' information which were clearly related to the intelligence Kraemer was passing to Berlin. Of some 30 such reports obtained in November, which dealt mainly with the RAF and the US Army Air Forces, two were attributed to a secret agent in England and were inaccurate. But the remainder were more reliable than most of the other material transmitted by the Japanese Attaché. They revived the suspicion that Kraemer's source might be in the Swedish embassy in London, and this conjecture was supported in December when an Abwehr officer defected in Sweden. He claimed that Kraemer was obtaining his intelligence from the Swedish Foreign Office, and that it had dried up during the suspension of diplomatic communications from London in preparation for *Overlord*. He also said that Kraemer was suspected of basing some of his order of battle reports on

---

* In December 1944 *Garbo* was made an MBE
† Between May 1942 and April 1945 the Germans paid *Garbo* more than £31,000 to meet the expenses of his network.

information already in German intelligence summaries to which he had access and that this suspicion was being investigated.*

Access to Kraemer's reports was further improved from January 1945, when the SIS recruited an employee of the German legation in Stockholm who was able to supply carbon copies of Kraemer's teleprinted messages to Berlin. Until Kraemer left Sweden in April with other members of the German legation, these continued to convey a steady stream of inaccurate information. But the suspicion that he had contacts in the Swedish government and that they were drawing their information from London was kept alive by occasional messages of disturbing accuracy; for example, his forecast on 31 January that there would be an Anglo-American offensive between Venlo and Aachen in the first week of February looked uncomfortably like a reference to Operations *Grenade* and *Veritable*.†

On 14 April Kraemer was arrested in Denmark and taken to Camp 020 for interrogation. He at first claimed that the Japanese Military Attaché had been the main source of his military information, and that he had obtained industrial and commercial intelligence from the German representative of Lufthansa, from a contact in the Swedish airline and from a naturalised Swedish businessman. He denied that he had had access to Swedish official sources. He also denied that he had had agents in the United Kingdom: *Josephine* and *Hektor* had been his code-names for different kinds of intelligence. Under further questioning he added that two journalists had helped him – one of them, a German, having good sources in Swedish official circles – but that the naturalised businessman, a former Austro-Hungarian intelligence officer who had kept in touch with Hungarian intelligence agents in the Iberian peninsula, had been his most valuable accomplice. This man had arranged in 1942 that reports from a Hungarian network in Madrid, known as *Fulep*, should be sent to Stockholm via the Hungarian legation in Madrid, and Kraemer had continued to receive them till the Hungarian legation in Stockholm closed at the end of 1944; they had purportedly been supplied by high-ranking British officers, but Kraemer had been highly sceptical of this claim. The SIS continued to disbelieve Kraemer's account, but after further examination in Germany,

---

* GAF documents found after the war confirmed that in the autumn of 1944 an enquiry was held into the possibility that Kraemer's intelligence was either deception material or wholly fraudulent. Schellenberg claimed during his interrogation at Camp 020 that he had shielded Kraemer.

† This report (some details of which were wrong) could have been an intelligent guess from a study of the strategic and tactical situation. It could also have been fabricated from recent German appreciations of Allied intentions. See Hinsley et al, op cit, Vol III Part 2, pp 671–673.

where Kraemer remained in detention till April 1946, the British interrogators judged that he no longer had any motive for withholding information and that he was not doing so. In the summer of 1946 the Allies interrogated Joseph Fullop, who had been Press Attaché at the Hungarian legation in Madrid, and established that he had been involved in a small way with an intelligence group named *Fulep*, probably run by the Military Attaché, which had supplied both Kraemer and the Japanese. Fullop's contribution had consisted of reports put together with considerable ingenuity from *Life* and *Fortune* magazines, *Flight*, *The Aeroplane*, *Aero Digest*, *The Economist* and the newspapers. This was not inconsistent with the picture obtained from Kraemer and it seems probable that in his later statements at Camp 020 he was substantially telling the truth with some normal and some tactical lapses of memory. However, this conclusion leaves two problems without wholly satisfactory answers.

Post-war research into German records relating to Operation *Fortitude* disclosed that Kraemer's reports from *Josephine* had contained a good deal of the deception material passed by the double-cross agents. References to FUSAG and to notional formations created for *Fortitude* appeared regularly. The warning from *Garbo* on 8 June that the assault on Normandy was a diversionary attack was paralleled by a *Josephine* message and it was the conjunction of the two messages which prompted the Germans to halt the transfer of 1st SS Panzer Division from Belgium.* In view of the suspicions which the Germans themselves entertained about Kraemer, the most likely explanation seems to be that he saw the material in German intelligence reports, reported it to Berlin with his own embellishments and drew the conclusion from it which the authors intended.

The other problem concerns the source of a message from Kraemer to Berlin on 16 September 1944 forecasting an airborne landing in the Arnhem area which, because of a technical hitch in Berlin, was not available to OKW until after Operation *Market Garden* had begun on 17 September. The existence of this message and its crucial delay were first reported in January 1945 by the Abwehr defector mentioned above and were confirmed by Schellenberg and others after the war. At Camp 020 Kraemer said that he had received the intelligence from *Fulep* via the diplomatic mail on 15 September, and that he had also learned from the Japanese Military Attaché two or three days before *Market Garden* that he had information from the Swedish General Staff that an airborne operation in Holland was imminent. Even if Kraemer's general

---

* See Hinsley et al, op cit, Vol III Part 2, p 182.

truthfulness is accepted, as the operation was only authorised on 10 September and the date for it was not fixed and formation commanders in England were not briefed till 12 September, it is very hard to believe that the information could have reached Stockholm via the Iberian peninsula in three days. The Japanese Military Attaché's information and study of the map might possibly have provided the basis for Kraemer's report. Probably because his account was not available until some time after the event and the message had in any case had no influence on it, no formal enquiry was carried out. In October 1945 the SHAEF Counter-Intelligence War Room concluded that the forecast was almost certainly 'an intelligent guess'.

Ostro's activities, like Kraemer's, continued to cause anxiety even after the success of *Overlord* had removed the fear that he might clash with the Allied deception programme and the Allied operational plans. In the autumn of 1944 ISOS decrypts contained reports from him which claimed to be based on information from an agent in Londonderry, and the SIS made an attempt to discredit him with the Germans (which proved abortive) through one of its Lisbon agents. The reports continued, as did differences of opinion as to how seriously he should be taken. The SIS felt that he was not particularly dangerous, while GC and CS found his voluminous traffic positively helpful, but the deception authorities, supported by the DNI, regarded him as a menace. In February 1945, when he sent a message correctly reporting the transfer of Canadian troops from Italy to the SHAEF front, the Twenty Committee, which discussed him at no fewer than 19 meetings between October 1944 and April 1945, finally recommended that, as an exceptional measure, direct action should be taken to eliminate him. 'C' declined to approve this course until an attempt had been made to bring *Ostro* over to the Allied side, but the war ended before he could be approached.

Some uncertainty as to *Ostro's* sources continued after he was arrested by the Americans in Austria in 1946. Under interrogation he stoutly maintained that he had had one valuable source in the United Kingdom and another in the Middle East, though he refused to give information about them or his means of contact with them. His account was disturbing, the more so as Schellenberg, interrogated in July 1945, had described him as the best source of military intelligence the Germans had had in Portugal, and one of their four top agents. After months of intensive enquiries, however, MI 5 concluded that, as had always seemed probable, his reports had been concocted by an acute and lively mind from newspapers and other overt sources and from the sometimes well-informed gossip of Lisbon and Madrid.

□

The fact that the British security authorities, after the middle of 1944, were mainly preoccupied with the activities of men like Kraemer and *Ostro* reflected the continuing success of the counter-espionage organisation in defending the United Kingdom against enemy infiltration during the Second World War. But wrong conclusions might be drawn from its success during the war unless it is emphasised that it depended on a combination of factors which ceased to operate when peace arrived, and which is unlikely to be repeated.

Great Britain being an island, it was possible in war-time to impose strict control of entry which could not be easily evaded. The vulnerable back door via the uncontrollable frontier between Northern Ireland and Eire was protected by the Eire government's vigorous action against the IRA and its determination that Eire should not be used as a base for espionage or sabotage against the United Kingdom. Besides this geographical advantage, in 1939 and throughout the war the United Kingdom had a homogeneous population in which patriotism was still regarded as a cardinal virtue and which, apart from a numerically insignificant minority, was deeply hostile to the Nazi regime. What the Security Executive described as the 'different loyalty'* of the leadership and indoctrinated cadres of the CPGB helped Germany only incidentally, and only until she attacked the Soviet Union in June 1941.

Germany, on the other hand, had made no effective preparations by 1939. She had neglected the opportunities offered by the large influx of refugees; she had not attempted to exploit such elements in British Fascism as might have been exploitable; she had made only feeble attempts to establish effective links with the IRA; and her stay-behind organisation, such as it was, depended on the doubtful loyalty of one mercenary agent – *Snow*. These missed opportunities can be attributed partly to the fact that until late in 1937 intelligence operations against the United Kingdom were restricted in the hope that some political accommodation would be reached and partly to the shortcomings of the Abwehr.

It was on account of those shortcomings that Germany was unable to make up lost ground when the unexpected German conquest of north-west Europe in the spring and summer of 1940 brought with it the immediate threat of invasion. The crisis revealed the weakness of security organisation in the United Kingdom but it also provoked urgent measures to strengthen it. These were begun in time to frustrate an offensive hastily mounted by the Abwehr in circumstances for which it was equally

---

* See below, p 285.

unprepared, and by the autumn of 1942 they had been developed into an efficient machine much of which would necessarily be dismantled when the war ended. Not less important, however, the development of these measures was accompanied by a massive build-up of intelligence about the German intelligence services.

Analysing the poor performance of the Abwehr in a report of December 1945, the SHAEF Counter-Intelligence War Room attributed it in the first place, on the basis of a wide range of evidence, to corruption and disaffection and to competition with the RSHA, these in their turn being due to bad leadership and the Nazi system of government. Admiral Canaris was a bad judge of men and a bad organiser. There was gross personal and professional corruption in Abteilung I (the espionage division) and its reports were not effectively scrutinised. The armed services knew little about the Abwehr and its sources and were unable to distinguish between good and bad. This lack of co-ordination and control was characteristic of the German intelligence organisation and reflected the 'vortex of competing ambitions' in high political circles. The RSHA was similarly 'a loose agglomeration of warring personalities.' It scored a few isolated successes on the intelligence side – in Vichy, Rome and Ankara – but by and large 'insignificant agents were recruited to no purpose by officers who had little or no knowledge of what they wanted'. The absorption of the Abwehr into the RSHA in the summer of 1944 made little practical difference. At this late stage no thorough-going re-organisation was possible. Contrary to expectations no plans were made to preserve the German Intelligence Service after military defeat.

In view of these weaknesses, which were far greater than had been expected and too fundamental to be off-set by the fact that the German intelligence services had many honest and industrious members and did not lack technical expertise, the SHAEF report concluded that the Allied success in the war 'was not due solely to Allied counter-measures, important though these undoubtedly were'. It was aware, however, that Allied knowledge of the enemy's activities in the western theatres of war, which had been 'very imperfect' up to 1940, was 'adequately representative' from 1940 to 1943 and 'probably complete' from 1943 to 1945. And it recognised that among the sources of this knowledge, which was so central to the effectiveness of the Allied counter-measures, ISOS had been pre-eminent.* The recognition of the invaluable assistance received from ISOS underlay, indeed, the distinction it drew

---

* The report made no explicit reference to ISOS, so as not to restrict its circulation, but it was in fact written in a section of the War Room staffed by members of the Radio Intelligence Section of the SIS.

between the failure of the Abwehr and the RSHA in the acquisition of intelligence and their very considerable successes in co-operation with the Gestapo in security operations against the Resistance movements and the Allied agencies that relied on them: the intelligence operations, carried out mainly beyond Germany's inner lines, involved the use of wireless and the availability of ISOS, whereas the security functions had been exercised mainly in occupied Europe and did not call for the use of radio till late in the war.

As the war came to an end a prudent security service would thus in any case have realised that the fortunate concurrence of the acceptability of crisis measures in the United Kingdom especially after the Fifth Column panic of 1940, of an inefficient opponent and of the priceless bonus of Allied Sigint was unlikely to be repeated, and that success in counter-espionage is always more difficult to achieve in peace-time conditions. And it was all the more likely that MI 5 would be prudent; already by the spring of 1943 it believed it had grounds for concluding that the Communist Party, while continuing to be a force for subversion, was becoming a serious threat as a source of espionage.

CHAPTER 17

Security against the Communist Threat in the United Kingdom to the End of the War

IN TERMS of the size of its membership, the end of 1942 marked the high-water line in the Communist Party's advance. Membership remained static during 1943 at about 50,000, a recruiting drive which brought in some 12,500 new members doing no more than make up for an increasing rate of wastage. In March 1944 the registered membership was 46,000, and it remained at that level for the rest of the war. But by the security authorities the Party was naturally regarded as constituting a continuing source of subversion and its members became an increasing threat as a channel for espionage.

The Communist Party's change of line following the German attack on Russia had been greeted sceptically, as merely a change of tactics, by the security authorities; and as we have seen, they had kept a close watch on its activities and obstructed its efforts to increase its influence.* They recapitulated the grounds for their suspicion in February 1943 when the Home Secretary, who was no doubt prompted by the Party's impending application for affiliation to the Labour Party, asked MI 5 for an up-to-date report. This reviewed the Party's policy from its announcement of qualified support of the war in September 1939; the change of line a month later, after long and serious debate, on instructions from the Comintern; the pursuit of the policy of revolutionary defeatism from October 1939 until Germany attacked Russia; the first confused reactions to this unforeseen development; and the eventual clarification of the Party's attitude at the beginning of July 1941 in the announcement that it was 'fighting for the establishment of a united national front of all those who are for Hitler's defeat'. Since then, the report continued, the Party's first aim had been to contribute everything in its power to the defence of the Soviet Union. There was, however, clear evidence in the possession of the authorities (in the form of statements made to classes held in various part of the country to train candidates for positions of trust) that the immediate urgency of the salvation of

---

* See above, p 82ff.

the Soviet Union had not changed the long-term revolutionary aims of the Party which involved the violent seizure of power. The Party believed that a revolutionary situation might develop in the comparatively near future. This report was circulated to the War Cabinet accompanied by a memorandum about Mosley's British Union, setting out the case for the Home Secretary's action against it in 1940.[1]

MI 5 had suggested in February 1941 that documents about the debate in the Communist Party's Political Bureau in September 1939 should be published as evidence of the Party's subjection to Moscow, but Swinton had brushed the idea aside.* Now the possible publication of the two memoranda came under discussion, but MI 5 was again rebuffed. The Foreign Office objected that publication would damage relations with the Soviet Union and provide ammunition for Goebbels. In the Home Office Maxwell, while regretting that more could not be done 'to open the eyes of the innocents', agreed with the Foreign Office, and also advised that publication would be seen in some quarters as an attempt to defeat the Communist campaign for affiliation to the Labour Party – as 'the act of a politician rather than a statesman' and as 'a move designed to gain an immediate end . . . rather than a policy based on long-term views'. In the War Cabinet discussion on 28 April 1943 ministers agreed that while there was much to be said in favour of publication the objections must prevail. They recognised too that difficulties would arise if, as was likely, Mosley claimed the right to reply to the memorandum on the British Union and that libel proceedings might result if private individuals quoted extracts from the memoranda, and that action for libel would probably succeed unless the government was prepared to produce the evidence on which the memoranda were based.[2]

Reviewing the situation in May 1943, MI 5 drew attention to the danger from Communist penetration of the Labour movement – 'a fundamental part of the Party's revolutionary theory without which the seizure of power would be impossible' – and to the further danger that the ostensibly patriotic Party line might lead to a relaxation in the precautions taken to deny Communists access to secret information. It knew that since the end of 1941 the Party had strengthened its arrangements for maintaining contact with members in the armed forces, had set up a secret interviewing room in London under cover of the Workers' Musical Association, and was receiving a considerable amount of secret information about weapons and operations from members of the armed forces, the civil service and industry. Nor did it doubt that 'Party members

* See above, p 81.

still put loyalty to the Party first ... and the Party will use that information irresponsibly according to its own lights ...'. Turning to details, it knew that the Party had obtained figures about the strength and dispositions of the RAF; a report on War Office assessments of the Dieppe raid; advance information about Operation *Torch*; information about combat equipment that was still under development; a copy of a paper prepared by the Association of Scientific Workers for the House of Commons Select Committee on Estimates which contained references to jet propulsion and other details about aircraft production that were still secret. Even more disturbing was the fact that leakage from junior staff in MI 5 itself to members of the Communist Party had led to the loss of one of its agents and the recent discovery that a detailed account of the War Cabinet's discussion of 28 April about the Communist Party, which could have been supplied only by someone with access to the minutes, had reached Pollitt two days later.

The intended dissolution of the Comintern was announced on 22 May 1943. The War Cabinet decided two days later that it would be undesirable to make known its view on this event 'at this stage'. On 2 June, after the announcement had been considered by the Wall Committee,* the Security Executive concluded that the principles of the Communist Party remained unchanged, that the Party must still be regarded as having a 'different loyalty' from that of other parties and that government departments should accordingly be advised to continue to treat it with as much caution as before.[3] As before, however, the departments continued to treat it with less caution than the security authorities believed to be necessary.

On 16 June the Labour Party conference rejected the Communist Party's request for affiliation by a large majority. The Communist Party had waged a vigorous campaign for affiliation, arguing with increasing intensity the need for unity in the struggle against Fascism, for maximum industrial output and for a People's Front for post-war reconstruction. But the Labour Party was not convinced that the Communist Party had ceased to be a creature of international Communism, and the arrest next day of D.F. Springhall, National Organiser of the Party since 1940, and his trial and conviction under the Official Secrets Acts, was a prompt reminder of the Party's 'different loyalty'.

Springhall's meetings with Mrs Olive Sheehan, the cadres leader of the secret Communist Party group in the Air Ministry, had aroused the suspicions of her flat-mate, who had confided in a friend in the RAF. The RAF man was present on 15 June when

---

* See above, pp 83–84.

Mrs Sheehan gave the flat-mate an envelope for 'Peter', and he opened it. It contained a note explaining that Mrs Sheehan was ill and could not see Peter, together with a list of the names and postings in the Air Ministry of six Party members and information about 'Window', the radar jamming device which was then highly secret. Arrested on 16 June, Mrs Sheehan identified Peter as Springhall and described her dealings with him; he had contacted her in the autumn of 1942 and after being persuaded by him that the British government was not keeping the Soviet Union fully informed about technical developments, she had supplied him with details about 'Window' since February 1943. She claimed that she did not think she was acting wrongly since he was passing the information to Moscow, where it would be used against the Germans. She was charged under DR 3 and received the maximum sentence of three months' hard labour. Springhall was sentenced to seven years' penal servitude.

His arrest led to the identification of several other contacts who had given him information. They included Captain Ormond Uren, an officer in the SOE, who had been introduced to him by the organiser of the Russia Today Society in Scotland as someone who wanted to help the Communist Party. In a series of meetings Uren had provided him with a written account of the organisation of the SOE and described his work there. Uren was tried by court martial in October, cashiered and sentenced to seven years' penal servitude.

As a result of these arrests the Party curtailed the conspiratorial side of its activities. Springhall was expelled; it was decided that no prominent member should engage in espionage; the interviewing room in London was closed down, together with the organisation responsible for contacts with members of the armed forces and many of the under-cover groups among junior civil servants; and the news that under-cover work was being abandoned was disseminated in Party circles. In July 1943 the 16th Communist Party Congress made cosmetic changes to emphasise the Party's national character. Its name was changed to the British Communist Party, the Central Committee became the Executive Committee, the Political Bureau, where effective power lay, was re-named the Political Committee, and the Control Commission (the disciplinary organ) became the Appeals Committee. As the Home Secretary informed the War Cabinet in a memoradum of 3 August, however, the Springhall case underlined the 'great risk of the Party trading on the current sympathy for Russia to induce people . . . to betray [secrets]', and it re-opened the problem of barring Communists from access to secret information.[4] In the spring of 1942, asked for advice on this problem by the Bridges Panel, the Security Executive had recommended that all new entrants into offices involved in work classified as Secret or Most Secret should be vetted, and that MI 5 should advise heads of departments as to whether the Communist affiliations of any individual were such as to warrant his exclusion.[5] The Panel had adopted the recommendation, but the pressure on manpower, the demand for special skills, especially those of scientists, procedural breakdowns and, in MI 5's opinion, 'a certain lack of appreciation of the risks involved' led to a considerable number of known Communists being employed on secret work by government departments and in the Services. At the same time, MI 5 had been troubled by the fact that no steps had been taken to exclude Communists from posts offering scope for recruitment and subversion. In the autumn of 1942 it had drawn attention to the penetration by Communists of the Army Education Corps.

In April 1943 MI 5 had recommended that some twenty Party members should be removed from the Education Corps. The Secretary of State for War had decided after discussion with the Lord President that while Communists should be excluded in future, no transfers should be made unless and until overt acts by individuals justified their dismissal. MI 5 returned to the matter in a paper in October, but its main purpose then was to argue that, whereas there had previously been a natural reluctance to move Communists from secret work, the Springhall case had provided grounds for taking action with public support against possible Parliamentary and Press criticism. The paper listed 57 known Communists who had access to secret information, in some cases to information of the highest secrecy; they included 23 in the Ministry of Supply, 18 in the Army and 8 in the universities of whom 3 were employed on the Anglo-US atomic project. It urged that action should be taken to remove them on two grounds. 'In the first place there is the risk that information of immediate operational importance which has not been communicated to the Soviet government may be passed on to that quarter'. In the second place, it was known that the Communist Party collected secret information for its own purposes and that members obtaining it communicated it to the Party leaders whether or not it was of direct or immediate interest.

In a minute of 28 October Duff Cooper, the chairman of the Security Executive, repeated these arguments to the Prime Minister, adding that it would be a comparatively simple matter to arrange the transfer of all known Communists from secret work and that the Communist Party was known to be expecting such action since Springhall's conviction. The Prime Minister minuted that 'As at present advised I agree with this', and asked the Home Secretary to pursue it. The Home Secretary also agreed. He replied on 9 November that any leakage of secret information to unauthorised persons was dangerous, that it was a mistake to condone it on the grounds that the leakage was to an ally and that the entire machinery of government would be impaired if any toleration was given to the doctrine that people engaged on confidential work were entitled to betray the confidence for an end which they personally regarded as good; and he recommended that all departments engaged on secret work should be advised to transfer known Communists, as notified by MI 5, to other departments. He added that this advice would have to be carried out with discretion and a sense of proportion and that in itself his proposal would not solve the problem. Before leaks could be stopped, the Communist Party had to be convinced that espionage discredited it, and government servants had to be convinced that loyalty to the Communist Party stood on a different footing to membership of other parties. He suggested that a public statement on behalf of the government might achieve those objects.[6]

The Prime Minister brushed aside the suggestion that there should be a public statement. On the advice of Morton, moreover, who commented on the Home Secretary's reply that 'MI 5 tends to see dangerous men too freely and to lack that knowledge of the world and sense of perspective which the Home Secretary rightly considers essential', he ruled that MI 5 should not be responsible for notifying alleged Communist employees to the departments. He set up instead a secret panel consisting of the chairman of the Security Executive, its two unofficial members (Wall and Foot) and Morton as his own representative which would decide what action was necessary on cases submitted to it by MI 5. In further discussions the Home Secretary secured the co-option to the panel of a Treasury expert on staff matters and a representative of the department involved in each case, and established that final responsibility for the employment or transfer of a Communist must rest with the department. This was made clear to departments when they were notified of the institution of the panel in February 1944.[7]

MI 5 was dissatisfied with the new procedure. It believed that the members of the panel were insufficiently knowledgeable about underground Communist activity and feared that the submission of briefs about individual Communists would require it to take unacceptable risks in revealing its sources. For these reasons it submitted only one case before the panel was wound up, together with the Security Executive itself, in July 1945. It arose in December 1944 from the discovery that an under-cover group including a number of civil servants was providing the Party with political intelligence and helping it to produce policy pamphlets. The panel agreed that one of the civil servants, who had access to Cabinet papers, constituted a security risk. But the Minister and the Permanent Under-Secretary of his department expressed complete confidence in him and declined to adopt the recommendation that he should be transferred.

Because it was unable or unwilling to produce evidence of individual cases for the panel MI 5 had to be content with the fact that the government had taken a more resolute stand on a more public issue relating to the employment of known Communists – their accreditation as war correspondents for the *Daily Worker*.

The *Daily Worker* had applied for the accreditation of a correspondent for north Africa and another for the United Kingdom in the spring of 1943. After consulting the Home Secretary, who had referred the matter to the War Cabinet, the War Office had rejected the applications, though it had not indicated, as MI 5 had advised, that correspondents nominated by the *Daily Worker* would never be accepted. At the end of 1943 it had rejected two more nominations from the paper, and when Mr D N Pritt had put down a Parliamentary question on the subject to the Secretary of State for War, the Secretary of State had recommended to the War Cabinet that the paper should at last be told that it would in no circumstances be permitted to accredit correspondents to the armed forces. 'It is not a question', he had argued, 'of information being given to Russia – that may or may not be desirable. It is solely a question of the danger of leakage of information to the enemy which may affect operations and cost the lives of British soldiers. It is certain that accredited correspondents . . . will obtain knowledge of plans . . . which if imparted to the enemy might endanger their success'.[8]

On 10 January 1944 the War Cabinet accepted the recommendation and a week later it approved the draft of a reply to Pritt which had been drawn up in consultation with the Home Office. This stated that 'in view of the paramount importance of security measures in connection with military operations His Majesty's Government are not prepared to accord special facilities to this newspaper which is the propagandist medium of the Communist Party of Great Britain. In recent times some of its members have shown that they are ready to subordinate the security of the State to the purposes of the organisation'. It added that the editor of the *Daily Worker* had been informed that on these grounds, which had been reinforced by recent experience including the Springhall and Uren cases, 'no correspondent of the *Daily Worker* will be regarded as suitable for the position of accredited correspondent to the armed forces'.[9]

In February 1944, a petition asking for reconsideration of the decision, signed by 49 MPs and referring to several Trades Union resolutions in support, was submitted by the *Daily Worker* to the Secretary of State for War. He rejected it after consulting the

Prime Minister and the Home Secretary, and despite recurrent pressure – in the form of complaints in the Commons debate on the adjournment in July 1944; a protest resolution carried at the Trades Union Congress in September 1944; a TUC deputation to the Prime Minister in March 1945 – the War Cabinet maintained its ruling till the end of hostilities.[10]

In an assessment issued in August 1944 of the likely development of the Communist Party's post-war policy MI 5 accepted that many who had joined the Party since June 1941 did not contemplate unconstitutional behaviour, but was convinced that the Party, whatever its public professions, had not abandoned its belief in the eventual seizure of power and that its members were expected to put loyalty to the Party above loyalty to their country. By the end of the war MI 5 had seen no reason to change its views. It accepted that time might show that the Party had chosen the path of constitutional reform, but believed that it could not yet be trusted to act loyally; that its not inconsiderable propaganda machine would support every move of Soviet foreign policy; that the risk of leakage from Communists to the Party, or of espionage on behalf of the USSR, constituted 'a very present menace'; and that therefore Communists ought not to be employed on secret work.

CHAPTER 17: REFERENCES

1. CAB 66/35, WP(43) 109 of 13 March, 148 of 14 April.
2. CAB 65/34, WM(43) 60 of 28 April.
3. CAB 65/34, WM(43) 75 of 24 May; CAB 93/5, Wall Committee 92nd Meeting of 1 June; CAB 93/2, SE 89th Meeting of 2 June 1943.
4. CAB 66/40, WP(43) 359 of 3 August.
5. CAB 98/48, S(42) 20 of 15 June; CAB 93/6, SE(CGD) 1st Meeting of 5 March 1942.
6. PREM 3/64/4.
7. ibid.
8. CAB 66/45, WP(44) 7 of 7 January.
9. CAB 65/41, WM(44) 4 and 7 of 10 and 17 January; Hansard, Vol 396, col 55.
10. CAB 65/49, WM(45) 3, 25 and 33 of 9 January, 26 February and 19 March; CAB 65/50, WM(45) 44 of 13 April; CAB 66/62, WP(45) 107 and 115 of 22 and 24 February; CAB 66/63 WP(45) 155 of 12 March; CAB 66/64, WP(45) 238 of 11 April; Hansard, Vol 402, col 1742; HO/255881/865003/139.

APPENDICES

APPENDIX 1

The German Intelligence Services

(i) The Organisation of the Abwehr*

FROM THE outbreak of war, until its absorption into the Reichssicherheitshauptamt (RSHA) on 1 June 1944, the principal German intelligence service was the Abwehr which, with the Amtsgruppe Ausland, constituted the Amt Auslandsnachrichten und Abwehr, one of the directorates of the OKW, the military staff of the Commander-in-Chief, Armed Forces. The Amtsgruppe Ausland co-ordinated the Attaché sections of the Service ministries, which collected intelligence by open and lawful means. The Abwehr was the Secret Intelligence Service of the High Command.

The Abwehr owed its name to the Treaty of Versailles which stipulated that Germany should not possess an offensive espionage service, but might have a counter-espionage and security organisation. Consequently, when Germany organised an espionage service in breach of the Treaty, she did so under cover of security, and continued to use the term Abwehr ('defence') to include both the offensive and defensive functions. Up to about 1935 the Abwehr was a comparatively small organisation: thereafter it grew considerably.

The Abwehr was mainly composed of officers of the old imperial Army and Navy, officers of the First World War recalled from the reserve, and officers of the post-war Reichswehr. All these groups tended to hold themselves aloof from the Nazis – even if they approved of Hitler's efforts to shake off the fetters of Versailles. Like the British clandestine services, the Abwehr was essentially the chief's private army, largely recruited through personal contact.

The chief of the Abwehr when war broke out was Admiral Wilhelm Canaris, who had been appointed in January 1935 at the age of 47. He came of a middle class evangelical family – his father managed an iron works – of Lombard origin, but Germanised for two centuries. Entering the Navy in 1905 he was serving on the south American station in 1914 and was present at the battles of

---

* See WO 219/5276, *German Intelligence Services* (SHAEF EDS 9/9 of 4 October 1944); *A History of the German Secret Services and British Counter-Measures* (Ogden, Utah 1986); P Leverkühn, *German Military Intelligence* (1954); C Abshagen, *Canaris (1956)*.

Coronel and the Falkland Islands. Afterwards, he escaped from
internment in Chile and managed to get back to Germany,
surviving an examination by British security control at Plymouth
on the way. He then spent a year in Spain on naval espionage
under civilian cover, but ended the war in command of a submarine in the Adriatic. In 1919–1920 he supported the Ebert-
Noske government against the Spartacists, sat on the court martial
which acquitted the alleged murderers of Karl Liebknecht and
Rosa Luxemburg, supported the Kapp Putsch and earned a
reputation as an intriguer, a reactionary and a crypto-monarchist.
After the failure of the Kapp Putsch he returned to naval service
and spent some years in the Ministry of Defence where, like many
others, he took an active interest in circumventing the Treaty of
Versailles. He visited Japan in 1924. By 1934 he had reached the
end of a moderately successful naval career. The vacancy at the
head of the Abwehr arose fortuitously.

Canaris played an important part in German-Spanish relations
during the Civil War when he established personal friendships
with General Franco and other leading personalities including
Count Jordana, Generals Vigon and Ascensio, and General Mar-
tinez Campos, the Chief of Intelligence. An Abwehr team accompanied the Condor Legion of German 'volunteers' and provided
the basis for the Abwehr's organisation in Spain during the Second
World War. Canaris also established good relations with the Italian
military intelligence service. He reported to Keitel, the head of the
OKW, through whom he had access to Hitler.

The Abwehr was organised in four principal departments or
Abteilungen (Abts). Abt I was responsible for espionage; Abt II
for sabotage and subversion; and Abt III for counter-espionage
and protective security. In very general terms it would be true to
say that Abt I performed the functions of the SIS (less Section V);
Abt II those of SOE and, to some extent, PWE; and Abt III those
of MI 5 and Section V. Abt Z was a general administrative
department serving the whole organisation.

The departmental heads in September 1939 were Colonels
Pieckenbrock, Lahousen, von Bentivegni and Oster. When interrogated after the war Lahousen, who came of a distinguished
Austrian military family and had been taken into the Abwehr after
the Anschluss, described Pieckenbrock as a 'clever, open, generous
and cheeful Westphalian ... a Reichswehr type, ie the typical
unpolitical expert'. He was a close friend of Canaris as well as his
deputy in the early years of the war. Bentivegni, 'a somewhat
ambitious Prussian', was also 'a typical Reichswehr officer'. Oster,
in Lahousen's words, was 'a single-minded and purposeful man of
action'. (However, his energies were primarily concentrated on his
Resistance activities.)

Abt I had five principal sections, each responsible for obtaining a particular kind of information: I/Heer (Foreign Armies); I/Marine (Foreign Navies and Mercantile Marine); I/Luft (Non-technical information about foreign Air Forces); I/Technik Luft (Technical Air Intelligence); I/Wirtschaft (Economic Intelligence with particular reference to war potential).

Abt II was not divided into Service sections, but drew a distinction between two types of operation – sabotage proper and 'Insurgierung', that is to say projects involving the exploitation of disaffected elements in an enemy country.

Abt III, like Abt I, had three Service sections responsible for protective measures in the armed forces; and a section III (Wirtschaft) responsible for the security of war industry. The section concerned with counter-espionage was IIIF, which in the Second World War was to prove much the most successful part of the organisation.

When war broke out the headquarters of the Abwehr – some 650 all ranks – was at Tirpitzufer 72, Berlin, close to the OKW. Headquarters was concerned with organisation and planning. The executive work was done by subordinate stations, known as Abwehrstellen, and there was an Abwehrstelle (Ast) in each Wehrkreis (military district) into which Germany was divided for military purposes. An Ast often had smaller subordinate stations known as Nebenstellen (Nests).

Every Ast reproduced the pattern of Abwehr headquarters with variations dictated by local circumstances. Its constitutional responsibility was to supply the Wehrkreis with operational intelligence and maintain military security. In theory all Asts were equal and independent. In practice their activities varied with local conditions, personalities and historical and geographical factors. Thus, before the war, Ast Hamburg was specially concerned with work against the United Kingdom and the USA, and Ast Wiesbaden (400 strong in 1939) with work against France and the Low Countries.

In 1940–1941 the Abwehr's organisation extended with the German conquests. In occupied territory each unit of military administration had an Abwehrstelle – Ast Norwegen, Ast Belgien, etc. When there was more than one unit of administration, as in France, each of them had its Ast. Where there was a supreme military commander for a large area, a head Ast, Astleitstelle (Alst), was established with his headquarters. Thus in France there was an Astleitstelle Frankreich to which all other Asts in France forwarded their reports as well as passing them to Abwehr headquarters. Nests, usually replicas of their parent Ast, were established as required in the same way as in Germany. There were also smaller offices, known as Aussenstellen, specialising in particular aspects of Abwehr work.

In neutral countries the Abwehr representation, mainly under embassy cover, was known as a Kriegsorganisation (KO). The most important KOs were those in Spain, Portugal, Sweden, Switzerland and Turkey. They were organised on the same lines as an Ast (ie with representatives of Abts I, II and III); had out-stations corresponding to the Nests; and reported direct to Berlin. Most of the male staff, including local German residents recruited by the KO, belonged to the armed forces although maintaining the outward appearance of civilians. A KO's work was not generally directed against the country where it was situated, which was merely used as a springboard for operations. In Italy and Hungary, which were considered to be responsible for organising intelligence operations from their own territory, liaison officers were established for the exchange of intelligence.

On paper the organisation of the Abwehr looked impressive. The reality was rather different. Central control was extremely weak. Each Ast was independent. There was no division of targets between them. Any Ast might send an agent to any part of the world, and might embrace any likely enterprise even though it concerned a country far removed from its normal sphere of work. It was possible for two Asts to have agents in the same place without either being aware of it. A British report of 1944 remarked that the Abwehr often had the appearance not of a single large intelligence service, but of a loose association of many small ones, competing and sometimes conflicting with one another.

In combat areas the Abwehr provided militarised units, known as Kommandos (attached to Army Group HQs) and Truppen (assigned to lower formations), to perform, broadly speaking, the functions of Abts I, II and III. In the early years of the war the Abwehr, and Abt II in particular, was closely associated with the special Brandenburg units. For the Polish campaign Kampftruppen of franc-tireurs were organised by Ast Breslau for special tasks, such as the seizure of important industrial installations to prevent their destruction. The experience gained led to the formation in October 1939 of the Lehr und Bau Kompagnie zbV 800 (Special Duty, Training and Construction Company No 800) which rapidly expanded to battalion strength. Recruited mainly from Germans who had been living abroad, the unit was designed for operations of a commando type, exploiting ruses de guerre such as wearing enemy uniforms or civilian clothes. There were several successful operations of this kind during the campaign in the Low Countries. In October 1940 the battalion became the Lehr Regiment Brandenburg. It was active in the Yugoslav campaign, and undertook the protection of the Romanian oil fields and shipping on the Danube.

In December 1942 the Brandenburg Regiment expanded to a division. In the early years of the war agents recruited from the regiment by the Abwehr were used against the United Kingdom and in the Middle East, but the Abwehr connection progressively weakened. The Brandenburg units were supposed to be used only for special operations, for example against the Yugoslav partisans and hunting down prisoners of war released in Italy after the Armistice of 9 September 1943.

(ii) The Sicherheitsdienst*

The Nazi Party developed its own intelligence service, the Sicherheitsdienst (SD) of the Reichsführer SS (RFSS) which in 1936 was formally recognised as an intelligence organisation of the Party and the state. From 1933 Party control of the normal Police apparatus was progressively extended. In 1936 Himmler (already RFSS) became Chief of the German Police which was divided into two categories, the Ordnungspolizei (ORPO) and the Sicherheitspolizei (SIPO). The latter, which comprised the Kriminalpolizei (KRIPO) and the Geheime Staatspolizei (GESTAPO) originally formed by Göring in 1933, was placed under Reinhardt Heydrich who was already head of the SD. In September 1939 the Reichssicherheitshauptamt (RSHA) was established under Heydrich to control both the SIPO and the SD. Heydrich was assassinated in 1942 and was succeeded after an interval of some months by Ernst Kaltenbrunner.

The RSHA was organised in seven departments, or Amter, of which only III, IV and VI were of counter-intelligence interest. I and II were purely administrative; V controlled the KRIPO in its non-political role; VII was no more than a perverted research institute for the protection and dissemination of Nazi culture. Amt III directed the activities of the SD within Germany, that is the supervision, as the information service both of Party and state, of every sphere of the nation's life. Its task was 'to see that the state of the people is sound and no harmful tendencies emerge'. Executive action was the responsibility of Amt IV, the original Gestapoamt by which name it was still sometimes known. It had the dual task of detecting political crime and taking preventive measures against treasonable acts or conspiracies, a formula covering almost any kind of activity by individuals or parties. Finally Amt VI was the SD in its capacity as a secret foreign political intelligence service.

There was a clear possibility of overlapping between Abt III F of

---

* See WO 219/5276 (SHAEF EDS 9/9 of 4 October 1944); and *A History of the German Secret Services and British Counter-Measures*.

the Abwehr and Amt IV, and between Abt I and Amt VI. When the war began relations between the RSHA and the Abwehr were governed by an agreement made at the end of 1936 between Canaris and Heydrich, known in the Abwehr as the Ten Commandments. The broad lines of this agreement were that on the offensive side the Abwehr should restrict its activities to purely military intelligence, and pass to the SD any political intelligence which happened to come its way, while the SD would reciprocate by passing to the Abwehr any military information which it might acquire fortuitously. On the defensive side it was recognised that counter-espionage was the Abwehr's business (though it depended on the Gestapo for executive action), while political investigations belonged to Amt IV. Any case of espionage handled by the Abwehr which involved a political element would be referred to Amt IV; conversely the Abwehr would be associated with any political investigation which revealed a case of espionage.

The war gave the RSHA scope for the steady expansion of its activities as a rival to the Abwehr. From the kidnapping by Amt IV of the SIS officers, Stevens and Best, at Venlo in December 1939, when the trap was baited with the prospect of contact with an anti-Nazi underground movement, and inevitably in occupied Europe, counter-espionage had a quasi-political flavour. Amt IV, which extended its organisation throughout occupied territory, could not be kept out of the act. The balance of power tilted increasingly in favour of Amt IV and Heydrich was pressing Canaris for further concessions as early as December 1941.

At the start of the war Amt VI was still an insignificant department. Himmler had decided to have a foreign intelligence service of his own, but the RSHA lacked the right kind of men for the work. In 1942 the character of Amt VI changed with the appointment of Walter Schellenberg as its head. This able and ambitious man, who had attracted attention by his successful handling of the Venlo kidnapping and was a favourite of Himmler, appreciated the weaknesses of the German intelligence machine and looked forward to the creation of a unified intelligence service. Under his direction Amt VI activities expanded steadily. Though on a much smaller scale than that of the Abwehr, Amt VI representation was established throughout occupied and neutral Europe, in Turkey and in south America. Its representative in Vichy France was exceptionally well informed in 1942; after the fall of Mussolini its representative in Rome correctly forecast Badoglio's intentions (in contrast to the Abwehr) and his intelligence made possible the rescue of Mussolini by an Amt VI officer, Otto Skorzeny; at the end of 1943 the *Cicero* case in Ankara redounded to its credit. Political intelligence continued to be its principal assignment, but in Russia, in the Middle East and north

Africa, in Persia and in Italy Amt VI began to trespass into the field of subversion and sabotage hitherto the exclusive preserves of Abt II.

(iii) The Fall of the Abwehr

The reputation of the Abwehr stood very high in Germany in September 1939 and, although on an objective assessment its achievements in the early years of the war were not very impressive, its performance was not seriously questioned until 1942 was well advanced. The success of the German armies was naturally taken to imply good intelligence. The Abwehr met the requirements laid on it for the Polish campaign, the invasion of Denmark and Norway and the Blitzkrieg in the west. It was very successful in Yugoslavia in the spring of 1941 in sabotaging the mobilisation of the Yugoslav forces and in preventing the destruction of communications and otherwise assisting the German campaign. With Spain non-belligerent on the side of the Axis, and buttressed by the privileged personal position enjoyed by Canaris, the Abwehr used the country almost as it chose as a base for intelligence and sabotage operations. In co-operation with the Gestapo and the radio interception services, the Abwehr scored major successes against the Resistance movements in western Europe and the Allied agencies which relied on them. Three of the most important networks in France, *Interallié*, *Autogiro* and *Prosper*, were completely penetrated in 1941; SOE operations in Belgium were badly damaged, and in Holland were totally controlled for twenty months from March 1942. Russian espionage rings operating in France, the Low Countries and Germany (named the *Rote Kapelle* or *Red Orchestra*) were smashed and some 200 of their members executed.*

Operation *Torch* in November 1942, when the Allies landed in north Africa, marked the beginning of a period of crisis which led to the fall of the Abwehr. Its failure to forecast the Allied target correctly was followed by a similar failure over Operation *Husky*, the invasion of Sicily, in July 1943. It failed again after Mussolini's fall, when its advice was that Badoglio offered all the advantages of a Pétain and must not be weakened or frightened by a misconceived attitude of suspicion. Meanwhile the balance of power in Germany was tilting more and more against the General Staff and

---

* See WO 219/5276 (SHAEF EDS 9/9 of 4 October 1944); *A History of the German Secret Services and British Counter-Measures*; Abshagen, op cit; Leverkühn, op cit; MRD Foot, *SOE in Europe* (1966); L de Jong, *The German Fifth Column in the Second World War* (1956); H J Giskes, *London Calling North Pole* (1953); P Hoffmann, *The History of the German Resistance 1933–1945* (1977); H Höhne, *Codeword Direktor* (1971).

other conservative elements in favour of the Nazi Party and of Himmler in particular. The rise of Himmler at the expense of the General Staff entailed the rise of the SD at the expense of the Abwehr. The latter was rightly suspected of being generally defeatist and harbouring elements which, from the Party's point of view, were actively disloyal.

The first half of 1943 saw extensive changes at the top of the Abwehr. Pieckenbrock and Lahousen were replaced as heads of Abt I and Abt II by Hansen and von Freytag-Loringhoven. Oster, the head of Abt Z, was suspended on charges of corruption. In the summer his close associate Hans von Dohnanyi, like him deeply involved in the German Resistance, was arrested. Canaris survived until January 1944, when his approach to his Spanish friends to counter heavy British pressure for the restriction of Abwehr activities was rebuffed. He was relieved of his post in February and Hansen (described by Lahousen as 'an absolute foe of the system and of Hitler') became acting Chief of the Abwehr. The same month Hitler ordered the creation of a unified intelligence service.

Negotiations ensued between Hansen and Schellenberg for the assimilation of the Abwehr with the SD. In mid-May Himmler informed representatives of both organisations at a conference in Salzburg that a new organisation, the RSHA Militärisches Amt (Mil Amt) would be established as from 1 June 1944. The arrangements contemplated at this stage would have preserved much of the original form of the Abwehr under the authority of the RSHA, but the July Plot completed its ruin. Hansen, the head of Ast Vienna who was his colleague in the negotiations with Schellenberg, and other lesser figures were executed; Freytag-Loringhoven committed suicide. Canaris and Oster were imprisoned. They survived until April 1945 when both were executed at Flossenburg. The remains of the Abwehr were swallowed by the RSHA.

But although the Abwehr had been completely destroyed, its 'broken and fossilised relics lingered on'. Schellenberg presided over both Amt VI and the Mil Amt, but they were organisationally distinct. Amt VI continued to concern itself mainly with political intelligence and its natural overspill – the exploitation of collaborationist elements both for intelligence (including operational intelligence) and sabotage. The Mil Amt's functions were those of Abt I and Abt II of the Abwehr. It consisted largely of former Abwehr personnel, who retained their Wehrmacht ranks and uniforms, and was organised internally on much the same lines. But its directing staff were RSHA personnel and it had no distinct policy or personality of its own.

The regional organisation of the Mil Amt was taken over bodily from that of the Abwehr. The Abwehrstellen were re-named

Kommandos des Meldegebietes (KDMs) and the subsidiary Nebenstellen became Aussenstellen (Austs). Abroad, the Kriegsorganisationen and their subsidiary stations were similarly redesignated. Both at home and abroad there was a marked increase of central control. KDMs abroad were drastically pruned and brought into close contact with Amt VI offices which took over their counter-espionage responsibilities. The Abwehr Kommandos and Truppen with the field armies became Frontaufklärung Kommandos and Truppen (FAKs and FATs), but their functions were unchanged and they remained essentially dependent on the Wehrmacht formations to which they were attached.

Sabotage and subversion were placed under Skorzeny. He was already head of the sabotage section of Amt VI and during the last nine months of the war was in effective control of all sabotage and subversion behind the Allied lines, and of special commando-type operations. For these purposes he had at his disposal new units, known as SS Jagdverbände, which absorbed the role, and many of the personnel, of the Brandenburg Division.

The re-fashioned German Intelligence Service was no more successful than the old Abwehr. Schellenberg realised the need for central planning and did his best to impart new drive to the formally unified service. But he took over no espionage source of any value in the United Kingdom or the USA and did not succeed in developing any. The stay-behind networks organised by the Abwehr and Amt VI in France, the Low Countries and Italy, and attempts to infiltrate agents by parachute and other means for intelligence or sabotage purposes, failed almost without exception. The only potentially important success – information on the eve of the Arnhem landing that the Resistance in the Eindhoven area had been ordered to stand by for action on 16 September and that a major airborne operation was imminent – was obtained through the Abwehr's penetration of the Dutch Resistance movement.*

The German Intelligence Service collapsed totally with the Wehrmacht. It had been forbidden to envisage defeat and there was no contingency plan for survival and resistance. Schellenberg and Skorzeny both surrendered.

---

* For the details see Appendix 14.

APPENDIX 2

The CPGB's *Volte Face* in October 1939

DOUBTS ABOUT the correctness of the line initially adopted by the CPGB were being felt by the middle of September by some of the more erudite Marxists. The German-Soviet pact itself raised a large question mark. On 14 September the *Daily Worker* received a telegram containing the formulation 'There is no doubt whatever in the minds of the Soviet people that this war is an imperialist and predatory war for a new re-division of the world'. The Soviet intervention in Poland followed on 17 September, and Moscow Radio broadcast an interview in which an American Communist declared that the war was an imperialist war and not a war against Fascism. Then came Soviet support for Hitler's 'peace offer'. In these circumstances it was decided to postpone a proposed national conference to rally the CPGB to its war-time tasks until it was known what Springhall,* a member of the Central Committee who happened to be in Moscow at the outbreak of the war, had to say on his return. This postponement was explained to the Central Committee on 24 September by Pollitt, the General Secretary.† He called for a frank discussion, '. . . without any wondering about what Stalin is going to say in a couple of weeks time, but as responsible leaders of a political party in this country', and argued that they should stick to the line proclaimed at the outbreak of war. He was opposed by Dutt,‡ one of the CPGB's leading theoreticians, who thought that the Party's line would have to be revised after contact with the

---

* Douglas Frank Springhall (1901–1953). A founder member of the CPGB Member of the Executive Committee of the Young Communist League 1922–1927. In Russia 1928–1931 when he attended the Lenin School. On return he became a member of the Central Committee of the CPGB. Became national organiser of the CPGB in January 1940. Convicted of espionage in 1943. Died in Moscow.

† Harry Pollitt (1890–1960). A founder member of the CPGB and by 1926, after imprisonment for sedition, its generally acknowledged leader. He held the position, despite some criticism from Moscow, until his replacement as General Secretary at the end of September 1939. He resumed office after Germany attacked Russia in June 1941. Chairman of the CPGB 1956–1960.

‡ Raymond Palme Dutt (1896–1974). A founder member of CPGB and a member of the Central (later the Executive) Committee for more than 40 years. Member of the Comintern's Executive Committee in 1933. The author of numerous books, he was made an honorary Doctor of Moscow University in 1962.

international comrades had been re-established. The war was an imperialist war conducted by the ruling classes, and not a people's anti-Fascist war. The main struggle of the working class should be against its own imperialist government.

In the ensuing discussion most speakers agreed with Pollitt, but virtually all wanted to hear the authoritative voice of the Comintern, as relayed by Springhall, before reaching a final conclusion.

Springhall reported on the following day. He said that he wanted to give the essence of conversations he had had with Dimitrov* and other Comintern leaders and of a telegram containing a 'short thesis' drawn up by the secretariat of the Comintern, which had been sent to the Sections (ie the Comintern's constituent Communist Parties) on 10 September, but which had not yet reached the CPGB. This short thesis characterised the war as an unjust imperialist war, which could not be supported by the working class or the Communist Party in any country. Germany's aims were European and world domination, but Poland was a semi-Fascist country and her disappearance would not be a terrific misfortune. In any case, Britain was not genuinely concerned with Polish independence, but only with preserving her imperial interests. Now the working class and Communist Parties must act so as to shatter the capitalist system and, in Dimitrov's words, become 'grave-diggers at the funeral of capitalism'. The Communist Parties of France, Britain, America and Belgium must change their line. It was recognised that this would involve dangers for the CPGB and it should proceed cautiously to begin with; there was no question of jumping in and speaking of turning imperialist war into civil war.

In reply to questions Springhall confirmed that, as this was to be treated as an imperialist war, the CPGB was to work for Britain's military defeat. He added that Dimitrov had not yet thought out the line in the event of Britain being defeated and Fascism being imposed on the country from within and from without.

When the Central Committee re-assembled on 2 October Pollitt had been replaced as General Secretary by a triumvirate. The Comintern's short thesis had been received and a resolution which closely followed its wording was introduced by Dutt. He explained in detail how the old line was wrong and had brought out dangerous anti-Soviet and anti-international tendencies in the Party, which must now become a real section of the Comintern

---

* George Dimitrov (1882–1949). Bulgarian revolutionary who joined the Executive Committee of the Comintern in 1919. Lived in Berlin 1929–1933 and was one of the accused in the Reichstag fire trial. Went to Moscow after his acquittal and was Executive Secretary of the Comintern from 1934 until its dissolution in 1943. Became Prime Minister of Bulgaria in 1945.

'with every member a fighting member of the Communist International'.

There was opposition from Gallacher,* the only Communist MP, Campbell,† acting editor of the *Daily Worker*, and Pollitt. Gallacher made a fierce attack on Dutt's 'unscrupulous and opportunist' speech. Campbell rejected the complete *volte face* which Dutt was now demanding from the Party. Whereas 'we started by saying that we had an interest in the defeat of the Nazis, we must now recognise that our prime interest is in the defeat of France and Great Britain, because that will furnish the suitable conditions for a revolution in this country'. The result, said Campbell, would not be revolution, but the extension of Fascism in western Europe, and the defeat of France and Britain would be a mortal blow to the British working class movement. Pollitt thought that in the long run the Comintern line would do the CPGB very great harm; he could not therefore continue as General Secretary.

In the end loyalty to the Soviet Union and the Comintern was the overriding consideration. The voting was 20 to 3 in favour of Dutt's resolution. Gallacher said that he had been overwhelmed by his personal feelings and asked that his vote should after all be recorded for the resolution. Pollitt and Campbell went into the wilderness. A month later both recanted in letters of dutiful self-criticism to the Central Committee. The CPGB in turn abased itself, confessing its grave error, due to an 'insufficiently Marxist-Leninist approach . . . lack of vigilance in relation to opportunist tendencies . . . concessions to vulgar liberal democratic conceptions . . . blurring of the distinction between the national interest of the British people and the imperial interest of the British ruling class . . . weakening of the class basis of the Party'.

---

* William Gallacher (1888–1965). A leading member of the Social Democratic Federation which merged with the CPGB in 1921. Imprisoned in 1925 for sedition with other members of the Party. MP for West Fife 1935–1950. President of the CPGB 1956–1963.

† John Ross Campbell (1894–1969). A founder member of the CPGB. In 1924 as editor of *Workers Weekly* was charged under the Incitement of Mutiny Act, 1797. The abandonment of the prosecution led to the fall of the first Labour government. Imprisoned in 1925 for sedition with other members of the party. Editor of the *Daily Worker* 1949–1959.

Technical Problems Affecting Radio Communications by the Double-Cross Agents

Notes written by a former MI 5 officer from his personal experience

1. For those used to watching colour television pictures of men on the moon, and listening to the conversation of astronauts, it is not easy to imagine the state of the art of radio at the outbreak of the 1939–1945 war. True, there was television in black and white, communication by radio throughout the world was commonplace and radio amateurs ('hams') kept in touch with each other in all countries of the world using low power, but transistors had not been invented, computers were unknown and recording on long steel wire, not on tape, was only carried out by the BBC and other professional recording organisations.

2. Radio communication between the UK and Germany was carried out on the high frequency bands from 5–7 MHz. As the propagation of radio waves varies between night and day, frequencies should be on the low side at night and higher during the day. This meant that a radio agent should not stay on the same frequency but move up and down the spectrum for his communications to be fully effective. The snag for the receiving station was that the agent's signal had to be picked out of other interfering signals so that time might be used up establishing communication before the message began. Time on the air is danger time for being intercepted by the enemy and should be kept to the minimum. Another factor was that the most efficient aerial for these frequencies would be about 30 metres long and erected high in the air free of obstructions. The strength of a transmission is low if the aerial is close to the ground and if the transmission path is obstructed.

3. Accordingly agents in this country using radio transmitters would be operating under difficulties. In order not to draw attention to themselves they would have to erect aerials which would not be obtrusive, or excite comment, and these were likely to be inefficient. It would not be easy for a man to take lodgings, put up an aerial and lock himself in his room for a period each day

while he sent messages and received replies on equipment which, if it were seen by the landlady, would certainly cause her to call the Police. Indeed, on reflection it seems amazing that the Germans could believe that a man would find it possible to arrive by parachute or boat in a country alert for spies, find lodgings and set himself up in this way.

4. Besides the difficulty of establishing and maintaining contact there were the problems presented by (a) direction finding and (b) 'fingerprinting' and control signals.

(a) The most accurate 'fix' of a transmitting station is obtained if not less than three receiving stations are spaced round the transmitting station. The Germans could not use stations all round an agent in England, but they could get a long base line with receiving stations at Nantes and Bordeaux in the west and Hamburg and Bremen in the east. We could not therefore take any chances although there was (as always) some inability among the experts to agree how accurate 'fixes' could be. Could a station be 'fixed' within a mile radius or was it as much as 10 miles? Like many other intelligence appreciations all one could do was to play safe and assume that the Germans were at least as good as us and maybe a bit better, and that if bearings were taken every day and found consistently to point to a location other than the one from which the agent said he was transmitting, they might smell a rat. We therefore had to assume that if a German agent told them he was transmitting from, say, Aylesbury, he would actually have to be located at or close to Aylesbury.

(b) Morse sent on an ordinary morse key by an individual has individual characteristics which any one familiar with the operator's 'fist' can recognise. All the radio agents who were sent to this country had been trained by the Germans who were going to listen to them after their arrival in England. So the principle on which we had to operate was to 'turn' the agent so that he would agree to send his own messages, and to have another person, who knew the morse code, to listen to the transmission and watch carefully what was being sent so as to be sure that there was no deviation from the message agreed upon. We knew, for example, that the Germans had envisaged the possibility of some agents being 'turned' and had instructed them to agree to co-operate, but to insert 'control' signals in a message. For example, the agent might say that he was always to put the word 'greetings' at the end of his message, whereas the inclusion of the word meant that he was operating under duress. There were variations of subtlety on this theme. If an agent was under control he might add – or omit – an X or a full stop or something small. It was difficult to know whether an agent was telling the truth about this. There were precedents to be consulted in previous cases, but the Germans (sensibly) did not seem to follow any consistent pattern – sometimes a sign was to be put in and sometimes omitted – and occasionally the agent couldn't remember his instructions properly. Even when the 'control' signal was included the Germans were inclined to say that the agent must have become confused in his excitement and to take no notice of it. Because they wanted to believe his transmission was genuine (and get the credit for it) they might not even report to their HQ that the control signal had been included.

If an agent went 'bad' and refused to continue, or if we had misgivings about his truthfulness and did not think we could trust him, we had to consider whether his 'fist' should be impersonated by the operator who had sat at his side listening to him. Another possibility was to say that the agent had managed to recruit 'a friend' to do the transmitting leaving the agent more time to engage in reconnaissance. Much depended on the circumstances of the case and what we thought we could get away with. But it was always difficult to decide whether it was safe to make a change or not. If an agent was under suspicion of having been 'turned', to bring in a new operator might confirm suspicions. There are examples where agents were successfully replaced by other operators. (I do not know if there were cases where the agent became suspect through making a change of operator).

5.   Nearly all the equipment made by the Germans for their radio spies could be contained in a small suitcase. The power of the transmitter was no more than 3 watts on batteries and 5/10 watts when running from a mains power supply. But the Germans realised that, although transmitters with higher power might help the reliability of communications and cut down transmitting time, higher power also presented a hazard to the agent himself in that the transmitter might cause local interference to domestic radio receivers and be more easily intercepted by the British authorities who, certainly in 1940, were bombarded with reports from all sides from people who thought they had heard 'morse' signals coming from suspicious houses. All such reports were investigated and most were discovered to be the product of a lively imagination, noisy water pipes or a central heating plant.

One ingenious design of transmitter required the substitution of a plug into the back of an ordinary radio receiver to convert it to a transmitter. Another agent brought to this country what appeared to be an ordinary radio set which contained (underneath the chassis) a small transmitter which could be brought into operation by turning a switch on the back of the set labelled 'radio/gramophone'. Other agents were instructed how to purchase components in England which would enable them to build their own transmitter. So far as is known none ever did so with success.

6.   *Snow* was the first agent to communicate with the Germans by radio soon after the outbreak of war in 1939. His radio set was installed in a cell in Wandsworth prison where he had been detained under DR 18B. The radio was operated by a warder who knew the morse code, although the Germans assumed it was *Snow* himself who was transmitting. The warder also listened around on his receiver and reported that, noticing the style of the operator in Germany and the characteristic morse note of the transmitter, he

recognised that communications were taking place at times other than when *Snow* was on the air. This gave our intercept stations a most important clue to the German spy communications network in Europe.

7. The first spy to bring a radio set with him was *Summer* who landed by parachute not far from Aylesbury on 6 September 1940. He was captured within a few hours of landing, interrogated and revealed his code and instructions. An immediate attempt was made to operate his transmitter in the area in which he landed and to establish communication with the Germans. His equipment was set up in a field, at the back of the house of the Chief Constable of Buckinghamshire, with each end of a short aerial tied to a couple of longish sticks projecting from a pig-sty. At 3 o'clock in the morning the spy lay on his stomach in a damp field tapping away on his morse key, watched over by a technical expert (a 'ham') who had been brought in to monitor the transmission to ensure that nothing was sent which would indicate to the enemy that *Summer* was under the control of MI 5. After two nights of failure to establish contact the expert recommended that the transmitting equipment should be given a better chance to show its paces by being installed in Aylesbury Police Station, with the aerial erected higher, clear of obstructions and tuned up carefully with an additional meter to read the aerial current. After a time communication was established in this way and *Summer* took his place as the second radio double agent in England.

8. *Tate* arrived by parachute soon after *Summer*. He too was captured and 'turned'. He was on the air almost continuously from October 1940 to May 1945. His radio equipment was installed in a house with the aerial clear of obstructions and tuned up carefully.

9. Ter Braak, *Zigzag* and *Mutt* and *Jeff* were also equipped with radio. Ter Braak killed himself in an air-raid shelter in Cambridge in April 1941. The state of his set indicated that he had almost certainly failed to establish communication with Germany. *Zigzag's* transmitter was set up in a house in a north-west London suburb with a good high aerial and contact was established with little difficulty. The set with which *Mutt* and *Jeff* transmitted to Norway was later moved to this location.

10. In the *Garbo* case we chanced our arm by using more power than in any other operation to ensure reliability of radio communication. Reliability was essential for the deception plans which we had to get across to the enemy at the time of *Overlord*. *Garbo* told the Germans that his operator had obtained a good powerful set. The set was in fact a BC 610, a well known all-band transmitter of American military manufacture capable of an output of 600 watts though it was used in the low power mode of 100 watts. This was 20 times the power of the sets used by *Summer* and *Tate*. The

transmitter was first operated from a house owned by *Garbo's* case-officer. Towards the end of the case it was moved to the flat on top of MI 5's London HQ, a very convenient arrangement for everyone concerned!

APPENDIX 4

List of Subjects Considered by the Security Executive

1. ESPIONAGE

Arrangements with Police and military Commands for dealing with suspected enemy agents.
Facilities for interrogation and detention.
Guidance to the Police on the technique of enemy agents.

2. SABOTAGE

Preventive measures, general and special.
Control of explosives and chemicals.
Arrangements for co-ordinated investigation and regular reports.

3. SUBVERSIVE ACTIVITIES

The British Union of Fascists.
The Communist Party of Great Britain and satellite organisations.
Trotskyist organisations.
Pacifist, 'Religious' and Conscientious Objectors organisations.

4. OTHER FIFTH COLUMN ACTIVITIES

Precautions against bogus notices, pamphlets, messages, etc.
Control of uniforms, badges, emblems, etc.
Action against the spreading of malicious or defeatist rumours.
Watch on enemy broadcasts masquerading as British.

5. ALIENS

Policy of internment and release.
Registration with the Police and the Ministry of Labour and National Service.
Restrictions on movement, employment, etc.
Privileges for Allied nationals.
Registration of former aliens.

6. PRISONERS OF WAR

Safeguard of employment on agriculture, forestry, etc.
Security conditions in camps.
Security arrangements for sending overseas.
Security of communications to British prisoners.

7. CONTROL OF INFORMATION AND COMMUNICATIONS

Censorship: Press: Postal, Telegraph and Telephone: Travellers.
Special censorship of mail from internment camps and Protected
Areas: between Great Britain and Ireland: of documents carried
by ships' crews.
Control of cameras, binoculars, telescopes, radio equipment and
high frequency electrical apparatus.
Control of codes, secret inks, light and flag signals, pigeons, etc.
Propaganda against careless talk.
Special control of information about the location and activities of
factories, government departments, military establishments, etc,
movements of population, port facilities, air-raid damage.
Special control of information obtainable from government
departments, government contractors, labour recruiting agents,
fire insurance proposal forms and the published accounts and
reports of companies, public utilities, local authorities, etc.

8. IDENTITY CARDS, PASSES AND PERMITS

Value of identity cards for security purposes.
Production of identity cards at hotels and boarding houses.
Special identity cards for seamen, and other special classes.

9. SECURITY OF SPECIAL LOCALITIES

Security measures in:–
    Operational or training areas.
    Government and Service establishments, aerodromes,
    internment camps.
    Factories, depots, public utilities, etc.
    Ports, docks, marshalling yards.

10. CONTROL OF ENTRY, EXIT, TRAVEL FACILITIES

Issue of visas: examination of arrivals.
Exit permits: repatriation policy.
Port control: co-ordination of port security services.
Control of air and steamship lines.

11. SHIPPING SECURITY

Prevention of subversion of crews.
Special measures to control information regarding convoys.
Special anti-sabotage precautions.

12. OVERSEAS SECURITY

Security measures in and for:–
    British colonies (West Africa and West Indies).
    British dominions.
    British interests in foreign countries.

APPENDIX 5

Prosecutions Under the Defence Regulations

(i) The British Union

The following is a list of cases of offences of varying gravity against the Defence Regulations in which former BU members were concerned –

1. The Duvivier/Crowle case: see above, p 38n.
2. William Swift and Mrs Ingrams, both active members of the BU, were convicted on 2 July 1940 of conspiracy to assist the enemy, and sentenced to long terms of penal servitude.
3. Olive Baker, a former member of BU and The Link, was convicted in July 1940 on charges of distributing postcards advertising the enemy-controlled New British Broadcasting Service, and sentenced to five years penal servitude.
4. In August 1940 G Trengrove, the former BU district leader in Cornwall, was convicted on a charge of having in his possession a document of such a nature that its dissemination would be a breach of the Defence Regulations. The document, composed by Trengrove, aimed at inciting soldiers and others not to discharge their duties. He was sent to prison for two months.
5. J Lloyd, who had been discharged from the Army because of his Fascist opinions, was convicted on 11 November 1940 for an offence against the blackout regulations, having lit a bonfire in his garden during an air raid. He gave the magistrate the Nazi salute.
6. T H Beckett, a former member of the BU, was sentenced to three years penal servitude in November 1940. He was found to be in possession of a list of 604 aerodromes in the British Empire, compiled from Air Ministry records, and had purloined an Air Ministry map showing aerodromes in No 4 works area.
7. In December 1940 detention orders under DR 18B(1) in respect of 'acts prejudicial' were made against former BU members who were reported to be preparing to carry out acts which might be of assistance to the enemy, including arson and other damage and the preparation of a map of important objectives in the Leeds area, with the apparent intention of communicating it to the enemy.
8. In June 1941 Molly Hiscox, a former member of the BU, the Right Club and The Link, and Nora Briscoe, a sympathiser, were

each sentenced to five years penal servitude for offences under the Defence Regulations. They had communicated to a person whom they believed to be a German agent confidential information to which Mrs Briscoe had access as a shorthand-typist in the Ministry of Supply.

9. In April 1943 W F Craven, a former member of the BU, was sentenced to penal servitude for life under the Defence Regulations. He had written to the German legation in Dublin offering his services.

10. In 1946 Arnold Leese, head of the Imperial Fascist League, and some of his associates were convicted of breaking the Defence Regulations by assisting escaped German prisoners of war and sentenced to imprisonment.

(ii) The Communist Party

The only case in which a member of the CPGB was detained under DR 18B was initiated by MI 5 with the agreement of the Ministry of Labour. The man concerned was John Mason, a Party member since 1934 who was employed by the English Steel Corporation. Information from secret sources showed that he was actively obstructing measures to increase production, and he was detained on 15 July 1940 under DR 18B on the grounds that he had been concerned in 'acts prejudicial'. In September the Advisory Committee recommended his continued detention. The Executive Council of the Amalgamated Engineering Union protested, but meetings at the Home Office served to convince them that detention was justified. Protests continued, however, from Communists and Communist-controlled organisations. Following a meeting between Mr Will Gallacher, MP and Maxwell, the former gave assurances that if Mason was released he would not engage in further activities impeding the war effort, and that his release would not be exploited by the CPGB. On 8 May 1941 his case was again referred by the Home Office to the Advisory Committee, which accepted his assurances about his future conduct and advised that his continued detention was not necessary. The detention order was accordingly revoked on 7 June 1941.

APPENDIX 6

Abwehr Agents: Autumn 1940

The first parties arrived in the early hours of 3 September when Waldberg and Meier landed near Dungeness, and Kieboom and Pons between Dymchurch and Rye. They had crossed the Channel in fishing smacks which were towed most of the way by German minesweepers, sailed to within a short distance of the English coast, launched dinghies, and rowed ashore. Each party had a wireless transmitter (but no receiver), revolver, material for secret writing with which to make notes for their own use, local maps and £60 in £5 notes. They were to pose as refugees and to report on troop dispositions and armaments, aerodromes, anti-aircraft defences, damaged ships in ports and civilian morale. When the invasion started they were to retire with the civilian population and continue to report, and they were given a pass-word for use when they eventually contacted invading forces.

Jose Waldberg was a German national, who had been on the Abwehr's books since May 1937 and had already worked for them in France; Karl Meier, a naturalised Dutch subject of German extraction, was new to the game having been recruited through the NSDAP in July 1940. Stoerd Pons and Charles van den Kieboom were both Dutch subjects who had been coerced into becoming agents with the threat of being sent to a concentration camp for currency offences. All four were arrested within a few hours, largely as a result of their own stupidity.

The first party came to grief swiftly. Having beached and unloaded their dinghy, Meier went off to Lydd where he fell into conversation with an air raid warden who asked him for his identity card. Meier told his cover story, ie that he was a refugee who had arrived on the previous night. Inadvertently he said '*we* arrived here last night', thus disclosing that he was not alone. He was taken into custody and interrogated and finally told the Police where they could pick up Waldberg. The latter, while waiting for Meier's return, had already sent out two messages on his transmitter and was just about to send a third when he was arrested.

The second party fared no better. While unpacking their boat on arrival, Pons approached some bystanders and asked where he was – not surprisingly they handed him straight over to the Police. Van den Kieboom was challenged by two officers in a car as he was carrying gear across the road to hide it.

All four agents were tried under the Treachery Act. Waldberg,

Meier and Kieboom were executed in December 1940. Pons was acquitted – rather luckily since his case was virtually on all fours with that of Kieboom – the jury apparently accepting that he had acted under duress. He remained in detention until the end of the war when he was handed over to the Dutch authorities.

Summer had been recruited by the Abwehr at the end of 1938, and had already made two visits to England on its behalf, ostensibly as a journalist representing Swedish newspapers, returning from a second trip in December 1939. He was dropped on 6 September in Northamptonshire; his instructions were to report on the area Oxford-Northampton-Birmingham, with particular reference to air raid damage in Birmingham. He was captured within a few hours of landing, having knocked himself out with the wireless set he was carrying; in addition to the set (transmitter and receiver) he had with him a code, materials for secret writing, a forged identity card in his own name with a number provided by *Snow*, a revolver and £200.

On 9 September *Summer* was offered his life in return for assistance in transmitting messages to the enemy and agreed to co-operate. On 17 September he told the Germans that he had been hiding in the open since his arrival, but now proposed to find shelter, posing as a refugee. The Abwehr vetoed this idea, and instructed *Snow* to contact him and arrange his accommodation, thus confirming that MI 5's continuing belief in the *Snow* case was justified. This manoeuvre was accomplished notionally by *Snow's* sub-agent *Biscuit*. At the end of September the Germans instructed *Summer* to cover the area London-Colchester-Southend. On 23 October he reported that he was established in lodgings near Cambridge.

An important piece of information given by *Summer* was that, while under training, he had become friendly with another agent who would follow him to England. In return for a promise that his friend's life would be spared he disclosed that they had arranged to meet outside The Black Boy Inn at Nottingham. The friend, a Danish national of German origin, arrived in England on the night of 19–20 September. He had been recruited by the Abwehr at the end of 1939, but this was his first mission. He was a determined and resourceful man, with a good knowledge of English and might well have been a dangerous agent. However, he sprained his ankle on landing in Cambridgeshire, and aroused suspicion when he hobbled into a village to make some purchases. He was arrested and found to be in possession of £132 and $160 in notes, a genuine Danish passport in his own name, and a forged British identity card embodying particulars supplied by *Snow*. Under interrogation he claimed to have left Denmark because of trouble with the Germans, travelled to England by boat and spent three months tramping from the neighbourhood of West Hartlepool. Although unable to account for himself since his supposed arrival, or to explain how he had kept his clothes clean and well-pressed and where he had last had his hair cut, he did not give way till confronted with the information which *Summer* had supplied about him and their projected rendezvous at The Black Boy.

Once broken, *Tate*, as he was named by MI 5, collaborated wholeheartedly. Under his guidance, his wireless set, parachute and other equipment were recovered. On 16 October he told the Germans that he was established in lodgings near Barnet; thereafter he maintained wireless communication with the Abwehr in Hamburg until twenty-four hours before the fall of the city in May 1945. His case was of great value, first for counter-espionage purposes and later for deception.

On 23 September the cutter *La Part Bien* arrived in Plymouth having surrendered voluntarily to a naval patrol boat. On board were three men of whom two, Hugo Jonasson, a Swede, and Gerald Libot, a Belgian, were German agents – or at least potential agents. They had certainly been recruited by the Abwehr: Jonasson had been paid 2,500 Belgian francs. Libot, who had been a member of the right wing Rexist Party and a Nazi propagandist, had volunteered his services. Their mission was probably sabotage.

A more serious, and more tragic, expedition came a week later. On 30 September Vera Eriksen, Karl Drucke and Werner Walti landed in a rubber dinghy near Port Gordon on the Moray Firth, having been flown from Norway in a seaplane. At about 0800 Drucke and Vera Eriksen appeared at Port Gordon railway station, where they aroused suspicion because of their bedraggled appearance and obvious ignorance of their whereabouts. The Police were called and the couple were arrested and found to be in possession of a wireless transmitter and receiver, maps showing most of the aerodromes in Great Britain, forged identity and ration cards based on particulars obtained from *Snow* and *Biscuit*, a revolver and about £400 in English banknotes. Soon after their arrest the dinghy was found, and enquiries were at once begun to discover whether it had brought any other passengers.

Almost at once there was a report of a man carrying a suitcase, wearing a wet mackintosh, and displaying complete ignorance of the locality, who had taken a train from Buckie station to Edinburgh that morning. The same afternoon a suitcase, bearing traces of having been put down on wet sand, was found in a cloakroom at Waverley station, Edinburgh; it had been left there by a man whose description tallied with that of the individual seen at Buckie, and proved to contain a wireless transmitting and receiving set. In the evening this man, who turned out to be Werner Walti, a Swiss subject, claimed the suitcase and was immediately arrested, though not before he had attempted to draw a revolver. In addition to the wireless equipment and the revolver, his property included £190 in English banknotes, forged identity and ration cards, a Swiss passport which was genuine but lacked an entry visa and immigration officer's stamp, a chart marking all aerodromes in Scotland and eleven ordnance maps of east Scotland, Norfolk and Suffolk.

Both men resisted interrogation stubbornly. Vera lied continually in an attempt to shield Drucke. It was not until eighteen months after the arrival of this party, and some six months after the execution of the two men* that Vera gave anything like a coherent account of her own adventurous history and the preparation of this disastrous mission.

Born in Kiev in December 1912, of parents (probably partly Jewish) named Staritzky, Vera was adopted by a German family called von Schalbourg which left Russia for Denmark at the time of the Revolution and assumed Danish nationality. In 1927 she went to Paris, where she joined the ballet, and three years later married a man by the name of Ignatieff, who combined the careers of Soviet agent and drug pedlar. For some while she acted as his courier but the association ended when he attempted to murder her. She tried to return to Denmark and enlisted the help of her step-brother, von Schalbourg, a Nazi, who brought her to the attention of the Abwehr's Dr Ritter. In October 1937, according to her story, she married, perhaps bigamously, a member of the Abwehr called variously von Wedel, zum Stuhrec or Oberleutnant Dierks. Ritter had hopes of using her as a penetration agent against the Soviet Intelligence Service but, when this failed, despatched her to London in the early part of 1939. Here she acted as a companion to an elderly lady, who had originally been introduced to Ritter by My Eriksson,† and who was erroneously believed by him to have valuable social contacts from whom Vera could obtain information. In fact no such opportunity existed and she returned empty-handed to Germany. There she met Drucke, who was acting as 'an occasional agent', and fell in love with him.

The scheme of sending the pair of them to England on an espionage mission was conceived by Ritter in August 1940. It was looked on as a hopeless enterprise by everyone else involved, including Vera's putative husband von Wedel, who decided to appeal personally to Admiral Canaris to have the trip cancelled, but was killed in a car smash. Various plans for landing the mission, now joined by Walti, in the United Kingdom were tried out before the seaplane/rubber dinghy plan was finally put into effect.

---

* They were tried under the Treachery Act and hanged on 6 August 1941.
† See above, p 41.

Vera maintained that her instructions were to pilot Drucke, who spoke virtually no English, to London and to establish him there, either with or without the assistance of her former employer, and wait until some unnamed person collected the wireless set from them. She insisted that Drucke knew no morse and could never have operated as a spy because of his lack of English. It is, however, quite likely that he had received a further briefing from Ritter which he did not disclose to her. Vera stated that Walti, who spoke fairly good English, was always intended to operate alone, probably reporting by wireless on Scottish aerodromes; she added that he was working purely for money.

The expedition achieved nothing but the deaths of the two men. Vera herself remained in detention for the rest of the war.

Next to arrive was another German, christened *Gander* by MI 5, who landed by parachute on 4 October, and was found by a farmer sheltering in a barn. He had a wireless transmitter but no receiver, £140, a forged identity card which did not, and a ration book which did, correspond with particulars obtained through *Snow* and *Biscuit*. He was wearing civilian clothes, but was carrying German Air Force unform and an Army paybook, and proved to be a member of the Lehr Regiment Brandenburg zbV 800,* a special unit closely associated with the Abwehr. His instructions were to cover the Midlands from Bedford to Liverpool, including Birmingham and Coventry, and to rejoin the invading forces which he could expect in about a fortnight. He was to transmit daily weather information and report on morale. He agreed to act as a double-cross agent, but having only a transmitter could be used by MI 5 only for a few weeks until his mission was exhausted. Nevertheless his willingness to co-operate, together with the fact that he had never been a member of the Nazi Party, saved him from prosecution and he was detained for the duration.

The fourth dinghy party landed from a seaplane off the coast near Nairn and came ashore on 25 October. It consisted of Gunnar Edvardssen, a Norwegian journalist who had been working as an interpreter with the German occupation forces, and two companions both of whom had been press-ganged – Otto Joost, a German who had fought for the Spanish government in the Civil War, and Legwald Lund, an elderly Norwegian seaman who had assaulted a German policeman.

Of all the spies sent in preparation for the projected invasion, these were the most ill-prepared. They had no papers, had had no training and were given no means of communicating with their base. Their instructions were to bicycle across Scotland (their

---

* See Appendix 1(i), p 298.

bicycles had had to be jettisoned during the landing), and cut telephone wires, thereby creating alarm and despondency, and to join up with the invading forces which they were told to expect in about three weeks.

The discovery of a parachute at Haversham, Berkshire, on 3 November signalled the arrival of another agent who, alone of the 1940 spies, evaded immediate capture. This was the man whose emaciated body was found on 1 April 1941 in an air raid shelter in Cambridge with a self-inflicted bullet wound. There was a Dutch passport (without an immigration stamp) on the body in the name of Jan Wilhelm Ter Braak, and a British identity card in the same name with one of the serial numbers supplied by *Snow* and exhibiting several gross errors (for example the name of a non-existent street was placed *after* the name of the town) which alone would have been enough to reveal it as a forgery. A search in the parcels office at the railway station disclosed that a case containing a wireless set similar to that brought by other parachute agents had been deposited by Ter Braak on 29 March.

It was possible to reconstruct Ter Braak's movements in some detail. He arrived in Cambridge on 4 November and obtained lodgings where he remained until 31 January 1941. During this period he went out most days, but never slept a night away. He told his landlady and her husband, with whom he was on good terms, that he had come from Holland during the evacuation from Dunkirk, that he was connected with the Free Dutch forces and was employed by a Dutch newspaper in London where he went occasionally for the purpose of his work. Ter Braak did not register with the Police as an alien, and though his landlord told the Assistant Aliens Officer that he had a Dutchman staying with him, this information was not followed up.

At the end of January 1941, Ter Braak was alarmed by enquiries from the Food Office about his ration card. The forged one he had brought contained particulars supplied by *Snow*, and Food Office records showed that the card had been issued to someone else. He therefore told his landlady that he had to leave Cambridge for London. In fact he only changed lodgings and the pattern of his behaviour continued to be the same up to 30 March.

On his arrival in Cambridge Ter Braak had a considerable sum of money and paid his bill regularly in cash. In March he changed five $10 bills through a fellow lodger employed at the bank. The only money found on his body was 1/9d and he owed his landlady for the current week.

It is impossible to say what Ter Braak accomplished for his masters during the five months he was at large. His suicide when his money was exhausted, the condition of his wireless set and the fact that no attempts were made to assist him through other channels apparently open to the Germans, strongly suggest that he failed to establish contact with them.

On 12 November the fishing smack *Josephine* put into Fishguard. Her captain, Cornelius Evertsen, a Dutchman, had been recruited by the Abwehr in August. On board were three anti-Fascist Cubans who had been recruited in a concentration camp in northern France and trained as saboteurs. They were to be landed by raft on the west coast and to find work in the neighbourhood of Bristol or Liverpool. Evertsen decided to surrender as he had no wish to work for the Germans.

APPENDIX 7

Two Seamen Agents

On 4 February 1941 the Censorship authorities intercepted a letter to a Lisbon address betraying signs of secret writing which, when developed, contained an account of an attack on a convoy. The writer was identified as Joseph Auguste Laureyssens who was arrested on 17 February and taken to Latchmere House. He was in possession of material for secret writing. His interrogation was described as 'difficult'. He proved himself 'a prolific liar with an abundance of low cunning', who skilfully sent the authorities off on a wild goose chase after other alleged agents. It was eventually established that he had been at large for several months and had written some 16 letters to Lisbon. He escaped trial because of evidential difficulties – by mistake the original intercepted message had been faded out and could not be re-developed – and was detained for the duration.

Alphonse Timmerman, was less fortunate. He was torpedoed in April 1941, picked up by a Spanish fishing boat and repatriated to Belgium. He was recruited by the Abwehr in the spring of 1941, trained and escorted to Huelva in July. There he was given money and false papers and told to find his way to England. He signed on as a steward in a ship which arrived in Glasgow on 1 September and was arrested, an SIS source having reported his Abwehr connections. He was found to have a considerable amount of money in sterling, dollars and pesetas, materials for secret writing, and a document purporting to certify that he had been detained in a Spanish prison camp. He made a full confession, was tried under the Treachery Act and executed.

APPENDIX 8

Tate's Report on Bomb Damage at Coventry, July 1941

(i) *Summary of Tate message as submitted for approval*

The centre of the town looks very bad. Many streets completely disappeared. Many roads up. Very many police. Very good food. Barrage balloons over the town.

There are many large factories with huge activity. A great deal of them undamaged. Thousands of labourers everywhere.

Rootes Security Ltd. Aircraft Division, No 1 engine factory, in Aldermoor Lane. Huge factory, very well camouflaged. Bomb damage not very important. Very great activity.

Next door in Aldermoor Lane is *Auto Machinery Co Ltd.* Same applies as to *Rootes*.

In same street is the *Lucas factory*.

Behind the houses in Brompton Road is a very large factory which seems to be new. Very well camouflaged.

In Parkside there are *Maudsley Motor Co Ltd*, and the *Rover Co Ltd* and the *Armstrong Siddeley Motor Co Ltd*. Motor car manufacturers, aircraft dept. offices and motor body works – all in one large factory site. Huge activity – unimportant bomb damage.

Gulson Road, very large factory. Seems to be *Jurys Crown Electrical Works*. Heavy damage, working full speed.

Quintin Road – *Maudsley Motor Co Ltd*, and the *British Pressed Panels Ltd* – slight damage. *Morris Motors* bodies branch – slight damage, much activity.

Little Park Street – Everything completely destroyed, including what seems to have been *Speedwell Gearcase Co.*

Earl Street and West Orchard Street – blown to bits.

Smithford Street – the *Triumph Cycle Co Ltd* completely destroyed.

Gosford Street – the *General Electric Co* Whitefriars Works, completely destroyed. Next door, the *Mechanisation and Aero Co Ltd*, practically undamaged, working full speed.

Bell Green Road – *Morris Motor Co*, Courthouse Green Works, badly damaged in parts, but working full speed.

Smith Street – the *Thomas Smith Stamping Works Ltd*, as well as the *English Electric Co*, are heavily damaged, but are working full speed.

Lower Ford Street – some damage, but little to factories. The *British Thompson Houston Co Ltd*, is in this street.

Humber Avenue – *the Aeronautical Equipment* (Thomas Smith's Stamping Works) are working full speed.

Aldermoor Green – about three miles north-east from Coventry, power station with three large chimneys and seven Wohl cooling towers – no bomb damage.

The report adds information about factories and roads in the vicinity of Coventry.

(ii) Message as finally approved

I have been in Coventry but had to stop operations after my first preliminary run round because I found the Police were conducting an identity card drive and I thought that I should have difficulties in clearing myself if picked up.

In my preliminary survey I found that the centre of town was badly damaged. Many streets completely disappeared, many roads are up. The outskirts seem to have suffered less so far as I could see from the train and from one bus ride. Balloon barrage over the town. This area is interesting to me and seems productive, but I must have a street plan. It may be worth while returning when the security drive is over.

There are many large factories. Some of them are undamaged, but there seems also to have been a great deal of industrial damage. I found much less activity than I had expected even taking into account the extent of the damage, and from such enquiries as I had time to make the answer seems to be that the authorities were so frightened by the raid of last November that they have put into operation a large-scale dispersal policy. As regards the direction in which this has taken place, I hardly know where to start. For example, GEC, which was badly damaged in November, has transferred operations to a new factory in Lanarkshire. Some of Morris Motors subsidiaries have also gone, but I could not find where. Although from the conversation I overheard in a bus, it is possible that they have transferred to the outskirts of Manchester.

I was able to get the following detailed information:

Little Park Street – Everything completely destroyed – no activity. Everything burnt out. One factory seems to have been the *Gearcase Co Ltd*.

Earl Street – Blown to pieces.

Smithford Street – The upper half blown to pieces.

West Orchard – Completely blown to pieces.

Priory Street – Cycle works completely destroyed and burnt out.

APPENDIX 9

Some 1942 Spies

(i) Enemy Double Agents

Several cases illustrated the threat to security in the UK that arose from the penetration of the clandestine organisations which operated for the Allies in occupied Europe.

(a)   Jean Charles Pelletier, a young man who had escaped to the United Kingdom after the French armistice and had been sent back to unoccupied France in March 1941 to assist with the communications of Gaullist agents, arrived back in England from Gibraltar in April 1942. The Free French were by then deeply suspicious of him and under their rigorous interrogation he confessed that he had been captured by the Germans and sent back to Vichy France to resume contact with his network and report on Gaullist and British activities. At the request of the Free French he was sent for further examination to Camp 020, where he repaired some of the damage he had done by submitting a number of useful proposals for the improvement of Allied radio security in France. He remained at Camp 020 until he was deported to France in 1945, a French court martial having found him guilty of treason and sentenced him to life imprisonment.

(b)   At the end of February 1942 a French woman, known as *Victoire*, who was a member of a large network of agents headed by a Polish officer, and a Frenchman, known as *Lucas*, who was head of an SOE network, were taken off a beach in France by motor torpedo boat and brought back to England. They had been brought together by *Lucas's* need for a radio link with London, but *Lucas* had discovered that *Victoire* had betrayed her network and transferred her services to the Abwehr, and that the link she had provided was under German control. He had alerted London to these facts and had concocted for the benefit of the Abwehr a plan by which, ostensibly to enable her to obtain information for the Germans but in fact either to get her out of their hands or to enable her to return to them as a triple agent, she would accompany him on a visit to London. After examination by MI 5, the SIS and SOE, it was decided that she could not be allowed to return to France. Though she co-operated, apparently wholeheartedly, in keeping the Abwehr-controlled link alive for long enough to protect *Lucas's* return, the Abwehr arrested him in May. *Victoire* was detained until she was handed over to the French authorities in June 1945. In 1949 she was found guilty of intelligence with the enemy, but the death sentence was commuted to life imprisonment.

(c) At the end of 1942 Tor Gulbrandsen, a Norwegian escaper who had gone back to Norway for the SOE in the previous February, returned to the United Kingdom from Sweden. His story was that when captured by the Germans in May he had named a few people in one section of his organisation but had otherwise divulged nothing to them before making his escape. The SOE believed him but MI 5 had reservations about the amount of information he had divulged; and these were borne out when another escaper reported in January 1943 that Gulbrandsen had talked freely and that his escape and return to England had been arranged by the Germans. He confessed that under the pressure of threats to his fiancée and his parents he had agreed to work for the Germans, his mission being to report in coded letters about the organisation of SOE and the despatch of agents to Norway. He remained in detention till the end of the war, when he was handed over to the Norwegian authorities.

(ii) Simoes

Ernesto Simoes arrived in Poole in July 1942 having been granted a visa under a scheme operated by the Ministry of Labour for recruiting foreign mechanics for the aircraft industry. At a routine examination at the LRC nothing emerged to suggest that he was a spy and he was released for employment with a firm in Luton. By then ISOS decrypts had disclosed that he had been recruited by the Abwehr, and MI 5 had decided to use his case to test the efficiency of the counter-espionage machinery and find out whether he contacted any unidentified agents. He wrote a letter to Lisbon in clear text, which merely gave his address, and received a reply which, by an oversight in Censorship, was not tested for secret writing. Intensive surveillance of him had otherwise produced no evidence that he was spying by the end of October. Since not even intensive surveillance had been able to obtain total coverage of his movements, and since he might be lying low until he had acquired valuable information, he was arrested in November. He confessed that he had been recruited by the Germans, who had instructed him to join the armed forces or get a job in an aircraft factory and report in secret writing on aircraft and ship construction, economic conditions and the arrival of US troops, but maintained that he had as yet submitted no reports. He was detained for the rest of the war.

(iii) Executed

(a)   On 18 May 1942, when decrypts had disclosed plans for the despatch to England of a seaman, probably Dutch, who would write to cover addresses in` Dutch or English and sign himself Karel van Dongen, three Dutchmen who said they were refugees were taken from a yacht found drifting off Harwich. One of them, a Dutch postal official, was named Dronkers. He and his companions were thoroughly examined over a period of three weeks. The LRC examiner, who did not know the ISOS information, was inclined to reject Dronker's very detailed story, in the course of which it emerged that he had been a seaman for a few years, as a plot to get him into Britain as a German agent. On 16 June the Senior Intelligence Officer minuted that on the whole he was inclined to think that the men were not agents, but Dronkers was the most likely to be one and best fitted the description of Karel van Dongen. The same day Dronkers was confronted with a Dutch intelligence officer, who had evidence that he had had contact with the Abwehr before the war, and he confessed that he had been sent by the Germans. The Abwehr had provided the yacht – and two genuine escapers to give him cover – and had instructed him to offer his services to the Dutch authorities in England and report in secret writing on a variety of military subjects to addresses in Stockholm and Lisbon. He was tried and sentenced under the Treachery Act and hanged at the end of the year.

(b)   Alexander Scott-Ford, a Writer in the Royal Navy who had been court-martialled and sentenced for embezzlement and forgery in March 1941 and who had subsequently been employed as a merchant seaman, was already under suspicion when his ship arrived in Liverpool in June 1942; ISOS decrypts had referred to him. He was left alone after maintaining that he had been approached by the Germans but had rejected their proposals. On his next arrival in Liverpool in a convoy from Lisbon in August he was interrogated again and made a full confession. The Germans had recruited him to report on convoys and had been dissatisfied with his first effort. In July in Lisbon they had threatened to denounce him to the British Consul if he failed to disclose the course followed by his next convoy and particulars about its escorts and to provide information about shipbuilding in Britain. He was tried and found guilty and executed in November 1942.

(c)   Johannes Winter, a Belgian ship's steward of German descent who arrived in Glasgow at the end of July via Gibraltar, had already aroused suspicions at Gibraltar; he claimed to have escaped from Belgium but had arrived by an unusual route. Under examination at the LRC and Camp 020 he admitted that he had been instructed by the Abwehr to sign on as a ship's steward

and report by secret writing on the convoys he sailed in. He was
hanged in January 1943.

APPENDIX 10

Interrogation Techniques

(i) The London Reception Centre

The LRC soon came to be regarded as a reception centre, not an internment camp. Aliens sent there for examination were 'guests', albeit involuntary. Some 95 per cent of them were loyal to the Allied cause, and many had faced dangers and hardships in order to reach the United Kingdom. They had a right, therefore, to reasonable comfort and courteous treatment which, moreover, were found to contribute importantly to persuading guests to divulge all the information in their possession. Accommodation and amenities were adequate if simple. The only real hardships were detention and the prohibition of visits and communications with the outside world. There was no personal search on arrival. Property was examined to discover whether the alien had anything with him directly incriminating, and so as to have available any item, particularly documentary evidence, which would help to confirm or contradict his story.

Interrogation would be a misnomer, at least for the initial process of examination conducted by uniformed intelligence officers. The aim was to extract a coherent story about the alien's background, recent activities and journey which could provide the basis for further questioning if this was judged necessary. No special interrogation techniques were employed. Results were achieved by checking the alien's story against factual information already recorded and the examiner's special skill lay in the selection, interpretation and assessment of the key features of the story and the adroit use of all the information at his disposal.

All orthodox travellers required visas, and a copy of the visa application was passed to the LRC when the visa was granted. This might be supplemented by a report from the consulate granting the visa, or from SIS or SOE if the traveller had been in touch with either of them. In every case, whether the traveller arrived through regular channels, or by escape boat or plane, there would be a report from the Immigration Officer and the SCO, and such information as could be derived from the inspection of the traveller's property. The MI 5 central registry was seldom helpful, since the LRC was concerned essentially with people and events outside MI 5's normal sphere of activity. The B1 registry, Section V's central ISOS index and the SIS central registry were of great value. But at best these provided information about suspects. They did not contain the depth of information about people, organisations and addresses, both hostile and friendly, living conditions, travel controls and so on which was needed to check the stories of the numerous refugees from occupied territory, any one of whom might possibly be a German agent. To fill this gap, in a form which also met the requirement for immediate accessibility, an MI 5 office circular of January 1942 announced the creation at the LRC of an index for recording all information likely to be of continuing value to its work. This eventually comprised some 100,000 cards. A great many sources contributed to it but the most valuable, both in quality and quantity, were the guests themselves. Although the index came to be used extensively outside the LRC, the overriding test for recording in it was whether or not a particular piece of information was likely to be of use in LRC work. The recording of favourable information was a unique feature.

With the assistance of these resources and his own knowledge and experience, the examiner considered the alien's detailed statement about his personal history, recent activities and journey, which every guest at the LRC was invited, and if necessary persuaded, to make. In the case of an escaper from enemy occupied territory the key points in the story would include previous employment, contacts of any kind with the Germans or with Resistance movements, the motive for the escape and the journey to the United Kingdom. A full and precise description of the route taken was of cardinal importance. Genuine escapes tended to follow a consistent pattern and could frequently be checked in detail by reference to the LRC index. On the other hand the 'escapes' of German agents were often very clumsily contrived or even entirely fictitious and incapable of standing up to a detailed check against the index and a large scale map. Length of stay in neutral territory, and in particular the contacts made there, were also likely to be significant. If the story was unsatisfactory the guest might be anything from a German agent to a mere nuisance, who was obviously lying but in whose case there was no genuine security interest of any kind. Where the story was unsatisfactory for whatever reason a very careful detailed report would be required as a springboard for further investigation. In particular the examiner would ask himself whether the man seemed a likely recruit for the German Intelligence Service by reason of his background, activities or political views, and whether there were any points in his story, such as an abrupt change of fortune, a sudden cessation of Resistance activities, a rather vague account of his escape or a marked variation in the density of circumstantial details about some recent period in his life, suggesting that he had in fact been recruited. If the examiner concluded that this was so the alien would be removed to Camp 020 for interrogation.

(ii) Camp 020

Camp 020, set up in 1940, and the reserve Camp 020R which opened in January 1943, were run as military establishments. The intelligence staff provided by MI 5 were all commissioned and wore uniform, while the administrative staff, the warders and the perimeter guard were soldiers. But apart from providing the administrative staff and guard force, and being answerable if there was an escape,* the War Office had no responsibility for the camps which came wholly under the Home Secretary. The Home Office exercised a right of inspection and the Camps were visited by the successive chairmen of the Security Executive which, in Petrie's words, had been 'so-largely . . . instrumental in bringing Camp 020 into existence'.

The administration of Camp 020 as a military establishment was deliberately designed to produce an impression of efficiency and above all of rigid discipline. A prisoner destined for Camp 020 was collected by an escort commanded by an officer and brought to the Camp in handcuffs. On arrival he was stripped, given a body search, dressed in prison clothes and placed in solitary confinement. The next stage was his formal admission to the Camp; brief particulars were taken, his weight, height and physical particulars were recorded and he was given a medical examination, including a dental inspection after it was discovered that material for secret writing was sometimes concealed in hollow teeth. Throughout this procedure, which was brief and businesslike but gave an indication of the prisoner's demeanour and the language in which he might be interrogated, officers and warders (picked men from the guard company) dealing with the prisoner were under instructions not to answer any questions he might ask. There was to be 'no chivalry, no gossip, no cigarettes'. After admission the prisoner returned to solitary confinement, without reading matter or cigarettes. Careful precautions were taken to prevent suicide.† Unless circumstances made immediate interrogation essential this step was postponed for two or three days. The delay allowed the prisoner's suspense to build up in complete solitude, and gave time to prepare the case. This meant obtaining and digesting every scrap of information which might assist interrogation and assessment of the prisoner's story. His personal property was minutely examined for incrimi-

---

* There were three attempted escapes. All failed.
† There were three serious attempts at suicide. One succeeded.

nating evidence such as material for secret writing, forged papers, cover addresses and aide-mémoires, codes or passwords, as well as clues to personal history and movements – photographs, bus tickets, and clothing tabs.

The agreement made at an early stage with Section V that the interrogators would not be allowed to see the undisguised texts of relevant ISOS messages was abrogated after long argument.

The first interrogation was considered crucial. The prisoner was brought before a board of four or five officers. He was marched in and remained standing at attention throughout an interrogation designed to impress upon him the omniscience and omnipotence of the British Secret Service; the hopelessness and isolation of his own position; and that the penalty for espionage was death and the only way he could help himself was to tell the truth. Violence was never used, either at the first interrogation or later, and questioning never extended beyond the endurance of one interrogator. Nevertheless the ordeal was formidable.

Camp 020 disposed of many resources which could be used if a prisoner did not break immediately and for exploiting and checking his story when he finally gave way. Under Home Office regulations solitary confinement could be prolonged up to 28 days, though this limit was only once reached in practice and a much shorter time usually sufficed. The prisoner might be confronted with confederates also in captivity, though experience apparently showed that this was 'a most dangerous expedient', or statements made by them. He might yield to a sympathetic approach; he might be persuaded to talk by a stool-pigeon or give himself away to another prisoner with whom he was allowed to associate in a cell covered by microphones.

The recording of interrogations was invaluable, but intelligence provided by covered associations was on the whole disappointing, apart from one case when a covered association established a prisoner's innocence. Prisoners were generally microphone conscious and rarely gave away anything which they had not already admitted in interrogation. But these facilities were important for indicating the general demeanour of prisoners and in covering the stool-pigeons at work.

Once a man's case was completed, if he was not executed, released as innocent, or released to B1A to act as a double-agent, life in Camp 020 was far from intolerable. Accommodation was good; association with other prisoners indoors and at exercise was freely allowed; there was a library and other recreational facilities. Internees could petition the Home Secretary if they wished, and many did so. Apart from the denial of visitors and letters, conditions there compared favourably with those in any other internment camp.

APPENDIX 11

Six Spies Caught in 1943 and 1944

(i) Five 'escapers'

(a) Frank Damien Steiner, a man with a Belgian father and a British mother who had spent some of his childhood in England, had begun his training for the Abwehr in December 1941. He had joined either from conviction – he had previously joined the Flemish SS and got a job in Germany – or because of threats to his German wife, who had associated with Jews and anti-Nazis. He had been taken across the Spanish frontier in March 1942, but had been intercepted by the Spanish Police, interned and deported to the Hague. After further training, he had succeeded in getting to Lisbon; on arriving there he had reported both to the German legation and to the Belgian authorities, who had passed him to the SIS representative. By then the Belgian and the British authorities had received reports that he was probably a German agent from people who had been interned with him in Spain, but he willingly accepted the suggestion that he should be flown to the United Kingdom to make a statement. At Camp 020, where he was interrogated in April 1943 (by which time he had also been referred to in ISOS decrypts) he proved to be co-operative, producing no less than 28 reports on various aspects of his contacts with the Germans, and there was some thought of using him as a double agent. But his personality defects ruled this out and he was interned.

He was handed over to the Belgian authorities in February 1945. They tried him for treason and sentenced him to death, but commuted the death penalty to life imprisonment when he appealed to the British authorities for confirmation of the fact that he had voluntarily helped them.

(b) In April 1943 ISOS gave warning that another Belgian, Raymond Laloux was due to arrive in Spain en route for the United Kingdom. Detained on his arrival from Lisbon, he admitted that he had been recruited by the Abwehr at the beginning of the year. His wife was to be paid 5,000 francs a month while he was in England. He claimed that he had never intended to carry out his mission but had kept silent about it for fear of reprisals against his wife and had disposed of his secret writing materials before his arrival. In view of the difficulty of rebutting this claim he was not proceeded against under the Treachery Act but was interned at Camp 020.

(c)   Johannes Huysmanns, another Belgian arrived in May 1943. He and his wife had been arrested by the Portuguese Police in Lisbon and deported to England after refusing a request from the Belgian authorities, prompted by Section V, that they should continue their journey to the Congo via the United Kingdom. ISOS decrypts had disclosed as early as September 1942 that he had been recruited, and that the Abwehr hoped to send him to the United Kingdom if he could get the necessary visas; in December they showed that the couple had moved to Barcelona. At Camp 020 he made a full confession after first putting up a stubborn defence of mistaken identity. He had accepted service in the Abwehr early in 1941 to escape trouble with the Gestapo in Brussels; and equipped with different questionnaires covering the United Kingdom, the USA, Brazil and Mexico, had spent the winter of 1942–1943 in Barcelona unsuccessfully trying to get visas for one or another of these destinations. His interrogation showed him to be a capable man, well-trained as a spy, and he supplied a vast amount of valuable information about the Abwehr. Prosecution was ruled out by the circumstances in which he had been deported to the United Kingdom and he was employed as a stool-pigeon at Camp 020 till the end of the war, when the Belgians, taking the view that his services for the British did not atone for his offences against Belgium, sentenced him to life imprisonment.

(d)   Oswald Job, who had been born in London of German parents and had lived in Paris since 1911, came to Poole from Lisbon in November 1943. He told the immigration authorities that he had been interned, but had escaped into Spain after being allowed out on parole the previous June. Before he arrived, however, the Germans had informed *Dragonfly*, who was pressing them for money, that they were sending a reliable person to him with jewellery, which they described in some detail. SCOs who had been alerted to this news found the jewellery on him during the search at Poole, and he was placed under strict surveillance to see whether he carried out his mission. When he made no move to do so he was summoned for interviews and eventually admitted that he had accepted a mission to report on bomb damage and public morale only as a means of getting out of France. But he insisted that the jewels were his own property, and had nothing to do with the mission, until he was shown the address to which *Dragonfly* had asked that they should be delivered. He then made a full confession. He had been recruited by the Abwehr, received training in secret writing (materials for which were hidden in his keys and the handle of his safety razor) and been given a code on which messages would be passed to him in German broadcasts from Paris; and he had agreed to deliver the jewels. His status as a spy was confirmed at the end of November by an ISOS decrypt. The story that he had been told to report on bomb damage and morale seemed improbable until, later on, it was learned that the V-weapon offensive had originally been scheduled to begin in January 1944. He was hanged in March 1944.

(e)   Josef Van Hove, a Belgian, arrived by air from Stockholm in February 1944 to join the Belgian forces in the United Kingdom. He claimed to have deserted in Gothenburg while serving as a steward on a ship out of Stettin, and to have been passed on by the British Consul to the Belgian authorities. As he also claimed that he had acquired the job as steward after being despatched to Hamburg for forced labour following a long record of trouble with the German police, and as his reputation as an unpleasant hanger-on around Antwerp night-clubs had preceded him to England, he was temporarily detained at the LRC. Re-examined in April, he confessed that he had worked for the Abwehr since early in 1942 and had been sent to England via Sweden to report on military intelligence by secret writing to the same cover addresses as those given to Neukermans.* He had written about 15 letters to these addresses while waiting in Stockholm. He had worked for the Germans solely for the money. He was hanged on 15 July, the last spy to be executed in England during the war.

(ii) A parachutist

Nicolay Hansen, a Norwegian coalminer, gave himself up immediately on landing near Frazerburgh on the night of 3 September 1943, handing over one radio set and indicating that another, which was soon recovered, had been dropped on another parachute. He claimed that he had been blackmailed into accepting the mission, in which he was to give himself up, confess to being a spy and hand over one radio set, having previously buried the other, and, after obtaining employment, to dig up the other set and use it to report on military and naval matters to Oslo. Under questioning he admitted that he also had secret writing material, concealed in a hollow tooth, but denied that he had been provided with a cover address. Further enquiries established that he had more writing material in another tooth and he confessed that he had been given the material and cover addresses in case he had to surrender the second of his radio sets.

Despite these indications of a treacherous intention, MI 5 was reluctant to prosecute since officers from Camp 020 would have to give evidence, but it eventually submitted the case to the DPP. He decided against proceedings and Hansen was interned.

---

* See above, pp 193–194.

APPENDIX 12*

Important Items Which It Is Undesirable For Visitors To See

Most Secret Equipment:

1. MULBERRY, PHOENIX and BOMBARDON:

Probably the greatest single factor of surprise in the operation.

(a) *Construction Sites* – Portsmouth, Stokes Bay, Alverstoke, Southampton, Hayling Island, North Point (Hants), Rainham, Tilbury, Erith.

(b) *MULBERRY Group Training Sites*:
  i. MULBERRY   – Christchurch and East of Selsey.
  ii. PHOENIX   – Christchurch Bay.
  iii. BOMBARDON   – Weymouth Bay and Ringstead.

2. PLUTO (including REL, DUMBO, SOLO and BAMBY):

(a) *Construction Sites* – Tilbury, Lydd, Dungeness, Rye, Hamble, Fawley, Lepe, Gurnard, Shanklin and Sandown.

(b) *Training Area* – Christchurch to Lymington.

3. R.G.: D.D. TANKS: C.D.L. TANKS AND OTHER MOST SECRET MILITARY ASSAULT EQUIPMENT TRAINING AREAS:

King's Lynn, Sheringham, Great Yarmouth (Broads Area), Ipswich, Colchester, Maldon, Sandwich, Dover, Folkestone, St. Leonards, Beachy Head, Hove, Storringham, Havant, Fareham, Southampton, Beaulieu–Fordingbridge, Broadstone, Swanage, West Lulworth, Dorchester, Budleigh Salterton, Paignton, Kingsbridge, Ivybridge, Penrhyn.

---

* Reproduced from CAB 121/381, OP(44) 2nd Meeting of 9 February, Enclosure II.

4. COMBINED OPERATIONAL TRAINING AREAS:

There are 28 of these areas from The Wash to Lands End, of which the Southwold Beaches, Studland Bay and Start Bay are major training and rehearsal areas.

5. HARDS:

There are 56 separate hards and 10 more under construction in sheltered waters from The Wash to Penzance for the embarkation of AFVs, guns and vehicles. Each accommodates one to four landing ships or equivalent in landing craft, and are designed to supplement port facilities.

6. EMBARKATION AREAS:

Great Yarmouth, Ipswich, Felixstowe, Tilbury, Gravesend, Deal, Dover, Folkestone, Hythe, Hastings, Newhaven, Shoreham, Portsmouth, Gosport, Southampton, Stanswood Bay, Beaulieu, Lymington, Poole, Weymouth, Portland, Torquay, Brixham, Dartmouth, Plymouth, Devonport, Fowey, Falmouth.

7. MARSHALLING AREAS:

Measuring about 20 miles by 10 miles behind the Embarkation Areas and contain camps where the final briefing of the troops, assault divisions, supporting troops (tanks, etc) and immediate follow-up divisions, takes place.

8. SECRET NAVAL STORES FOR THE ASSAULT:

There are 28 civil firms between The Wash and Lands End which hold these stores.

9. DECOYS:

There are 96 Air Decoys within 10 miles of the coast from The Wash to Lands End, which represent air fields, large fires, dummy dockyards, etc. Many more lights representing dummy hards are being installed.

APPENDIX 13

SHAEF Intelligence Directive No 7: Counter-Intelligence

Contents

(*Note*:   The following abbreviations are used throughout –
CI for Counter Intelligence
CA for Civil Affairs.)

Section I – Definitions

The following are definitions of terms used in this directive –

1. *Counter-Intelligence.* The collection, collation, evaluation and distribution of information, as well as all executive action, including civil and military security measures, to counter enemy intelligence or subversive activities.

2. *Counter-Intelligence information.* All information relating to CI work.

3. *Counter-Intelligence Staffs.* British Ib Staffs and US CI Branches of G2.

4. *Chief Counter-Intelligence Officer.* The Officer in charge of any CI Staff.

5. *Counter-Intelligence Personnel.* British Field Security and US CI Personnel.

Section II – Spheres of Responsibility

1. *In the Planning Stage*

(a) SHAEF will be responsible for –

    i.   Formulating CI policy

    ii. Co-ordinating CI policy with ANCXF and C-in-C Allied Expeditionary Air Force

    iii. Co-ordinating the collection, collation and distribution of CI information as between the producer agencies in London and subordinate headquarters

    iv. The security of the mounting of the operation. Co-ordination between Forces under the Supreme Commander and static agencies in the United Kingdom will be effected through the Sub-Committee of ISSB.

(b) Headquarters of Army Groups will be responsible for –

    i.   Detailed CI planning, including the selection of CI targets within their respective spheres.

    ii. The dissemination of CI information to subordinate Headquarters.

    iii. Maintaining liaison on CI measures with AEAF and ANCXF.

    iv. All normal security measures within their Commands.

2. *In the Field*

(a) SHAEF will be responsible for –

    i.   Deciding general questions of CI policy.

    ii. Co-ordinating the CI activities of Army Groups.

    iii. Maintaining close liaison with the producer agencies in

London to ensure that the Army Groups receive all the information they require.

   iv. Maintaining liaison on CI policy with AEAF and ANCXF.

(b) Headquarters of Army Groups will be responsible for –

   i. The organisation and operation of CI within their respective zones.

   ii. Collating and distributing CI information from all sources relating to their respective zones.

   iii. Maintaining close liaison with each other to ensure co-ordination of their activities, and the fullest exchange of CI information.

   iv. Rendering to SHAEF such reports as may be called for.

   v. Maintaining liaison on CI matters with TAF and 9th US Air Force, and with appropriate Naval authorities.

Section III – Military Security
Part I – The United Kingdom

General

1. Military Security is at all times the responsibility of Formation and Unit Commanders who will ensure that all ranks are cognisant of, and well trained in, all normal military security procedure. Operational success is vitally dependent on the strict observance of the basic principles of Military Security.

In the United Kingdom Formations and Units will concentrate, move and embark within the security framework set up by the existing Static Security organisations and with which Formations and Units will not need to concern themselves, except where liaison is necessary.

Existing Security Framework in the United Kingdom

2. It is important, however, that Formation and Unit Commanders should be aware, in broad outline, of the component parts of this framework in order that they may be reassured and may confine their security activities to military matters only. To this end, Commanders should be informed of whatever points are considered necessary concerning –

(a) The functions of the ISSB–OVERLORD Sub-Committee.
(b) The Coastal Belt Security Committees.
(c) The existence of the Regulated Areas and Visitors' ban.
(d) Civil Security activities of the Security Service.

(e)   The existence and functions of the Regional Security Liaison officers.
(f)   The Military and Civil Censorship plan.
(g)   Security responsibilities of GHQ, Home Forces.
(h)   Division of security responsibility at Ports.

Detailed information concerning the above headings can be supplied on request to G2, SHAEF.

Security Points Requiring Special Attention

3.   Experience has shown that in the training and preparation for an operation the following points of Military Security require special attention –

(a)   The safeguarding of all information relating to the objective and date of the operation, together with the strength of the Force and methods to be employed.
(b)   The observance of strict security discipline in offices, and with maps and documents.
(c)   The proper security of telephone conversations.
(d)   The restriction of knowledge of a cover plan to the minimum number of personnel.
(e)   The proper observance of all censorship regulations.
(f)   The importance of selecting a diligent and painstaking Unit Security Officer who will, helped by CI personnel, properly train his men in the basic principles of security.
(g)   The security discipline of troop movements.
(h)   The complete segregation of all combat troops once briefing has taken place, and the rigid enforcement of all security regulations.
(i)   The denial to unauthorised pressmen and photographers of access to troops.
(j)   The safeguarding of all information and the discouraging of speculation about any special devices to be used for the operation.
(k)   The importance of publicising any punishment allotted for security infringement.

Regulated Areas

4.   The power to impose restrictions in Regulated Areas rests with the GOC-in-C of the Command concerned, and it is his responsibility to impose the necessary restrictions. If further restrictions are considered necessary, the GOC-in-C of the Command concerned should be approached, but this should not be done on lower than an Army level.
5.   [Omitted.]

Co-ordination

6. Certain security activities connected with the operation are undertaken through the co-operation of Service and Civilian authorities. These activities are co-ordinated by the ISSB–OVERLORD Sub-Committee and, on a lower level, by the Coastal Belt Security Committees. These Committees will assign, in cases of doubt, responsibility for the co-ordination of any necessary security measures. The Coastal Belt Security Committees are convened under the Chairmanship of the GSO(I) of the Command concerned, and any cases of doubt or difficulty should be referred to him.

7. All action taken by the Coastal Belt Security Committees is reported to the ISSB–OVERLORD Sub-Committee whose responsibility it is to ensure that all Service and Civilian authorities affected are duly informed.

Counter-Intelligence Personnel

8. CI Personnel in the United Kingdom, relieved by the existing security framework of the responsibility for Civil Security, devote themselves to the training in Military Security of all Formations and Units. It must be realised, however, that CI personnel operating overseas will have heavy Civil Security responsibilities, and that good Military Security will largely depend on the effectiveness of the individual measures taken by each unit, which in turn depends on efficient training prior to going overseas.

Security Reports

9. It is essential that any breach of security which might endanger the success of the operation should be reported immediately to SHAEF.

10. Any general tendencies affecting Military Security, or the prevalence of any minor form of security breach, should also be reported to SHAEF in case it may be necessary to issue a supplementary security instruction or to take any necessary counteracting measures.

Liaison

11. All Formation Commanders are responsible for ensuring that their CI Staff establish liaison, on their own level, with the CI Staff of the static formation in whose area they are situated, or to whose area they move.

Cessation of Leave

12.　Normal privilege leave will cease some time before D-Day. The impression should be conveyed that this cessation differs in no way from previous cessations which will have occurred for the purpose of intensive training or exercise.

Part II – In Continental Europe

General

13.　Military security overseas will continue to be the responsibility of Command. The primary danger to the security of the Allied Forces will arise from Civil sources, and as a result CI personnel will be largely occupied with Civil Security duties. Commanders, therefore, must realise that CI personnel will not be available to check and advise on routine Military Security measures to the same extent as in the United Kingdom.

Duties of CI Personnel

14.　CI Personnel of Corps and Divisions will not be diverted to duties which may retard or interfere with their proper role.
15.　In the assault, the primary duty of CI Personnel is to secure CI targets in the area of the objective. The selection of such targets will be the task of the appropriate CI staff. Foremost among these targets will be –

(a)　Known and suspect enemy agents.
(b)　Known enemy collaborationists, sympathisers, and other persons whose presence menaces the security of the Allied Forces.
(c)　Buildings, billets and installations known or suspected to contain documents of CI value.

16.　Other duties of CI in forward areas will include –

(a)　Co-operating with Military Police in marshalling refugees and other civilians arriving from enemy occupied territory, and directing them to interrogation posts.
(b)　Contacting local authorities and persons known to be friendly to the Allied cause, to secure all possible CI information.
(c)　Advising and assisting in security against sabotage all public and private installations whose continued operation is essential to the Allies.
(d)　Checking upon the observance by the civil population of all security provisions contained in the proclamations and orders issued by Civil Affairs Staffs and Detachments.

(e)   Assisting in the discovery and collection of any hidden armaments or equipment which have not been surrendered or reported in accordance with proclamations.

(f)   The seizure of civil communications until they are taken over by other authorities.

(g)   Seizing and impounding civilian mail until it is taken over by censorship personnel.

(h)   Advising on the immediate establishment of guards at all captured ordnance and ammunition dumps, especially those which may be accessible to the local population.

17.   It must be realised that CI personnel, if limited to their own resources, may be unable to carry out all necessary security measures under adverse circumstances. Consequently, they may require the assistance of other troops in seizing suspect premises and in the execution of other CI duties where necessary and practicable.

18.   The seizure of enemy documents which may contain information of CI value is a primary CI target. Often, however, such documents will contain information of value to Combat Intelligence, or documents desired by the Documents Sections may be found with other documents of CI value. In such cases CI personnel will co-operate with and assist Document Sections and CI staffs in the procurement of such material.

19.   Certain documents containing statistical data will be of primary interest to Civil Affairs. Every effort should be made to preserve them intact and in place.

In Other Areas

20.   In other areas (including Lines/Zones of Communication) under jurisdiction of Allied Force, the duties of CI personnel will include –

(a)   The investigation of cases of espionage and of disaffection among the Armed Forces.

(b)   The detection and investigation of all cases of subversive influences emanating from the civilian population and likely to affect adversely the Allied Forces.

(c)   The institution of necessary checks on security control of the civil population.

(d)   Advising and assisting in all other general security matters.

In an Evacuation and Withdrawal

21.   In the event that Allied Forces are forced to evacuate any position, CI personnel will perform the necessary measures to

prevent valuable information from falling into the hands of the enemy.

Liaison

22. Liaison between CI personnel and all other Allied Intelligence agencies is the responsibility of security staffs. It is essential that there be the closest co-operation both in planning and operation with –

(a)   Civil Affairs staffs and detachments.
(b)   Naval and Air Force Security Officers.
(c)   Military Police (Provost Personnel).
(d)   Special Counter Intelligence and Special Forces Personnel.
(e)   W/T Detection Units.
(f)   Document collection and evaluation units.
(g)   Political Survey Officers.
(h)   Attached Allied CI staffs and Personnel.

Disposition of CI Personnel

23.   The disposition of CI Personnel units and the allocation of areas in which they will operate is the responsibility of the Commanders of Army Groups.

24.   Subject to the operational necessity, AC of SG2, SHAEF, may designate CI targets outside the areas assigned to the respective Army Groups.

Section IV – Port Counter-Intelligence

1.   *Port Counter-Intelligence.* For the purpose of this directive the term 'Port Counter-Intelligence Officer' will include all officers in charge of CI personnel stationed at seaports, airport and frontier posts who have to deal with travel control.

2.   *Organisation.* Port CI operations are of two kinds –

(a)   Military and Civil Security in the local military area.
(b)   Travel Control.

3.   *Military and Civil Security in the Local Military Area.* On all matters of –

(a)   Military security, including the security of military installations.
(b)   Civil security concerning local static population, including all necessary investigations into cases of espionage, sabotage and subversive activity.

The Port CI Officer will be responsible to the Base Sub-Area (Br) or Port (US) Commander.

4. *Travel Control.* As regards travel control, and all ancillary matters, the Port CI Officer will work under the direction of the AC of SG2, SHAEF. The Port CI Officer will keep his Commander informed of travel control matters concerning which he deals direct with SHAEF.

5. *Geographical Responsibility of Port CI Officers.* The normal area of responsibility of the Port CI Officer is that of the Base Sub-Area/Port Commander. AC of SG2 SHAEF, with the advice of the CI Staff responsible for Military and Civil Security in the zone, may however increase these areas for any Port CI Officer.

6. (a) *Army.* The security of the dock area, including control of exit and entry, is the responsibility of the Base Sub-Area/Port Commander.

(b) *Navy.* The security of all Naval installations and stores ashore and the CI precautions for all HM, US and Allied Naval ships and craft in the Port is the responsibility of the Naval Officer in charge. He, with the advice of the Port CI Officer, will issue instructions regarding harbour craft, fishing vessels, etc. manned by local civilian crews. The Superintendent Sea Transport Officer is responsible that Masters of merchant vessels conform to the security regulations of the port and mount adequate guards and sentries. The US Naval Port Security Officer (Commerce and Travel Officer), under the direction of the Naval Officer in charge, will be responsible for the internal security of US Merchant ships.

(c) *Royal Air Force.* Dock Sections of RAF Security personnel will be available for supervising the disembarkation of RAF personnel and stores. In CI matters they will operate under the direction of the Army Port CI Officer.

(d) *Co-ordination.* All security measures will be co-ordinated by the Port CI Officer. While attached to the staff of the Base Sub-Area/Port Commander, the Port CI Officer will act as adviser on CI matters to Naval and other authorities in the Port.

7. *Duties of Port CI Officers*
Port Control. Within the Port the CI Officer will be responsible for –

(a) Planning and supervising the control of entry to and exit from the dock area, from the landward side from ship to shore.
(b) Recommending measures for the protection of ships and installations from sabotage.
(c) Establishing the necessary security check and control of civilian labour and personnel, and persons with business in the port, to whom passes are issued for entry into the dock area.

(d)   Checking crew lists of merchant ships and advising on security measures relating to crews, including shore leave.
(e)   Searching any small craft for CI purposes.
(f)   The security control of all civilian travel through the port.

8.   *Civil Security*. The civil security responsibility of the Port CI Officer will include –

(a)   The investigation and reporting upon all suspected cases of sabotage, espionage and leakage of information.
(b)   Such immediate action in regard to suspects, including arrest, as may seem expedient or, after reference, may be ordered by CI staffs.
(c)   Advising the Base Sub-Area/Port Commander on security measures to be imposed on the civilian population in the area.
(d)   Liaison with the local police, and any civil port authority on CI matters.

In all matters relating to Civil Security, the Port CI Officers will maintain close liaison with the appropriate Civil Affairs Detachments. CA Staffs will be responsible for the preparation of passes for issue to civilians allowed to enter port areas. Regulations covering their issue will be formulated by the Port CI Officer.
9.   *Coast Line Security*. Within the sector assigned to the Base Sub-Area/Port Commander, the Port CI Officer will be responsible for the establishment and co-ordination of measures to prevent illicit communications between sea and shore, and illegal entry or exit by sea along the coast-line. Measures ashore relating to the security of the coast-line will be co-ordinated with any security measures taken by the Navy.
10.   *Travel Control*. The duties of Port CI Officers in regard to travel control is dealt with in SHAEF instructions.
11.   *Records and Intelligence*. Port CI Officers will be provided by AC of SG2 SHAEF and CI Staffs responsible for Civil and Military Security in the zone with all necessary Intelligence that is available, including lists of known and suspect enemy agents, suspect officials in the district and suspect seamen.
12.   Reports as required will be made as follows–

(a)   Military and Civil Security in the area, to the Base Sub-Area/Port Commander.
(b)   Travel control matters, direct to AC of SG2, SHAEF, with copy to Base Sub-Area/Port Commander.

Section V – Security Control of Civilian Traffic

(Note. This long section is not reproduced here. Briefly, in the very early stages of the operation, the only civilians to be brought to England were known or suspected enemy agents; those required and volunteering to enter the United Kingdom for interrogation; and leaders of Resistance Groups, and Allied agents. Later, when travel control had been properly organised, certain others would be allowed to enter the United Kingdom. These were limited to key individuals whose presence was required by British, US and Allied Government Agencies. No private applications from the civilian population would be considered.

To visit North West Europe, civilians (by which was meant those not forming part of the Allied Expeditionary Force or the Naval and Air Forces) to whom permits might be issued were distinguished persons nominated by SHAEF and such civilians as were requested by Army Groups and the Naval and Air Commanders. No private travel would be allowed.

As the campaign progressed, regulations were relaxed by degrees).

Section VI – Relations With Other Intelligence Authorities

Naval and Air Force Security Authorities

1.   CI Staffs and CI personnel will maintain close liaison with all Naval and Air Force security authorities in their area.
2.   The co-ordination between Naval and Military CI authorities in regard to Port Security is dealt with in Section IV.
3.   The security of airfields and control of entry thereto is an Air Force responsibility, but CI personnel will be available to assist Air Force security authorities in carrying out investigation.
4.   CI staffs and personnel will, in discharging their responsibility for the security control of the civil population, safeguard the interests of the Navy and Air Force. The following are the main duties which will be performed on behalf of the Navy and Air Force where desired –

(a)   Liaison with representatives of Civil Affairs on CI.
(b)   Liaison with local civil authorities, including the civil police.
(c)   Security control of the civil population, in conjunction with Civil Affairs.
(d)   Investigation (outside airfields) of incidents involving civilians, reported by Naval and Air Force personnel.

5.   Whilst the Army is responsible for Civil Security in the Theatre of operations, RAF security will, generally speaking, be ensured by RAF Security Personnel, who will co-ordinate their activities at all levels with the Army, and keep them fully informed on all matters relating to Civil Security.

Special Intelligence Agencies represented in the Field

6. The Secret Intelligence Service and OSS will provide Special Counter Intelligence Units for attachment to the CI Staffs of British and American Army Group and Army Headquarters. These work as an integral part of the CI Staffs of the Headquarters to which they are attached. For duties see Appendix B to this Directive.

SOE/OSS

7. Special Force (SF) Staffs, which are integrated, will be attached to Headquarters of Army Groups and Armies. Their CI functions consist in –

(a) Providing the CI Staff with CI information from Resistance Groups, together with an estimate, based on previous knowledge, of the reliability of the source.
(b) Assisting CI staffs and personnel in matters where their specialised knowledge of Resistance Groups would be of help. This will include assisting in establishing the bonafides of persons claiming to have been working for Allied underground movements or Resistance Groups. It is emphasised that while SF Staffs will be able to provide assistance in such cases, the responsibility for determining the bonafides and for recommending as to disposal rests with the CI staffs.

Mobile W/T Detection Units

8. Mobile Units for locating illicit wireless transmitters will be supplied by the Radio Security Service and US Signal Corps. For functions and employment see Appendix C to this Directive.

Allied Intelligence Services

9. Allied Intelligence Missions will be attached to Army Groups and will contain a CI element. Detailed directions on the relationship between CI Staffs and Allied CI Services will be issued in due course. During the planning stage, no operational plans will be discussed with Allied Intelligence Services, except under the direction of SHAEF.
10. It is envisaged that the role of Allied CI Personnel will be –

(a) Assisting CI Personnel in the examination and disposal of miscellaneous suspects and suspect refugees.
(b) Assisting in the collection of CI information in the Field.

Political Survey Officers

11. Political Survey Officers are Officers of the Psychological Warfare Branch engaged in the collection of information for propaganda purposes. They will be attached to Army Groups and certain lower formations.

12. Their duties will include the collection in the Field by overt methods (e.g. direct observation, interrogation of civilians and refugees, examination of documents, etc) of –

(a) All forms of Civil Intelligence required by PWB, units and staffs of OWI, PWE, and OSS for the purpose of propaganda output and guidance of propaganda policy.

(b) Information required by Civil Affairs and other interested bodies, relating to conditions of life in the countries concerned and the attitude of the people to these conditions which is not otherwise provided.

13. Political Survey Officers and CI Staffs will make available to each other such information of interest as they may acquire from their own sources.

Censorship Staffs

14. The Army Censorship Organisation will undertake the censorship of certain civilian communications. This will include the examination of captured mails in the combat area. Close liaison should be maintained with the Censorship Staffs to ensure that the maximum CI information is obtained from such censorship. CI staffs will provide the Censorship Staffs with 'Watch Lists' containing the names and addresses of persons and organisations over whom censorship supervision is desired in the area concerned.

Section VII – Security Control of the Civil Population

Spheres of Responsibility

1. The Security Control of the civil population will be a joint responsibility of CI and CA Staffs. As a general rule, CI Staffs will be responsible for formulating security policies, but they will co-ordinate with and consult CA Staffs when these policies affect the civil population. CA Staffs will be responsible for implementing security policies through CA Detachments and the indigenous authorities.

Relations between CI Personnel and CA Detachments

2. CI personnel and CA detachments will maintain close liaison in the Field to ensure co-ordination of action and avoid duplication of effort. When the entry into a town in which CA Detachments are to operate is contemplated, the closest co-ordination must be maintained in the planning and execution of their respective roles. CI Staffs may establish in any locality a Security Committee to review and co-ordinate all matters of security interest. This Committee may consist of Military, Naval and Air Force CI Staffs, Provost Marshal Staff, CA Detachments, and when desired, indigenous police.

Proclamations

3. Proclamations imposing restrictions upon the civil population of liberated territory will be promulgated by the Supreme Commander. These will include the usual war time security restrictions. The drafting of these proclamations will be the responsibility of CA Staffs who will determine the necessary restrictions in conjunction with CI Staffs. Such regulations as may be issued by subordinate Commanders within the framework of these proclamations will also be prepared by CA Staffs in consultation with CI Staffs.

Security Regulations

4. CI Staffs will be responsible for recommending to CA Staffs security regulations affecting the civil population. CA Detachments will be responsible for implementing such regulations through the local civil administration. CI Personnel will initiate checks to ensure that such regulations are carried out and will report any infractions to CI Staffs and CA Detachments.

Relations with indigenous police

5. It is the responsibility of CA Detachments to supervise, and where necessary reactivate all police forces in liberated territory. Supervision of the security branches of indigenous police forces will be carried out in accordance with policies laid down by the CI Staffs.

6. Wherever possible CI Personnel will make their initial contact with indigenous police in conjunction with CA Detachments. Thereafter CI Personnel will maintain direct contact with the indigenous police at all levels on day to day routine matters.

7. CA Detachments will ensure that CI Personnel have at all

times free access to the records of the local police. If it is found necessary to seize any records, the CA Detachments will be informed and the records returned as soon as practicable.

Relations with other civil authorities

8. CA Staffs and Detachments will, wherever possible, be the channels for dealing with other civil authorities. After the initial contact has been made in conjunction with CA, CI Staffs may make direct contact on day to day matters.

Officials

9. The supervision and appointment of Civilian Officials will be a CA responsibility. CI Personnel will furnish CA Detachments with any information they possess of the reliability of officials, and CA Detachments will consult with CI Personnel in cases where the reliability of an official is doubtful from the security aspect. CI Personnel will only arrest those officials who might continue to assist the enemy or be required for interrogation, and in such cases they will keep CA Detachments informed of any action they take.

Suspect Political Organisations

10. If there is evidence that any political organisation is subversive in character and that its activities constitute a menace to the security of our Forces, CI Staffs will be responsible for recommending action to be taken, e.g. whether its activities are to be suspended, the members arrested, or the records seized. Where the activities of such an organisation do not endanger the security of our Forces, but tend to promote unrest among the civil population or to be politically disruptive, CA Staffs, in consultation with CI Staffs, will be responsible for recommending action to be taken.

Denunciation

11. Where denunciations of individuals are received by CI Personnel, the cases will first be examined to determine whether suspicion is based on political, personal or security grounds. If it is clearly established that no violation or danger to security exists, the names of such persons will be given to CA Detachments for any further investigation or action. Where convenient CA Detachments and CI Personnel may establish a joint system for the preliminary investigation of denunciations. Security grounds will be the only justification for the detention of denounced persons by

CI Personnel. Mere membership in a particular organisation will not necessarily provide sufficient grounds for detention.

Black and White Lists

12. CI Staffs will receive detailed information prior to D Day designed to assist in the Security Control of the civil population. This will include –

(a) Black Lists of officials and other individuals known to have assisted the enemy, and lists of European political organisations in which membership is sufficient to present a prima facie case against the individual.
(b) White Lists of individuals and officials believed to be reliable.

13. CI Staffs and Personnel will bear in mind the fact that this information is primarily intended to serve as a guide only and that in most cases the information should be verified by local investigation before action is taken.

Security Check of civilian labour

14. Thorough security checking of mass labour is impracticable. Such precautions, however, as are feasible, such as checking by CA Detachments with civil police, care in selection of foremen, and the establishment by CI Personnel of a system of informants, will be instituted wherever such labour may be in a position to endanger security. In the employment of individuals within Headquarters or in other places where they may have access to confidential information or vulnerable points, CA Detachments will be responsible for preliminary checking with local police. No such individuals will be employed, however, until their names have been checked against the suspects lists and cleared by the CI Staff.

Passes and Permits

15. CA Staffs will be responsible for, but will work in close co-operation with CI Staffs in the preparation and issue of civilian passes and permits and of plans for their use.
16. CA Detachments will supply CI Personnel with forms to enable them to issue passes and permits to civilians in special circumstances. CA Detachments, not CI Personnel, however, will be primarily responsible for issuing such passes and permits, and they may use the indigenous police for this purpose.

Section VIII – Procedure for Interrogating Refugees and Civilian Suspects in the Operational Zone

General

1.   In the operational zone the following classes of persons must be regarded as suspect and will require examination and interrogation for CI purposes –

(a)   Refugees reaching our lines from enemy territory.
(b)   Civilians who have aroused suspicion and failed to establish their bonafides.
(c)   Released or escaped alien PW and civilian internees.

The object of such interrogation is to provide an effective screen to prevent the infiltration of enemy agents.

2.   In addition, interrogation will be conducted with the aim of collecting CI information as well as Intelligence for operational, propaganda and other purposes.

3.   The evacuation of civilians from the forward areas for relief purposes or for operational reasons will be the responsibility of the Provost Marshal and CA Staffs. For this purpose refugee clearing stations will be established in the forward areas, where refugees will be marshalled and directed to their refugee camps which will be established as required, by the CA Staffs at Army Headquarters.

Security Control Posts

4.   CI Personnel in the forward areas will be responsible for establishing security control posts to divert from the main stream of refugees those who will be required for interrogation, and for directing them to the Refugee Interrogation Posts. The security control posts may often be conveniently established at the Refugee Clearing Stations. It must be made clear to all concerned in handling refugees in forward areas that security interests must have priority over welfare.

Refugee Interrogation Posts

5.   It will be the responsibility of CI Staffs to determine where to establish the Refugee Interrogation Posts. It may be found convenient to establish them as annexes to the Corps PW cages, since civilian suspects may then be attached to parties of PW and escorted with them from the forward areas and, if necessary, evacuated with them to the Army PW cage.

6. Refugee Interrogation Posts will provide the principal machinery for 'screening' suspect persons and it will be at this stage that the bulk of the information of Intelligence value will be obtained. The interrogation staff at the Refugee Interrogation Post may be provided from the Central Reserve of CI Personnel at the disposal of CI Staffs at Army Groups, and from CI Personnel of the Allied National Intelligence Services operating with the CI Staffs. Combat Intelligence and Political Survey Officers should be given facilities for interrogating persons passing through the Refugee Interrogation Posts.

Civilian Interrogation Centres

7. Persons whose cases clearly require detailed examination will be passed back from the Refugee Interrogation Posts to the Civilian Annexe to the Army PW Cage. Civilian Interrogation Centres will be established at these Annexes and suspects will here be interrogated and investigated at length, and reports furnished to the CI Staffs for decision as to final disposal.

Section IX — The Handling and Disposal of Known or Suspected Enemy Agents

1. The first responsibility of CI Staffs in the Theatre of Operation is the detection and apprehension of enemy agents. Detailed planning of measures against the German Intelligence Service (GIS) must be undertaken well in advance. Such plans will be based on information supplied by SCI Units and will be formulated in consultation with officers of those units. While SCI Units will render advice and furnish information, executive action is the responsibility of CI Staffs and personnel.

2. GIS targets having been designated by the CI Staffs, success will depend on the speed and thoroughness of initial action. Plans should therefore include attacks on GIS targets by personnel operating in many cases with advanced units.

3. Whenever GIS personnel are captured, SCI Officers must be notified and afforded the earliest opportunity to interrogate them. All documents, records or equipment of GIS Personnel captured will be turned over to SCI Units for examination. SCI Units will be consulted as to the disposal of each individual case. It is only by making the fullest use in this way of SCI Units that the maximum information can be obtained, and the detection and arrest of other agents secured.

4. It is important to conceal from the enemy the amount of knowledge concerning the organisation and activities of the GIS which we have acquired through captured agents. The arrest and

disposal of known and suspect enemy agents must therefore be attended with the maximum degree of secrecy. No mention should be made in the Press of the capture of or action taken against an enemy agent without the express authority of the AC or SG2/BGSI Army Groups.

5. In order to ensure secrecy, CI Staffs should arrange for the provision of suitable guarded secret premises in which captured enemy agents may be segregated and detained.

6. CI Staffs should arrange to be kept informed of the arrest of enemy agents by the indigenous authorities, whether Military or Civil. The power of CI staffs to demand that any such agent be handed over to them for examination or disposal will be the subject of agreements to be reached with the Allied National authorities.

7. The ultimate disposal of a captured enemy agent should be decided by the CI staffs after consultation with the SCI Unit.

8. The Field Interrogation of arrested enemy agents should be carried out immediately. The more important cases should, on advice from SCI Officers, be returned to the United Kingdom for further and more special interrogation by the Security Service Interrogation Centre in London.

9. Where evidence is available and military necessity demands, prosecutions can be instituted against captured enemy agents of any nationality in US or British Military Courts. CI Staffs should constantly bear this possibility in mind in all cases of sufficient importance. Captured enemy agents may in some cases be tried in the Civil or Military Courts of the indigenous authorities in liberated territories when these are reconstituted. Advice as to the legal procedure should be obtained from the CA Legal Officers.

Section X – Counter-Sabotage

Prevention

1. The protection of all stores, equipment, installations, etc against sabotage will be the responsibility of Command. CI Staffs will be responsible for advising Commanders in regard to measures for the prevention of sabotage. For this purpose personnel will conduct surveys and inspection of vital points and will recommend protective measures.

Investigation

2. The investigation of all cases of suspected sabotage will be the responsibility of CI Staffs, and all suspected acts will be reported to them without delay.

3. Investigation will normally be undertaken by CI Personnel, but in special cases an expert investigator may be obtained from the Security Service, London, at the request of the Chief CI Officer at Army Group Headquarters.

4. Liaison will be maintained with Bomb Disposal Units for assistance in connection with sabotage equipment.

Enemy Sabotage Agents

5. Information from special sources covering the activities of enemy agents will be made available to CI Staffs by SCI Units, who will advise on the action to be taken in respect of such agents.

6. Any captured saboteur known or believed to be an enemy agent will be handled in the same manner as other enemy agents (Section IX).

Liaison with the Security Service

7. CI Staffs at Headquarters of Army Groups will maintain direct liaison with the Counter-Sabotage Section of the Security Service. Security Service will furnish CI Staffs with all available information of enemy sabotage methods and equipment, and with advice as to measures for the prevention and detection of sabotage and interrogation of saboteurs. CI Staffs will similarly notify Security Service of sabotage developments discovered in the Field. Where necessary such information will be passed through Section V of the Secret Intelligence Service.

Section XI – Channels of Counter-Intelligence Information

(Note. This Section is not given here. It lays down in great detail the methods of handling and passing information. These methods are based on common sense, and must vary with the Staff organisation of the Force.)

Section XII – Suspect British Indian Nationals

(Note. This Section dealt with a problem peculiar to the campaign, the examination of Indian prisoners, both military and civilian, to discover whether they had been suborned by the enemy.)

Appendix A to SHAEF Intelligence Directive No 7
Areas Subject to Special Restrictions

(Note. This Appendix detailed the various Regulated, Protected, Defence and Restricted Areas in operation in the United Kingdom. It is not included here.)

Appendix B to SHAEF Intelligence Directive No 7
Special Counter-Intelligence Units

General

1.   Information relating to enemy Secret Intelligence Services in enemy, enemy occupied and neutral territory, is available in London mainly in Section V of the Secret Intelligence Service, X2 Branch of OSS, but also in other Departments such as the Security Service and MI 14d of the War Office. Owing to the special nature of this information and the great discretion required in its use, it is not suitable for passing to the CI Staffs through normal Intelligence channels. Special CI Units will therefore be supplied by Section V of the Secret Intelligence Service for attachment to British Army Groups and Armies. These Units will act as a channel for passing information to CI Staffs about enemy Secret Intelligence Services and will advise them as to its use.

2.   All producer Departments of information of this type in London will work in the closest collaboration and will pass their information to SIS/OSS for transmission if necessary to SCI Units.

Organisation

3.   (a)   British SCI Units are of two types –

  Type A (4 Officers and 6 ORs) suitable for attachment to Army Group HQ
  Type B (2 Officers and 2 ORs) suitable for attachment to Army HQ or smaller independent detachment.

  (b)   US SCI Units are also of two types –
  For an Army Group. 4 Officers and 11 EM
  For an Army. 3 Officers and 4 EM.

Administration

4.   SCI Units will be administered for all purposes by the Headquarters to which they are attached.

Duties

5.   The duties of SCI Units in the planning stage are –

(a)   To assist in the preparation of all available information about enemy Secret Intelligence Services in the form required by the CI Staffs.

(b)   To advise CI Staffs in the selection of the immediate CI targets and in the method of dealing with them to ensure the maximum Intelligence results.

6.   The duties of SCI Units in the Field are –

(a)   To distribute and interpret to the CI Staffs all counter-espionage information received by them from London and from other SCI Units, and advice on its most effective and secure use.
(b)   To afford the maximum protection to special sources of secret counter-espionage information.
(c)   To advise CI Staffs in the selection of counter-espionage targets whose capture is likely to yield material of value.
(d)   To assist CI Staffs in the examination of captured enemy documents or material of special counter-espionage interest.
(e)   To assist CI Staffs in the interrogation of captured enemy agents.
(f)   To pass to London all information on enemy Secret Intelligence Services collected in the Field, including such captured documents and other material as is no longer required in the Field.
(g)   To serve as a direct channel between each Army Group HQ for information on enemy Secret Intelligence Services collected in the Field.
(h)   To serve as a channel between the Army Groups and from the Army Groups to London for any other CI information which cannot be passed through normal Service channels.

Employment of SCI Units

7.   SCI Units are normally attached to the CI Staffs of a Headquarters and are directly responsible to the Chief CI Staff Officers.
8.   Although not technically forming part of the CI Staff, the officers of SCI Units will work in closest liaison with the component sub-sections of the Staff. The functions of the SCI Units are advisory and not executive. Executive action on information supplied by SCI Units is the province of the CI Staffs and Personnel.
9.   SCI Units will normally pass their information direct to the appropriate sub-section of the CI Staff. However, in furtherance of the responsibility to safeguard special sources, they will have the right to withhold any particular item of information derived from such sources from any but the Chief CI Officer, and to represent to him the necessity for prohibiting or limiting action upon it, where action or unrestricted action might prejudice the security of these sources. The ultimate decision as to whether action is or is not taken in the Field will rest with the AC of SG2 or BGSI of the Army Group, except when an express prohibition of action is issued by SIS or OSS in London.

10. Personnel of SCI Units should not be employed in any area where there is a danger of capture and therefore of interrogation by the enemy. They should normally move with the Headquarters to which they are attached.

11. It may be profitable to attach CI Personnel to SCI Units for short periods of training for special tasks, e.g. the seizure and inspection of CI documents. Personnel of SCI Units may also accompany CI Personnel on such tasks subject to the proviso in the previous paragraph.

12. Personnel of SCI Units are specially qualified and must not be employed on any other than CI duties.

Communications

13. SCI Units are furnished with special communications and codes and are not normally dependent on Army Signals.

14. Each SCI Unit will be in direct communication with its London Headquarters, and all Units within the same Army Group zone will be in direct communication with one another. In addition, each Unit with an Army Group Headquarters will be in direct communication with the Unit at the other Army Group.

Appendix C to SHAEF Intelligence Directive No 7
 Mobile W/T Detection Units

1. *Function.* The detection of illicit wireless transmitters is carried out in two phases; first, the recognition of a wireless signal as originally from an enemy agent and its rough location by long range direction finding; and, second, the accurate location of the illicit transmitter by local direction finding. The first stage involves the large scale analysis of wireless signals based on a fixed D/F system which in this Theatre is carried out in the United Kingdom. The second stage, in the Field, is carried out by a team of D/F vans, mobile, and operating under the direction of the central control in England with its attendant analysis and fixed D/F. Six vans each are provided at 21 Army Group and 1st United States Army Group respectively, linked by special W/T to a common central control. The function of these vans is to locate from comparatively short range the source of a radio signal into which they are directed in terms of frequency, rough location, etc. by the central control. They are not suitable for the initial detection of an agent's signal, a task which for technical reasons can hardly ever be accomplished by local action.

2. *Organisation.* The personnel and vans at HQ 21 Army Group will form part of the Special Communications Unit supplied by the Secret Intelligence Service. Those at 1st US Army Group will be

supplied by the US Signal Corps. While these units will be technically controlled from the United Kingdom, they will be under the operational command of the Chief CI Staff Officers at Army Group Heaquarters. The Officer in charge of the mobile vans will be responsible for their technical employment. They will at all times work in close liaison with SCI Units and CI Personnel.

3. *Local Intelligence.* Experience has shown that CI Staffs may expect to receive numerous reports alleging illicit use of W/T behind our lines. Many of these reports will be obviously absurd or the result of ulterior motives on the part of local inhabitants, but all reports that are not obviously ridiculous must be investigated. An Officer experienced in investigating such cases will be available at each Army Group HQ and any reports which appear to merit investigation will be referred to him. He will be able to call on any further technical help necessary. Mobile D/F vans will not normally be employed in investigating cases arising from local Intelligence without prior reference to the central station in the United Kingdom.

APPENDIX 14

The Case of *King Kong*

Christian Lindemans was born at Rotterdam in 1912. From 1929 to 1940 he worked as a motor mechanic in his father's business. In 1936 he had a very bad accident, sustaining severe leg and arm injuries and a fractured skull. The head injury had permanent effects. He suffered from blackouts and was also epileptic. Tall and heavily built, he was nicknamed *King Kong*. He spoke French and German well, and English slightly.

The garage was completely destroyed by the German attack on Rotterdam in May 1940. In August *King Kong* found a job as a lorry driver on the Lille–Paris route carrying petrol for the German Air Force. Through the daughter of the house in which he lodged at Lille, by whom he had two children and whom he regarded as his wife, he came into contact with Resistance activities in which he became increasingly involved from about the middle of 1941. During the years 1942–1943 he worked with Resistance groups, among them one in Rotterdam in which his younger brother was active. In this period he performed good work of the kind undertaken by many other patriots. By the middle of 1943 he was living in Paris with his 'wife', who was still an active Resistance worker. At the end of 1943 his brother was arrested in Rotterdam. About the same time a member of the group with which *King Kong* was working in Paris was also caught. Among the arrests that followed was *King Kong's* 'wife'; he himself was away at the time. He moved to Rotterdam and then to Brussels. In March 1944, being without work and with his 'wife' and brother in the hands of the enemy, he either sought contact with, or was contacted by, the Abwehr. In return for a promise that his brother and his 'wife'* would be released he became an Abwehr agent. Control of his case was ultimately in the hands of Oberstleutnant Giskes, at Brussels.

King Kong was instructed initially to return to Holland and keep in touch with the Resistance movement. This he did, and disclosed a mass of information about Resistance and espionage organisations in Holland, France and Belgium.

At about the end of April 1944 Giskes decided that he should

---

* There is some question whether his 'wife' was included in the bargain. *King Kong* claimed that she was. Others concerned in the transaction only specified his brother. The latter was released by the Germans. The former was still in prison in France under sentence of death when she was released by the Americans.

373

move to Belgium. He was to use his Resistance contacts to obtain information, such as the date of the invasion and the orders that were being given by the Allies to the Armée Blanche. He did not discover the date of the invasion, but he had some successes. An ISOS decrypt of 22 August from Giskes to a colleague contained a report received from *King Kong* about instructions given to Belgian Resistance leaders by British officers at a meeting the previous day.

At the beginning of September Giskes instructed *King Kong* to stay behind in Belgium and try to penetrate the British Intelligence Service. *King Kong* quickly obtained an introduction through the Armée Blanche to a unit in Antwerp working for IS 9. Probably about 12 September he was despatched on a mission to pass through the lines to Eindhoven and inform chiefs of the Resistance there that they were to stay quiet. Such Allied pilots as they had in their care were not to move as the Allied armies would liberate the territory shortly.

King Kong was captured by the Germans between the lines. He disclosed that he was working for the Abwehr and, after being questioned by Army intelligence staff, was passed on to the Abwehr unit at Driebergen, where he was interviewed by the officer commanding, Major Kiesewetter. (Giskes was now in charge of Abwehr activities in the sector of the West Wall between Cleves and Trier). After de-briefing, *King Kong* was told to return across the lines and find out whether the German stay-behind agents in Brussels had carried out the sabotage that had been planned. He was escorted to Eindhoven and stayed there until it was liberated by the Allies.

About 22 or 23 September *King Kong* was taken to Prince Bernhard's headquarters where he was questioned by an officer on the Prince's staff who had known him in the Resistance and suspected that he had turned traitor. The interview was inconclusive. For the next five weeks *King Kong* continued to operate as a liaison agent with the Dutch Forces of the Interior. During this period he visited Prince Bernhard's HQ from time to time. According to the evidence given to the Dutch Commission of Enquiry into the conduct of the government 1940–1945, he was kept at arm's length as he was under suspicion.

On 26 October *King Kong* was denounced as a German agent by a Dutchman who was himself an Abwehr agent and had been instrumental in *King Kong's* recruitment. *King Kong* was arrested on 28 October at Prince Bernhard's headquarters. It was thought that his case would be of considerable counter-espionage interest. His betrayals were alleged to have been on a massive scale, and it was feared that, because of his access to the Prince's HQ, he might have been able to give the Germans valuable military intelligence.

Accordingly, on 3 November he was transferred to Camp 020 for interrogation.

King Kong's mental and physical condition made the investigation very difficult. A report was issued on 18 November with a covering note in which MI 5 said: 'Although the man has broken in the sense that he has admitted to working for the Germans, denouncing patriots and passing military information, it has not been found possible to maintain the pressure on him owing to the fits from which he suffers. The result has been that Camp 020 have been unable to report what information regarding Allied plans and military dispositions *King Kong* has passed to the enemy. Furthermore, his memory of events and dates is so weak that it has not so far been found possible to obtain such a detailed story of his movements as to enable any safe deduction to be made as to the opportunities he had for passing on particulars of the information which he must have been in a position to acquire . . . We can only advise that *King Kong*, if he had the opportunity, probably informed the enemy of all operational information which he had'. The only operational information specified in the report was in the passage dealing with *King Kong's* mission to Eindhoven in mid-September; *King Kong* admitted that he had given Kiesewetter information about the numbers of British troops and tanks he had seen. A revised and amplified report, issued on 6 December, added nothing to this aspect of the case. *King Kong's* four confessions, made on different dates, contained admissions of disclosing operational information in general terms only.

On 7 December *King Kong* was handed over to the Dutch authorities. He committed suicide in July 1946 while awaiting trial.

Allegations that, when *King Kong* reported to the Abwehr on 15 September at Driebergen, he betrayed Operation *Market Garden*, and this was responsible for the disaster to the 1st Airborne Division at Arnhem and for the failure of the operation, were first made in February 1945. There are two questions to be answered. The first is whether the betrayal took place. The second is whether, if it did, it had the results attributed to it.

The best witness to what *King Kong* said on 15 September, and what action was taken by the Abwehr, might have been Kiesewetter. However, there is no evidence from him in the records of the case, presumably because he never became available for questioning. In June–July 1945 Giskes and his former subordinate, Huntemann, were interrogated at Camp 020. The examination was primarily concerned with the large-scale penetration of SOE activities in Holland but the opportunity was also taken to probe the *King Kong* case. The two German intelligence officers substantially confirmed the account of *King Kong's* recruitment and work for the Abwehr which Camp 020 had extracted from him. With regard to the information which *King Kong* gave to the Germans on 15 September Giskes said that he had heard about 20 September that *King Kong* had been at Driebergen, but that 'it was only weeks later' that he had received 'incomplete reports' of what *King Kong* had said. The gist of them had been that a British attack, direction Eindhoven, was timed for 17 September. Airborne troops in large numbers were in readiness. Huntemann's testimony was that he had been in Kiesewetter's office at Driebergen on 15 September when news of *King Kong's* arrival in the German lines with important information was telephoned through, and that he had told Kiesewetter who *King Kong* was. Huntemann had had to leave to keep an appointment and had not been present when *King Kong* was brought to Driebergen, but he had been told the next day by Kiesewetter that *King Kong* had brought information about an Allied airborne action which was expected shortly in the Munster–Dülmen area of Westphalia. Arnhem had not been mentioned, but in February 1945 Giskes had talked to him about *King Kong*, and had said that *King Kong* had given information about the Arnhem landing.

In reply to further questioning Giskes confirmed what he had said in a written statement: 'A report by [the Abwehr] in Driebergen reached me towards the end of October 1944 and I remember the following about the information given by *King Kong*. *King Kong* had reported on 15 September that –

"1. The English attack in the direction of Eindhoven was imminent. (As far as I can remember *King Kong* gave the time and date as being early on 17 September).
2. For the attack, which was imminent, large forces of airborne troops were standing by. (The place or sector where these troops were to be committed was not given.)" '.

Huntemann now said that on returning to Driebergen in the evening of 15 September he had found the Abwehr unit busy compiling a report on *King Kong's* information. *King Kong* had succeeded in getting in touch with the enemy intelligence service and had been instructed to deliver an order to the Resistance leaders in Eindhoven to the effect that they should cease activity as the Allies would be there in a few days' time. Huntemann stated that his memory was confused about the reference to an airborne landing in Westphalia. It was possible that this reference had been made by a man with whom he had had an appointment in the afternoon of 15 September, 'who always knew about many rumours'. 'Certainly' he went on, 'nothing was talked about in my presence that evening and the following day concerning an imminent airborne landing in the Arnhem area . . . Only much later, about February 1945, Giskes told me that *King Kong* . . . had reported about the entire Arnhem operation beforehand.'

In his book *London Calling North Pole*, Giskes gave the same account of the information brought by *King Kong* as he had done at Camp 020, and remarked that 'King Kong was not the betrayer of Arnhem simply because he was not in the position to betray it'.

Another of Giskes's subordinates, Richard Christmann, was arrested by the French in 1946. When first interrogated he stated that he had been sent to Driebergen in September 1944 by Giskes to wait for *King Kong* to return across the lines. On hearing that *King Kong* had been captured Christmann 'had him brought' to Driebergen. 'When he arrived', Christmann's statement continued, '*King Kong* reported to me on the tasks entrusted to him by Giskes'. Among other things, *King Kong* had learnt that massive parachute landings were planned on the line Eindhoven–Amsterdam–Zuider Zee, without precise details on the exact dropping zones, round about 18 September. 'The departments concerned realised immediately that Arnhem and Nijmegen were the two key points . . . This information was sent that same night to the different Army Corps and to General HQs. This permitted the despatch to the region of Arnhem and Nijmegen of hastily collected reinforcements consisting largely of SS and Police, with some tanks . . .'.

Christmann was subsequently interrogated by the Americans, whose report in September contained the following passage: '[*King Kong*] further reported that he had succeeded in getting American and British officers to talk of a big aerial landing on 17–18 September . . . The aerial landing was to take place in the Eindhoven, Nijmegen and Arnhem areas. In case of success of this landing, several other landings had been planned in the Amersfoort, Ostrand and Zuider Zee areas . . . On all these reports made up two summaries . . . the second one covered the prospective aerial landings . . .'.

Christmann claimed that the second report was sent out at once to several HQs including OKW Berlin. However, 'the notified department did not know . . . if there was any truth to the prospective aerial landings and refused to send troops for counter-measures. Only the auxiliary troops, SS School Arnhem, Holland Militia and other troops were ordered to be ready. Without the presence of these troops in the Arnhem area, the aerial landing on 17 September would have succeeded'.

Joseph Schreieder, also a former subordinate of Giskes, told the Dutch Commission of Enquiry that on 17 September Kiesewetter had mentioned *King Kong's* visit two days earlier, and had said that he had brought information about an impending attack on Arnhem.

The evidence of these witnesses establishes that *King Kong* betrayed Operation *Market Garden* to the extent that he gave warning that the British would attack towards Eindhoven on 17 September and that airborne troops would be used in connection with this offensive. Whether Arnhem (which lies some 30 miles north of Eindhoven, with Nijmegen in between) was mentioned as a target of the airborne assault is very doubtful. The evidence of Giskes and Huntemann that it was not carries much more weight than that of either Christmann, who changed his story on this point between his interrogations by the French and the Americans, or Schreieder, whose belief that *King Kong* referred to Arnhem, and not to Eindhoven, may well have grown up after *Market Garden*. But the question is in any case academic since it is certain that *King Kong's* information, whatever it was and in whatever form it was reported, had no practical consequences. The Germans were expecting a break-out from the XXX Corps bridgehead at any moment, and were making such preparations as they could to meet it. The possibility that the Allies might employ airborne troops to assist their advance into Holland or Germany was recognised, but the Germans were not expecting an airborne landing at Arnhem. Field Marshal Model, commanding Army Group B, happened to be at a headquarters close to the town and narrowly escaped capture. The presence in the neighbourhood of 9th and 10th SS Panzer Divisions was accidental – they had been ordered there early in September to re-organise – and they were not alerted before the 1st Airborne Division landed on 17 September.*

It is profitless to speculate how *King Kong* obtained the information which he delivered on 15 September. In the euphoria which prevailed at the time, when the rapid end of the war was confidently expected, there may well have been widespread carelessness. However, attempts have been made to fix responsibility on the headquarters of Prince Bernhard. It is therefore right to repeat that *King Kong's* first contact with this HQ was not made until after Operation *Market Garden* had failed.

---

* For the details see Hinsley et al, *British Intelligence in the Second World War*, Vol III Part 2 (1988), pp 383–384, 387.

APPENDIX 15

Some Double-Cross Agents Run in the Field

Dragoman was a Spaniard born in 1895. His father was in the hotel business and he visited the United Kingdom and Germany to learn the languages. From 1934–1939 he worked for the American Express Company in Cherbourg. In 1936 he met an Abwehr agent, for whom he obtained overt information about shipping and other matters. In September 1940 he was formally recruited as an Abwehr agent. He was trained to operate radio and made regular transmissions, apparently without being given any specific task. In April 1944 he was told that when the Allies invaded he was to stay behind in Cherbourg and transmit information of operational interest and meteorological reports.

ISOS revealed that the Abwehr had recruited *Dragoman* as a stay-behind agent, and that he had been on the air between 7 and 20 June 1944. On 15 June the Germans promised to send him a reinforcement with the code name of *Desire*. When Cherbourg fell on 28 June the OSS/X2 SCIU made a special search for *Dragoman* without success. However, by good fortune, it was learnt coincidentally from *Dragoman's* first contact, who by now was in touch with the OSS in Portugal, that a man answering to *Dragoman's* real name was being trained as a stay-behind agent in Cherbourg. With French help, *Dragoman* was discovered working as an interpreter with the US Service of Supplies. He was arrested on 8 July. The fact that he had a letter in his possession addressed to one of his cover-names broke him, and he volunteered to work for the Allies. He established contact with the Germans on 25 July and, after some argument, was sent to Camp 020 for interrogation. Camp 020 considered him 'unreliable', but he was nevertheless returned to France on 20 August to operate under American control.

Desire arrived on 22 August; he was duly arrested, confessed, and revealed the presence of another agent. This was *Charles*, who had helped to train *Dragoman*. He too was arrested. In September the Germans began asking *Dragoman* what had happened to *Desire* and *Charles*, and at the beginning of October urged him to visit *Charles*. *Dragoman* therefore reported that he had met *Charles* (from whom he had collected 60,000 francs) and gave explanations, which the Germans found satisfactory, of *Desire's* disappearance and *Charles's* silence. The Germans were grateful and sent *Dragoman* a detailed naval questionnaire. Regular contacts were continued. In mid-December the 212 Committee was told that the case was 'running quietly'. In February 1945 money and new signal plans for *Dragoman* and *Charles* were dropped by the regular mail plane between Germany and the Channel Islands. At the beginning of March *Dragoman* was being questioned about the pipeline at Cherbourg, and it was thought that the Germans might possibly be contemplating an attack on it by troops from Jersey.

Charles became the double-cross agent *Skull*. It was intended that he should begin transmissions at the end of September, but only partial success had been achieved by the end of November, when it was clear from messages received that the Germans thought highly of him. In December they instructed him to move to Brest and he made a notional visit there over Christmas. The 212 Committee was told on 9 February that he had been asked to meet a German intelligence officer who was to visit one of the pockets still resisting on the Atlantic coast, and on 23 February that he had been asked to pay other agents in Rouen and Le Havre. On 6 April it was reported that he had gone down to Bordeaux in connection with the German intelligence officer's visit. He was still being given important assignments by the Germans in the closing days of the war.

The credit for the capture of *Muleteer*, a Frenchman who had the German alias *Tazy*, belonged entirely to ISOS. An agent with the name *Tazy* was known to be transmitting in July 1944 when the reception of his traffic was taken over by the Abwehr station at Wiesbaden. The early messages were confined to weather reports. *Tazy's* effective career as an agent began after the liberation of Paris. He sent messages containing information about conditions in the city and some operational intelligence about Orly airfield and other matters. At the beginning of October the Germans instructed him to ring a telephone number in Paris from a public call box. He did so, was arrested the next day and came under the control of the OSS/X2 SCIU with 12th US Army Group. His story, as told after his arrest and later at Camp 020, was as follows.

He was born in 1905, performed his military service from 1924–1926, and from 1926–1929 earned his living as a radio electrician, also acquiring a criminal record for various minor acts of dishonesty. He was recalled to the colours in 1939, taken prisoner in 1940, escaped, and from 1940–1944 worked in his trade. In 1942 he played what, according to his own account, was a minor role in supplying radio sets to the German Air Force. Many of these proved faulty and in February 1944 he was arbitrarily required to pay a penalty of 68,000 francs. He was now unemployed and sought the help of a contact whom he knew to be in touch with some organisation run by the Germans. He was introduced to a German who questioned him about his qualifications and the type of employment he wanted and held out hopes of work in an aircraft factory. In May he was given 6,000 francs for expenses and signed a receipt with the name *Tazy*. This was followed by training in radio, cyphering and meteorology. He claimed that at this stage he realised for the first time that he was employed by the German Intelligence Service and accepted the situation in the hope of recovering his 68,000 francs. He broached this matter to his German contact who promised to arrange a refund.

During his training, which continued in June and July, he received two payments of 8,000 francs each. On 6 August he was given a transmitter and instructed how to operate it if the Germans evacuated Paris. Between 6 and 16 August he exchanged call signs with his control, and passed meteorological reports to keep his hand in, using his spy name. About 17 August, finding that his contact had left Paris, he sent a signal asking whether there was anyone in the city from whom he could get instructions. During the next six weeks, besides sending regular meteorological reports, he exchanged some three dozen messages with the German Intelligence Service. He passed military, political and economic intelligence, and pressed for the money which he thought was owed to him. The Germans encouraged him to persevere and claimed to have despatched 30,000 francs by a reliable friend.

Tazy claimed that he had accepted a mission from the Germans solely in order to recover the money which had been unjustly extorted from him. The 212 Committee was told on 9 October that he might be useful for counter-espionage and he was put into operation as a double-cross agent under the code name *Muleteer*.

As the account which *Muleteer* had given of his traffic with his control station omitted, or minimised, the operational intelligence which he was known (from ISOS) to have transmitted, on 24 October he was sent to Camp 020 for further interrogation. The conclusion reached there was that he had served the Germans faithfully as a stay-behind agent until his arrest, and he was returned to France on 2 November with a recommendation that he should not be used further for double-cross work.

The recommendation was disregarded and *Muleteer* was run with some success until the end of hostilities. An agent who had been dropped by parachute near Chartres with the mission of paying him and obtaining intelligence about the effect of the Ardennes offensive on Franco-American relations, was arrested in his apartment on 24 December. In February 1945, in response to repeated demands for money, *Muleteer* was sent directions for finding a buried valise containing 50,000 francs and a radio set. The money was for him; the set was to be held until he received further instructions. The location of the cache on Route Nationale 3 had been tardily indicated to *Brutus* in response to a suggestion that he might be posted to France.*

ISOS recorded the regular circulation of *Tazy* messages by his Wiesbaden control to other stations. In mid-February Wiesbaden was told that the German High Command was interested in the whereabouts of 101st US Airborne Division, which was thought to be in the Soissons area, and was instructed to ask *Tazy* to make investigations on the spot. He duly paid a notional visit to Soissons, and another to the Rheims area in response to repeated questions about Allied airborne troops. A message on 10 March showed that the Germans were inclined to believe that he was genuine, and they arranged a further remittance for him at the end of the month. For his part he reaffirmed his loyalty to 'the cause of Europe', and expressed his willingness to continue the struggle after the end of hostilities. His case was handed over to the French at the beginning of April.

Derrick, a Belgian, was a hydrographer by profession. In October 1940 he visited Brussels and joined a Resistance group there. In April 1941 the Germans ordered him to continue his survey work on their behalf. He referred them to his employers in Brussels, who instructed him to comply in order to keep an eye on Belgian state property. The employment enabled him to gather useful information, and he passed this regularly to the Resistance network which was by now in contact with London. He travelled all along the Belgian coast and made a very detailed map of the German positions; he also managed to get a chart of the minefields from a German office in Ostend.

In the course of his work *Derrick* became very friendly with some German naval engineers, and some of his Belgian friends thought that he had become a collaborator. In March 1944 he was asked to join a 'Fifth Column' of men whom the Germans knew to be reliable and who would send information by radio for the use of the German Air Force after the expected Allied invasion of the continent. For this service he would receive 3,000 francs per month. *Derrick* asked for a few days to think this over and sent a trusted messenger to his Resistance chief in Brussels reporting the approach. He was told that he was not obliged to take such a risk, but that it would be a very good thing if he did; London had approved his accepting the task and he would be contacted on the arrival of British forces.

The Abwehr gave *Derrick* six weeks' training in Brussels in morse and cyphers and in reporting meteorological information.

---

* See above, p 273.

He was also to report on shipping in Ostend, Allied headquarters and military installations, aircraft, aerodromes, anti-aircraft guns and the results of German bombing. The Germans brought his radio set to him, rented a room for him in Ostend and fixed up his aerials.

Derrick made his first contact with the Germans under British control on 27 September 1944. The case ran until the end of hostilities and proved especially valuable to GC and CS.* In May 1945 the case-officer reported that more was owed to *Derrick* than to any of the other double-cross agents in Belgium, and that the case had yielded a substantial dividend.

Deputy, a Belgian born in 1903, was a ship's radio operator who volunteered for clandestine work and was recruited by SOE. He was instructed to return to his normal occupation, jump ship in a neutral port, approach the Germans and ask to be repatriated. After a roundabout journey, which took so long that SOE paid him off, *Deputy* got himself recruited by the Abwehr in Lisbon. He was sent to Brussels, where the Abwehr kept in touch with him, and at the beginning of September 1944 was instructed to act as radio operator for an agent in Antwerp.

Deputy at once reported this mission to the British and, under instruction, worked with the agent who gave him reports on the naval, military and political situation in Antwerp, the state of the port, and the results of the V 1 and V 2 attacks in which the Germans were particularly interested. The agent told *Deputy* that he had worked for the Germans since 1942 and had been trained in the use of secret writing but not given any material; he was violently pro-German and wanted to do everything in his power to help them. At the end of November 1944 the port of Antwerp was about to be reopened and it was decided to eliminate the agent by arranging for him to be arrested as a German spy. However, on Christmas Day the agent, a woman and a dog were found dead from asphyxiation by gas in the woman's room in Antwerp. The Belgian police were satisfied that this was an accident. *Deputy* made his last contact with the Germans on 30 April 1945.

Frank was called up to the Belgian Army in October 1939 and trained as a radio operator. After demobilisation, he worked for the Water Board in Brussels, and in April 1942 joined the right wing Rexist Party with the intention of passing information about its members and activities to a Resistance organisation. In due course this brought him to the notice of the SD, which recruited him in June 1943 as a stay-behind agent. He confided this to an

---

* For example, in reading the cyphers of mobile intelligence units, see above, pp 182, 266–267.

elderly Englishwoman, resident in Brussels, whom he had known for a long time.

Frank was briefed by the Germans for his mission in July 1944, given 3,000 francs and a promise of 1,000 francs a month, and instructed to report military, political and economic information. He arranged that his English friend would tell the Allies about him as soon as they arrived. She duly did so and he was run as a double-cross agent from 20 September 1944. His case proved valuable, and his information on the SD stay-behind network was a prime factor in its early break-up. In February 1945 it was still thought important to provide a high standard of traffic for an agent of his calibre. *Frank's* last contact with the Germans was on 16 April 1945.

The case of *Sniper*,* which was becalmed in June 1944, took a new turn when SHAEF Ops B said that it would like to have him in France and asked MI 5 to arrange with the Germans for a radio transmitter to be made available for him there. A letter from the Germans saying that they were taking immediate steps to deliver a set to him in the United Kingdom caused some delay, but nothing happened and the Germans were accordingly told that *Sniper* was being posted to the field and were asked to name a place where he could pick up a set in Belgium. On 1 December directions were received for finding a set which had been buried for him at Turnhout, whence it was retrieved on 12 December. *Sniper's* arrival in Belgium was reported to the 212 Committee on 5 January 1945, but owing to technical difficulties communication with the Germans was not established until March. There was also difficulty with the Belgian authorities over *Sniper's* personal position, and in the end he did not operate the radio himself. The last contact with the enemy by a controlled agent in 21st Army Group's sector was made on the *Sniper* link on 2 May.

---

* See above, pp 218–219.

Index